ENVIRONMENT AND SUSTAINABLE ECONOMIC DEVELOPMENT

ENVIRONMENT AND SUSTAINABLE ECONOMIC DEVELOPMENT

Editor

RAJ KUMAR SEN

Published on behalf of the
Centre for Studies on Environment and Sustainable
Development (CSESD), Rabindra Bharati University

DEEP & DEEP PUBLICATIONS PVT. LTD.
F-159, Rajouri Garden, New Delhi - 110027

ENVIRONMENT AND SUSTAINABLE ECONOMIC DEVELOPMENT

ISBN 978-81-8450-365-4

Typeset by THE LASER PRINTERS, 8/15, 3rd Floor, Subhash Nagar, New Delhi-110027.

Printed in India at MAYUR ENTERPRISES, WZ Plot No. 3, Gujjar Market, Tihar Village, New Delhi - 110 018

Published by DEEP & DEEP PUBLICATIONS PVT. LTD.,
F-159, Rajouri Garden, New Delhi-110027. Phones: 25435369, 25440916.
E-mail: ddpbooks@yahoo.co.in • ddpubs@gmail.com
Sales Showroom: 2/13, Ansari Road, Daryaganj, New Delhi-110002
Phone/Fax: 23245122

Contents

SECTION V
Institutions, Management Practices and Social Responsibilities for Sustainable Development

List of Contributors

1. **Dr. Raj Kumar Sen:** Professor of Economics and Director, CSESD, Rabindra Bharati University, Kolkata.
2. **Dr. M.M. Goel:** Professor & Chairman, Economics Department, Kurukshetra University, Kurukshetra.
3. **Ms. Sanchita:** Department of Management, GGS Indraprastha University, New Delhi.
4. **Dr. B.N. Ghosh:** Professor of Economics, East Mediterranean University, North Cyprus.
5. **Dr. Sudarshan lyengar:** Vice-Chancellor, Gujarat Vidyapith, Ahmedabad
6. **Dr. Santosh Kumar Ghorai:** Director, DDE, Vidyasagar University, Medinipur.
7. **Dr. Ramprasad Sengupta:** Professor of Economics, J.N.U., New Delhi.
8. **Dr. U. Sankar:** Professor of Economics, Madras School of Economics, Chennai.
9. **Dr. Gopal K. Kadekodi:** Hony. Professor, Centre for Multi-Disciplinary Development Research, Dharwar.
10. **Dr. Clem Tisdell:** Emeritus Professor of Economics, Queensland University, Brisbane, Australia.
11. **Dr. Debal Ray:** Chief Environment Officer, Govt. of W. Bengal, Kolkata.
12. **Dr. N.C. Sahu:** Professor & Co-ordinator, Department of Economics, Berhampur University, Orissa.

13. **Dr. C.D. Panda:** Department of Economics, Gunupur College, Orissa.
14. **Dr. L.P. Panda:** CSREM, Paralakhemundi, Orissa.
15. **Dr. V.B. Jugale:** Professor of Economics, Shivaji University, Kolhapur
16. **Dr. L. Venkatachalam:** Madras Institute of Development Studies, Chennai.
17. **Dr. Pradeep K. Katiha:** Senior Scientist, Central Indian Fisheries Research Institute, Kolkata.
18. **Ms. Sanchita Sarkar:** Formerly of CIFRI, Kolkata.
19. **Dr. Joyashree Roy:** Professor of Economics, and Co-ordinator, GCP, Jadavpur University, Kolkata.
20. **Moumita Roy:** Research Associate, Jadavpur University, Kolkata.
21. **Ms. Shreya Roychowdhury:** Research Associate, Jadavpur University, Kolkata.
22. **Dr. Somnath Hazra:** Program Manager, RCDC, Bhubaneswar.
23. **Dr. Kanchan Chopra:** Former Professor and Director, Institute of Economic Growth, Delhi.
24. **Dr. M.N. Murty:** Professor, Institute of Economic Growth, Delhi.
25. **Dr. Bishwanath Goldar:** Professor, Institute of Economic Growth, Delhi.
26. **Dr. Shrawan Kumar Singh:** Retd. Professor of Economics, IGNOU, New Delhi.

Environment and Sustainable Economic Development: An Overview

Raj Kumar Sen

For sustainable economic development one can not deny the role of environmental ecology which is either not considered or not adequately emphasized in the mainstream approach of economic growth for the developing economies since the second half of 20th century though the situation is gradually changing slowly since 1972 when incidences like acid rain and industrial pollution were recognized in Europe as harmful to the level of living of the common people and the ecology and environment surrounding them. At the beginning, economic development and economic growth were considered to be nearly the same but it was felt later in a decisive manner that economic development is different from economic growth as it includes something more than economic growth only. At one stage it was felt that poverty is the greatest polluter and environmental considerations are nothing but luxury for the poor countries and poor people, but gradually it has been agreed that by following the approach of sustainable economic development the interests of both the poor and rich people belonging to both types of countries not only of the present generation but also of the future generation are protected. This is aptly described in both ancient and modern Indian economic thinking and these conceptual issues are available from scriptures like Gita on the one hand and Gandhian economic thinking on the other. Besides, there are also various issues and concepts as described by different authors in this context.

Of course, for sustainable economic development one must consider the application of environmentally sound technologies and use of ecosystem accounts for allocation of resources. It is also important to understand the ecological limits that are relevant in them. For these reasons the role of the natural resources and their use is important to be taken into account for achieving the target of sustainable development. Among the natural resources the question of agriculture and the use of new products (like GMOs), protection of forest and biodiversity conservation, tribal village ecosystem and relationship with bio-diversity for sustainable development, soil salinity and its effects due to cultivation of particular crops, sustainable water management and limitations of tradeable water rights including the sustainability of fisheries are some of the major issues that need our attention. Many articles on these issues have considered them in the context of India and also some of the regions in it.

In recent periods the unsustainabilities of the present growth pattern is observed so far as the impact of climate change is concerned. It is necessary to discuss this problem on the one hand from sectoral stand point as such impacts might be regional and local rather than national. Similarly, on the other hand, the considerations for trans-boundary problems are also important as in many cases such regional impacts are not limited by national boundaries.

The role of institutions, management practices and social responsibilities are no less important for achieving the goal of sustainable development. Prices, legal institutions, participatory practices for environmental management are also relevant in this context. The situation is taking such a turn that one has to remind the corporate sector their responsibilities to achieve sustainable economic development in the true sense of the term.

An attempt is made in this volume to understand the problems related with environment, ecology and sustainable economic development. Though the thrust of this volume is on the importance of these themes in general, yet many of the articles included here have given special emphasis on the problems of India in particular and developing countries in general. As many as 19 articles, all of which are invited from recognized experts in the subject are distributed over 5 sections considering the focus of these articles and these are briefly introduced in the following paragraphs. However, for the benefit of the readers all articles are accompanied by an abstract along some keywords relevant for them. Interested readers can obtain a bird's eye view of these articles from their respective abstracts.

After this overview the section I opens with "Issues in Sustainable Development: Some Reflections". This section contains altogether 4 articles. The first article is on "Issues in Sustainable Development for Indian Economy" (**M.M. Goel and Sanchita**) where the authors have dwelt upon the valuable wisdom contained in the ancient Indian scriptures specially in Gita and discussed its current relevance for the sustainable economic development of India. The next article is by **B.N. Ghosh** who has discussed the issue of sustainable development from the Gandhian Perspective. Some reflections on sustainable development by **Sudarshan lyengar** are given in the next article which has taken up the issue from both the modern and ancient view points. The last article in this sub-section is by **Santosh Kumar Ghorai** who wanted to deliver in it a few new words on sustainable development. One can obtain a number of new ideas on sustainable economic development from this set of four articles.

The section II of this book is on "Ecological Limits and Environmentally Sound Technologies and Ecosystem Accounts". We have three articles in this section. **Ramprasad Sengupta** has offered a new approach to ecological limits and its relationship with economic development. Environmentally sound technologies for sustainable development of India is the theme of the article by **U. Sankar**. On the other hand in the next article **Gopal K. Kadekodi** has discussed a framework for sustainable development on the basis of ecosystem accounts for resource allocation.

The section III of this book is quite exhaustive and includes as many as six articles dealing with natural resources and sustainable development. Among these natural resources we have discussions on Agricultural Sustainability and the Introduction of GMOs (**Clem Tisdell**), Forest and Biodiversity Conservation in West Bengal (**Debal Ray**), Biodiversity and Sustainable Development in a Tribal Village Ecosystem (**N.C. Sahu, C.D. Panda and L.P. Panda**), Degrading the Development or Developing the Degradation? (**V.B. Jugale**), Sustainable Water Management in India and Tradeable Water Rights (**L. Venkatachalam**) and

Sustainability of Indian Fisheries (**Pradeep K. Katiha and Sanchita Sarkar**).

Section IV of this volume is relatively slim and contains only two articles dealing with mitigating impacts from climate change. One of them deals with sectoral approach for negotiating these and its relevance from the Indian economy (**Joyashree Roy, Moumita Roy and Shreya Roychowdhury**). The other article by **Raj Kumar Sen and Somnath Hazra**, is on Indo-Bangladesh co-operation to mitigate climate change impacts on Sundarbans which is extended over both these neighbouring countries.

The last section of this book consists of four articles and they deal with institutions, management practices and social responsibilities for sustainable development. **Kanchan Chopra** has discussed the role of prices and law as institutions for sustainable development in global and national perspective. **M.N. Murty** has emphasized in his article on the participatory institutions for environmental management in India. Impact of environmental management practices on profitability and market value of Indian industrial firms has been discussed by **Bishwanath Goldar** in his article. Finally a new theme dealing with corporate social responsibility and sustainable business has been discussed by **Shrawan Kumar Singh** in his article.

This volume is one of the important publications completed in 2009-10 by the newly established CSESD of the Rabindra Bharati University. We are thankful to the University authorities for providing physical and financial inputs to organise its activities. We are extremely thankful to the renowned authors for submitting these valuable articles without which this volume could not see the light of the day on the important subjects of Environment, Ecology and Sustainable Economic Development, many of which have important relevance for the Indian economy. The directors and advisors of the CSESD deserve the heart felt thanks for their co-operation and support extended to this publication. Last but not the least we are extremely thankful to the publisher for undertaking the publication of this volume. We sincerely hope that this volume will be useful to the researchers, academicians, policy-makers and to the general readers who are interested in this important area and we hope that it will be both light and fruit bearing by expanding the frontiers of this growing subject.

SECTION I

ISSUES IN SUSTAINABLE DEVELOPMENT: SOME REFLECTIONS

Issues in Sustainable Development for Indian Economy

M.M. Goel and Sanchita

To understand, analyse, interpret and adopt the concept of sustainable development (SD) in Indian economy we need to introspect seriously the various related issues of concern which falls under the domain of the present paper. The history of India is replete with innumerable initiatives undertaken by people that demonstrate not just concern for environment, but also the awareness of the need to balance it with livelihood resources. This 'tradition' of care, conservation and preservation of environmental resources is also reflected in the spirit of India. Our traditions of worshipping our mountains, rivers, ponds, and the three elements of our existence—earth, fire, and water confirm our commitment to sustainability. Scriptures recorded the pristine beauty of the environment when the simple folk used to worship mountains, rivers, and ponds. We heard chanting of verses of Peace: *dyauh shanti* (Peace in Sky), *antariksha shanti* (Peace in the atmosphere), *prithivi shanti* (Peace on Earth), *apah shanti* (Peace in water), *aushadhay shanti* (Peace in the herbs), *Vanaspataya shanti* (Peace in trees)—this is verily an appeal to protect the Environment. We need to treat dynamics of environment as water which search its own profit for everyone today for safe tomorrow to ensure intra-generation and inter-generation equity. We believe that for every ill in Indian economy in 21st century there are Vedic pills and Bhagwad Gita is the panacea. Truly, Bhagwad Gita is a treatise on welfare economics and needs to be accepted as a sacro-secular epic for the entire humanity for the survival of human race. We need to understand the relationship management between nature and human being in all aspects of life which needs to be SIMPLE in strict sense of the mode explained herein.

To understand, analyse, interpret and adopt the concept of sustainable development (SD) in Indian economy, we need to introspect seriously the various related issues of concern which falls under the domain of the present paper.

The history of India is replete with innumerable initiatives undertaken by people that demonstrate not just concern for environment, but also the awareness of the need to balance it with livelihood resources. This 'tradition' of care, conservation and preservation of environmental resources is also reflected in the spirit of India. Our traditions of worshipping our mountains, rivers, ponds, and the three elements of our existence—earth, fire, and water confirm our commitment to sustainability. Scriptures recorded the pristine beauty of the environment when the simple folk used to worship mountains, rivers, and ponds. We heard chanting of verses of Peace: *dyauh shanti* (Peace in Sky), *antariksha shanti* (Peace in the atmosphere), *prithivi shanti* (Peace on Earth), *apah shanti* (Peace in water), *aushadhaya shanti* (Peace in the herbs), *Vanaspataya shanti* (Peace in trees)—this is verily an appeal to protect the Environment. We need to treat dynamics of environment as water which search its own profit for everyone today for safe tomorrow to ensure intra-generation and inter-generation equity.

Sustainable development (SD) is a process of change, in which exploitation of resources, the direction of investments, the orientation of technological development, and institutional change are all in harmony and enhance both current and future potential to meet human needs and aspirations. It ensures not only intra-generation but inter-generation equity in all walks of life in every economy of the World including India. Interdependent and mutually reinforcing pillars of sustainable development are economic development, social development, and environmental protection.

The bottom line of SD is Quality of life of present and future generations. To achieve the objective of SD, it is of utmost importance to increase quality of life and utilize efficiently the natural resources. Keeping environment clean and protecting the economy from pollution are other important requirements

We need to understand the method of measuring SD. The Measurement of SD is being done by Green National Income and Genuine Savings as under:

Green National Income = (Net National Income) – (Depletion of Natural Resources+ Environmental Degradation.)

Genuine Savings = Rate of Savings – Depreciation of Man Made Capital – Depreciation of Natural Capital (Depletion of Natural Resources and Degradation of Environment).

The basic issues of Sustainable Development Process for the present generation to understand are: efficient use of natural resources, quality of life of the future generation, pollution does not delimit the concept of development, distributional equity and preservation of three types of capital—human capital (education and technical advance), physical capital (machines, tools, etc.) and natural capital (i.e. natural resources, clean air, clean water, etc.)

For qualifying a development process as 'Sustainable' the essential requisites includes Rs. 5. All developmental processes must essentially pass through the test of Rs. 5 to be qualified as 'Sustainable'. The Rs. 5 have been thought off to show that it is in our hands to design the developmental programs so that they pass the Rs. 5 test.

- **Resistance.** The process of development must be resistant to degradation and generate economic growth equitably not only intra-generational but also inter-generational keeping the future generations in mind.
- **Resilience.** The process should have flexibility to adapt and ensure least degradation of environment.
- **Regeneration.** The development process should have the capacity to regenerate the natural resources consumed during its implementation so that the net effect on the environment is minimized.
- **Redesign.** The development process should evolve after design—feedback-redesign cycle so as to ensure that the goals of sustainability are adequately addressed.

- **Replenishment.** The process should attempt to replenish the natural capital rather than destroying it.

We need to perceive environment as human resource development (HRD) activity and is necessary infrastructure for sustainable development. Environment is the summation of all conditions and influences that affect the development and life of organisms. Physical (non-living) and biological (living) environments are the two sides of the same coin (human environment) and both interact with each other. A change in physical environment brings a change in biological environment and *vice versa*. The environment is being affected by many factors and affects living beings.

SD is basically dependent on Sustainable Human Development (SHD) which has been defined in *Human Development Report, 1994* by the United Nations Development Programme (UNDP) as "the development that not only generates economic growth but distributes its benefits equitably; that generates the environment rather than destroying it; that empowers people rather than marginalizing them. It is development that gives priority to the poor, enlarging their choice and opportunities and providing for their participation in decision that affects their lives". Human Development can not be sustained without introducing Indian ethos primarily taken from Bhagwad Gita which is neutral religion free treatise on management and welfare economics.

To adopt and accept the normative approach to SHD in Indian economy it is essential to understand SIMPLE model of SHD consisting of six human development activities such as Spiritual Quotient (SQ) development, Intuition development, Physical development, Mental level development, Love yourself attitude development and Emotional quotient (EQ) development. The synergy of these six aspects of SHD is essential requirement of the desirable professionals for the Indian economy to emerge and realize its full potential. Now, we venture to discuss the components of our model in reverse order one by one.

1. EMOTIONAL QUOTIENT DEVELOPMENT

Everyone wants success in life. What determines success then? A recent spate of management thoughts and practices champion the cause of EQ (Emotional Quotient) as that arm, which when added to IQ, define success. How simple is it to test, measure and take steps to increase your IQ: But we usually run into difficulties even in defining EQ, let alone getting to the bottom of it. A variety of words and phrases have been used to define the factors which governs EQ. The ability to get along with people and situations. 'A positive and proactive attitude towards all aspects of life.' 'The ability to command respect by building relationships.'

EQ focuses on the softer skills of building and maintaining human relationships. This aspect of life assumes a lot of importance since no where is a person detached from the human element. Be it the work place, the home front or the social circle, human interactions are inevitable and our success depends to a large extent on what we make of these interactions and relationships. For this *shloka* number 15 of Ch. 17 of Bhagwad Gita needs to be adopted. Persons with high EQ can be great leaders, get promoted and thrive during uncertainty and change.

There are four cornerstones for emotional intelligence. Executing EQ begins with 'emotional literacy' as the first cornerstone which develops self-confidence through emotional honesty, energy, emotional feed-back, initiation of responsibility and connection. The second cornerstone is of 'emotional fitness' which strengthens our authenticity, believability and resilience. The third cornerstone of 'emotional depth' explores way to align our life and work with unique potential and purpose. The fourth cornerstone advances to 'emotional alchemy' through which we extend our creative instinct and capacity to resolve problems constructively.

There are three major components to improve EQ such as motivating oneself, motivating others and empathising with others? which clearly prescribe the functional areas which determine the EQ of a person. All these three components of EQ are related to the teachings of Bhagvad Gita to a greater extent. We can motivate ourselves by understanding, analysing and adopting the teachings of Bhagvad Gita in our life. We can motivate others by directing them to understand, analyse and adopt Bhagvad Gita in their life. The increasing acceptance of EQ as an important contributor to SHD helps in taking momentous decision, or even decisions which are not repetitive in nature. EQ takes the participants through the process of improving their positions in life to achieve a win-win situation.

2. LOVE YOURSELF ATTITUDE DEVELOPMENT

In Bridharanyak Upanishad, Yagnavalka says to his wife Maitri that—"Husband loves his wife not for wife's sake but for the sake of the self and a wife loves her husband not for husband's sake but for own sake; mother loves her child not for child's sake but for own sake and a child loves his mother not for mother's sake but for own shake." It means all the activities which we are doing in our ordinary business of life are guided by self-interest, i.e. Love for our own self. It is a love of own self that urges to take those activities where we get pleasure and discard all those activities where pain is there. So every-where self-interest or love for own self is the guiding force.

According to Swami Ram Tirth, there are two types of selves—Little self, i.e. our body which is composed of all sense organs and the purest self, i.e. our soul.

Now in the first chapter of Bhagvad Gita when Arjuna throws away his *Gandiv* and wants to run away from his Dharma that is he is not ready to fight for the sake of truth by arguing that there is no use of killing our own relatives, friends, gurus even for the kingdom of three lokas. Now this is the little self which is speaking in Arjuna. He is in the grip of Moha. He does not realise that his foes want dominion. This type of Moha distracts one from one's dharma (duty) and have been oppressors and have heaped inequities on the just and the innocent. Arjuna justifies his dereliction of duty with fancy rationalisations.

Bhagvad Gita teaches us self love of the highest order. So, a person is to develop himself so that he can shun love for little self and act according to the dictates of the purest self, i.e. soul. So it is the realisation of the purest self when a person loves his soul then his actions and he becomes a useful member of the society. Then he has no desire and no object to gratify him. His karmas are automatic as the sun shines. As sun gives light to everybody irrespective of caste, creed and religion, in the same way, he works for the welfare of everybody and he observes the same purest self. In brief, a journey from little self to purest self constitutes SHD.

3. PHYSICAL DEVELOPMENT

An old and wise saying—'A sound mind lives in a sound body'

makes the justification for physical development. Having a sound body is very essential for the proper development of one's life. If our body is not working properly it is diseased. We can not perform our duty well and will be inefficient in our work, the growth and development of one's life depends upon the development of physical powers. Physical development contributes a lot in human life and hence necessary for SHD. Physical development is possible by understanding, analysing and adopting Bhagvad Gita in our life.

For the proper maintenance, growth and development of the body, first of all, we must have knowledge about constituents of the body. In sloka 4 of 7 of B.G. Lord Krishna clearly explains the constituents of body—

bhumir apo nab vayuh
kham mano budhir eva ca
Ahankara itlyam me
bhinna prakrtir astadha

(Earth, water, fire, air, mind,
intelligence and ego;
These constitutes my nature eight
Fold divided)

The body which is transient and changing consists of five elements, fire, water, air and earth; within which five sense objects are included. They are manifestations of the physical sound, touch, form, taste and smell. If these senses are active and competent, then we will have a sound body. Air must be devoid of pollution and it is possible through yagnas as prescribed in Bhagvad Gita. Some of the bodily diseases are due to polluted water. Rainy water is considered pure containing many useful elements for the bodily development. In the past, we used to perform yagnas for rain which is also the basis of our agricultural development.

To have a healthy body, we must know, what are its needs? It needs proteins, vitamins, carbohydrates, minerals and fats for its proper growth and development. It needs a balanced diet. Balanced diet is one that contains all these elements in a right proportion required for proper growth of the body. This balanced diet provides energy to our body which in turn provides us the power for our routine work. The purpose of food is to increase the duration of life, purify the mind and aid bodily strength. In the past, great authorities selected those foods that best aid to health and increase life's duration; such as milk products, ghee, wheat, fruits and vegetables. In Bhagvad Gita, (17: 8, 9, 10) food which is agreeable to different men according to their innate nature is of three kinds.

ayuh-saytva-balarogya
suk-priti-vivardhanah
rasyah snigdhah sthira hrdya
aharah sattvika priyah

(Foods which promotes life's duration, intelligence, vigour, health, happiness and cheerfulness are dear to 'Sattavika' type of man; such foods are juicy, fatty, wholesome and pleasing to the heart)

Katv-amla-lavanaty-usna
tiksna-Rusuksa-vidahinah
ahara rajasasyesta
duhkh-sokamaya pradah

(Food which are bitter, acid, salty, over hot, pungent, dry and burning and which cause suffering, grief and sickness are dear to the 'Rajasika' type of man)

Yata-yamam gata rasam
puti paryusitam ca yat
ucchistam api camedhyam
bhojanam tamasa-priyam

(Food which is half cooled or half ripe, insipid, putted, polluted and stale is dear to a men of tamasika disposition).

As already stated that our body needs such a balanced diet which contains all the essential components required for bodily growth. So a diet must contain all these; such as cow milk and ghee. The cow milk contains protein (3.4 percent), lactose (4.1 percent), solids (13.7 percent), fats (4.9 percent), solids without fats

(8.8 percent), minerals (10.7 percent). That is why cow milk has been prescribed by Krishna in Gita as a food which promotes intelligence, vigour and bodily strength. On the other hand, the third type of food liked by tamasika has adverse effect on our body. It increases infection and diseases. Such food stuffs although very palatable to the persons but the conclusion of a systematic medical study shows that it is not an essential diet for human and is unsuitable diet. It actually has harmful effects on various parts of the body.

Lastly, regulation of diet and sleeping is recommended for healthy body. Too much eating and sleeping, both are injurious to health. In B.G. (6.16) it has been clearly explained that—

Naty-asnatas tu-yogo' sti
na caikantam anasata
na cati svapna-silasya
jagrato naiva cariuna

(There is no possibility of one's becoming yogi, if one eats too much or eats too little, sleeps too much or does not sleep enough).

Extravagance in the matter of eating, sleeping, defending and mating, which are the demands of the body, can block advancement of physical development. We should be regulated in our eating, sleeping, mating and all other bodily activities for proper growth and development.

4. MENTAL LEVEL DEVELOPMENT

Without the mind's help, nothing can succeed. So in the process of development, the cooperation of mind is essential as a means of growth, external actions and inward attitude of mind, both are needed. Action is must if you want to test your mind. External actions reveal the quality of mind. The surface of the water is clear, but throws a stone into it and at once mud rises up. Our mind is just like that.

Now the question arises—what makes our mind polluted? When we do any work, we are guided by our senses which in turn are guided by our mind and mind ultimately is guided by our discriminating intelligence/(Vivek). If our mind has a mixture of lust, krodha and illusion, it will not guide us in proper direction so these three can be treated as obstacles in the way of mental development.

The most important thing what one should cultivate in his life is the need to purify the mind. We have to cleanse mind of its dirt. To light a lamp, one needs not only the oil and wick, but a flame. When the lamp is lit, the dark disappears. Purity of mind is the will to dispel darkness in our life. To attain purity of mind, many things are prescribed. Firstly, there is 'yagna', and 'dana' (sacrifice and gifts), jap (prayer and penance), and dhyan (meditating and concentration). These means can be compared with washing soda and soap. But Bhakti is water. Without water, these other things are useless, but even without these, water can cleanse. If in yagna, yoga, dhyan and jap, the heart does not enter, how can purity of mind result ? It is the involvement of heart that is Bhakti. Bhakti is essential for all kinds of efforts. If a trained nurse, attending on a patient, has not the Bhavna, the mental attitude of service, how can it be true service? In work without heart, there is neither strength not satisfaction. Secondly, the things we practise day and night stick to us. We will have to train the mind right from childhood. Take constant care that food impressions alone come to the mind. By letting the mind go as it pleases, we will defeat ourselves. Then we will never acquire good impressions. Similarly, wisdom should be gathered without wasting even a single moment. Noble thoughts should pass through our mind so that good impressions should be created. These should go on constantly. Thirdly, purity of mind can be attained by assuming erect posture. All our activities should be pure. To purify activities, its motive should be transformed. Activities should not be performed for one's individual profit, for satisfying the instinct for outward object but for the whole world. In B.G. (17: 16),"

"Manah prasadah saumyatvam mounam atmavinigraha bhav samsudir ity etat tapo manasam uceyate"

Meaning thereby a calm and contented mental clarity, kindness, silence, self-control and purity of character constitute the austerity of the mind.

5. INTUITION FOR INTELLIGENCE DEVELOPMENT

As students, how often have we heard the dismissive statement, "if you do not do well in class, you can never be successful." And while in job, how many times we have been told, "your success is not related to your performance in class." It was a very surprising statement by a senior official of the examination board which went on to say the same thing in the light of the recent furore over the Mathematics paper in an examination. Taken together, the two statements send very contradictory messages to those who are striving for success.

What determines success then, if it is not Intelligence Quotient (I.Q.)? By stating otherwise, are we not shifting from an old age paradigm which has permeated the very consciousness of every parent, child and educationist? A recent spate of management thoughts and practices champion the cause of EQ (Emotional Quotient) as that warm which when added to IQ define success.

When sailing in the life-boat, we have to face many hurdles and obstacles. For the successful journey, one must be aware of all hurdles and obstacles that come in the way of journey of life. Now even to have a very correct and precise picture of all these obstacles, intelligence is required. Intelligence refers to the power to analyse things in their proper perspective. The individual is the passenger in the car of the material body, and intelligence is the driver. Mind is the driving instrument and senses are the horses. The self is thus the enjoyer or sufferer in the association of the mind and senses. Intelligence is supposed to direct the mind, but the mind is so strong and obstinate that it often overcomes the intelligence sometimes, although the mind is supposed to be subservient to the intelligence. The ability not to read many books on different subjects but understand them and apply them when necessary is intelligence.

It is krodha that hinders in the way of intelligence development. In (B.G. 2.63):

Krodhad bhavati sammohah
sammohat smrti vibhramah
smrti bhramsad buddhi-naso
buddhi-nasat pranasyati

(From anger, complete delusion arises, delusion to bewilderment of memory. When memory is bewildered, intelligence is lost and when intelligence is lost one falls down again into the material pool.)

So, to attain sustainable development, it is very important for us to develop intelligence to understand and accept situations, people and the changes happening around us through intuition which is possible only by undertaking bhakti.

6. SPIRITUAL QUOTIENT (SQ) DEVELOPMENT

Spiritual development is essential for the removal of stress and strain as well as social and economic health of the society. Spiritual development must be performed in order to convert human beings into human capital. Besides the development of senses and mind, there is one thing more which is most important that is spirit, soul or atma. We are to realise it which is the spiritual path.

The figure which we see with our eyes, we call it body or image. But even after seeing with our eyes the outer form, we still have to enter into the object and see it from within. We have to remove the armour, the skin of the fruit and the pulp within. Despite the rough sharp exterior of the coconut, the fruit is full of sweet juicy pulp. When look at ourselves or others, we have to distinguish the inside from outside. Soul can be compared to a driver and body to a vehicle. It is the spark of life that makes the body appear. The Soul pervades the body with consciousness as a lamp fills a room with light. The lamp that gives light to the entire room may be in one corner of the room. Similarly, the soul is situated in the region of our heart. The soul is not removed during heart transplantation as soul is spiritual. For example, when stepney or radiator of a car is changed, nothing happens to the driver.

In B.G. (2: 23) Krishna tells:

nainam chindanti sastrani
nainam dahati pavakah
a chinam kledayanty apo
a sosavati marutah

(The soul can never be cut to pieces by any weapon, not burned by fire, not moistened by water, nor withered by the wind).

Now Lord Krishna says that we are to realise our soul; once a person realises his/her soul, then his/her outlook becomes quite different from that of the worldly people and s(he) becomes the source of inspiration to all. It is the ideal state of spiritual development. So long we do not realise the soul, we remain absorbed in ordinary activities. We know nothing beyond eating, drinking, sleeping and mating. For these, we fight; in this way, we are involved in activities relating to the body. Progress begins only later. All this time, soul remains merely watching like a mother watching her child crawling near the well. With some care, the soul watches us. One day the soul wakes up and knowledge dawns upon it that it has been living like an animal. When the soul begins to think like this, the foundations of ethics are laid. It starts exercising the power of discrimination. Discipline takes the place of self-inelegance. When the soul thus enters the domains of ethics, the soul does not merely stand aside and watch. Then it expresses approval from within saying—'well done.' In the next stage, a man through doing his duty tries to cleanse his mind and heart. When he feels tired, then the soul begins to pray—'I have come to the end of my efforts. Give me more strength.' Until a man realises that he can not achieve success by his own efforts, however hard, he can not understand the secret of prayer. Then a man by own efforts to do a work prove inadequate, he should call on the supreme with a sad and yearning heart as Draupadi did. The stream of Lord's compassion and succour flows continuously. This is the third stage. The supreme now comes very close. He comes running now to help you.

Thus progressively, we should learn to experience the Lord; the Lord comes towards us for our help. After this, we have to give over to the Lord the fruit of action, and make Him the enjoyer. And in the end, we should surrender to him the right to resolve and thus fill all our life with him. This must be the ultimate goal of a person and it is the ideal stage of spiritual development. In true sense, HRD is possible through self-realization and spiritual development.

In brief, I wish to emphasize that for every ill in Indian economy in 21st century there are Vedic pills and Bhagwad Gita is the panacea. It is believed that the river Sarasvati has dried because the totality of knowledge was complete and given with no more to come; but the spiritual river is now flowing so may be the Sarasvati river flow again in order to quench the thirst for proper knowledge which is required urgently for the international community. It is believed that the period of consciousness has already started.

To create work culture in India, there is need of converting holiday culture in to holy-day culture. It is firmly believed by the author that the rate of progress in spiritualism is faster than the rate of progress in materialising; therefore, there is need of accepting spiritually guided materialism making a case for 'needonomics' and not 'greedonomics' as a solution of various problems in the country in 21st century. There is no doubt that India will emerge as a super power of the world on its spiritual strength only and not on the basis of any thing else. To make it happen we should adopt an evolutionary approach and should not expect miracles. Truly, Bhagwad Gita is a treatise on welfare economics and needs to be accepted as a sacro-secular epic for the entire humanity for the survival of human race.

To ensure transparency, quickness and accountability, the manpower in the Central and State Pollution Boards must be trained to work under pressure cooker environment as most of the women do in the kitchen for the great cause with honesty and integrity.

To do real justice with environment, we need to understand the Agenda 21 which addresses the pressing problems of today and also aims at preparing the world for the challenges of the next century. It reflects a global consensus and political commitment at the highest level on development and environment cooperation. It is a dynamic programme. It is carried out by the various actors according to the different situations, capacities and priorities of countries and regions in full respect of all the principles contained in the Rio Declaration on Environment and Development.

Environmental Protection Act, 1986 in India is a landmark in legislation of environment. It is informative as well as preventive. It has provided necessary powers to the Government to deal effectively with the prevention and control of pollution but the provisions are not sufficient for creating environment culture. There is a continuous need to review and update the Act as per requirements of the time. We have to go a long way in environmental legislation to reach the highest standards in prevention and control of environment in India.

The State Pollution Control Boards have merely proved to be data collecting machinery. The honest environmental assessment reports can certainly seal the fate of many industrial units which are running but polluting the water and must not be allowed to operate as water is our need of the day to survive, exist and sustain.

We need to understand the relationship management between nature and human being in all aspects of life which needs to be SIMPLE in strict sense of the model explained herein.

REFERENCES

1. M.M. Goel (2009): Academic Concerns for Environment, Central Chronicle. *www.centralchronicle.com*, June 5.
2. M.M. Goel (2009): Academic Concerns for World Environment Day, The Home Pages, Vol. 12, No 170, *www.homepagesindia.com*, June 5.
3. M.M. Goel (2007): An Introduction to 'The Portrait of Mahatma Gandhi': A Drama by Er. Himendra Thakur of USA, *Antarjyoti*, New Delhi, October.
4. M.M. Goel (2005): Corporate Value System for Social Responsibility; Lessons from Bhagwad Gita, Book of Abstracts and presented in 4th International conference on Corporate Social Responsibility at London Metropolitan University, London, 7-9 September.
5. M.M. Goel (2002): Excellence Models for Teachers in the Changing Economic Scenario. University News—*a weekly Journal of Higher Education*, Vol. 40, No. 42, October 21-27.
6 M.M. Goel (2002): Lessons from Bhagvad Gita for Banking Industry, *Economic Dateline*, Volume II, No. 1, January.
7 M.M. Goel (1999): Implications of Bhagvad Gita for Sustainable Human Development, Samarika by Gita Kendra, Kurukshetra Development Board.
8. A.C. Bhaktivedanta Swami Prabupada (1983): *Bhagvad Gita—As It Is*, The Bhaktivedanta Book Trust, Bombay.

Sustainable Development: The Gandhian Perspective

B.N. GHOSH

The concept of sustainable development is now a very popular expression to development theorists and policy-makers. Interestingly, Gandhi, though not a theoretical economist, had the feel of the expression, and did explain it in his discourses on development. However, the concept of development that Gandhi elaborated upon was not one of pure economic development but conflated with the concept of social development. To Gandhi, economic development, as it appears, is subsumed under societal development. Economic development, social development and moral development are integrated categories in the Gandhian schema. Gandhi's concept of sustainable development is based on the provision of *basic needs* for all the people in a country like India. Unless poverty and unemployment are wiped out, Gandhi is not prepared to accept that the country has really attained prosperity, freedom and sustainable development. For Gandhi,

> Real wealth does not consist of jewellery and money, but in providing for proper food, clothes, education, and creating

The present paper is a modified version of a part of the author's book, *Gandhian Political Economy*, Ashgate Publishing Co., UK, 2007.

healthy conditions of living for every one of us. A country can be called prosperous and free only when its citizens can easily earn enough to meet their needs.

(*Gandhi*, 1947, 13 May)

Gandhi never presented any full-boiled theory of sustainable development. However, one can cull out his ideas to weave a definite pattern for a meta-theoretic construct of sustainable development (SD) in the rather nebulous area of Gandhian epistemology from his numerous writings, speeches and interviews. This is the basic purpose of the present paper.

THE ONTOLOGY OF GANDHIAN CONCEPT OF DEVELOPMENT

M.K. Gandhi's ideas on sustainable development can be appreciated well, if one delves deeper into his theory of development. The Gandhian theory of development can be called the stage theory of development or the evolutionary theory of development. Gandhi conceived of three distinct stages of development. Officially, the idea of *swaraj* (independence) was adopted in the Nagpur Congress in 1920 and the Lahore Congress made a public declaration of it in 1929. Gandhi was making serious plans about *swaraj* (independence) in 1928 (*Gandhi*, 1928, 12 January) and *sarvodaya* and *Ramrajya* (ideal polity) in 1947 (*Gandhi*, 1947, 4 July). However, the *constructive programmes* which contained the ideas of *sarvodaya* were completed in 1941. The works for reform and constructive programmes started long before the attainment of actual independence (*Gandhi*, 1940, 25 August). In fact, constructive activities and reforms were part and parcel of the Gandhian paradigm of development from the very beginning, and these started from the first stage of his development programmes. Gandhi made this very clear in 1931, long before the attainment of freedom. He wrote: "We have everywhere emphasized the necessity of carrying on the constructive activities" (*Gandhi*, 1931, 2 July).

The three distinct stages of development in the theory of Gandhian development are: the stage of rural development (reformation of the sector through constructive programmes), development under *swaraj* and the last stage of development is called *sarvodaya* (the development for all). In each one of these stages, the purpose and aim of development was different. For instance, in the first stage, the aim was to reconstruct the villages through the development of village industries and handicrafts *(khadi)* to generate more employment and income and to reduce the level of overall poverty. The basic idea was to make villages self-sufficient and self-reliant. Gandhi wanted self-reliance in everything (*Gandhi*, 1947, 13 May). In the second stage of development, it would be necessary to eliminate the colonial structure and attain *swaraj*. This stage also aimed at eliminating the city-village dichotomy through decentralisation. The workers would own the means of production in this stage. In the last stage, there would be *sarvodaya* for benefits of all classes of people; their basic physical needs would be provided for, and there would be enough scope for the development of body, mind and spirit. Gandhi's development paradigm follows *the principle of balanced development*. It would be a stage of holistic balanced development. It should, however, be noted that the stages cannot be segregated clearly in apple-pie order; there may be possible overlapping of some stages. To a discerning reader, Gandhi's concept of SD encompasses self-sufficency, self-reliance, *sarvodaya* and balanced development. Let me elaborate on these issues.

The following were the basic objectives of the Gandhian schema of holistic development:

- First, human development (including moral development) for capability expansion.
- Second, development in a balanced way through manual and intellectual labour (development of body, mind and soul) (*Gandhi*, 1946, 8 Sept.)
- Third, development with social justice, rights and freedom. This is in accordance with the *principle of social and human development*.
- Fourth, attainment of self-sufficiency and self-reliance through rural development.
- Fifth, reduction in poverty through the generation of additional income and employment.

The fifth objective was basically short-run in nature and was interrelated with the fourth objective. The first three objectives were to be achieved in the long-run. The second and third objectives are interconnected in the sense that holistic balanced development should subsume justice, freedom and rights. Since eradication of poverty and achievement of self-sufficiency need a long time, these can also be categorised as long-term objectives. In the short-run, these objectives can only be partially achieved. Most of these types of development had to be actualised through various types of reforms. The most important concept of progress in the Gandhian theory of development is the same as the one in the Hegelian version of Marxism concerned with the humanist goal, that is, a journey towards the emancipation of mankind from the realm of necessity to the realm of freedom. In the scheme of development that Gandhi was contemplating, the achievement of freedom was closely identified with the welfare of under-privileged people (*Gandhi*, 1945, 15 June). Gandhi laid much emphasis on the achievement of freedom which could give a man the full opportunity to develop himself (*Gandhi*, 1947, 13 May). But he suggested that the real hard work to eradicate poverty and deprivation would begin only after independence; and although it is very hard to achieve perfection, one can make life better through efforts and discipline (*Gandhi*, 1918, 13 January). Gandhi is like Kant who propounded that a true ideal can never be achieved in one life, but there should be progress towards it.

However, unlike the Marxian concept of development which is production-centric, Gandhi's concept of development is human-centric and it delimits production to basic needs. Gandhi's theory is not concerned with the perception of newer and newer human needs and the consciousness to satisfy these needs. But like Marx, Gandhi believed that capitalist development by its very nature is uneven, exploitative and unequal, and the poor colonies which are linked with the metropolitan countries ultimately become the hewers of wood and the drawers of water.

Gandhi's basic idea of SD was to have an all-round development of society which included human development along with socio-economic-political development. For him, human development and social development are inseparable because the two are interactive in more ways than one. Development is essentially a type of freedom (*Sen*, 1999). Development as freedom encompasses freedom to pursue one's own goals without domination or dependency, freedom of choice, freedom of social interactions and the like. Human development in Gandhi's schema does not only include capability expansion through the improvement of human capital and uplift of morality but also human contestability that can be raised through empowerment, entitlement and endowment by inculcating ethical and moral principles to make the capability expansion operational. Contestability is the manifested overt ability to prove the inherent or acquired capability. Gandhi's idea of the *principle of transformational growth* put more stress on the improvement of human capability consistent with moral and ethical principles so that human beings can be more contestable in facing all types of real challenges not only in the present but also in the other world.

Capability and Contestability

Capability and contestability are two different conceptual notions. All contestability includes capability but all capability may not include contestability which is a broader concept. Capability is esoteric but contestability is exoteric. Contestability is optimum capability (body and mind) plus moral and spiritual strength. In the context of Gandhian development, a person acquires *soul force* through practice of all the four nomological rules that include truth, *anasakti, ahimsa* and *sarvodaya.* A strong soul-force is the necessary precondition for success in any important endeavour which is just and moral. Once this is achieved, a person has the required contestability in any venture which is for the benefit of all people. Here lies the importance of knowledge, information and proper education. To Gandhi, proper education not only includes knowledge of the subject but also devotion to duty, spirit of service and, most importantly the training of character (*Gandhi*, 1932, 10 July). Gandhi advocated the dissemination of knowledge among common people through the spread of adult education programmes, part-time schooling and also programmes for women's education in India. For ensuring command over resources, he suggested the development of village and cottage industries. However, it should be noted that Gandhi did not use the term contestability but it can be culled out from his various writings and speeches. His idea of contestability cannot be used in the sense of material gain in the arena of the market but it is more a moral force without which there may be the problem of capability failure.

In the Gandhian theory of development, the village is the primary organizational unit and the development of the village or the rural area is the primary concern in any successful scheme of development of the country. The methodology of development here is the *bottom-up approach*. In such a schema of development, *khadi* or village industries will predominate and it will generate a number of desirable advantages. First, the development of village industries will create sufficient employment and income for the rural population. The level of income and productivity generated by these industries may not be high but it will be sufficient for the rural population if their meta-needs are controlled. Many economists including A.K. Sen criticized the Gandhian scheme of village and cottage industries by saying that such industries are inflationary in character because the wage is higher than productivity (*Sen*, 1962). Such a line of argument does not hold water once one takes into account the objective function and true nature of a village economy. It should be noted that these industries are familial in nature and labourers are all sharing the family-based work and eating from a common kitchen. In such a context, the imputation of market wages for evaluating the performance of the employed workers is wholly unrealistic. When the family workers are employed on family-based enterprise, be it *charkha* (the hand-spinning machine) or *khadi* industries, they are not paid any wage. The basic objective function of a rural family under the situation of unemployment and zero opportunity cost of labour is to maximise employment and total familial output even at the low level of per capita productivity and income. Forced unemployment hinders the individual not only from attaining the moral duty of participation in the divine act of creation but also from serving his family and neighbours through work. To a neoclassical economist, the profit maximizing employment is determined at the point where the wage rate and the marginal productivity of labour become equal. This line of approach can be castigated as irrelevant from many analytical angles for the rural development of a country which has been facing the problem of surplus labour.

In the case of family-based production functions in rural areas, capitalistic production relations do not at all enter into the system and evaluation through the yardstick of the market is totally incongruent. In the rural areas of a developing over-populated country like India, family farms are the abode of semi-proletariats who are struggling day in and day out to make both ends meet. In such a context, the concept of profit maximisation is not only grossly irrelevant but also patently wrong. The concept of marginal productivity is useless and somewhat preposterous. A more relevant concept that may have some applicability is the concept of average productivity. It should be noted that rural farm family members in a bid to maximise the family output and employment, may work on farms and spend family labour till the marginal productivity is zero (to use the neoclassical concept). This is not meaningless because the family farm is guided by consideration of total output and because, when the marginal productivity is falling, the average productivity lies above the marginal productivity, and at the point where marginal productivity is zero, the total productivity becomes maximum. Thus, the objective functions of rural family farms are quite rational in relation to their circumstances including high man-land ratios, limited capital and technology endowment. Capitalist production relations are overly inappropriate for the cottage and village industries that Gandhi was recommending for increasing rural income and employment. To Gandhi, SD should ensure that income and employment must go hand in hand even if they are at the low level.

What is more appropriate in the over-populated rural sector in a country like India is the *peasant* or *household made of production* where there occurs over-exploitation of family labour for the production of the cheapest food articles that can make possible the reproduction of *labour power* at a very low cost. The capitalist state very often implements programmes of agrarian reforms to support simple commodity production; but these do not help the poor small farmers who remain tied to limited resources and live the life of *semi-proletariats* (*Ghosh*, 2000). During the *British Raj* in India, the help from the state did not create a definite precondition for agrarian accumulation. Capitalist relations did not touch family farms, and thus, functional agrarian dualism continued.

The small family farms continued to exist in spite of many limitations because, the small size of the farms generated many comparative advantages, e.g. low cost of production, better supervision, maximisation of employment and output and so on. They optimised their gains by substituting labour for capital, and remained small enough to reap economies of better supervision and flexibility. Since small farms were insufficient in generating full employment and income, Gandhi advocated the establishment of village and small industries to supplement the income. These industries could provide the *bread labour* for the members of the family. Gandhi advocated the development of village and cottage industries primarily because such industries would be able to eliminate poverty, hunger, unemployment and human degradation.

Secondly, to help village level development, Gandhi popularised the concept of *swadeshi* (home-produced goods). Once people are inspired by patriotic sentiments to buy India-made goods, the indigenous industries can be expanded to a considerable extent and the levels of income, output and employment could develop satisfactorily. However, investment is limited by the extent of the market. As the market expands, investment would go up, and all the salutary changes will follow through the operation of the multiplier effect. This idea of Gandhi is quite inconsonance with the modern theory of economic development.

Gandhi, therefore, realised that although economic development was necessary for a country like India, capitalist industrialisation was unwanted. He made it clear that it was not necessary for India to be industrialised in the modern sense of the term (*Gandhi*, 1977:165). According to him, industrialisation is fraught with many evils, and no amount of socialisation can eradicate them. Capitalist industrialization in many countries is sustained through *the principle of enabling myth* that it would create a win-win situation for everybody. But Gandhi thought that industrialization leads to active or passive exploitation of villagers (*Gandhi*, 1936, 29 August). In this context, Gandhi writes: "Hitherto the industrialization has been so planned as to destroy the villages and their crafts. In the State of the future it will subserve the villages and their crafts". (*Gandhi*, 1940. 27 January)

Industrialization goes hand in hand with centralisation and it ruins the village economy and its self-sufficiency. Industrialization involves passive exploitation of villages as the problems of competition and marketing come in. In Gandhi's conceptualisation, industrialisation depends entirely on the capacity to exploit, on the opening of foreign markets and also on the absence of competition (*Gandhi*, 1931, 12 November). Capital-intensive methods of industrialisation also lead to the impoverishment of villages and an increase in unemployment. Moreover, capitalist development breeds a permanent conflict between labour and capital. It is because of the possibility of inequality that Gandhi did not want industrialization. He asserts: "I do not believe that industrialization is necessary in any case for any country. It is much less so for India". (*Gandhi*, 1958-84: 63, vol. 92).

Gandhi was not completely against the use of machinery or capital but pointed out that its use must be restricted and it must not replace human beings (Gandhi's views on machinery are discussed in detail later in this chapter). In his view, machinery creates a *disembedded economy.* This argument was particularly relevant in the labour-surplus economy of India. Through economic development, Gandhi wanted to generate full employment of mind, body and spirit for everybody. The question was: how to bring about economic development without tears? As pointed out earlier, the dependency model of development was, according to Gandhi, not suitable for india as it led to many economic evils in the past. What then should be the paradigm of development in India?

PARADIGMS OF DEVELOPMENT

As conventional wisdom teaches us, there are basically the following three models of economic development that can be pursued by a developing country (see *Das*, 1970):

1. Capitalist model (without dependency) with emphasis on large-scale capital-intensive techniques of production. This method is based on higher capital-output ratio, it is labour-saving and increases the productivity per worker and generates re-investible surplus.
2. Capitalist model (with dependency) where, for the supply of capital and technology, the developing country has to depend on the metropolitan centre (which is generally a developed country).
3. Command economy model where the entire task of development is directed by the state and the surplus for

development is extracted from the agricultural sector. In a communistic type of development, the agricultural sector may be collectivised, and many schemes of forced savings may have to be devised from time to time.

In all these models, there is a primacy of growing production for satisfying the increasing needs of people, and therefore, the resource requirements are pretty high every year. However, Gandhi did not like any of these models. Since his reasons for the rejection of capitalistic methods of development have already been enumerated, it will suffice to mention here briefly a few cogent arguments from the Gandhian perspective. Gandhi did not recommend the capitalistic path of development mainly because it is exploitative in nature and generates economic inequalities and conflicts, and all these evils of *transformational growth* are accentuated under a dependency type of development. According to Gandhi, the private sector capital accumulation needed for development is impossible without exploitation, and there lies his basic objection. On the other hand, state-directed development increases the economic sufferings and sacrifices of the rural people and leads to concentration of power in a few hands and destroys individuality, rights and freedom.

Gandhi, therefore, presented his own paradigm of development which was distinct from all traditional models and which represents the crux of his ideas on SD. In presenting his model of development, he was confronted with two main constraints. First, how can one achieve a rate of growth of output sufficient enough to provide the basic needs of the people both in the present and future (taking into account the rate of growth of population)? Second, how can one mobilise the necessary resources for generating and sustaining that critical rate of growth?

The answers to these strategic questions were starkly simple for Gandhi. The answer to the first question was that a high rate of growth was not at all necessary. Gandhi was not in favour of an exorbitantly high rate of growth of output *per se*, but he wanted a fairly good amount of production to satisfy the increased rate of population growth. He was right in appreciating the truth, evidently, that a high rate of growth is not necessarily the optimum rate of growth. This truth is now being appreciated by the miracle economies of the East Asian countries. For these countries, a high rate of economic growth has indeed exacerbated many socio-economic evils like economic inequalities, recession, financial crisis, and the neglect of the social sector (*Ghosh*, 2001). Indeed, when economic growth rate is kept within manageable limits, many of the problems in the domains of production and resource management become comparatively easy.

The answer to the second question in the perspective of Gandhian political economy is rather interesting. Gandhi advocated the control of desire for meta-needs and bringing down the scale of wants to the *ethical minima*, or what can be called the *basic necessities of life* (*Gandhi*, 1947, 15 April). This is necessary in the context of the staggering poverty of India and requires some changes in life style (*Gandhi*, 1940, 25 August). These basic necessities included people's right to a proper house, an adequate and balanced diet for the family and the supply of locally made clothes, facilities for the education of children and adequate medical relief (*Gandhi*, 1946, 24 January). His concept of basic needs is more or less similar to the modern concept. To Gandhi, economic development does not mean that one should have more but that one should be more.

The total demand being moderate, the rate of growth of supply of output need not be very high. Production was not for export but for home consumption and self-sufficiency. For the fairly closed economy model that Gandhi had in mind, development management did not require extra stresses and strains. The production conditions of the basic necessities of life would be under the direct control of people.

The necessary resources at the national level could be mobilised in the following four ways: first, taxing the rich and the owners of large industries; second, capital accumulation by extracting surplus from state industries and nationalised enterprises; third, increased income from the rural sector may also contribute to the generation of savings and investment. When the rural sector is fairly developed, it would be able to contribute to further development and expansion, and fourth, through trusteeship and social control, a good amount of resources may be mobilised for social development.

The production of basic needs has to be employment-generating and income-creating, and what was needed was mutual help and cooperation without exploitation at the levels of both production and distribution. *The principle of cooperation* is all-pervasive in GPE. In the Gandhian schema, development must have a moral basis. It needs discipline and moral responsibility as well as a particular type of personality pattern.

In the first stage, as Gandhi proposed, development must start from the grass roots level—the lowest rung of the ladder (*Gandhi*, 1946, 28 July). Since most Indians lived in villages, the focus of initial development must be on the development of villages. He suggested in this connection, the development of handicrafts, and small and villages industries *(khadi)*. The mode and technique of production for the development of these industries would be familial, or household modes of production with labour-intensive techniques. The village industries included the whole range of rural industries having various types of inter-linkages such as weaving, pottery, shoe-making, clothes manufacturing, food production and so on. The surplus product of these industries could be marketed out elsewhere in the country.

The development of handicrafts and *swadeshi* (indigenous) goods could lead to a number of advantages. These included three main benefits. First, the creation of additional income and employment to reduce disguised unemployment, overt underemployment, seasonal unemployment and surplus labour. Gandhi wanted each rural family to have maximum levels of output which was possible by extending employment to all eligible family labourers *until the marginal productivity of labour becomes zero* (my emphasis). This principle is not applicable to a profit maximising farm; but to Gandhi, it seemed to be justifiable because at the point of zero marginal productivity of labour, average productivity is still higher than marginal productivity, and the total productivity is maximum. Moreover, family labourers are not paid any wages. In fact, for family economics, more often than not, the neoclassical market principle does not apply. Secondly, the possibility of substantial capital savings would help the generation of sustainable growth in the long-run. Since these industries have a low capital-output ratio, they are very suitable for a capital-poor country. Thirdly, these industries involve a short fruition lag or gestation period. Fourthly, the labour-intensive method of production that these industries use would ensure industrial peace by minimising industrial disputes which are generally associated with capital-intensive large scale production.

Fifth, Gandhi's India contained a huge amount of surplus labour with zero opportunity cost *(labour of zero value)*. The shifting of surplus labour to more productive occupations provided by village industries did not entail any opportunity cost. Therefore, following Chenery's *social marginal productivity criterion* (*Chenery*, 1963), it would be clearly advantageous to encourage labour-intensive methods of development to absorb surplus labour for higher rates of capital formation. The development of village industries would decrease the dependency on the urban sector and its exploitation. Sixth, Gandhi said that the immediate advantage of the development of these industries is that these would bring about self-sufficiency and a self-reliant method of development. Lastly, development through the spirit of *swadeshi* will help to prepare the ground for the attainment of economic independence out of the clutches of alien rule.

Swadeshi was essential for banishing India's pauperism (*Gandhi*, 1921, 8 December). Rural development was also thought to be a means for correcting the urban bias. Gandhi's main argument for the development of village industries was to remove poverty through the generation of sufficient employment opportunities for the unemployed, underemployed and surplus (idle) labour. The problem of surplus labour or disguised unemployment was indeed very acute and serious in India during Gandhi's time. It is intriguing to examine how the Gandhian paradigm of village-centric development could contribute to solving the problem of surplus labour.

Surplus labour or labour of zero value is a very broad concept encompassing open unemployment, underemployment and disguised unemployment. (Disguised unemployment being overwhelming in nature and extent, as alleged by some, is regarded as being synonymous with surplus labour). It is generally believed that disguised unemployment in India during Gandhi's time affected about thirty percent of the labour force in agriculture. This was indeed a drag on rural development. The question is: how could this huge amount of surplus labour be utilised for capital formation and economic development? Before examining Gandhi's views on this issue, a couple of models are briefly outlined here.[1]

Ragnar Nurkse (1953) believed that disguised unemployment

contained disguised saving potential. It is, in fact, a blessing in disguise, for it can be used for capital formation. Mere reallocation of surplus labour from agriculture to the industrial sector would ensure capital formation in underdeveloped countries, and at the same time, would turn unproductive consumption into productive saving. Be that as it may, Gandhi's plan for the utilization of rural surplus labour was diametrically different from that of Nurkse's. Gunnar Myrdal (1968), like Gandhi, observed that it would be wholly unrealistic to shunt the rural surplus labour out to the cities. It is better, according to him, to provide productive works to these surplus labourers in the agricultural sector itself. In fact, the underemployed workers can be organized on their own and their neighbours' farms on reciprocal aid for capital building, and they need not be given a wage. Surplus workers can be utilized for land improvements by organizing cooperative farming societies in the rural sector. In most underdeveloped countries, there is greater scope for the utilization of better farming facilities (see, *Myrdal*, 1968: 1285).

What was really needed in agriculture was a suitable land reform policy encouraging an owner-cultivator system along with labour-intensive methods of production, as Gandhi seems to have suggested in his trusteeship programme (see, *Gandhi*, 1939, 6 May). Gandhi suggested non-violent land-reforms. He assures that "It is possible, without a violent redistribution of land to secure for tenants rights which virtually amount to ownership" (*Gandhi*, 1958-84, Vol. 64:258)

He rightly suggested that a developing agriculture must be made to be the primary employer of an increasing population as in the case of India, and this was possible if rural agro-industries were given encouragement. The Gandhian type of development seems to be feasible and realistic, given the basic objective functions, the possible parameters of action and the economic milieu of his time. Assuming a very modest growth rate of 3 per cent per annum, and given the capital-output ratio of around 3:1, a rate of investment of about 9 per cent was all that was necessary for the growth to be sustainable.[2] The three per cent rate of growth was more or less consistent with the rate of growth of population during Gandhi's time. A nine per cent rate of growth of savings was not at all unrealisable in a situation when almost all the people had jobs throughout the year, and the savings by the state from the sources mentioned earlier were also available. In that case, the growth rate could be gradually increased and it would be completely self-sustainable: investment would be equal to domestic savings. The numerical assumptions made here, however, are not the ones proposed by Gandhi but simply illustrative of the feasibility of his paradigm.

ROLE OF MACHINERY

In the context of the choice of technique of the Gandhian theory of development, a discussion on the use of machinery becomes immediately relevant. Gandhi was not so much against the large-scale industries as he was against the use of machinery. To Gandhi, as much as it was to Marx, machinery is an instrument that dehumanises and alienates labour, and technological determinism leads to the enslavement of the labouring class. Machinery replaces labour from its rightful position and capital is always in conflict with labour. Here his views are similar to those of David Ricardo (*Ricardo*, 1817).

In the Gandhian scheme of development, "there is no room for machines that would displace human labour and that would concentrate power in a few hands" (*Gandhi*, 1946, 28 July), Gandhi is, however, in favour of those machines which are helpful to the workers for their work (*Gandhi*, 1919, 17 Sept.). What he did not like was the craze for machinery, as Gandhi said: "I hold that the machinery method is harmful when the same thing can be done easily by millions of hands not otherwise occupied" (*Gandhi*, 1931, 2 July).

Indian handicrafts were destroyed by the use of machinery. Machinery makes labourers slaves. It produces horrible working conditions. It displaces human labour and increases unemployment. Gandhi states that it is criminal to displace labour by the introduction of power-driven machinery. It is wrong to think that machinery saves labour. Machinery improves the lot of a few persons only but it deteriorates the conditions of the common people who are unemployed and exploited. Small-scale types of family industries help to increase employment and output more than the large-scale industries. Under large-scale industries, employment is always lower to which Gandhi objected. The employment differences between these two types of industries show that large-scale industries have the possibility of generating more unemployment. Gandhi was perhaps influenced by the better labour absorptive power of cottage and village type of industries. This thinking was rational in the perspective of the existence of a large number of surplus labour in India (*Ghosh*, 1988: 322-23). But unfortunately, post-colonial planners including Jawaharlal Nehru rejected the endogenous development alternatives proposed by Gandhi, and depended on the Western model of capital intensive technology (*Mehmet*, 2001:211).

Gandhi seems to be opposed to machinery because machines establish mastery over man and make him their slave. He believed that machinery is permissible if it does not deprive masses of men the opportunity of labour, increases efficiency and does not make people slaves. Machinery also encroaches upon the individuality of labourers. But Gandhi was not against the use of all machinery. He welcomed that type of machinery which helped the workers and which posed as servants. Mechanisation is good particularly for labour-deficit countries. It is bad for labour-surplus economies. Gandhi's basic objection to the large-scale industries in India was that such industries always work on the principle of profit maximisation which leads to the amassing of wealth by the owners through exploitation of labour.

Immiserisation of the working class is considered to be the ultimate outcome of the capital accumulation process. As more and more capital is accumulated, the size of the industrial reserve army (IRA) goes up and the pauperism of the working class also goes on increasing. This is technically called the *absolute general law of capitalist accumulation*. According to this law, capital accumulation leads to both the relative and the absolute deterioration in the lot of the working class. The relative deterioration can be seen from the fact that as capitalism grows, the share of wages in national income goes down. Secondly, the rate of growth of profit exceeds the rate of growth of wages. Thirdly, the share of profit goes up relatively and a greater part of national income is concentrated in the hands of a few capitalists. There may be an *absolute deterioration* of the conditions of the working class. This is expressed in declining wages, increasing unemployment, poorer living conditions and so on. This is possiblly due to the fact that workers are an exploited class. Their conditions may get worse by increasing unemployment, lower wages and palpable working conditions.

Under capitalism, poverty exists in its acute form, both physically and socially. *Physical poverty* includes malnutrition, under-nutrition, poor housing and living conditions and the like. Social poverty implies discrepancy between wages, inequalities in consumption, in social expenditure and in opportunities, and also in resource endowments and allocation. The position of workers in the percentile ranking of society's income distribution falls at the bottom. The pent-up demands of the workers are not satisfied. As the analysis *of path dependency and hysteresis* shows, the tendency towards deterioration of economic conditions of the working class is a socio-economic law of capitalism. The capitalist relations of production determine this law. Nothing short of a revolution can change such rigid relations. But unlike Marx, Gandhi, however, advocated gradual change and reform of the industrial sector to change capitalist relations in the realms of production and distribution.

REFORMING THE INDUSTRIAL SECTOR

Gandhi went a step further than Marx in suggesting some reforms for large-scale industries so that these industries can contribute to the welfare of everybody without harming anybody else—a state of bliss through Pareto improvement. He suggested better industrial and human relations and profit sharing between labour and capital, and wanted the formation of better rapport and relations between labour and capital. As Gandhi put it, "I have always said that my ideal is that capital and labour should supplement and help each other" (*Gandhi*, 1925, 14 August).

While the capitalist system stands for allocative efficiency, it hopelessly lacks equity. Therefore, if it is possible to find out a trade-off between efficiency and equity, it will eliminate much of the evils of the capitalist system. Gandhian political economy is an attempt to construct a trade-off or compromise through: (i) industrial reorganization and decentralization, (ii) the development of cottage and village industries, and also (iii) the scheme of trusteeship. His advocacy of *trusteeship* seems to be an extremely important idea.

On the question of unhealthy competition between machine-made goods and goods produced by the village industries,

Gandhi advocated heavy taxation on machine-made goods (*Gandhi*, 19 August, 1939: 242). The cities should not be allowed to produce what villages could produce, and the cities should act as the clearing house for village products. The protection to village industries would, however, be time-bound. If self-sufficiency is maintained, modern machinery and rationalisation could be introduced in villages. In Gandhi's view, technological improvement could be introduced to village industries to make capital more efficient. In fact, appropriate technology was needed for the regeneration of the village economy, and such technology would not be an anachronism but could be well-embedded in the system.

Gandhi's forceful advocacy of labour-intensive technology in his paradigm of development was entirely rational for the labour-surplus and capital-deficient economy of India of his time. In fact, the question of choice of technology, whether capital-intensive or labour-intensive, should not proceed from any preconceived notion in favour of one or the other alternative. There is no *apriori* solution to the choice of appropriate capital intensity in a development program. Such a choice depends not merely upon the actual economic and technical conditions and potentialities but also upon the political and social objectives that a country wants to achieve. In the case of "Gandhian development", the basic objective being full employment even with a low level of per capita income and economic independence with social justice, the appropriate technique of production could not have been anything other than the labour-intensive method. The debate on the question of appropriateness of labour-intensive *versus* capital-intensive techniques of production for a labour-surplus country like India is indeed a sham debate (see, *Sen*, 1962).

As A.K. Sen (1962) has stated, no technique of production is always distinctly superior to the other and there is nothing like a once-and-for-all choice of technique. The choice of technique will ultimately depend on value judgements regarding the preference of either the immediate present or the future. Sen observes that if a premium is put on the present and the future discounted, a labour-intensive method of production will be the appropriate technique; on the other hand, if a premium is put on the future, and the present discounted, a capital-intensive line of production should be preferred. In view of Gandhi's serious concern for the immediate solution to rural India's massive poverty, unemployment and underemployment problems and his socio-economic plans for achieving self-sufficiency, the obvious choice was the labour-intensive method of production. It was indeed the most appropriate technique of production in Gandhi's India, and its economic appeal is by no means less even now in modern rural India in the context of massive surplus labour, unemployment, underemployment and rural poverty.

In the Gandhian system, there would be a tripartite division of industries, and the village, cottage and handicraft industries would be dispersed in rural areas. The urban industries may be privately owned, but will not compete with the rural industries, and the heavy, basic and nationally important key industries would be run on a no-profit-no-loss philosophy under the control of the state. In his schema, minor and major industries are to supplement each other (*Gandhi*, 1934, 26 July). Some vital key industries could be nationalised or socialised (*Gandhi*, 1946, 1 Sept.). In the case of socialised industries, the control would be in the hands of people (*Gandhi*, 1968: 346, Vol. 4). The advantage that can be derived from the development of cottage and village industries of the type that Gandhi was advocating is the self-reliance of the village economy (*Gandhi*, 1947, 13 May). The self-sufficiency may not be perfect but that will give a sense of independence. During the period when Gandhi was writing and fighting in his own way, the country was not only ruled by a foreign government but was also heavily dependent on that foreign country for almost everything. His concept of *swaraj* or independence included both political and economic *swaraj.* It is said by Karl Marx that economic power is the key to political power. Needless to add, the Marxian and the Gandhian concepts of political economy have many important commonalities. These commonalities are so significant that sometimes Gandhi is regarded as Karl Marx minus violence.

Limited self-sufficiency in the village economy can give rise to many types of exchange relations among the neighbouring rural and semi-rural areas that can be helpful for satisfying the mutual needs for the basic necessities of life, and at the same time, the rural economy would be able to enjoy economic freedom which is a prelude to political freedom. Once rural areas, which constituted the significant dimension of the Indian sub-continent, are more or less independent and self-sufficient though on a limited scale, they can have many types of interactions and externalities nationally and internationally. Gandhi conceived of the possibility of such interactions in the 1940s (*Gandhi*, 1946, 28 July). Such interactions could help reduce dependency and dominance. Political economy is indeed a study of interactions and interrelations, and Gandhian political economy is no exception to this broader characterisation of political economy. Another feature of political economy—the study of dependency and dominance, is also well-articulated in GPE. The dependence-dominance relationship may be endogenous in the system for which Gandhi suggested decentralisation at many levels.

DECENTRALISATION

The second stage of development in the Gandhian plan would be marked by an increasing degree of decentralising the industrial structure which was initiated in the first stage of rural development. Gandhi advocated decentralisation for reaping the advantages of flexibilization of technology and organisation. Decentralisation was not meant for capital goods but only for consumer goods industries. Decentralisation was not only recommended for industries but also for political power in order to make it more advantageous for the common people. The decentralised structure of the politico-economic system was presumed to be necessary for preventing exploitation, inequality and conflicts. The structural change suggested in the second stage of development after the attainment of self-sufficiency was to eradicate urban bias in development and to destroy the colonial market that was so expansive in India during Gandhi's time. The predominance of *swadeshi* (home-made goods), in both production and consumption, was a step forward towards attainment of *swaraj* (independence).

Decentralization forms the organizational method of the Gandhian working plans. Gandhi wanted a decentralized pattern of development because such a pattern is better, socially and spiritually. Decentralized industries can play a crucial role in the development of a country like India with least disturbance and dislocation. The philosophy of decentralization conforms to the *principle of minimum dislocation*, and small and village industries could serve the purpose of decentralisation. The centralised industries are generally large-scale industries. These industries are anti-democratic and lead to regimentation. Village industries are highly democratic and conducive to the growth of amicable relations between labour and capital. However, some industries are by nature large-scale. They cannot be avoided. In that case, Gandhi advocated strict state control over such industries.

Another important reason for the policy of decentralization was its ability to avoid violence. Large-scale industries needed to be decentralized to avoid violence. Gandhi suggested dispersal of industries as against their concentration in particular areas. He was of the view that village industries could be mechanized gradually. Large-scale industries are sometimes found to be wasteful. These industries are unrelated to the rest of the economy. Gandhi thought that, by and large, people should try to use indigenous power and material for development of the economy. Power has to be used in small-scale and cottage industries very cautiously, lest it should generate exploitation.

Decentralisation is advocated for at least four basic reasons: First, for better administration, control and supervision. Second, for eradicating the possibility of violence, as centralised organizations or institutions are generally prone to violence. Centralisation cannot be fully defended and protected without adequate force (*Gandhi*, 6 May, 1939: 39). Third, centralisation leads to concentration of power and authority which can be misused by the possessor of such power in the name of settling socio-economic problems. Fourth, decentralisation stands for maximisation of individual freedom. However, Gandhi was prepared to give more power to people's organizations like *panchayats*.

The Gandhian pattern of decentralisation is to correct the evils of a centralised economy. The decentralisation of economic power through the development of cottage and village industries was a means to eradicate the concentration of economic power in a few hands in India. During his time, some large-scale capitalist industries had been concentrating wealth and monopoly power amidst the growing poverty of the masses. He was against the growing income and wealth disparities of this type arising out of the growth of large-scale industries. Capitalistic industrialisation was castigated by Gandhi because it does not help the growth of

Figure 1: Holistic Development in Gandhian Political Economy

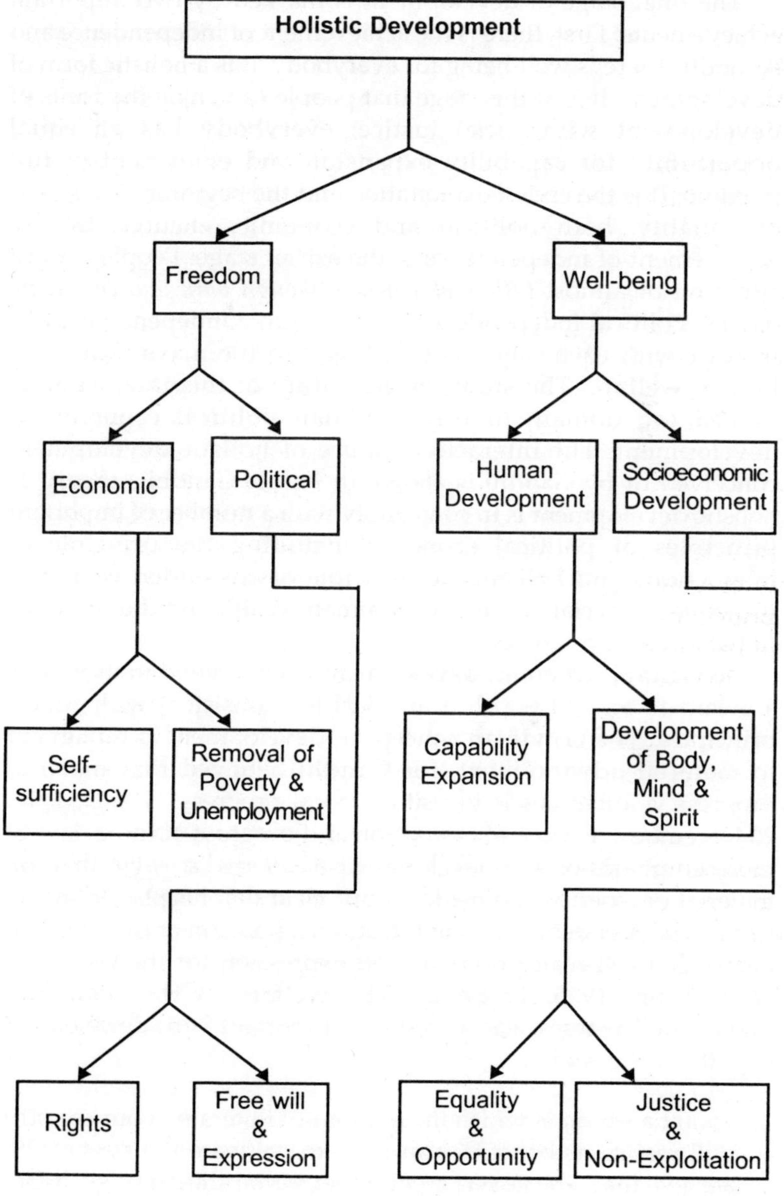

personality: it simply favours material progress. The goal of life, after all, is not material progress.

The final stage of development is marked by two important achievements. First, there is the achievement of independence and secondly, there is well-being for everybody. It is a holistic form of development. It is at this stage that people can enjoy the fruits of development with social justice; everybody has an equal opportunity for capability expansion and enjoyment of full freedom. It is the end of exploitation and the beginning of the era of equality, both political and economic, ensured by the achievement of independence in the earlier stage. People enjoy a situation of almost *full employment although with low per capita income.* Political independence and economic independence will interact with each other and will lead to the maximisation of human welfare. The study of the nature of this interaction is indeed the domain of the Gandhian political economy of development. The interactive nature of holistic development conceived of by Gandhi is shown in Fig. 1. Gandhi's theory of holistic development is in conformity with a number of important principles of political economy including the principle of interactions and holism, the principle of embedded economy, principles of social-cultural and human wealth and the principle of balanced development.

To Gandhi, economic development is not an end in itself; it is a means to an end which is an ideal life consistent with ethical principles. The Gandhian concept of development is repugnant to material advancement, for Gandhi believed that material progress is antagonistic to real or moral progress (*Gandhi*, 1916, 25 December). For the liberalisation and progress of India, he put more emphasis on the development of *internal strength* than on material prosperity, and made it quite clear that his plan to secure *swaraj* (independence) was not to attain a position of isolation but one of full self-realization and self-expression for the benefit of all (*Gandhi*, 1925, 17 Sept.). The welfare of the poor and uneducated masses was always an important consideration for Gandhi, as he said:

> I want a *swaraj* in which the millions of illiterate in our country will realise its benefits. You have to cultivate the strength to achieve that. The government under *swaraj* should be such that

people may clearly see the distinction between the arbitrary and autocratic British rule and the democratic government run on non-violent lines.

(*Gandhi*, 1947, 17 April)

Here lies the importance of *sarvodaya* (welfare of all). Gandhi's *sarvodaya* is a stage of balanced development. In the first stage of the Gandhian development paradigm, development is unbalanced in favour of the rural sector, village industries, and handicrafts, but subsequently, with the attainment of *sarvodaya*, development becomes balanced in many ways, e.g., sectoral balance, balance in terms of socio-economic equality, balanced development of human beings, and so forth. In this stage, there is the conspicuous deliverance of men in the realm of freedom which is the primary aim of Gandhi's paradigm of development. This was also the aim of Mao Tse-Tung's model of economic development (see, *Mao Tse Tung*, 1966).[3] The *principle of transformational growth* from the regime of enjoyment through materialism to the regime of enjoyment through renunciation has remained indeed very critical in Gandhi's theory of socio-economic development.

IN FINALE

Gandhi never explained explicitly the concept of sustainable development. However, it is possible to construct his views on this issue from the literature on and by Gandhi. In his universe of discourse on socio-economic development which is holistic in nature, Gandhi's ideas on SD can be gauged from his advice on the basic necessities of life, ethically minimal demand, balanced life with a special focus on the spiritual dimension of life and the moderate level of required production through the labour-intensive method that brings self-sufficiency and self-reliance by generating a level of near-full employment situation in congruence with the level of income needed—a situation that guarantees balanced development where there is complete freedom and no exploitation, class conflict or class struggles.

NOTES AND REFERENCES

1. It is possible to have capital formation with the help of surplus labour. There are various models showing such a possibility. Some of these

models are: the Nurksean model, the Myrdal model and so on. For an elaborate discussion on these models and also on the possibilities of more labour absorption in labour-surplus agriculture as in India, see, B.N. Ghosh (1977, Ch. 5).

2. This can be derived from the following basic equation of the Harrod-Domar model of growth:
   G = S (or I) × 1/ k (where G = Growth rate; S = Saving; I = Investment; 1/k = Reciprocal of capital-output ratio).
3. Mao's idea was to make China a powerful country by following the path of socialism, but at the same time, he wanted to make Chinese men the perfect type of men. The achievement of these two objectives may involve a lesser rate of economic growth.

REFERENCES

Chenery, H.B. (1963), "The Application of Investment Criteria", *Quarterly Journal of Economics*. February.

Das, Amritananda (1970), "A Reintroduction to Gandhian Economic Thinking" in M.P. Sinha (ed.) *Contemporary Relevance of Gandhi*, Nachiketa Publications Ltd., Bombay.

Emmanuel. A. (1972), *Unequal Exchange*, Monthly Review Press, New York.

Gandhi, M.K. (1918), "Letter to Esther Faering", 13 January.

Gandhi, M.K. (1919), "*Swadeshi* v. Machinery", *Young India*, 17 September.

Gandhi, M.K. (1921), "The Secret of Swaraj", *Young India*, 19 January.

Gandhi, M.K. (1921), *Young India*, December, 8.

Gandhi, M.K. (1925), "Speech at Indian Association", Jamshedpur, *Amrit Bazar Patrika*, 14 August.

Gandhi, M.K. (1924), *Navajivan*, 7 September.

Gandhi, M.K. (1925), *Young India*, 17 September.

Gandhi, M.K. (1925), *Young India*, 28 May.

Gandhi. M.K. (1928), *Young India*, 12 January.

Gandhi, M.K. (1929), *Young India*, 6 June.

Gandhi, M.K. (1930), "Draft Declaration for January 26", in *Collected Works*, Govt. of India, New Delhi, vol. 48: 214, 10 January.

Gandhi, M.K. (1931), "Superstitions Die Hard", 2 July.

Gandhi, M.K. (1931), *Young India*, 2 July.

Gandhi, M.K. (1931), *Young India*, 12 November.

Gandhi, M.K. (1932), "Education", MMU/II, 10 July.

Gandhi, M. K. (1934), *The Hindu*, 26 July.

Gandhi, M.K. (1936), *Harijan*, 29 August.

Gandhi, M.K. (1939), "Answers to Questions at Gandhi Seva Sangh Meeting", Brindaban, 6 May, as cited in *Collected Works*, Vol. 77.

Gandhi, M.K. (1939), *Harijan*, August, 19.

Gandhi, M.K. (1940), "Ahima in Practice", as in *Collected Works, 11*: 244, 27 January.

Gandhi, M.K. (1940), *Harijan*, 25 August.

Gandhi, M.K. (1945), "My Life is My Message", *The Hindu*, 15 June.

Gandhi, M.K. (1946), "Workers' Conference, Madras", 24 January as in *Collected Works*. Vol. 89: 296.

Gandhi, M.K. (1946), "Independence", *Harijan*, 28 July.

Gandhi, M.K. (1946J, *Harijan*, 1, Sept.

Gandhi, M.K. (1946), "Address to Trainees Basic Teachers' Camp", *Harijan*, 8 Sept.

Gandhi, M.K. (1947), "Talk with Manu Gandhi," 15 April. Gandhi Camp, Patna.

Gandhi, M.K. (1947), "Talk with Congress Workers," Gandhi Camp. Patna, 17 April.

Gandhi, M.K. (1947), "Advice to Construction Workers", 13 May.

Gandhi, M.K. (1947), "Speech at Paryer Meeting", July 4, New Delhi.

Gandhi, M.K. (1958-84), *Collected Works*, Govt. of India, New Delhi, Vols. 92, 32, 64, Vol. 80.

Gandhi, M.K. (1968), *Selected Works*, edited by Sriman Narayan, Vol. 4, Navajivan, Ahmedabad.

Gandhi, M.K. (1977), *Hind Swaraj*, Cambridge University Press, UK.

Ghosh, B.N. (1977), *Disguised Unemployment in Underdeveloped Countries*, Heritage Publishers. New Delhi.

Ghosh, B.N. (1988), *Concise History of Economic Thought*, Himalaya Publishing House, Bombay.

Ghosh, B.N. (2000), *The Three Dimensional Man*, Utusan Publications, Kuala Lumpur.

Ghosh, B.N. (2001) (ed.), *Global Financial Crises and Reforms*, Routledge, London and New York.

Ghosh, B.N. (2007), Gandhian Political Economy, Ashgate Publishing Co., England

Ghosh, S.K. (1984), "Marx on India", *Monthly Review*, January.

Habib, Irfan (1969), '"Problems of Marxist Historical Analysis", *Enquiry*, Monsoon.

Mao Tse-Tung (1966), *Selected Works* (as quoted in *Peking Review*, Nov.).

Mehmet, Ozay (2001), "Globalization as Westernization: A Post-colonial Theory of Global Exploitation" in B. N. Ghosh (ed.), *Contemporary Issues in Development Economics*, Routledge, London and New York.

Mohri, Kenzo (1979), "Marx and Underdevelopment", *Monthly Review*, April.

Myrdal, Gunnar (1968), *Asian Drama*, Allen lane, Penguin Press, London.

Naoroji, Dadabhai (1901), *Poverty and Un-British Rule in India*, Swan, Sonnenschein & Co., London.

Nurkse, R. (1953), *Problems of Capital Formation in Underdeveloped Countries*, Oxford University Press, London.

Ricardo, David (1817), *The Principles of Political Economy and Taxation*, Cambridge.

Sen, A.K. (1962), *The Choice of Technique*, Basil Blackwell, Oxford.

Sen, A.K. (1999), *Development as Freedom*. Knopf. New York.

Sustainable Development: Some Reflections

SUDARSHAN IYENGAR

Sustainable development is a relatively new concept in Development Economics. Rapidly growing economies with large population base have caused concern among the ecologists and the economists both. Despite an assurance from the economists about the infinite possibilities of production and consumption of the goods and services, it is increasing realised that the environmental externalities have started taking its toll. In this paper an attempt is made to review the issues involved in the understanding of the concepts of sustainability and outline the limitations that the economists would face in tackling the issue of natural resources crisis. There is a brief review also of the world economies to show that perpetual growth of the economy is likely to be a myth and the human societies will have to be careful in using these sources. If all the poor and low income countries try to achieve the income levels of high income countries with the use of energy efficient technologies, the end result is likely to be disastrous. In the final analysis there is a discussion with which the scope of the subject is enhanced to new horizons where conventional economics does not go. It is argued with the help of Gandhian thought that there were cultural traditions in societies such as Indian where the need itself was moderated to achieve long-term sustainability.

INTRODUCTION

Shift from soil economics to oil economics brought in dramatic change in the rate at which natural resources were used by the humanity. With industrialisation economic growth became very fast. The rise in income was rapid and so also the consumption. Rapid and substantial rise in consumption in turn led to increased demand for the natural resources for production. Forests, water resources and most importantly fuel sources started being used at a very rapid rate. Obviously, there were hardly any serious efforts to replace and regenerate what was being drawn from the nature. Use of metal and minerals also was with same high intensity and rate. It dawned upon the humanity that many of these natural resources were exhaustible and might not be available to the coming generations.[1] Further, if they were exhausted, the economic activities might also almost come to a standstill. Interestingly, even when soil economics was dominant and agriculture and allied sector contributed more than 90 per cent to the Gross Domestic Product (GDP); rise in population faster than food production became a matter of serious concern and debate among the then thinkers known as classical economists. Robert Malthus, put it most dramatically when he said that the population grew in geometric progression and the food production grew at arithmetic progression and therefore population would easily overtake the food production and humanity would slip into great misery. Malthus's *Essay on Population* was published in 1798. Lionel Robbins thought "his (Malthus) was direct result of a hostile reaction to the uprush of Utopian speculation, Utopian optimism, which accompanied the first years of the French Revolution."[2] More than the mathematical precision Malthus was hinting at the diminishing returns in agriculture.

The dooms day clergy-economist proved wrong largely because progress in technology delayed the decreasing returns in agriculture, and the population depending on agriculture for employment also declined sharply in UK and other European countries that were going through the industrial revolution. The

Industrialising world then never looked back. Expanding markets, trade and distribution of wealth generated in the economy were the major areas of intellectual quest that kept the economists occupied for nearly two centuries. Human misery was brought in differently by Karl Marx but only to argue that capitalism was inherently exploitative because the only way to extract more surplus to invest was giving less and less to labour. The argument was most potent and hardly any other idea in recent human history has been so dominant in the society. We all know that whether the capitalism matured or not, revolution occurred, communism came and the iron curtains were drawn after the October Revolution, and it took another 70 years for it to come down.

Whether capitalist mode of production, where individual with all freedom—*lassiez faire*, or the communist mode, where the state was the master controller of resources and output, the objective was creation of wealth by exploiting nature resources and converting into material development. In the capitalist mode the issue of distribution of material wealth was raised, but the overarching argument was that this type of material development led to the welfare of the humanity. The course being chartered had been born out the age of 'Enlightenment' and was the course for humanity. For more than two centuries with the beginning of industrialisation the occidental societies did not ever think that the development path which it taken would confront the issue of sustainability. In fact as we will see in the following sections, even today the economists' argument of sustainability reflects the arrogance born out of capabilities of science and technology to tide over all and any type of crisis.

SUSTAINABLE DEVELOPMENT: ISSUE AND CONCEPTS

It is important however to note that the issue of sustainability was also first raised by some scientists' who articulated concern over the rapid use and depletion of natural resources including minerals that was being used for production and consumption. A remarkable document named *The Limits to Growth*[3] was produced by a small team at the Massachusetts Institute of Technology, in 1972, which studied the fundamental limits to growth In global population, agriculture, resource use, industry and pollution. The report showed interactions between different factors and concluded that even under the most optimistic assumptions about advances in technology the world cannot support present rates of economic and population growth for more than a few decades from the time of the publication of the report. Needless to say the report generated a huge worldwide debate. There have been many optimists who have questioned the assumptions, estimates and conclusions of the report and provided different scenario. The most prominent among those who took the Club of Rome Project report head on was Julian Simon (1981) who in his famous book *The Ultimate Resource* almost proved the case for more economic growth and more population growth without limits. There arc fair amount of serious people who agree with the position that unbridled accumulation of wealth by individuals should be no problem and believe in 'keeping the governments off the people's back when they accumulate wealth'. This position is not tenable for all the countries and all the time is what evolves as the criticism to Julian Simon's overenthusiastic position. Simon's fundamental position is the denial of resource finitude. Herman E. Daly (1999) produces a piquant critique on the position of Julian Simon. The first argument is theoretical and prominently mathematical. According to Daly, Simon reasons from infinite divisibility to infinite amount, which is wrong because the infinite divisibility of a line segment does not imply infinite length. Daly says that the illustration of copper metal used by Simon is thus wrong. Well. I would not like to bother you with this rather mathematical argument and go on to Daly's critique of Simon's empirical argument. It is also important and relevant in the context of the issues that I propose to raise.

The empirical argument of Simon is about the infinite substitutability. Even if copper were finite (which indeed all minerals are in the foreseeable future), Simon would argue that there were infinite possibilities of substituting other resources for copper. It is important at once to understand that if each substitutable resource was finite, as copper is in this illustration, the set of substitutable resources cannot be infinite! Unless of course it is argued that production without any natural resource was possible. That is man made resource is made without natural resource. Daly points that more important problem in Simon's argument arises because he (Simon) does not mention the assumptions that have been made by the original proponents of the thesis. Simon's argument is based on a study by Weinberg and Goeller and titled *The Age of Sustainability*. The basic assumption is that of a steady state. Levels of population, energy consumption and low-cost abundant energy source are assumed. The society thus is at a high consumption level (the global average per capita energy consumption is 70 per cent of the per capita energy consumption of the United States) but at a steady state implying thereby that there is no further increase either in population or in the energy consumption levels. If the societies have to move to higher levels then it could happen only under extensive planning. If Simon has argued about unlimited economic growth and population growth there appears a clear problem. Daly concludes his critique by saying, "in sum, both the theoretical and empirical arguments against finitude fail utterly. Since everything else in Simon's position depends on the abolishing finitude, the game is effectively over." (*Daly*, 1999, p. 28).

While the international research team form MIT was examining the finite and infinite resources of the world in a very meticulous fashion, United Nations Conference on the Human Environment, Stockholm, 1972 was discussing what should be considered under the sustainable development concept.[4] It was broadly agreed that interdependence of human beings and the natural environment needs to be recognised and studied, links between economic and social development and environmental protection must be explored and there has to be global vision and common principles for moving towards sustainable development. With the passage of time United Nations appointed the UN Commission in 1983 for Sustainable Development chaired by Norwegian Prime Minister Gro Harlem Brundtland, who after the publication of the report was strongly identified with its key messages.

The World Commission on Environment and Development, (Brundtland Commission) (*United Nations*, 1987) defined sustainable development simply as—*Development that meets the needs of the present without compromising the ability of future generations to meet their own needs.* In more detail, the Commission said, *sustainable development is a process of change in which exploitation of resources, the direction of investments, the orientation of technological development, and institutional change are all in harmony and enhance both current and future potential to meet human needs and aspirations.*

Many international organisations have since then worked on the concept and have tried to give varying definitions. The point for discussion is how have the economists tried to react to these definitions. I wish to pick Robert Solow on this because he has dealt with the subject professionally and he has also addressed a lecture for common citizens. For all those who are seriously interested in the subject I would recommend reading this lecture carefully. It is a brilliant lecture[5] although I disagree with him on the finer position he takes on the subject. Let me first deal with a point with which I also agree with him, It is related the way UNESCO understands of the sustainable development. If the UNESCO indeed means what Solow has picked up from the document as the definition of sustainable development, that is, '... every generation should leave water, air and soil resources as pure and unpolluted as when it came on earth' or alternatively, "each generation should leave undiminished all the species of animals it found on earth," then there is serious problem with the understanding. It is good to listen to but not worth-considering at all. The human specie has already violated this for thousands of years and secondly, nature itself as its evolution shows does not seem to be holding on to all the species that appear on the face of the earth. Going back to the cave age is not one is suggesting nor would it be feasible for the human societies to accomplish it.[5]

The key question arises from the definition given by the report 'Our Common Future'. As is clear form the title sustainable development is related to our obligation to the future. In technical terms it has been posed as the issue of intergenerational equity. This does not mean that intra-generational equity is not an issue in the sustainability development debate, but the tough not to crack is the inter-generational equity issue. 'Our Common Future' defined sustainable development as *Development that meets the needs of the present without compromising the ability of future generations to meet their own needs.* To Solow's mind even this is vague and his position is that the concept of sustainability is indeed vague and has very limited policy implications. Hence, one should not read more than it allows. He says, "the best thing I could think of is to say that it is an obligation to conduct ourselves so that we can leave to the future the option or the capacity to be as well off as we are."[6] This kind of injunction to sustainability is also not totally acceptable to him simply because he thinks that we would not be in a position to know about the tastes and preferences of the future generations say 100 years from now, nor we would know the technology that the generations would be using for production and consumption. At best what we can do is to imagine that more or less people will be like us and we can extrapolate the present technological level to some extent and make some intelligent guess. Solow therefore, emphasises the point about vagueness in the concept of sustainability and not meaninglessness. I do not think that the concept is even vague. Now, before 1 say why it is not vague let me elaborate the Solow's concept of leaving the option or the capacity for the next generations to be at least as well off as we are.

Solow as we now know is very clear that we cannot leave the world as it is because that is not possible. From this premise he goes on to say that we do not have any responsibility to leave practically anything as it is. He includes preserving a piece of landscape or a species in this scheme of his too. For him preserving a landscape or a species is intrinsically valuable to us and therefore we may preserve, but preserving or conserving in the name sustainability is not on because you don't have to do it. It is also true about production for him. Society need not be guilty in using up of all the aluminium 'as long as we leave behind a capacity to perform the same or analogous functions using other kinds of materials—plastics or other natural or artificial materials'.[7] Thus, the entire emphasis in Solow's argument is on the general capacity for production and consumption and not on particular material or species. Implicit in the argument is the confidence and approval of substitutability of one input with the other. The argument of sustainability in economics is then built further with respect to total availability of capital. It is argued that in the initial stages of development natural resources capital is more and it is combined with man-made capital and human capital and eventually it is the man-made capital including the farms, improved land, machines, technology and human mind that determines the development prospects of the human society.[8] The Schultzian concept of capital has given such a tremendous courage to the economists that Julian Simon thinks that human capital combined with technology can never feel any constraint and hence no limits to growth and no limits to human population! Solow is not far behind. He practically says almost the same thing as Simon says except that he thinks that sustainability, as a concept is not meaningless. Only thing is that it is vague.

I think that both Julian Simon and Robert Solow ignore the ecology and its implications for economics. In fact, for Simon, Daly says, "not a single chapter in *The Resourceful Earth* was written by an ecologist. Simon sees the natural world mainly as source of vexations, not services."[9] The inter-generational equity issue is not simply limited to leaving the capacity to produce and consume by the future generations at a level at which the present generation does, but it is also to make sure that present actions do not lead to unintended total destruction of nature with which we live and thereby destroying the capacity of the future generation altogether or at least substantially. Now, this type of decision-making calls for some humility about the human knowledge and also more importantly some values that the humanity should uphold. Economist have agreed that even for retaining the same level of natural capital stock over a long period of time[10] it is essentially decision-making under uncertainty and it is proposed that safe minimum standards approach should be followed. When we do not know the environmental consequences of not conserving and if the social cost of conserving is not too high (all of course is subjective here), the recommendation is to conserve. It is under this wisdom we have International Union for Conservation of Nature (IUCN[11]). Some of our economist friends raise brows about the naturalists fighting to conserve species, but I think that it is simply the arrogance about the technology and perhaps over confidence that substitutes are available infinitely *a la* Julian Simon and Robert Solow.

Environment plays three types of roles in the survival game of human species. Its first role is as a *supplier of resources.* Its second role is to *provide local and global environmental and ecological*[12] *services.* Its third role is to *act as sink that receives the waste generated in the process of production and consumption.* Thus, environment has close linkages with the economy. All copper and all aluminium cannot be simply used up because there are substitutes or there is technological possibility of building substitutes. May be in particular case of both these metals the availability or otherwise may not be the issue, but the misconception that it is 'used up' is. Economists seem to have or at least they seem to attach very heavy weight to the 'source value' of the natural resource and not to the 'sink function'. The first law of thermodynamics does tell us that matter like energy can neither be consumed nor be destroyed. The first law is also known as material balance principle. It implies that matter can be converted into energy, one form of energy can be converted into another form of energy and in theory energy can be converted into matter.[13]

The first implication is that more the economy produces using the natural resources (first role of environment), more will be the waste generated. Let us remember that we can neither destroy matter nor energy, we simply change the form and hence residue form will increase with increase in production. The waste will have to be returned to nature. In this sense, whatever is 'produced' is not 'consumed' even in equilibrium situation because consumption in conventional sense is inadequate expression to what happens in reality in nature. If the sink function increases and assimilation capacity goes down there are threats to the availability of resources as inputs and also a threat to life support systems. Clean air and water are cases in point. With increased production and consumption the waste and emissions pollute the air and water and the sink function of natural resources go up. There is a natural capacity to assimilate and purification, but after the threshold values are crossed not only that they become useless for human survival, they may unleash unknown impacts threatening the very existence of human and other species.

Before I go on to talk about the second implication of the first law of thermodynamics let me make this point that for Simon and Solow both it is less important whether other species survive or not. In Solow's words 'if you do not eat one species of fish, you can eat another species of fish.'[14] He wants us to learn the lesson of substitution very steadfastly. If one extends the logic little more then you come to a position that why eat fish at all? Swallow a tablet or any other form of food that has same taste and nutritive value of fish. Forget even that mankind should not bother whether there is fish or not as long as there is some food by which she can survive! Let us imagine a situation where people of Nagpur region decide that they would agree to leave for the future generation a huge factory that will produce tablets tasting exactly like the sweet

Nagpur *santras* and discontinue all the *santra* cultivation. The next generations will get the nutrition and taste both of the *santra* from the tablets produced in the factory.

Would you have any problem? I have an ethical problem here. Does the present generation have any ethical right to decide for the next generation that it should be well off eating the *santra* flavoured tablets in Nagpur and *rohu* flavoured tablets in Kolkata? While it is true that we would not know about tastes and preferences of the next generations, how is it justified to leave them with lack of choice between a tree grown *santra* and pond bred *rohu* fish and the flavoured tablets? 1 would consider this set of choice for the next generations as violation of inter-generational equity as long as it is in the control of the present generation to grant this choice to the next generation. Let me be clear here that if as a process of evolution *santra* disappears or for that matter *rohu* disappears as many thousands species that man may have consumed in past have indeed disappeared, I have no problem and I would not consider it as inter-generational equity violation. But, if humanity destroys all the *santra* germ plasma from the face of the earth and destroy all the ponds in and around Kolkata and other wetlands that breed and grow *rohu* and thereby deprive the next generations of the choice of eating *santra* and *rohu* I would consider it violation of intergenerational equity. In Solow's scheme the violation does not take place because the next generations have the general technological capacity to produce and consume something that has all the qualities of *santra* and *rohu*.

The second implication is on the possibility of substitution of one resource in place of other under the first law of thermodynamics. The origin of the argument of 'limits to growth' is traced to this law. Economic production takes place, combining inputs from environment (the N in neoclassical model), man-made capital (K in the model) and human capital (L). The main exposition of the second implication of the first law is championed by Christensen.[15] He argues that the first law places definite upper limits on the substitutability between different types of resources used in production, and that neoclassical economics has ignored this fact because it has ignored physical features of production. According to him, the neoclassical notion of land, labour and capital as the primary inputs to production is poor reflection of reality. Christensen prefers to consider all material and energy forms used in production and not produced by human beings as primary factors. These factors are then combined with capital K and human capital L to produce output in endogenously determined structures (firms and markets). He argues further, that output can only be increased by varying all of these inputs, or at least more than one at a time. Thus, the concept of marginal product loses relevance. At all the times then it is joint marginal product. Since 'primary factors' have to be necessarily combined with some form of man-made capital, the substitutability between the two is extremely limited. That is elasticity of substitution between the two is close to zero. Thus, if we follow Christensen's argument, production in the economy without primary capital is not possible. Simon and Solow tend to argue that there is immense scope for substituting among the primary factors and also go on to argue that eventually there would be scope for substitution between primary and man-made capital. The latter position implies that mankind can do without any material and energy that it is drawing from other than man-made sources and rely totally on man-made capital. Thus, the Schultzian proverbial 'K' will have only man-made capital and labour (human capital) and yet will be able to produce all the goods and services that would provide at least same standard of living that the present generation has. As on today when almost 100 per cent of food material is derived from natural sources (of course in some combination of man-made capital) and 95 per cent of energy is from primary sources, Simon-Solow claim of passing on general capacities to the next generations with immense substitutability potential appears a tall order.

Let me also make another point. Apart from positing immense faith in the leaving the general capacities with the next generations Solow and Simon also appear to be extremely anthropocentric. In their enthusiasm to prove the point of substitutability based on human genius (read invested human capital) between primary factors and man-made factors they simply think that the planet earth is mean for the survival of human species only. They therefore, also ignore that while using the other species and finishing them from the earth, we may also finish other species that we don't use, but are dependent on the species that we use and that we may finish. They appear to be indifferent about the existence and survival of other species. Do they see and realise that such an approach might lead to destruction of human species too as part of some programming unknown to the human genius! Then why should Solow say that sustainability concept is a vague concept? In view of decision-making under uncertainty safe minimum standards appears to be a wise strategy. Let me close the discussion on the substitutability and vagueness with a story well known to all us Indians. An old man was planting a sapling of mango in the presence of his grand son. The King happened to pass by in disguise and asked the old man about the wisdom of his action because the mango would yield fruits only after fifteen years or so and the old man might be dead by then. The old man replied that the passerby was being foolish if he thought that he was planting mango tree with the hope to eat the fruit himself. Obviously, it was for his grand son. The old man's grandfather had planted a mango tree when he was a boy and he ate the mangoes all his life and thus he felt obliged to plant a tree for his grand son. This is our institutionalised understanding of inter-generational equity in practice.

Kindly allow me to digress here a little. The story has now lived perhaps for two thousand years or more. It is not contained in any textbook. It is also not part of curriculum of any school or university course. It has been passed on form one generation to the next orally in the oral tradition. It is also almost a household story. The younger generation among the audience may say that they have never heard it and they may be right also. That precisely is the point. The young generation have not heard it because parents have failed to tell them the story. If *Panchatantra* stories have been viewed as old fashioned regressive and backward by the parents in the present generation and the generation before them, we have committed a sad mistake. We should perhaps remind ourselves that the 'old man and the disguised king's story' has its basis in the Vedic hymns. There should not be any doubt about the development of philosophy about life and living in India thousands of years before the western society embarked on this course. If we take recourse to Swami Vivekanda's thoughts, religion has three parts: philosophy, mythology and rituals. Philosophy is basic for every religion. Mythology is developed to explain and illustrate religion with the help of legendary lives of great men and women in the form of stories, fables and folklore.

Rituals give the philosophy a concrete form so that every one may grasp it well. Swami Vivekananda says that ritual is concretised philosophy (*Iyengar*, 2001).

The old man and for that matter if there were many of them planting mango trees they were performing *karma* and *puranas* carried it forward for generations. It is important for us to understand that the Vedic gurus and rishis had gained some understanding about the human existence in the vast nature and had realised that given the *prakruti* (nature) of *manushya* (human species) *saha-astitva* (coexistence with nature) was the key to sustained (eternal) and happy life of human species on this earth. The Vedic period scholars not only understood the full import of ecological services provided by nature, but also realised the need for spiritual base for regulating human behaviour in respecting while using nature for survival. The reverence for nature was not created only for spiritual purpose, but it was also institutionalised for sustainable survival. Human specie being nurtured by nature and human specie in turn contributing its share of nurturing nature can be termed as *Samposhit Astitva*—mutually nurturing existence. In this context Indian term for Sustainable Development should be *Samposhit Vikas*. Simon and Solow miss this point completely, because as Daly has mentioned for they see the natural world mainly as source of vexations, not even services. Solow, as we have noted, is on a different plain than Simon because at least he recognised some meaning of the sustainability and therefore its relevance. Going further, he also opines that pursuing the goal of sustainability cannot be left to the market forces alone. He says, "it is often asked whether, at this level, the goal or obligation of sustainability can be left entirely to the market. It seems to me that there is no reason to believe in doctrinaire way that it can. The future is not adequately represented in the market, at lest not the far future."[16] He goes on to say that in principle government could serve as a trustee as a representative of future interests. I want to go a step further. Government is also made up of the people from the present generation and more or less carry same value systems. Thus both market (in which future generations are participating presently) and the government (read State) whose values are likely to be same as that of the present generation would not take care of sustainability from intergenerational equity point of view. And it is here that I want to argue that the issue of sustainability is not vague. The problem is that western philosophy is not able to handle it from the philosophy stage onwards. The *purana* of sustainability has not been created; the *karma* is not defined at all. In Indian tradition we have both *purana* and *karma* to back the philosophy of sustainability that is *saha-astitva* and *Samposhit Vikas.* Ishavasya Upanishad in its first verse makes this so clear in a rather spiritual way. It says: *Ishavasyam idam sarvam Yatkinchit Jagatyam Jagat; Ten tyaktena bhunjitha maa grudha kasya swid dhanam.* We in India are reluctant to put forward our concept of sustainable development reflected in our concepts and practices.

Solow and Simon perhaps take the positions that they take because of the philosophical grounding their society has received now for about 400 years or so. The 'Enlightenment Project', which the humanity began with renaissance visualised largely nature as something to be understood for use and exploitation. Capra quoting an extreme example mentions Francis Bacon's perceptions in the following way. "The terms in which Bacon advocated his new empirical method of investigation were not only passionate but often outright vicious. Nature, in his view, had to be 'hounded in her wanderings,' 'bound into service,' and made a 'slave.' She was to be 'put in constraint,' and the aim of scientist was to 'torture nature's secret from her."[17] In this approach man takes from nature and is not obliged to give back. In the Indian philosophy man not only is obliged to give back, but also takes with utmost respect and humility. It might be good to remind ourselves here that in all the religious ceremonies and rituals we follow, there are specified items of plants and other material that we utilise from nature. Insistence for religious purpose ensured that the species were retained in the environment a few as possible. Rigidities did enter over time and prescriptions for substitutes are also known, but the essential point is that we had to take from nature with respect and give back something as part of our obligation. By weaving human behaviour in the spiritual and religious fabric of the society, the governance was decentralised and the *Raja*—the King also had similar obligations. Unless each citizen in the society feels obliged and think about the responsibility towards the inter-generational equity with respect to resource base outside the market vortex, even government with all purposeful intents cannot be successful trusty. In my position this is a value issue and falls patently outside the realm of economics, but decisively impacts the economic behaviour. For me therefore, sustainable development does not simply mean holding the total capital stock intact with humanity, and thereby ensure general competence to provide at least the same level of livings for the next generations (sustainable), but influencing human behaviour in a way where the interface with nature is mutually nourishing (*samposhit*). I will now turn my attention to the Indian economic scene and examine the implications for sustainable development.

WORLD ECONOMIES AND SUSTAINABILITY ISSUE

India is still rated to be a low income and a poor country in the categorisation that is done by the World Bank. Table 1 below gives per capita income in US dollars and energy consumption in India, and averages for low-income, middle income and high-income countries during last 25 years.

I have taken two variables, per capita income in US dollars and energy consumption per capita. Use of energy should reflect the level of technology and industrial nature of the economy. Per capita income in India has grown over time. In 30 years it has grown 5 times. In case of lower income countries, the club to which India belongs to has experienced relatively smaller increase. The average per capita income has increased by 2.9 times, although in 1978, India's average per capita income was lower to that of the average for the low income countries. Growth in per capita income in India to that extent has been relatively faster. Middle-income countries have not been slow in experiencing growth in per capita income over time; they have experienced a rise by 2.29 times. High-income countries that largely comprise of the OECD countries have experienced a steady rise in the per capita income. Between 1978 and 2007, average per capita income increased by 4.1 times. While India and other low-income countries, which have about 40 per cent of the World population in 2000, are trying to run faster in the economic growth race, the high-income countries are ahead and fast. The gap between low-income countries and the high-income countries has widened between 1978 and 2007. It case of India the gap has declined marginally.

TABLE 1

Per Capita Income and Energy Consumption in Different Economies

Countries	*Per Capita Income in US dollars*				*Per Capita Energy consumption in kg oil equivalent*			
	1978	*1988*	*1999*	*2007*	*1978 Kg Coal equivalent*	*1988*	*1997*	*2006* British Thermal Unit (BTU)*
India	180	340	450	950 (59.81)	176	100	479	15.9
% to high income countries	2.23	1.99	1.75	1.86	2.49	1.96	8.92	5.75
Low Income countries	200	320	410	578 (36.35)	161	126	563	15.9
% to high income countries	2.48	1.87	1.59	1.58	2.28	2.47	10.49	5.75
Middle Income countries	1250	1930	2000	2872 (94.34)#	903	585	1368	127.2
% to high income countries	15.46	11.30	7.77	6.73	12.79	11.47	25.47	46.05
High Income countries	8070	17080	25730	37,566 (136.10)	7060	5098	5369	276.2

*Data for 2006 are for different set of countries. The low income country data is average for Africa, Middle income is for Middle East and High Income is for North America

The income figure for Higher Middle income groups has been taken for this analysis because Middle East incomes are in that range.

Source: World Development Reports, 1980, 1990, 2000/2001 and 2005. The World Bank, Washington, D.C.

The energy scene is interesting and instructive. Oil equivalent use data are for two points 1988 and 1997 and when one relates it with the per capita income, there is some surprise in the store. India and low-income countries appear to be achieving increase in income by using more energy per dollar earned. In 1988 India used 0.3 kg of oil equivalent for every per capita dollar earned and in 1999 it used 1.06 kg of oil equivalent of energy for earning one dollar per capita. In case of low-income countries the story is same. In case of high-income countries increase in income is accompanied by decrease in energy consumption. Clearly, the high-income countries are on clean technology path and India and low-income countries are with old and perhaps dirty technologies using more energy per unit of production. Although India has experienced increase in per capita income over last 25 years, poor people continue to exist. In the year 1999-00, 28 per cent of the population was below poverty line using the national poverty line, which is slightly less than a US dollar a day. Using the international poverty line one finds that India had about 35 per cent of population that earned less than one US dollar and day and 80 per cent of the total population earned less than 2 US dollars a day. In absolute numbers they are staggering figures of 350 and 800 million persons. Energy consumption data for 2006 is for British Thermal Units (BTU). The percent share to high income countries offers comparative picture.

Now let us enter into some speculative arithmetic for understanding the stupendous task the Indian economy faces. Suppose that US dollar 28,850 is what we wish to hit in order to join the club of high-income countries. How much time will it take? It took us 25 years to reach average per capita income of dollar 530 in 2003 from dollar 180 in 1978. This gives an annual compounded growth of 4.41 per cent. If the per capita income continues to grow at the same rate, it will take 93 years to reach the present level of the high-income countries average per capita income. One may note form Table 1 that rise in per capita income was faster between 1978 and 1988 and slowed down after that. In the last 15 years that is from 1988 to 2003 the PCI grew at annual compound rate of 3 per cent. If we take this rate then it will take 135 years for India to reach the level of PCI of high-income in 2003. However, it also assume that the high income countries will also continue to grow at the rate at which they grew in the time periods considered, then in 93 years high income countries will have PCI of dollar 30,77,820 as the per capita income in these countries grew at annual compound rate of 5.19 per cent. Again we consider last 15 years that is from 1988 to 2003, the high-income countries also experienced relatively slower growth in their PCIs. With that growth rate when India reaches the present high-income countries' level in 135 years, the high-income countries would touch dollar 29,68,611. Obviously, most of these numbers are absurd in some sense, because they are static scenes that are extrapolated. In a span of 25 years things change drastically. But it is important to note that it is a pipe dream for India and Low Income countries to imagine the average PCI levels of the high-income countries. Compared to 1997, share in energy consumption for India has registered increase. The share is same for African countries. The middle-east countries who are the major producer of energy, consume high level of energy, but yet their level is less than half of North America, which of course is the energy guzzler of the world.

The energy use scene is scarier. As we have shown in the table, between 1988 and 1997 per capita energy use in all economies other than high-income countries has grown dramatically. In India for instance the growth is at the annual average compound rate of 19 per cent! At this rate it would take only 14 years for India to reach the high-income countries levels of energy use. And we know that even the PCI grew at 4.41 per cent per annum, the PCI in 14 years may touch dollar 2500. And with such high level of energy use what will be the fate of environment? Simon and Solow and their likes have not perhaps thought through the problems. They may still argue about the substitutability and efficiency of resource use with the help of science and technology as the main drivers. There is some promise in it. By 2006 for instance the energy required to produce a dollar of income has reduced and will reduce further. But it is very unlikely that it will touch the present efficiency mark of North America. It is evident from the table above that in 2006 India produced 60 US dollars for one BTU of energy. Low income African countries produced dollar 36, high middle income countries produced dollar 94 and the North America produced dollar 136 for one BTU. It would be illustrative at this juncture to refer to Schumacher's work. Fuel consumption and its need for economic growth of the kind that the western world has embarked has so much clouded the minds of thinkers that almost every debate about sustainability revolves around it, perhaps rightly so. Schumacher also picks up fuel consumption and has shown in 1973 itself as to what gigantic quantities humanity is talking about when the standard of living of every citizen in the world has to be raised to the high-income countries' levels. Schumacher argues that even if it is granted that such reserves are there in the layers below the earth, they are not uniformly distributed. What Solow and Simon miss out in their enthusiastic economic analysis is that control, trade and use of natural resources such fuel is political economy. The Country having the source and control is not likely to trade is as easily as economists may assume notwithstanding global commitment to free market approach and existence of World Trade Organisation. India, the case that I am discussing now, is unfortunately not fortunate to have the oil reserves of the kind that would be required to put us on a growth path that will give annual compounded growth rate of 5 per cent in the Per Capita Income. I agree with Schumacher when he says, "exploratory calculation, of course, does not *prove* anything. A *proof* about the future is any case impossible, and it has been sagely remarked that all predictions are unreliable, particularly those about future. What is required is judgement, and exploratory calculations can at least help to inform our judgement."[18] It appears that in the context of sustainable development issue in India formation of judgment is also a very difficult exercise and it is also apparent that we are yet to begin the exercise in any right earnest. Here I would like to take recourse to a wonderful review article by Partha Dasgupta and Karl Goran Maler. Both of them have taken up the developing countries' case with highly substantial commitment and academic rigour.

In a recent paper[19] Dasgupta and Maler have argued that the economic growth issue is vexed and in a way calls for lot of care and caution. Commenting on growth experiences and growth models Dasgupta and Maler argue that it is a little heavy burden that economists are putting on the experience of last 250 years or so. If one takes a longer perspective in history, the effect is immensely sobering. The growth rates, including last 200 years, even for high-income economies are not much above zero. Then in a footnote they illustrate that taking the average PCI for all the countries taken together at US dollar 5000 in the year 2000 and considering that people had were just above poverty line with an average 1 US dollar a day income (because the international poverty line), the average PCI would be dollar 350 in year 1. The present income thus would be 16 times higher. It also means that the PCI doubled every 500 years. With these figures the average annual compounded growth rate would be around 0.14 per cent, which is not much in excess of zero. The point being made, as I understand is that in the sustainable development debate arguing for non-declining consumption or non-declining utility even in 100 or 200 years framework does not help. Non-declining natural capital stock approach, even if it is feasible to measure, is not a very meaningful exercise at an aggregate level because the impacts of environmental degradation are felt at local levels and on the local communities who eke out living out of it.

In a comprehensive review of the recent development in resource and environmental economics Dasgupta and Maler come out with conclusions that are extremely relevant for an economy as such India. They say that the natural scientists, who believe 'in humanity's current use of Nature's services a symptom of deep malaise, have talked past with another group of scientists (mostly economists) who document the fact that people today are on an average better off in many ways than they had ever been (so why the gloom?)."[20] The development in environment and resource economics and the technical vocabulary that has evolved does not give tools to both facilitating a dialogue, but help in bringing forth the disagreements on the evidence that is examined with agreed tools. The authors say that the frontiers of modern welfare economics have been expanded and the 'discussions on inter-generational welfare should be about institutions and policies that bring about changes and movements in *wealth*, whereby an economy's wealth we mean the social worth of its entire set of capital assets, including not only manufactured and human capital, but also knowledge and natural capital'.[21] They go on to show that recent evidence measuring changes in *wealth* in many countries has shown that industrialised countries such as the United States and the United Kingdom, have accumulated *wealth per capita*, sub-Saharan Africa and Middle East have suffered a decline. The Indian sub-continent appears to be a borderline case. Authors caution us that more work needs to be done on the subject, but these are the preliminary evidences.

In the above context further learning reported by the authors are vital for the discussions on the sustainable development of the Indian economy. The developments in concepts and methodologies in environmental and resource economics have facilitated the study of rural economies. Aggregate statistics at the national level suppress information pertaining to local natural resource bases. Recent evidence from the village studies on local resource base have shown how breaking down of traditional non-market institutions thereby deprive substantial section of people of their livelihood, while some thrive as markets grow elsewhere. The spatial characteristics of ecosystems have been emphatically emphasised. Well, in my understanding evidence already was there in ample even if one had looked at it in the conventional economic development studies' point of view. Particularly in case of India the implementation of the 'Green Revolution Technology' (GRT) in almost a mindless fashion in all the rural areas of the country has brought ecological disasters in many drought prone regions in the country. In the name of rural development and decentralised planning for development, the annual development plans were galore with GRT promoting schemes and they were indiscriminately implemented. Farmers were enticed to dig wells, bore wells, deep bore wells and get tractors and other mechanised equipments. For all this there were subsidies and loans. Further, there were subsidies and loans for electric pump sets, submersible pumps. And to top it all, there were promises for almost free electricity. 'Grow More Food Campaign' worked as long as it could. I am not belittling the achievements on that front. But the policies that the government pursued irrespective of the agro-climatic and geo-physical suitability, led to disastrous consequences.

Land related policies emphasised privatisation of common lands in a big way. No care was taken to see especially in the drought prone semi arid and arid regions whether the traditional and settled land use in the villages was the result of long drawn experience of the local population and whether the uncultivated lands that were left as such were solely because of lack of property rights or economic wherewithal require for cultivation or it was also left to serve ecological services of cohesive land and water management so that area under cultivation yielded optimum outputs. The so-called privatisation drive created tremendous pressure on the land that was left as common for fuel wood and fodder. India as a whole also experienced high population growth further adding to the pressure. Occupation of one and livelihood generation of one led to the killing of options to the other.[22] Simon and Solow should perhaps view this seriously that while the substitutability argument may hold at macro-level analysis and at a conceptual level, at local level competition does not offer substitution choices, it offers misery and further impoverishment when people compete for scanty and degrading natural resource base. This has happened in India. To put it again in the words of Dasgupta and Maler, contemporary models of economic growth are by and large dismissive of the importance of Nature. In their extreme form, growth models assume a positive link between the creation of ideas (technological progress) and population growth in world where the natural-resource base comprises a fixed, indestructible factor of production."[23] And we know for sure that natural resource base is not indestructible and *a la* Christensen cannot be substituted by man-made and human capital.

Let me finally bring Dasgupta and Maler before I embark on my final thesis because the passage I am going to quote will provide the link. Continuing the argument about the humility that is required to discuss economic growth rates in the long-run perspective, the authors say, "The foregoing remark bear on the aggregate economy (*refers to the 2000 years argument*). At a more micro level, we noted in section 3-5 that positive feedback in ecological (including individual metabolic) pathways are reasons why the prospects of economic betterment among the world's poorest are bleaker than among the rich. The non-convexities the poor face can be a reflection of their inability to obtain substitutes for depleted natural resources. Resource depletion can be for poor like crossing a threshold: their room for manoeuvre is circumscribed hugely once they cross. In contrast, the rich can usually "substitute" their way out of problems."[24]

This brings us to the issue of intra-generational equity as well. As we observed in the Table above the difference between the low-income and high-income countries is sharp and has grown over time. So is true in the case of an economy. The gap between rich and poor in all likelihood would increase with economic growth under the Julian Simon's scheme. Rich will find substitutes and poor would almost perish. It has already started happening. It is not uncommon to hear these days about the eco-conscious society promoting wood substitutes for living and furnishing in urban areas because we have almost exhausted the timber forests by cutting it at almost uneconomic prices (State or market forces, both would have under-priced it anyway). The rich have found "substitutes" thanks to science and technology. Only poor are left high and dry. Forests are gone and hence fuel wood, food and fodder have gone. Topsoil has eroded. Downstream land enrichment is gone and so is gone the cultivation prospects. So what do the poor do? Migrate. Free mobility of factors of production and we all want to promote for the prosperity of human being in general. What do they do? Where do they go? Obviously, they go to the urban areas. Crowd it further, make it filthier, create immense pressure on the minimum basic services and create all kinds of economic, social and cultural negative externalities. Let us remember that even in 2003 after 14 years of freeing the economy form the clutches of the government, which in any case was most desirable, 80 per cent in India, earn less than 2 US dollars per day per capita. Poor are thronging to urban areas without any meaningful substitutes left back in rural areas. In Schumacher's words people do not become mobile, they become footloose and get eventually lost. I am reminded of our yesteryears famous Hindi poet Rahim, whose couplet aptly describes the rich substituting and poor perishing. It says, *"keh Rahim kaise nibhe ker ber ko sang, ve dolat ras aapne inke fatat ang."*

Let me come back to the definition of sustainable development given to us by the World Commission on sustainable development about leaving something for coming generations. It contains within it two key concepts:

- The concept of "needs", in particular the essential needs of the world's poor, to which overriding priority should be given; and
- The idea of limitations imposed by the state of technology and social organization on the environment's ability to meet present and future needs.

I think both the points have been covered in this paper somewhat adequately. But all the discussion including rigorous academic analysis and debate miss out to finally point out that the debate also should be informed by the disciplines other than pure technical economics as we know today. All our efforts and intellectual quest is to carry out hard-headed analysis of how income and wealth are generated, how improvement in valuation of natural resources can improve decision-making under uncertainty and how study of distributional issue can provide policy guidelines for improving the income distribution and thereby increase the total social well-being in general. Obviously, we have no definite answers whatever approach we take; single final answer does not exist. But, in the case of sustainable debate we are looking for the proverbial key under the lamp post while it was lost in the darkness elsewhere!

Mahatma Gandhi had some inkling about this. In his scheme of interaction with Nature the basic Indian value of humility in use and obligation to give back both were prominently present. His use of a tiny tumbler on the banks of flowing Sabarmati River near his Ashram and his statement that he would draw only the amount he needs is both famous and telling about the value he held. His oft quoted remark about there being enough for everybody's need and not enough for everybody's greed is also very effective in communicating that the interaction with nature has to be two-way and with restraint. Mainstream economists have mostly treated tastes and preference of producers and consumers as given and demands as something that go on getting generated. With these given parametric behaviour of human being, the problem of allocation of resourcs was to be solved. We have seen above to some extent that how difficult this apparently simple looking problem is. One of the important lessons that we need to learn is that demands cannot be treated as unlimited. Obviously, State and government cannot formulate rules and regulations for this, but the individual behaviour will have to be influenced for this. Market would also not do it because of known reasons. In this context, the Vedic value of peacefully co-existing with nature and respect to all other species in nature becomes very important. In order to influence everybody's lifestyle obviously we need the *Darshana* (philosophy), *the Purana* (The Folk and popular form of philosophy) *and the Kriya Kanda* (rituals). Materialistically low living standard does not imply low quality of life. By choosing lower materialistic standard, a society would solve the sustainability problem to a significant extent. In this paper I would abstain from elaborating beyond this, as the space would not permit.

Finally, let me make a point about the micro-macro issue in creating society's *wealth a la* Dasgupta and Maler. Poor people in vulnerable regions are going to be hit by the swindling of the natural resources by the rich and then become totally without options for livelihood. Globalisation and marketisation is going to further hit some poor this way. Gandhi's choice for decentralised production and governance system was because of this reason. The more decentralised production and distribution system better is the control people will have on their destiny. There would be trade national and international, but not for meeting basic minimum needs. Such markets will have to be local and regional. The conservation and livelihood generation from the local ecology and natural resource bases would be possible only through such local development and mutual dependence. Interestingly, the latest drive in the rural development programme talks about watershed development, swajaldhara, small-scale industrial units, that supports indigenous knowledge systems and enterprise, all through people's participation. It is a good move provided it is seriously attempted. Government driven people's participation would not work. It would merely become a cliche. Gandhi's *Swaraj* was not rule by natives alone, but most importantly it was ruling self. For the sustainable development of the Indian economy, generating livelrhood by conserving natural resource bases in a decentralised governance mode including self-rule appear to be imperatives. It is perhaps time for second battle for *Swaraj*.

Notes and References

1. This paper is a revised version of the E.F. Schumacher Memorial Lecture delivered at Nagpur University in 2004.
2. This is mentioned in the 17th Lecture that Lionel Robbins delivered in the London School of Economics during 1979-80. See Steven G. Medema and Warren J. Samuels 1998. (p. 169).
3. For those who are interested please refer Donnella Meadows and others, 1972.
4. In fact, the concern had been already expressed earlier in 1970. A brief account of the timeline on this is contained in the following paragraph. Environmental movements are born and are active since 1970s. America celebrated 'Earth Day' on 22nd April 1970 to highlight the environment

and development contradictions. The United Nations organised environment summit on June 5, 1972 and formed United Nations Environmental Programme. The famous work 'Limits to Growth' of the Club of Rome was also published in 1972. In 1980 and 1983 'North South: A Programme for Survival', and 'Common Crisis' were published in that order. In 1987 the Brandt Commission published the widely acclaimed work 'Our Common Future'. The expression 'sustainable development' gained currency alter this publication. The First earth summit on environmental issues was held in June 1993 in Rio-de-Janeiro. Brazil and the second summit know n us Rio + 10 has been recently concluded on September 4, 2002 in Johannesburg.

5. It is the Eighteenth J. Seward Johnson Lecture to the Marine Policy Centre, Woods Hole Oceanographic Institution, delivered at Woods Hole, Massachusetts on June 14, 1991 and it is published in U. Sankar (edited) 2001. *Environmental Economics,* Oxford University Press, New Delhi.
6. *Ibid.*, p. 271.
7. *Ibid.*, p. 272.
8. Resource Scarcity has bothered the economists since last 300 years or so. Classical economists put the aggregate production function as $Y = f(D, K, L)$. Land D was defined broadly to include soil and mineral resources. For them land was important and thus its constraint was real and we have shown how Malthus predicted doom because of land's limited capacity. Industrial revolution brought technology and substitution and hence the aggregate production function for the neo-classical economists was changed to $Y = f(K, L)$. Here land broadly defined as natural resource was less of a constraint as it responded to investments. The human capital perspective developed relatively recently by T.W. Schultz and the one that is in vogue at present recognises capital as the only important input for the aggregate production function for the society. Both land (read natural resources) and labour are responsive to investments (human capital formation) and hence the function is expressed as $Y = f(K)$. For interesting details refer Randall Alan, 1991. *Resource Economics: An Economic Approach to Natural Resource and Environmental Policy,* John Wiley and Sons, New York.
9. Daly, *op. cit.*, p. 29.
10. Non-declining natural capital stock approach is one of the approaches discussed in environmental economics for sustainable development. The concept has been evolved by accepting the limited substitutability between natural and man-made capital stock. For details see Hanley Nick, *et. al.*, 1997.
11. IUCN's mission is to influence, encourage and assist societies throughout the world to conserve the integrity and diversity of nature and to ensure that any use of natural resources is equitable and ecologically sustainable.
12. There is yet another branch of economics namely, Ecological Economics. It deals with the two-way links between ecological and economic

systems. There is a difference between ecologist's perspective and economist's perspective in their approach to environmental problems. While the ecologist takes a holistic view considering all living organisms, the economist, trained in a utilitarian framework, takes an anthropocentric view to the problem.

13. A closed system cannot add to its stock of matter and energy. (It is crucial to understand that in case of both the laws of thermodynamics, they hold true only and only in closed system. That is, a system, which does not exchange matter or energy with its environment.) Is earth a closed system? Boulding calls earth a spaceship, which does not make it strictly a closed system. Boulding says, "closed systems, in fact, are very rare in human experience, in fact, by definition unknowable, for if there are genuinely closed systems around us, we have no way of getting information into them or out of them; and hence if they are really closed, we would be quite unaware of their existence". The spaceship earth then is partially powered by solar energy with given stock of matter and energy in the process of formation of earth. Earth's capacity to convert add to the stock of matter is yet very minimal at about 1% of the total sunlight we get. It is done by photosynthesis. In case of energy use too, solar energy forms a very tiny part of the energy that we use. The present energy use on earth is a transformed material from the activity of the past solar energy led photosynthesis, i.e. fossil fuels; oil, natural gas and coal. As per the World Resource Institute in 1991, these three sources accounted for 94 per cent of the total world energy use. Thus, despite Boulding's insistence on earth not being a closed system, for all practical purposes, given the level of science and technology capacity of the human society to add to the stock of matter and energy is extremely limited. It is in this context that we should examine the implications of the first law of thermodynamics on economics of resource use and conservation. See Boulding K., 1992, "The Economics of Coming Spaceship Earth", in Markandeya Anil and Richardson Julie (Editors), *The Earthscan Reader in Environmental Economics.* Earthscan Publications Ltd. London and Hanley Nick, Shogren Jason F. and White Ben, 1997, *Environmental Economics In Theory and Practice,* Macmillan India Limited, Delhi.
14. Solow *op. cit.*, p. 271.
15. Christensen P.P. as quoted in Hanely Nick *et. al. op. cit.* Chapter 1.
16. Solow in *op. cit.*, p. 273.
17. Capra Fritzof, 1983, pp. 40-41.
18. Schumacher E.F., 1977, p. 24.
19. Dasgupta Partha and Maler Karl Goran, 2004, Working Paper No. 7-04.
20. *Ibid.*, p. 40.
21. *Ibid.*, p. 40.
22. An aside point may be in place here. Some of the economists and other thinkers now vociferously attack the planning era and hold the huge government and State's control responsible for the ills including the environmental disasters. 1 am of the opinion that with respect to natural

resource degradation even under market regime would not have been very different. In this country a seed company can introduce genetically modified seeds without any tests and trials massively into farmer's field and risk the entire future generation in the name of giving a fair chance to farmers under marketisation and globalisation.

23. *Ibid.*, p. 41.
24. *Ibid.*, p. 42, first bracket is my addition.

References

Boulding, K., 1992, "The Economics of Coming Spaceship Earth", in Markandeya Anil, and Richardson Julie (Editors) *The Earth scan Reader in Environmental Economics*. Earthscan Publications Ltd. London

Capra Fritzof, 1983, *The Turning Point*. Flamingo, An imprint of Harper Collins Publishers, London, pp. 40-41.

Dasgupta, Partha and Maler Karl Goran, 2004, "Environmental and Resource Economics: Some Recent Developments". South Asian Network for Development and Environmental Economics (SANDEE) Kathmandu, Nepal. Working Paper No. 7-04.

Day Herman E., 1999, *Ecological Economics and the Ecology of Economics*, Edward Elgar Northampton MA, USA.

Donnella Meadows and others, 1972, *The limits to Growth: A report for The Club of Rome's Project on the Predicament of Mankind*. A Potomac Associates Book, Pan Books London and Sydney.

Hanley Nick, Shogren Jason F. and White Ben, 1997. *Environmental Economics in Theory and Practice*, Macmillan India Limited, New Delhi.

Iyengar S. 2001, "Karma as Dharma", in *Humanscape*, Mumbai. February Issue.

Medema Steven G. and Samuel Warren J. (Eds), 1998, *A History of Economic Thought: The LSE Lectures*, Oxford University Press, London.

Randall Alan, 1991, *Resource Economics: An Economic Approach to Natural Resource and Environmental Policy*, John Wiley and Sons, New York.

Schumacher, E.F. 1977, *Small is Beautiful: A study of Economics as if People Mattered*, Radha Krishna, New Delhi.

Simon Julian, 1981, *The Ultimate Resource*, Princeton University Press, Princeton NJ.

Solow Robert, 1991, Eighteenth J. Seward Johnson Lecture to the Marine Policy Centre, Woods Hole Oceanographic Institution, delivered at Woods Hole, Massachusetts on June 14, in U Sankar (edited) 2001, *Environmental Economics*, Oxford University Press, New Delhi.

United Nations, 1987, *Our Common Future: The World Commission on Environment and Development*, United Nations, Washington, D.C.

A Few New Words on Sustainable Development

SANTOSH KUMAR GHORAI

Nothing is absolute, nothing is perfect, 'sustainable development' is also not the 'last word' in the present society which is very much concerned about the environment. Inside the word 'sustainable' the two properties 'variablility' and 'adjustability' are intrinsically hidden. Inventive skills, creative ability and commitment will bring hope for reflection and resources sustainability. Discussion and criticism on 'sustainable development' have been outlined in the article.

The term *'sustainable development' ordinarily is defined as the development, which satisfies the needs of the present without compromising the ability oj future generation to satisfy their needs.* Thus it aims at balancing the needs of present and future generation and gives importance on *'eco-justice '* and *'eco-efficiency'*. While eco-justice ensures rights of all persons to environmental resources, eco-efficiency ensures conserving energy and input per unit of output.

The two buzz words of the new millennium lexicon are *'globalization'* and *'sustainable development'*. In the initial stages we were concerned with economic growth or prosperity which was mainly the indicator of the national wealth a country was producing year after year. It was thus a narrowly defined 'income' or wealth and 'prosperity' based view and its only parameter was country's real income, i.e. Gross Domestic Product (GDP). It, however, did not take much long to realize that it is not the country's wealth alone but the welfare of its people that is most important. Economic growth must become inclusive, every person, a common man at large, should be its stake holder. He should enjoy the betterment of his living standard. It is not wealth generation alone, but wealth distribution that is important. Thus we moved ahead from growth to growth plus equity.

$$\text{Growth} \Rightarrow \text{Growth} + \text{Equity}$$

This was the concept of economic development. Today we have moved beyond this. Equity as was conventionally understood was a static concept. It took into consideration the equality of opportunity to people at a given point of time. But what about equality of opportunity over a period of time? What if using the opportunity to improve the standard of living today reduces or destroys similar opportunities for generations to come? Are we using up the resources over which they also have their rightful claims? In other words, we need to look at the problem of equity not only among people at a given point of time, but among people across different generations over a period of time. That precisely is the concept of sustainability of development or *sustainable development*.

- According to Webster's New International Dictionary, "*sustain*—to cause of continue (as in existence or a certain state, or in force or intensity); to keep up, especially *without interruption diminution*, flagging, etc. to prolong."
- Considering the globe as a whole 'sustainable development' means—improving the quality of human life while living within the carrying capacity of supporting ecosystems.
- Sustainability is the 'long-term, cultural, economic and environmental health and vitality with emphasis on long-term, together with the importance of linking our social, financial, and environmental well-being.'
- Sustainability is the simple principle of taking from the

Earth only what it can provide indefinitely, thus leaving future generation no less than we have access to ourselves.

- Development refers to the continued improvement of living standards by economic growth, usually in the developing countries. Developed (industrialised) countries are usually more concerned about environmental sustainability, while the developing countries are more concerned about economic development.

It may be stated that sustainable development is constrained by:

(i) what the nature/earth has to offer *(carrying capacity),*
(ii) what we can take from it while not undetermining the future generations, and
(iii) improvements of standard of living for present generation within the above constraints.

- **Carrying capacity** of an ecosystem means the size of the population that can be supported indefinitely on the available resources and services of that ecosystem. *Living within the limits of an ecosystem* depends on three factors:

(a) the amount of resources available in the ecosystem;
(b) the size of the population; and
(c) the amount of resources each individual is consuming.

Illustration: Let us consider a case of survival in a lifeboat after a shipwreck. The survival of number of people in the lifeboat depends on how much food and water are reserved; how much each person eats and drinks each day; and how many days they are afloat. If the lifeboat is replaced by an island, how long the people survived would depend on the food and water supply on the island and how wisely they used it. A small desert island will support far fewer people than a large continent with abundant water and fertile soil for growing crops.

Here food and water are the *natural capital* of the island. *'Living within the carrying capacity'* means using those supplies no faster than they are replenished by the island's environment: using the 'interest' income of the natural capital. A community that is living off the interest of its community capital is living within the carrying capacity. A community that is degrading or destroying the ecosystem on which it depends is using up its community capital is living unsustainability. In this respect it can be mentioned:

> *"Nature has enough to satisfy every person's need not any persons greed. "*
>
> —Mahatma Gandhi

Community sustainability is living within the carrying capacity of the community's human, social and built capital. Carrying capacity is much harder to measure for these types of capital, but the basic concept is the same.

Some examples are:

1. A community that allows its children to be poorly educated, undernourished, and poorly housed is eroding its *human capital.*
2. A community that allows the quality of its social interactions to decline through lack of trust, respect and tolerance is eroding its *social capital.*
3. A community that allows its buildings, roads, parks, power facilities, water facilities and waste processing capability to decay is eroding its *built capital.* Additionally, a community that is creating built capital without considering the future maintenance of that capital is setting itself up for eventual decay. The population dynamics of the world is as follows:

TABLE 1

Time taken to add 1 billion Population on the Earth

1st billion population	2 million years
2nd billion population	130 years
3rd billion population	30 years
4th billion population	15 years
5th billion population	12 years

The massive population size and its mind boggling speed of growth has created serious concerns as to how and whether the earth's resources will be enough to ensure the sustainance to this growing population.

Modern Definition

Sustainable development is the ability to make development—choice which respects the relationship between the three "Es"—Economy, Ecology and Equality.

- *Economy:* Economic activity should serve common good, be self renewing and should build local assets and self reliance.
- *Ecology:* It should involve the realization that humans are part of nature, nature has limits and communities are responsible for protecting and building natural assets.
- *Equality:* The opportunity for all for full participation in all activities, benefits and decision-making of a society at a given point of time as well as protecting the rightful claims of future generations.

If these ingredients are incorporated in the national goals of all countries then it should be possible to develop *sustainable society.* Such a society would be characterized by an emphasis on preserving the environment, developing strong peaceful relationships between people and nations and an emphasis on equitable distribution of wealth.

If these three essential ingredients are treated separately, very often it presents dilemma like:

(i) *'if the environmentalist win the economy suffers'*; or
(ii) *'if business has its way the environment will be destroyed'*.

Actually *economy-environment linkage* is one area where we have to have *'win-win solution'* and not *'win-looser solution'*. Nobody can afford to be a loser, we all are on one side only, and there are no two sides to this coin of sustainable community development. There has to be a holistic solution and not a piecemeal solution.

Problems Related to Piecemeal Solution

(a) Solution to one problem can make another problem worse. *Example:* Creating affordable housing is a good thing, but when that housing is built in areas, it results increased traffic and the related pollution problems.

(b) Opposite groups are automatically created and they are always in a fighting mood.

(c) Short-term benefits can not give long-terms results.

Sustainability requires *integrated view* of the world—it requires multidimensional indicators that show the links among a community's economy, environment and society.

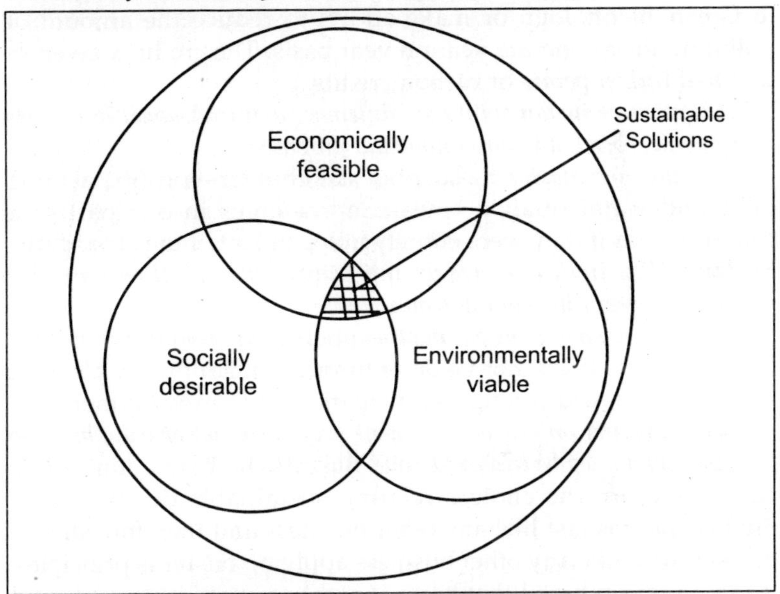

Integrated View of Sustainability

Green Accounting

Green accounting essentially concentrates on depletion of environmental capital. Conventionally the physical capital so much dominated the thinking, policy as well as practice that the natural capital and its depreciation was overlooked. This is corrected through the system of *Green Accounting*.

SNNP (Sustainable Net National Product)

On the basis of 'Green Accounting' one indication is developed which is known as *'Sustainable Net National Product (SNNP)'*. SNNP is calculated as:

SNNP = GNNP (Gross Net National Product) – (defence expenditure + cost of unmitigated pollution + depreciation of man-made capital + depreciation of environmental capital).

The corporate units are persuaded by pollution control boards in different countries to take steps to comply with the prescribed standards. They are awarded special incentives if they change over to Green Technology or make efforts to reduce the amount of pollution they generate year on year basis. The credit is given in terms of *carbon points* or carbon credits.

Indicators of sustainability are different from traditional indicators of economic, social, and environmental progress.

Traditional indicators:—such as stakeholder—profits, asthma rates and water quality—measure—changes in one part of a community as if they were entirely independent of the other parts. *Sustainability indicators reflect the reality that the three different segments are very lightly interconnected.*

First and foremost, we all must realize that environment protection is not a charity. It can not be done through philanthropy alone. It has to be achieved through participation and empowerment.

Secondly, *not only is environment protection not charily, but also a business and must be treated like one.* Business is about optimization choices, so are the choices relating sustainable development. Environment is just like any other business and therefore should be dealt with like any other business applying business principles. It can be remembered that basis of any business is exchange and the purpose of any business is not to maximize the outcome of business.

Some Tools to Assess the Impact

Efforts are being made to assess the impact of economy on environment by developing various tools. Some of them concentrate on the rate of use of earth's reproducible resources in different parts of the world to maintain their current standard of living. One such tool is *ecological foot print*.

Ecological Foot Print

Ecological foot print is defined as the area (hectares) of land required to sustain the present consumption levels considering the reproducible natural resources incorporated in it. Some rough estimates indicate that if the developed countries want to maintain their present rate of resource consumption we would need 10 to 12 earths to sustain it. That essentially indicates that the world is moving at rate faster than the one that can be sustained in the long-run.

Explanation

Let your house is surrounded by a small garden and wall around the compound. Can you isolate yourself in your home and continue to live indefinitely? Certainly the answer is—'no'.

How large a piece of land would you need, if you are to sustain yourself completely? That area is your **'ecological foot-print'**.

If a city is isolated (say Kolkata) and be covered. Then the carrying capacity of the city area is not sufficient to sustain the lives of the population. How large should the area covered be, if we want the city to survive indefinitely on the land, water and energy sources available within the hemisphere (which was imagined to cover the city). That area is the ecological footprint of the city. So, ecological foot-print of Kolkata city is many many times larger than its actual area. If we compare the ecological foot-print of a citizen of the U.S. with that of an Indian citizen, it is obvious that same is many times greater for U.S citizen. It is essential to reduce ecological foot-print in developed country and to increase the same in developing country.

Sustainable Development and Civil Society

We must treat environmental issues by making them a part of larger economic issues and develop a holistic approach. One broad mechanism is given below:

The problem of sustainable development need not be very untractable. We have various solutions looming on the horizon. As for example, the use and varied applications of solar energy gives us a new hope as a substitute for fuel problem. The constant research pertaining to **'green technology and chemistry'**, bio-technology and nano-technology now offers us a series of solutions to overcome the serious problem of depletion of natural resources and environmental degradation.

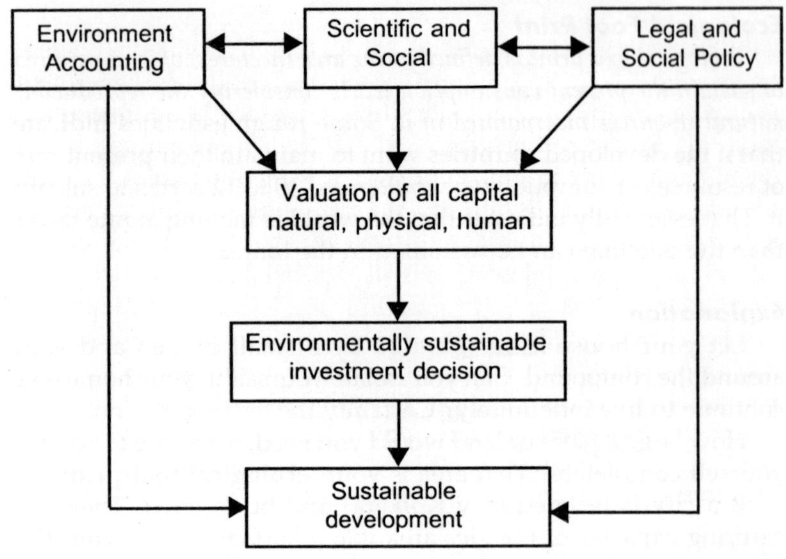

"The solution can not be that which bans the development of those who need it the most; the fact is that everything that contributes to underdevelopment and poverty is an open violation of ecology."

—*Fidel Castro*

References

Bailey, R., (ed), 2000. *Earth Report 2000*, New York: McGraw-Hill.

Bruntland, H.G., 1987. *Our Common Future*, WCED, New York: Oxford University Press.

Economic Research Association, 1992. 'Units Converted from Pounds to Metric Tons'. In R.W. Larson, F. Vignota and R. Westeds.

New York Times, 2000. World Almanae, 2000, New York.

Price, C., 1993. *Time, Discounting and Value*, Malden, MA: Blackwell.

Smith, G.W., 1987. *Engineering Economy: Analysis of Capital Expenditures*, Iowa State University Press.

"The Science of Money," 1998. *Discover*, Special Issue 19(10).

World Bank, 2003. *World Development Indicators* database at www.worldbank.org/data/

SECTION II

ECOLOGICAL LIMITS, ENVIRONMENTALLY SOUND TECHNOLOGIES AND ECOSYSTEM ACCOUNTS

Ecological Limits and Economic Development*

RAMPRASAD SENGUPTA

This paper reviews the difference in approach of the environmental economics and the ecological economics in addressing the issues arising from the interactive relationship between the human economy and the natural environment with special reference to the recognition of the role of ecological limits in economic development. It critically reviews in this context the basic concepts and presumptions of neoclassical microeconomics and macroeconomics to examine if they are adequate in handling the issues of environmental sustainability of economic growth and equity in development. After going through the arguments of the debates the paper finally concludes that the fundamental conceptual apparatus of neoclassical economics is adequate to analyse most of the environmental issues of choices in development by appropriately incorporating the concerned interdisciplinary factors of ecological and associated social behaviour into the analysis. The challenge one has to face in the context is one of ingenuity in the application of the neoclassical methodology

*I would like to thank my colleague Prof. Anjan Mukherji for very useful comments on the draft of the paper. I am alone however responsible for all the assertions made in the paper.

while defining the problems of choice and formally structuring analytical models in order to incorporate the interdisciplinary factors.

Key words: Ecological Economics, Ecological limits, Sustainable development.

I. INTRODUCTION

There have developed two schools of thoughts in economics which have addressed the issues arising from the interactive relation between human economy and the natural environment—*environmental economics* and *ecological economics*. The former has focused on the special problem arising from the public good nature of ecosystem services and the externalities arising from the residuals of the material resources during the various stages of the life cycle of their transformation in production, transportation and final use. These have been viewed mostly as problems of market failure. The largest case of market failure in the recent history has been the phenomenon of global warming and climate change due to anthropogenic emissions. The problem of pollution control has been considered by the school of environmental economics as a public economics issue. In order to resolve this problem this school has focused on monetizing the value of non-market eco-services of nature in order to internalize the environmental costs and solving for the optimal allocation of resources among economic activities and corresponding optimal pollution. It has also searched for the alternative regulatory instruments of environmental control and deliberated on the choice of the right regulatory policies. The analytical approach of these issues has been mostly one of microeconomic and general equilibrium of neoclassical economics.

The other school of ecological economics has criticized the environmental economics school as it does not explicitly recognize the serious implication of the entropy laws and its fall out in terms of ecological limits to scale of aggregate economic activity of a society. According to it the environmental economics takes a narrow reductionist view of the nature presuming the natural environment as one of the sub-sectors of the economic system whose flows of services are not marketable but monetisable. It is not however always clear whether ecological economists have in principle any objection to the evaluation of environmental or ecosystem services, nor what they would do for policy evaluation in the absence of such monetary evaluation. Their focus of analysis has however been on the macro-level issues of growth of income and wealth and their sustainability. Their thrust of analysis has been on the assessment of the environmental cost of economic growth if the equilibrium of the ecosystem is so disturbed that nature's capability of reproducing itself is eroded and the natural environment gets degraded. The sustainable accounting for the characterization of the dynamic process of economic change has to take account of the environmental resource, cost of growth and expand the concept of capital base to include not only the man-made or human capital but also the natural capital. Any criteria for the policy evaluation for sustainability would thus ultimately require all kinds of resources and capital to be evaluated. If however the knowledge and data-base regarding the behaviour of the natural environment in the particular context of its interaction with human economy and society are not considered to be adequate for reliable monetary valuation, hybrid physical-monetary macroeconomic environmental accounting system is often recommended or practiced in some countries. However, whenever any actual policy choice is made from among developmental options involving alternative environmental implications, the choice would immediately reveal the subjective preference and relative valuation by the society of environmental resources or ecosystem services *vis-a-vis* other marketable resources or products in terms of gains or losses of which the opportunity cost of protection of environment would be calculated. The value of interdisciplinary research for monetizing the value of the natural environment cannot be ignored or its importance belittled.

This paper reviews the approaches of micro and macro-level analysis of conventional economics in the context of environmental resource use and points to their limitations. It also reviews the approaches of environmental and ecological economics and emphasizes the moot point of debate in the context as centering around the recognition of the ecological limits to the scale and their significance in the valuation of resources and the sustainability of their use. The paper points out that the fundamental apparatus of neoclassical economics is powerful enough to address these issues. There is in fact not much point in the debate that goes on between the above two schools of thought. What is relevant and important is the appropriate definition of the problems of choice taking account of the latest scientific and socio-economic knowledge-based information which can capture the deep implication of the entropy law of nature and limits to the capacity of our planet in respect of sustainability or indefinite reproducibility of our economic processes.

II. ECONOMIC THEORY AND ECOLOGICAL LIMITS TO SCALE IN ECONOMICS

The central theme of analysis of economics has been the development of well-being of the people of a society. At the microeconomic level of analysis the major analytical issue has been the rational allocation of income resources by individuals as consumers among alternative product ends and that of productive resources by the individuals as producers or suppliers among those same different products. Each agent maximizes his/her measure of welfare—consumer's surplus for the buyers of product and producers' surplus for the sellers. This would result in a state of equilibrium allocation of resources. The characterization of this equilibrium allocation in terms of the aggregate welfare measure of social surplus (consumers' surplus + producers' surplus of all the individual agents) would depend on the state of perfection or imperfection of the institution of market or its failure for reasons of externalities, or public good characteristics of some of the product ends, or for other reasons of non-convex behaviour.

At the macroeconomic aggregative level the economists have been mainly concerned with the measurement of the aggregate level of all the productive activities as done in terms of Gross Domestic Product (GDP) or Gross National Product (GNP) and with the analysis of behaviour of aggregate income, employment, price level and the balance of payments. Although the GDP or GNP was designed to measure the aggregate volume of economic activities and not immediately to yield a measure of human welfare, the economists have assumed that the latter is positively correlated with the volume of aggregate activity or scale of GDP and therefore have per capita GNP as the prime indicator of development. The growth of GDP has thus been considered to be good for the people of an economy. Economic policies have therefore targeted the maximization of aggregate income and the attainment of full employment in the short-run and that of economic growth in the long run. The macroeconomics has also been concerned with the balance of payments equilibrium and price stability, for combining the goal of scaling up the economy with stability and better sharing or distribution of its benefit. The economic theory of capitalist development describes economic growth to be driven by the forces of accumulation of capital (machines and structures) and technical change resulting in higher labour productivity as supported by the consumerist culture based on the value system—that more is better. This would ensure that all that is produced would be sold.

II.1 Pre-analytic Vision of Microeconomic Theory and Scale

I here mean by pre-analytic vision our preconception or broad ideas with which we begin to look at a subject of analysis and which lead to the emergence of a paradigm of analysis or theory. The pre-analytic vision of economic theory would conceive rationality in terms of choice in favour of higher scale of consumption and production of goods and services of an economy. Besides, according to such vision the relation between human economy and the natural environment or the ecosystem characterizing it, poses no constraint in attaining the rational allocation of resources. It is now well-recognised that the human economy is dependent on the natural environment for the supply of natural resources or natural capital which provide either material throughput in production or crucial ecosystem services which provide direct support to human life and livelihood and create the physical environmental conditions to make the production of goods and services possible. On the other hand, the economy generates wastes at the end of the life cycle of all natural resources drawn from the ecosystems and these have to be inevitably disposed of into the sink of the natural environment. In the conventional microeconomic analysis the major issue of choice is one of finding out the *optimum scale* of consumption or production of a particular good or services, (and not necessarily its maximum feasible scale) which should correspond to the rational choice. As microeconomics discusses about the part of an economy, and not the whole, the equilibrium as well as the optimal resource allocation in each product market, has to consider both the benefit and the opportunity cost of engaging resources in producing and using that product. Marginalism has taught us that in a convex world of preference and technology production or consumption of a product should stop where the marginal benefit equals marginal cost of engagement of resources, while the second order condition would be appropriately satisfied due to convexity.

Neoclassical microeconomics has however, considered the primary resources to be consisting mainly of human labour and man made capital which itself is created by the labour in the past. In case land or any other natural resource is considered in any analysis, it would inevitably be characterized as a private good over which the property right is defined and has therefore a market, even if it is a non produced good. The ecosystem resources which do not fall under such category—particularly sink service of nature for waste absorption—are mostly ignored and do not mostly figure in the cost. This has the implication that all such natural capital or ecosystem services are either abundantly available or our pre-analytic vision is responsible for the erroneous cost calculation for the use of such resources failing to capture the true scarcity and resulting in either depletion of the scarce resources or over-pollution of the natural environment. The calculus of social surplus becomes inadequate or imperfect for arriving at the proper choice of scale of sectoral production and consumption.

II.2 Pre-analytic Vision of Macroeconomics and Scale

The pre-analytic vision of macroeconomics on the other hand assumes that a larger economic system is better and economic growth is good since such growth does not involve any cost. In the short-run macroeconomics we do not talk about the optimal scale of a macroeconomy. The policy thrust is on full employment of resources and removal of constraints in the way of such full employment. As macroeconomics discusses about the total economy, and not any part, there is no discussion of opportunity cost of employment of resources of labour and capital in the short-run static macroeconomic analysis. In the long-run economic analysis of growth, the choice of saving rate is one of intertemporal choice of consumption out of income. The cost of saving for tomorrow's higher income or consumption is the sacrifice of today's consumption. The optimum growth is characterized by the neoclassical economic theory to be the one which maximizes the present equivalent value of the intertemporal profile of current well-being (or instantaneous utility out of consumption) for any given social discount rate which amounts to the value of wealth or of stock of resources. Following a Ramsey framework of analysis, it is thus the maximization of wealth which is the major concern for the long-run analysis of macro-dynamics at any point of time on the historical time axis. Again as the discourse of macroeconomics already considers the unit of analysis to be the entire macro economy itself, there is no scope of discussion of opportunity cost of engagement of resources in the economy as there is no scope of their engagement outside it. It is the intertemporal engagement of resources which would matter in maximising the shadow value of the initial resource endowment or equivalently the wealth measure of intertemporal well-being over infinite time horizon. There is thus no discussion on the cost of growth, although there is one on the optimal pace of growth where the rate of discount gives the benchmark of the opportunity cost of use of income or social product for consumption in the current period *vis-a-vis* the same in the following period. Such pre-analytic vision of a macro-economy only recognizes the feasibility of wealth creation, but not its cost in any opportunity sense since there exists implicitly nothing outside the totality of the economy as conceived in analysis and/or outside the inter-temporal time frame.

III. ECOLOGY AND PARADIGM CHANGE IN ECONOMICS

The main limitation of the analytical framework of neoclassical economics arises from the missing aspect in the vision that it is not in fact the economy which describes the whole that would be relevant for the determination of the human welfare. It is, in fact, the economy and the natural environment together which would constitute the whole with reference to which we have to discuss macroeconomic growth and the optimal pace or pattern of growth. The relationship between the natural environment and the human economy is to be recognized for ascertaining the environmental and social cost of economic growth (*Brown*, 2001). In other words, the domain over which the choice problems of an economy is to be defined should be the whole or the universe comprising both the economy and the eco-system so that we can define the opportunity cost of action in one part of the system (economy) in terms of losses involved in the other part (nature). It is now well recognized that substantive amount of such cost of growth arises due to the depletion of minerals and fossil fuels, degradation of land and loss of top soil, pollution of air and water bodies, deforestation, loss of biodiversity and loss of various other related ecosystem services. As these would involve substantive costs due to negative externalities causing damage of health, species loss and loss of productivity in a range of primary economic activities in agriculture and other sectors, they need to be considered and not neglected to decide the pace and structure of growth. This would necessitate the consideration of the common property resources with public good character as asset with economic value taking account of the structure and the functional behaviour of the ecosystem which interact with the economy and influence people's choices. In other words, the expanded models of our economic choices and policies have to factor in the concerned interdisciplinary factors by appropriate articulation. (e.g., global temperature behaviour and climate change in an integrated model of global change and choice.)

One possible explanation of neglect of such social cost due to environmental externalities and social loss due to growth may be that the pre-analytic vision of economic theory is assuming the environmental capacity of the nature in supplying resources and absorbing waste to be still large enough relative to the requirement of economic growth. However, it is undeniable that the global economic growth combined with the growth of population during the last one hundred years has been causing increasing stress on the relationship between the natural environment and the human economy, as indicated by the regular data generated on shrinking forests, collapsing fisheries, eroding soil, degrading range land, expanding desert, rising CO_2, melting of arctic sea ice, rising sea level, dying coral reefs and vanishing species. While these are a few major illustrative phenomena with many of them having impacts across countries and regions, economic growth has had important environmental consequences at national or local level, as illustrated by the physical and chemical degradation of topsoil, salinisation of land due to water logging resulting from the growing irrigation activities, chemical pollution of water bodies, air pollution from mining and quarrying, automotive emission, emission from the fossil fuel, etc. While economy is thus in conflict with earth's natural systems, it is interesting that *economics is still relevant to estimate and account for all such costs of growth and develop true indicators of growth of wealth and real well-being and appropriate policies.* The environmental economics has developed over the last three decades as an extension of applied welfare economics which focuses on the methodology of valuation of environmental services and estimation of these costs due to their losses or damages, and on the regulatory instruments and institutions to internalize the costs of externalities of economic activities and to protect the public good of the environment.

III.1. Environmental Economics: Any Limit to Macro-economy?

The neoclassical environmental economics has been mostly confined to microeconomic level of analysis, where the existence of the possible limitation of environmental capacity to provide the supply of natural resources and absorb waste is recognized. The analysis of socially optimum scale of any sectoral activity and resource allocation as discussed there internalizes the costs of such scarcities and associated externalities. It is also assumed at the same time that the problems arising from such limitation can be abated by appropriate spending on (a) abatement of pollution, (b) discovery of more of the existing resources or their substitutes, and (c) resource conserving technical changes. This implies the admission of the fundamental possibilities of substitution of natural resources and eco-services by human labour, man-made physical and knowledge capital whose actual realization will follow the dictates of market prices of natural capital relative to that of other types of capital or inputs when it becomes scarce. The basic assumption of neoclassical economics with reference to the relation between the economy and the natural environment or ecosystem as underlying such postulates of substitution is that the *ecosystem is a sub-system of the economy as it is merely an extractive and waste disposal sector.* Economic growth can continue even if natural capital becomes scarce, as technology can grow around the sub-sector ecosystem by the substitution of natural capital by man made capital provided the price-tax system signals the true scarcity of the natural capital. As per such vision, nature is conceived to be a system which is supplier of indestructible building blocks which are substitutable and super abundant (*Daly*, 1999). At any stage of history all these building blocks are not well discovered or known. The real *limit to growth* has been the constraint of knowledge capital and technology. There is supposed to be no limit to the discovery of new technology as per such vision in the very long run, provided appropriate investment is made. Technology can provide substitution of natural capital by man made capital or knowledge capital and may raise the supply of ecosystem services in efficiency unit or degrade waste in an eco-friendly manner. A growing economic system would provide enough surplus which can be allocated for the growth of knowledge capital for such development of technology. The modern endogenous growth theory among others searches for the conditions for indefinite steady state economic growth through endogenous investment in knowledge capital, keeping the ecosystem in equilibrium. This would mean that economic growth is possible in the long-run without being constrained by its component eco subsystem.

III.2 Ecological Economics: Perspective of Macro-economic Growth

The pre-analytic vision of neoclassical macro theory as outlined above would however be contested by the ecologists and natural scientists. According to them human economy constitutes a sub-system of a larger ecosystem of the natural environment of this planet which is finite, non-growing and materially closed while it is open only to a flow-through of solar energy. This solar energy flow to our planet is also finite and non-growing per unit of time. While the solar energy flow and bio-geo-chemical cycles of the planet's ecosystem can regenerate resources and degrade wastes for the economy, there would be finite bound on the rates of such regeneration and waste absorption. The entropy law ensures continuous degradation of resources into waste as they are used in the processes of production and consumption in the economy. While the scientific and technological progress can moderate the rise of entropy with growth of GDP, it cannot be *a priori* ensured that the effect of indefinite growth of scale of an economy on entropy can be exactly offset by technical changes unless we reach a state where something more can be produced out of nothing, which conflicts with one of the basic postulates of the theory of economic production. The newly emerging paradigm of ecological economics visualizes economy to be a part of the total system of the natural environment. With the economic growth the empty world of the pre-industrial revolution ecosystem has now become almost a full or congested world with the economic activities and population filling up the eco-space. The human subsystem with such growth is now appropriating almost the entirety of the environmental capital providing ecoservices, leaving very limited natural resources and other natural capital services for other species and conservation of biodiversity. As macroeconomy is part of the total system as per the pre-analytic vision of ecological economics, it would recognize with consistency the existence of environmental and social cost of economic growth defined in terms of stress and strain of the natural environmental system particularly in a situation of full world occupation by the human economy. The ecological economics therefore focuses on the estimation of costs of growth in terms of loss of natural resources and environmental capacity and derive the measure of true accumulation of wealth and well-being of the people of a nation after taking care of costs of depletion and degradation of natural capital and ecosystem. As the macroeconomy grows, it would become a larger part of the total ecosystem and has to increasingly conform to the finitude, and non growth character and to the entropy level of the total ecosystem. The ultimate scale of the economy in the long-run would also be limited by the size of the total system of which it constitutes a part, even if the neoclassical assumption of substitutability between the natural capital and man-made or knowledge capital is possible at some stage of development.

III.3 Substitutability vs. Complementarity

The ecological perspective of macroeconomy raises however an important issue regarding complementarity vs. substitutability between the man-made and the natural capital. The GDP being the sum of all the value added by labour and man made capital in the different spheres and individual activities of production, a question may be asked: what is the base on which this value is added. There can be no GDP created by labour and man made capital in a vacuum. It is the natural resources of energy and material which provides the basis on which the value is added by labour and man-made capital for their service of conversion of these resources in products of material goods and services. There is thus a fundamental relation of complementarity between the labour and man-made capital on the one hand and the natural capital on the other. If a particular natural resource becomes scarce, the dictates of prices would often cause substitution of one resource by another natural resource and correspondingly there would be a switch in technology involving the use of the alternative resource. In response to such scarcity, there is, however, also the alternative possibility of substitution of techniques which uses basically the same natural resources in different proportion to man-made capital and other inputs, ultimately reducing the requirement of the concerned natural resource per unit of gross output or value-added (for example the resource and energy conservation). While dematerialization of economy and investment in technological change for material and energy conservation, discovery of new resources and resource substitution would contribute to the expansion of the scale of an economy in terms of the measure of the aggregate value of social product, the relationship of basic complementarity would not permit such indefinite substitution for sustaining growth. As the human system would expand and tend to move towards a full-world situation, the limits imposed by the requirement of complementarity would become stringent and binding. While any substitution possibility between the man-made and the natural capital can ease the constraint of resource scarcity in the short run, the long-run view of development should recognize the limit to scale in terms of GDP, arising from the finitude of the earth's system and the cost of conversion of the environment into social product. As the environment has also amenity value and the various biological species may have instrumental as well as intrinsic value as per our perception, these considerations along with the complementarity of natural capital with the other man-made one would lead to delimiting the size of the optimum scale of an economy.

In view of the ultimate limit to the scale of optimal size, we possibly need to conceptualise development differently by addressing more carefully the other dimensions of development and characterise optimality accordingly. The value or the preference system may require to be adapted to realize the nature and deep implications of the constraints that the environmental system poses. There may in fact evolve different views what well-being or a well lived life should mean in such ecological context. Human consciousness develops with the changing conditions of the environmental and material existence. In the changing environmental conditions the human consciousness is likely to guide the value system to so evolve that it is no longer considered to be exogenous to the environment and instead may be deeply influenced by the latter. The environment may be considered valuable not for instrumental reason, but valuable for being such an end in itself with which human self can relate and redefine a new relation of identity.

IV. ECOLOGICAL LIMITS AND EQUITY IN DEVELOPMENT

IV.1 Poverty, Income Distribution and the Environment

One important issue of development economics has been that of equity and distribution of income and wealth. In the historical process of socioeconomic evolution the concern for equity has inevitably created some space for every individual in the economy for his or her sheer survival and for the political viability and sustainability of any given socio-economic order. The space so created however has been quite inadequate for many *vis-a-vis* the requirement of basic minimum needs as illustrated by the existence of the poor in overpopulated developing countries like India. Economic growth has in fact been able to address the Malthusian problem of population through demographic transition. Investment stimulating growth has addressed the problem of Keynesian unemployment by raising the level of effective demand. It is, however, also worth-noting here that any environmental movement loses its force in any period of recession and unemployment as their redressal would inevitably cause greater resource use and waste arising at least in the short-run. Economic growth is also considered to contribute to the removal of poverty, but often at some environmental cost. However, if economic growth is driven by such investment and technical change which are environment conserving, economic growth and poverty removal may not conflict with environmental sustainability at least in the long-run.

In the current context of global policy formulation for the abatement of global warming and controlling climate change, a major argument for growth and greater allocation of any possible quota for green house gas emissions than the current emission level, as put forward by the overpopulated poor developing countries, has arisen from the concern for the fast removal of poverty from the world. The argument for growth in the context of equitable distribution has been that it raises the mean of the distribution of income along with that of the average of value of its poorest quantile. While economic growth may raise the bottom line of the distribution and remove poverty it does not however ensure that the measure of inequality, like Gini Coefficient or gap between the richest 20% and the poorest 20% of population will decline with growth. Besides, economic growth may be a necessary condition, but not a sufficient one for the speedy removal of poverty. It is also to be noted that any scaling up of growth with technology which degrades land and soil and depletes water resource affecting primary productivity of the ecosystem would stand in the way of food security of the growing millions of a developing country and be counter-productive in poverty removal.

If such concern for equity is to be addressed in the short or long-run developmental context within the finitude of the ecosystem, it is important to ascertain the range of choices in ensuring re-distribution of income and wealth within the current generation either remaining within an *a priori* set bound of scale (in a situation where exceeding such limits would bring catastrophe) at the least opportunity cost of sacrifice of growth or at the least environmental and social cost of ecosystem for surpassing the environmental capacity for delivering justice.

It is also worth noting here that apart from the relationship between the poverty alleviation and the expansion of scale of an economy and its implication on the scale of use of resources and ecosystem services, there also exists a complex relationship between the environmental state and the level of poverty, deprivation, and inequality. In the dual society of a developing economy with a sharp divide between the rich and the poor, the rich have conspicuous material consumption and contribute to substantive generation of wastes of various kinds like CO_2 emission, chemical effluents, solid wastes, etc. The poor and the deprived, on the other hand, live and survive directly at the cost of the environment by often forcible occupation and overuse of the various common property resources like forest, pasture land, and the agricultural land of marginal quality. The over use of such resources causes decline in their primary productivities and aggravates the economic condition of the poor further. Urban poverty as characterized by living in congested slums, lack of infrastructure for sanitation and safe water supply, etc. leads to both environmental and human degradation. The neoclassical economic logic also points out that it is the income-elasticity of environmental service and amenities which plays a determining role in the demand for environmental quality and services and the stringency of environmental regulation of a society. A redistribution of income with growth within the limits of scale as imposed by the finitude of the eco-system may go a long way in raising the environmental quality and the quality of life of the people. The preference structure, the value system and culture are in fact important not only in determining the allocation of resources between the environmental and the non-environmental sector, but also in determining the direct and indirect resource and pollution intensity of products consumed and of the aggregate GDP or income generated. The policy issues for environmental sustainability cannot thus be addressed independent of considerations of the state of development, distribution of income and wealth, values, preferences and culture of the people.

IV.2 Inter-generational Equity in Development and the Environment

The finitude of ecosystem also raises a problem of inter generational equity as any scaling up leads to the depletion of resources and growth of pollution. If the scale of economic activities causes extraction of resources at a rate exceeding the rate of its regeneration, or disposal of wastes at a rate higher than that of its absorption in the nature, it will deplete the resource stock or qualitatively degrade the natural environment which would in turn adversely affect the primary productivity of the ecosystem and the flow of ecosystem services in future. The higher current well-being of the present period would be attained at the cost of decline in the level of current well-being in the future. The consideration of inter-generational equity would thus require such inter-temporal distribution of use of natural resources and environmental capacity that the well-being indicator does not decline in value over time. If our welfare indicator or function pays weightage to the altruistic concern for the future generation yet unborn, the inter-generational equity would require the present equivalent value of inter temporal profile of utilities of current consumption of the different generations, or equivalently the value of the present stock of all kinds of capital assets—natural and man-made—not to decline over time. As the inter-generational equity requires the measure of aggregate value of wealth not to decline, the growing occupation of space of the total ecosystem by the economy is thus to reach a steady state (*Daly*, 1999, *Daly and Townsend*, 1994) or stationary state equilibrium by a monotonic movement leaving some space of the total system for other species and rest of the natural environment. The latter condition is required so that the ecosystem may be able to indefinitely recreate itself and provide a continuous stable flow of eco-services for the human economy, preserve biodiversity and protect also the resilience of our ecosystem. The maximization of the short-run scale of an economy or that of steady state growth rate will thus have to be replaced by the objective of sustainable development as characterized by the removal of poverty and the sustenance of the level of wealth over time for such intra-generational and intergenerational equity consideration.

IV.3 Ecological Economic Perspective of Macroeconomic Development: Shift from Scale to Quality—Concept of Sustainable Development

Unlike the conventional macroeconomics, the macroeconomics as viewed from the perspective of ecological sustainability will thus be concerned with the optimum allocation of resource space of the finite total system between the human economy and the natural environment. However, the same allocation of eco space of the total system of the universe for the humans can deliver different levels of human welfare depending on the choice of product mix, technology and natural resource use, preference structure and value system, state of knowledge and human capability development, and distributive mechanism, institutional norms and culture. All these determinant conditions internal to the human system would also contribute to the qualitative aspect of the human economy as characterized among others by the equity and fairness in sharing the benefit of macroeconomic development, cleanliness of the physical environment and the scale of availability of environmental amenities and services.

The ideology of the so-called ecological economics has thus shifted the focus of economic development from the scalar expansion to the qualitative changes of human society and equity in development processes. While ecological economics approaches the issue of substantiality with prime focus on the limits to scale imposed by the nature on the human system, it has searched solution for sustainable development through the means of achieving qualitative change in society by way of development of knowledge and technology, institutional innovations, policy reforms and radical change in the value system and preference structure, so that the society can realize its full potential and the economy can evolve to become an improved (and not necessarily larger) structure or system for delivering human welfare (*Daly and Farley*, 2004).

While there has now developed some clarity in the perception and conceptual approach of ecological economics to address macro economic development issues, the precise methodology of analysis required for the purpose is yet to be fully developed and complete. The so-called ecological economists attempt to use a multi-disciplinary knowledge base and inter-disciplinary methodology to address the problem of sustainability encompassing economic, social and environmental considerations with a holistic approach. This has involved quite complex analysis of interactive relations among the ecosystem, scale of an economy, society and institutions for developing models of policy research on sustainable development. Some section of such school of thought proposes a trans-disciplinary meta-framework for the analysis of sustainability issues with reference to economic efficiency of resource allocation, socio-economic equity and environmental conservation (*Mumasinghe*, 2005). However, given the current state of development of the subject of ecological economics and the wide range of multi-disciplinary issues it is trying to address, its over all conceptual framework of analysis as developed and methodology as practised have often been somewhat heuristic, incomplete and ever changing depending on the kind of problem addressed. The precise definition or notion of sustainability also varies often with the context. The subject as claimed to be different from the neoclassical environmental economics is in some sense is to yield a precise analytical framework and be commonly well-known and accepted for generating policy results on a range of issues which would not be conflicting with each other and not work at cross purposes.

However, it is nevertheless important to emphasize that the role of ecological limits to scale and the interactive relation between the human economy and the natural environment have to be recognized and understood in the context of our theory and application of macroeconomic development and policy. This would in any case require a unified scientific and integrative inter-disciplinary approach of analysis instead of a narrow reductionist one of conventional economics. The analytical apparatus of neoclassical economics of optimization in static or dynamic inter-temporal framework of choices would however remain the major useful tool for internalizing environmental cost of growth and expansion of scale or for evaluating the environmental consequences of poverty, deprivation and disparity. The validity and significance of such results of analyses and their usefulness for policy purposes would however depend on the quality of assumptions as well as on that of formulation of the concerned economic model of measurement and choice in development. The recognition of limits to scale require the universe of domain of constraints and their levels and possibly the specification of the objective function to be so defined as to factor in the concerned ecological factors into the models. This does not mean that the entire apparatus of neoclassical economics is of little value as often asserted by the ecological economists.

V. CONCLUSION

In order to improve the quality of assumption and formulation of economic models for the purpose we need to correctly internalize or factor in some of the ecological factors in economic models. Such internalization of ecological factors may introduce problems of non-convexities as the environmental goods often involve public good character and generate externalities, while some of the ecological variables show non-convexity in their nonlinear behavioral pattern. As searching for the global optimum becomes a difficult task in such situation, the search may have to be confined to the ascertaining of the local optima in the relevant domain of variation of the ecological and economic variables of the system.

The integration of ecological factors in economic model of systemic behaviour or policy enables us to define the notion of welfare, equity and environmental sustainability from holistic perspective and assess the economic cost of growth for better policies while retaining the essential methodological principle of economics for resolving the problems of choice. To my mind the main additionality of ecological economics over environmental economics although discussed in inarticulated manner in the literature, is the recognition of the limits of scale and factoring in more of inter-disciplinarity in its framework of analysis. I would like to claim that if such extension is to be called part of any discourse of "economic science" it should only be considered as an extension of applied neoclassical economics defined in a broader framework of analysis. If one model of economic choice cannot do justice to the adequate consideration of a number of interactions of ecological and economic factors, we may have a set of interactive models, with a central economic model and other satellite models considering the ecological driving factors or impact variables which are connected with the economic variables. Such models may talk to each other and represent an integrated system which need not always be mechanistically interconnected by any *a priori* assumption about the nature of interconnectedness of such models. The economic analyst can be allowed the freedom for deciding on how to use the result of one of the satellite models into another model of the system depending on the context and policy issues to be addressed. Similar conceptual approach has been taken in the UN system of Standard National Accounts (SNA) 1993 for integrating environmental accounting with the macroeconomic accounting.

We thus need not define several extensions of economic science—environmental economics and ecological economics—depending on whether we are addressing the problem of environmental valuation and taxes or other market based instruments of environmental control for correcting market failure, or that of the sustainability of economic growth as arising from the ecological limits. The theory of valuation of environmental services has in fact to clearly recognize the problems of limits of ecosystem because that lies at the fundamental root of market failure. Again no discussion on the sustainability of macroeconomic growth is possible unless one can value the environmental assets properly. It is thus essential that there is congruence in the approaches of addressing micro and macro-economic questions and unified principle of economic analysis is applied for the issues of environmental and resource economics. I would like to emphasize that if we are analyzing economic choices and economic policy related issues we need to have our feet firmly grounded in the basics of methodology of economic analysis which is quite amenable to the incorporation of inter-disciplinary factors. The latter can be done by appropriately broadening its framework and defining the assumptions and constraints carefully without searching for a trans-disciplinary meta-framework of supra-analysis. The main thrust that is required for the further development of the economics of the environment and natural resources is that it needs to be viewed as a branch of economic science—be it called environmental economics or ecological economics—that is to address the challenges of *ecological limits and entropy law* to the sustainable functioning of the economy. Such development and extension of economic science is possible without diluting the essentials of the neoclassical economic logic, nor being reductionist in our approach of sustainability analysis.

References

Brown Lester R. (2001), *Eco-Economy,* W.W. Norton & Company, London.

Daly, Herman E. (1999), *Ecological Economics and Ecology of Economics,* Edward Elgar, Cheltenham, UK.

Daly, Herman E. and Joshua Farley (2004), *Ecological Economics: Principles and Application,* Island Press

Daly, Herman E. and Kenneth N. Townsend (1994), *Valuing the Earth: Economics, Ecology, Ethics,* The MIT Press, Cambridge, Massachusetts, USA.

Munasinghe, Mohan (2005), "The Sustainomics Trans-disciplinary Meta-Framework for Making Development More Sustainable: Applications to Energy Issues", Pushpam Kumar (ed.) *Economics of Environment and Development,* Anne Book, New Delhi.

Environmentally Sound Technologies for Sustainable Development of India

U. SANKAR

This paper deals with the meaning, drivers and modes of adoption of environmentally sound technologies in developing countries. It critically reviews the technology transfer provisions in WTO agreements and assess their effectiveness. It also stresses the need for development of indigenous environmentally sound technologies for the South and considers the efforts taken in this regard and also capacity buildings in India.

1. INTRODUCTION

The World Commission on Environment and Development (WCED), in its publication *Our Common Future* (*WCED*, 1987), defines the concept of sustainable development as 'meeting the needs of the present generation without compromising the needs of future generations'. Solow (1991/2000) notes that sustainability has become a buzzword. According to him 'it is a vague concept. ... It is, at best, a general guide to policies that have to do with investment, conservation and resource use'. Sustainability was viewed as distributional equity between the present and the future i.e., inter-generational equity. Solow notes that when one thinks of equity one must 'think about equity not between periods of time but equity right now', i.e. intra-generational equity. The problem of reconciling intra-generational equity with inter-generational equity is yet unresolved as the former requires use of high discount rate while the latter requires use of low discount rate in choices among projects.

Despite the conceptual problem, this concept has been embraced by the U.N. Assembly and accepted by multilateral agencies dealing with trade, environment and poverty. Efforts have been made to operationalize the concept. The WCED publication clarifies that sustainable development is 'a process of change in which exploitation of resources, the direction of investments, the orientation of technological development, and institutional change are all in harmony and enhance both current and future potential to meet human needs and aspirations'. Now, there seems to be a consensus that sustainable development 'involves transforming decision-making and basing it upon the triple imperative of long-term ecological, social and economic security ("the triple bottom line"), specifically,

- living within the limits of local and global biophysical carrying capacity and biodiversity (the ecological imperative);
- ensuring that basic needs are met through democratic system of governance and equity (the social imperative); and
- ensuring a vibrant economy based on eco-efficiency and sustainability (the economic imperative). (*UNEP*, 2003).

Sustainability assessments of major projects and policy changes in many countries are being made using economic, social and environmental indicators.

The Preamble to Science and Technology Policy, 2003 recognizes the central role of science and technology 'in raising the quality of life of the people of the country, particularly of the disadvantaged sections of society, in creating wealth for all, in making India globally competitive, in utilizing resources in a sustainable manner, in protecting the environment and ensuring national security' [*Government of India (Department of Science and Technology)* 2003]. This policy also takes into consideration, among other things, economic, social and environmental objectives.

India needs environmentally sound technologies (ESTs) for sustainable development. Such technologies are needed for sustaining economic growth at 8 per cent or more, conservation of exhaustible natural resources, augmentation and sustainable use of renewable natural resources, compliance with domestic environmental regulations, compliance with Technical Barriers to Trade (TBT) and Sanitary and Phyto-Sanitary (SPS) measures of the World Trade Organization (WTO) and provisions in Multilateral Environmental Agreements (MEAs), overcoming market access barriers in the form of environmental requirements in importing countries, and sustainable management of natural resources.

Technology policy involves choice between borrowing technologies developed abroad and indigenous development of technologies. The choice depends on costs of imported and indigenous technologies, availability of technologies appropriate to our needs and terms of access, and long-term prospects of indigenous development with spin-off benefits. An assessment of trade-offs among economic, social and environmental goals is necessary before investment decisions on R&D and technology development/import of technologies is made to ensure sustainable development.

Section II deals with meaning of ESTs, differences between ESTs and other technologies, and drivers and the modes for adoption of ESTs. Section III deals with issues in transfer of ESTs. It summarizes provisions in the WTO Agreements and selected MEAs regarding transfer of ESTs, the extent to which the provisions have been implemented, and the problems India face. Section IV considers India's efforts in indigenous development of ESTs and domestic capacity-building in natural resource management. Section V contains concluding remarks.

II. ESTs: MEANING, DRIVERS AND MODES OF ADOPTION

Meaning

According to UNCED (1992), Agenda 21, Chapter 34, ESTs

'protect the environment, are less polluting, use all resources in a more sustainable manner, recycle more of their wastes and products, and handle residual wastes in a more acceptable manner than the technologies for which they were substitutes'. They cover "process and product technologies" for the prevention of pollution and "end of the pipe" technologies for treatment of *pollution* after it has been generated.

Chapter 34 says that ESTs 'are not just individual technologies, but total systems which include know-how, procedures, goods and services and equipment as well as organizational and managerial procedures'. Thus there are four aspects of transfer of ESTs: (a) infoware, including designs and blueprints which constitute the document embodied knowledge on information and technology; (b) technoware, which includes the physical aspects, i.e., machinery and equipment; (c) humanware, which includes skills, human aspects of technology management learning and adaptation; and (d) organware, which covers production arrangement linkages within which the technology is operated.

This chapter also notes that ESTs should be 'compatible with nationally determined socio-economic, cultural and environmental priorities'. Thus the concept of environmental soundness is relative; it is also an evolving concept changing with developments in technology and environmental standards. Some ESTs developed in the North may not be appropriate to some developing countries in the South because these technologies were developed keeping in view the environmental standards, factor endowments and factors prices prevailing in the North. Even when such ESTs are available, there may be export restrictions or their prices may be high or there may be costs associated with their adaptation. Thus there is a case for indigenous development of ESTs in the South.

ESTs and other Technologies

There is a vast literature on technology transfer dealing with access, terms, channels and home country and host country policies. See for example, Maskus (2004) and country submissions and discussions in TRIPS Working Group on Trade and Transfer of Technology (WT/WGTTT/M). Less and McMillan (2005), based on UNCTAD (2003), point out similarities and differences between ESTs and other technologies. We consider the roles of governments in developing countries in creating sound domestic environmental policy regimes, in facilitating successful transfer and adoption of ESTs, and in developing indigenous capacity for generation and use of ESTs.

Drivers

(a) Environmental Policy

Environmental problems arise largely because of "market failures," "institutional failures" and "government failures". Therefore, we need an environmental policy regime for internalization of environmental externalities in producer's and consumer's decisions. Each country has the right to determine its environmental standards based on its own needs and technical and financing capabilities.

Given the standards, there are three options for complying with the standards: (a) regulatory or command and control, (b) use of charges and fees, and (c) creation and operation of markets for pollution permits. Most economists prefer options (b) and (c) because they make use of the information available with the polluters about the sources of pollution and least cost methods of achieving compliance with the standards. India's environmental legislations come under criminal laws and hence both in enforcement of the laws and in the judicial decisions the issue is compliance or non-compliance with the regulations and not the extent of compliance. National Environmental Policy 2006 favours a shift from criminal liability to civil liability [*Government of India* (*Ministry of Environment and Forests*), 2006]. Such a shift is necessary for internalization of negative environmental externalities in decision-making and introduction of economic instruments like pollution charges and tradable pollution permits. However, in situations where irreversible damages are likely to occur or when pollution load is likely to exceed the carrying capacity of a region, precautionary approach favours the adoption of option (a).

An environmental policy regime will meet the environmental effectiveness criteria only if two conditions are met. The first condition is that prices of environmental resources reflect their social costs. The second condition is that the laws are enforced. Only when the two conditions are met, the polluting firms have an incentive to internalize all environmental costs in their decisions in such a manner that their private costs of pollution abatement equal the social costs of pollution abatement. An incentive for compliance beyond standards will induce firms to search for and apply ESTs.

Two other issues are relevant in design and implementation of environmental standards. The first issue is the nature of link between pollution load at the micro-level and pollution load at the macro-level. One major weakness of the concentration-based standards/or technology based standards is that even if every polluting unit complies with the standards, the aggregate pollution load will increase because of economic growth. We need periodic revisions for tightening the standards so that there are caps on aggregate pollution loads.

The second issue is the type of efficiency criterion used i.e. static efficiency or dynamic efficiency. Porter and Van der Linde (1995) argue that 'the notion of an inevitable struggle between ecology ,and the economy grows out of a static view of environmental regulation, in which technology, products, processes and consumer needs are all fixed' (p. 97). According to them, comparative advantage rests on 'the capacity for innovation and improvement that shift the constraint' (p. 98). They mention two kinds of innovation offsets. Product offsets occur when environmental regulation produces not just less pollution, but also creates better-performing products, safer products and lower production costs. Process offsets occur when environmental regulation not only leads to reduced pollution, but also results in higher productivity, material savings, better utilization of products, etc. Use of ESTs by firms will enable them not only to comply with domestic environmental requirements but also produce "better" and "safer" products and improve their corporate image. By adopting ESTs early they can push the environment agenda further.

Public policies such as creation of information exchanges on ESTs, lower tariffs on import of ESTs, tax holidays, accelerated depreciation allowances on the capital, loans at concessional rates for acquisition of ESTs and recognition of adoption of ESTs by firms provide incentives for firms to switch over to ESTs. Market pressures can also influence firms to adopt ESTs. Changes in accounting practices, i.e. from historical costs to economic (opportunity) costs, internalization of all external costs in pricing, and evaluation of outcomes rather than inputs are desirable for sustainable allocation of resources.

(b) Market Access

TBT and SPS Agreements and other environmental requirements in developed countries affect market access for products such as leather and leather products, textiles and processed food when the requirements are above the international norms. Environmental requirements in the forms of product specifications, permissible levels of chemicals, limits on emissions and waste discharges, packaging requirements, ecolabelling, and adoption of ISO-14000 standards in developed countries' markets put pressures on export-oriented units to adopt environment-friendly technologies, processes and inputs. The EU wants to leverage compliance with internal EU environmental standards against market access.

(c) New Market Opportunities

Markets are emerging for "green" products and goods produced based on ESTs. The demand arises because of growing environmental awareness among consumers about product characteristics and green movement highlighting the need for life cycle assessment for environmental protection. Success of Doha Round of negotiations on reduction of tariffs in environmental goods and elimination of non-tariff barriers for environmental goods and services will generate demand for ESTs.

(d) Compliance with MEA Provisions

Compliance with MEAs often requires legal and institutional measures and adoption of ESTs. For example, the Montreal Protocol requires parties to substitute technologies, processes and inputs which prevent depletion of the ozone layer. The Convention on Climate Change recommends adoption of energy efficient and less polluting fossil fuel technologies and renewable energy technologies.

Modes of Transfer/Production

We consider four different modes of EST transfer depending on industry characteristics and policy goals.

Mode 1: Large Firms

If ESTs are under IPR regime and the transferee is a large firm, then the transfer is feasible through licensing, foreign direct investment (FDI) or joint venture (JV). Licensing is desirable if it is a standard technology. FDI or JV is appropriate if the transfer involves info ware, techno ware, organware and humanware. The host country government's main responsibility is creation of a TRIPS-consistent environment for IPR protection, lowering of transaction cost of EST transfer and promotion of an open trading regime. Access to the ESTs on fair and concessional terms or/and transfers may take place under MEA obligations.

Mode 2: Small and Medium Enterprises (SMEs)

If ESTs are under IPR regime and the transferees are SMEs, then involvement of host government, inter-governmental agencies such as UNCTAD and UNIDO, industry associations and industry-specific research institutions is needed in the form of a partnership. This is necessary to overcome barriers to transfer of ESTs and their effective absorption in the host country. The barriers and problems are:

(i) lack of information about ESTs appropriate to domestic environmental standards;
(ii) need for adaptation and diffusion of borrowed technologies;
(iii) high costs of access to and transfer of ESTs because of small size, information asymmetry and financing problems in host country, and IPR protection and restrictive practices of EST suppliers in home countries;
(iv) non-internalization of environmental costs in investment and pricing decisions because of under-pricing of resources or/and poor enforcement of environmental regulations in host countries;
(v) presence of positive externalities in adoption of ESTs; development goals such as decentralized development and employment generation; and
(vi) addressing the last mile problem in creating access to scattered units and units in remote areas.

Agenda 21 Chapter 34 suggests the following options for

transfer of ESTs coming under IPR regime on favourable terms:

(a) compulsory purchase of ESTs from IPR holders and their transfer to developing countries for specified purposes on non-exclusive basis to meet their obligations under MEAs;
(b) government purchase at market prices from IPR holders and transfer them to developing countries on concessional terms to meet their "common but differentiated responsibilities" (CDR) and other obligations;
(c) prevention of monopoly and restrictive practices of patent-holders, e.g. high royalties, restrictions on exports/third-party sale, tie-in sales; and
(d) financial assistance on concessional terms by governments directly or through UN agencies.

According to UNCTAD (1992) about 40 percent of R&D in OECD countries in 1998 was publicly funded. Some resulting technologies are now available only to firms in their countries. As part of international cooperation, OECD countries could give access to these technologies to developing countries free of cost.

Conventional channels of technology transfer such as licensing, FDI and JV may not be appropriate under this mode because (i) there are many users, (ii) the technology must be made operational taking into account the ground realities, and (c) there will be spillovers.

Mode 3: Development Cooperation

Some ESTs developed in the North may not be appropriate to developing countries because of differences in factor endowments, size, environmental standards and other location-specific factors. Hence, it is desirable to develop indigenous ESTs to meet local needs. For easier access and rapid diffusion of such ESTs, it is desirable to place them in public domain. A development cooperation model involving many stakeholders—firms, industry associations, research laboratories, suppliers of different components of ESTs, governments of host countries and inter-governmental organizations is needed. The cooperation must be voluntary and mutually beneficial. This is possible when economies of scale and scope in the collective action result in cost complementarities and overall cost savings. We need incentive structures and cost-sharing arrangements to induce and sustain cooperation among the different stakeholders.

Mode 4: South-South Cooperation

There is a need for South-South Cooperation in the development and transfer of ESTs. The needs are obvious in agriculture where small firms dominate, operations are labour-intensive, and climatic conditions are similar; in industries where SMEs dominate, techniques are labour-intensive and environmental standards are similar; and in health where most of the diseases are tropical and access to drugs at affordable prices is important. Thus there is a case for public funding of R&D in these areas and keeping the technologies in public domain. A regional cooperation agreement under FTA or economic partnership with support from UN agencies is an institutional option

III. TECHNOLOGY TRANSFER PROVISIONS IN WTO AND MEAs AND THEIR EFFECTIVENESS

The WTO and most MEAs aim at sustainable development. They also incorporate development concerns based on Rio Declaration Principle 7 of common but differentiated responsibilities (CDR) in the forms of special and differential treatment (S&DT) of developing countries and supportive measures such as financial and technical assistance and capacity building for developing and least developed countries. The Doha Ministerial Declaration (DMD) WT/MIN(01)/Dec./7 dated 20 November 2001 reaffirms WTO members commitment to the objective of sustainable development and also their commitment to the WTO as the unique forum for global trade rule-making and liberalization. The DMD recognizes that majority of WTO members are developing countries and WTO members 'seek to place their needs and interests at the heart of the Work Programme' adopted in the Declaration. The Work Programme covers, *inter alia,* market access, trade-related intellectual property rights (TRIPS), trade and environment, and trade and transfer of technology.

(a) Technology Transfer in WTO

The WTO Agreements on Technical Barriers to Trade (TBT) and on Application of Sanitary and Phytosanitary (SPS) Measures recognize the importance of international standards and conformity assessments in improving the efficiency of production and facilitating the conduct of trade. These Agreements also give the option to states to prescribe standards which are higher than international standards when they are necessary. Article 11 of TBT deals with technical assistance regarding the establishment of national standardizing bodies and bodies for the assessment of conformity with standards adopted within the territory of the requesting member and participation in the international standardizing bodies. Article 12 states that members shall take into account the special development, financial and trade need of developing country members in the implementation of this Agreement. There is no specific mention of EST transfer.

Article 9 of SPS Agreement states that technical assistance to developing countries may be, *inter alia*, in the areas of processing technologies, research infrastructure, including the establishment of national regulatory bodies and may take the form of advice, credits, donations and grants, including for the purpose of seeking technical expertise, training and equipment to allow such countries to adjust to, and comply with sanitary or phytosanitary measures necessary to achieve the appropriate level of sanitary and phytosanitary protection in their export markets. Article 10 on SDT 'allows scope for the phased introduction of new sanitary or phytosanitary measures, longer time-frames for compliance should be accorded on products of interest to developing members so as to maintain opportunities for their exports'.

There are only a few cases of bilateral technical assistance between developed and developing countries. TBT and SPS standards fixed by developed countries are often higher than the international standards. Developing countries perceive that the higher standards and other environmental requirements prescribed by consumers and producers raise the cost of access to the markets and act as non-tariff barriers. Tariff escalation in products of export interest to developing countries, e.g. leather, textiles and processed food affect their exports. Further, the dependence of developing countries on substitutes for restricted/banned inputs which are generally costlier than the inputs available domestically and terms of access to the ESTs which come under IPR raise the unit cost of complying with the environmental requirements abroad. Developing countries can compete, despite the increased environmental compliance costs, only if they have comparative cost advantages in material and labour costs.

We illustrate the market access problem and the responses of India with special reference to leather exports. Sahasranamam (2006) argues that environmental requirements are proliferating particularly in the EU. As some of the inputs used in leather tanning are banned, leather exporting countries have to depend on the EU or other developed countries for access to the inputs. Tariff escalation in this sector in the EU and USA discourage exports of value-added leather products from India. Interviews with leather exporters in India reveal the difficulties they face with regard to switching to environment friendly processes, in getting access to banned inputs, packaging requirements, and certification and testing requirements. Even though India has the largest leather research institute in the world, better raw material base and UNIDO's Technology Modernization Programme for Leather Industry, Indian governments' policy responses to global changes in trading and environmental regime were relatively slow. (*Sankar*, 2006).

TRIPS

The preamble to TRIPS Agreement recognizes that intellectual property rights are private rights. It recognizes 'the needs of the least developed country members in respect of maximum flexibility in the domestic implementation of laws and regulations in order to enable them to create a sound and viable technological base'. Article 7 says that the protection and enforcement of IPRs should contribute to the promotion of technological innovation and to the transfer and dissemination of technology, to the mutual advantage of producers and users of technological knowledge and in a manner conducive to social and economic welfare, and to a balance of rights and obligations.

Article 66.2 requires that members provide incentives to enterprises and institutions in their territories for the purpose of promoting and encouraging technology transfer only to least-developed country members. Article 67 provides for technical and financial cooperation in favour of developing and least-developed countries in the preparation of laws and regulations on the protection and enforcement of IPRs as well as on the prevention of their abuse and support regarding the establishment or reinforcement of domestic offices and agencies relevant to the matters.

In the submissions to the Working Group on Trade and Transfer of Technology, developed countries stress on enforcement of IPRs and creation of an enabling environment in developing countries to facilitate technology transfer. Developing countries argue that the provisions for technology transfer in various agreements contain only "best-endeavor" commitments and not mandatory rules. They contend that 'the ongoing process of globalization is rather skewed. While barriers to investment are coming down rapidly and consequently capital is becoming highly mobile, the majority of other factors of production like labour and technology is becoming increasingly restricted'. They want the working Group "to examine the need for desirability of internationally agreed disciplines on transfer of technology with a view to promote trade and development and come up with appropriate recommendations". (WT/WGTTT/W/6. Communication from Cuba, India, Indonesia, Kenya, Pakistan, Tanzania and Zimbabwe, 7 May 2003)

Tariff Reductions in Environmental Goods

The DMD mandate Para 31(iii) provides for negotiations on tariff reductions (or as appropriate elimination) in environmental goods and services. The expectation is that this negotiation will result both in trade liberalization and improvement in environmental quality. Developed country members provided OECD and Asia Pacific Economic Cooperation (APEC) lists of environmental goods and services for tariff reduction. Developing countries contend that the lists are too long, consist of multiple end-use products, and if accepted will result in balance of payments difficulties. To break the deadlock India submitted the Environmental Project Approach (EPA). Under EPA, a project which meets certain predetermined criteria considered by the Designated National Authority will be eligible for a temporary tariff concessions granted for goods and services deemed necessary for achieving nationally identified environmental goals. The advantages of EPA are that (a) choice of the projects is based on national priorities, (b) it avoids the multiple end-use problems, and (c) the magnitude of loss in customs revenue is under government control. (See *WTO*, 2005).

Many developed countries have not endorsed the EPA. Now, they have come with a pruned list of 153 environmental goods for tariff reduction (See *WTO* (*JOB*, (07) 54). Many developing countries prefer trade liberalization of "single-use" environmental goods. India finds only 5 single use goods in the list. During 2007-08, India's exports of these goods amounted to Rs. 24,310 crore while its imports amounted to Rs. 49,859 crore. Also fast track liberalization will have adverse impact on the Indian environmental goods industry. The World Bank (2007) has suggested fast track trade liberalization of 43 climate-friendly products to achieve the goals of the UNFCCC. In this list also only 4 are single use goods and in many products India's imports exceeded her imports in 2007-08. If the tariff reductions are linked to access to ESTs on favourable terms, then a win-win situation is possible.

Technology Transfer Provisions in MEAs

Many MEAs contain provisions to encourage transfer of technologies which are necessary to comply with the obligations under the MEAs. We consider 4 MEAs.

The Montreal Protocol on Substances that Deplete the Ozone Layer (MP)

Article 10A of the Protocol requires 'the best available, environmentally safe substitutes and related technologies are expeditiously transferred' to developing countries, and that the transfers 'occur under fair and most favourable conditions'. The projects funded by the Multilateral Fund could relate to production, equipment manufacture, recycling and technical assistance and training in aerosol, foam, halons, refrigeration, airconditioning and the solvent sectors. This Fund aims to meet the incremental costs on projects. Scientific evidence on the ozone problem, availability of substitutes for ozone depleting substances (ODS) technologies, and financial support based on incremental cost to a large number of developing countries are factors responsible for the partial success of MP. However, the available multilateral fund is inadequate and as a result no financial support was available to SMEs switching to non-ODS technologies and to local technology development projects.

Kyoto Protocol

Article 10 of the Protocol deals with the transfer of, or access to ESTs, know-how, practices and processes pertinent to climate change, in particular to developing countries for the effective transfer of ESTs that are publicly owned or in the public domain and creation of on enabling environment for the private sector to promote and enhance the transfer of, and access to ESTs. Article 11.2 provides for new and additional financial resources to meet the agreed full costs incurred by developing country parties for the transfer of technology. Article 12.2 deals with the Clean Development Mechanism (CDM). The purpose of CDM shall be to assist parties not included in Annex 1 (developed countries) in achieving sustainable development and in contributing to the ultimate objective of the Convention on climate change, and to assist parties included in Annex 1 in achieving compliance with their quantified emission limitations and reduction commitments under Article 3. CDM has a strong orientation towards leveraging FDI for ensuring transfer of climate mitigating technologies. It has encouraged many bilateral technology transfer agreements between developed countries and developing countries in areas such as thermal power generation, wind energy and other renewable sources of energy.

Basel Convention on the Control of Transboundary Movements of Hazardous Wastes and Disposal (BC)

Article 10(3) requires parties to assist developing countries in the implementation of measures for (a) minimizing generation of hazardous wastes, (b) ensuring availability of adequate disposal facilities for environmentally sound management of these wastes, (c) ensuring prevention of pollution by persons involved in managing hazardous wastes, and (d) ensuring that the transboudary movement of hazardous wastes are reduced to the minimum consistent with environmentally sound and efficient management of such wastes and in a manner which protects human health and environment. Article 14(4) calls for the establishment of an appropriate funding mechanism of a voluntary nature. The BC provides for information exchange.

There are no provisions on technology transfer under most favourable terms. It does not provide financial assistance to developing countries. The BC favours ban on movement of hazardous wastes from OECD countries to non-OECD countries. Many developing countries would prefer ESTs for recycling used lead, zinc and steel so that they can recover valuable materials for industrial use and provide 'safe' jobs for the smelters.

Convention on Biodiversity (CBD)

Article 15.6 says that every contracting party to the CBD shall make efforts to develop and carryout scientific research based on genetic resources provided by other contracting parties with the full participation and to the extent possible within the countries supplying the genetic material. This provision would help enhancing the scientific capacity of the provider country and also avoid biopiracy. Article 19 provides for measures that could ensure effective participation in biological research activities by those contracting parties, especially developing countries. It says that access to technologies should be on fair and most favourable terms, including concessional and preferential terms where mutually agreed. Article 15.6 and Article 19 provide enabling clauses for development of biotechnologies in developing countries. The provisions relating to technological transfer are not mandatory. Conflicts between CBD and TRIPS could arise because (i) CBD's aim is to achieve sustainable development while TRIPS aim is strengthening IPRs which are private rights; (ii) Industrial R&D is protected by IPRs but biological resources and traditional knowledge in developing countries are under common property or public property regime, and (iii) there is no provision for inclusion of country of origin and prior informed consent of provider of biological resources or traditional knowledge in patent applications.

Among MEAs, only MP and KP have provisions for transfer of ESTs on favourable terms and financial assistance. Both China and India availed of these provisions.

In India, the Ministry of Environment and Forest's International Cooperation and Sustainable Division is the nodal point with the Ministry to coordinate all international cooperation and sustainable development issues. During the period 1991 till June 2006, India received US$ 184 million from the Multilateral

Fund supplemented by a co-funding of US$ 997 million for ozone-phase out projects. Funds were not available to support switch-over to non-ODS technologies by SMEs particularly in the foam sector. India's efforts to acquire the HFC 1349 technology for the refrigerator sector were not successful as the owners of the technology did not want to endanger their production base by rival production capabilities in developing countries. On the whole, compliance with MP obligations by India is satisfactory.

As for climate change, India has no emission reduction commitments under the Kyoto Protocol. However, India is aware of the adverse effects of global warming and as the CDM provides an opportunity to switch over to coal-based energy efficient technologies, and investments in renewable energy and other CO_2 reduction technologies, they have entered into the CDM market. As of June 2008, the CDM Authority of India has approved 969 projects including 533 in renewable energy, 303 in energy efficiency and 6 in forestry. 340 of the projects registered to the CDM Executive Board. India accounts for about 32 per cent of the world total. India's projects would generate 493 million certified emission reduction (CER) credits by the year 2012, if all the host-countries approved projects in India go on stream. [*Government of India* (*Prime Minister's Council on Climate Change*), 2008]

The Global Environment Facility provides funds for incremental costs in focal areas—biodiversity, climate change, land degradation, ozone depletion, and persistent organic pollutants. These projects require mandatory co-funding. From 1991 to 2008, these projects have leveraged co-financing of US$ 1,798 million till end of March 2008.

Our review of technology transfer provisions in WTO Agreements and selected MEAs reveal that generally the provisions are non-mandatory and hence non-binding. Even where funds are available, they are inadequate and can be used only for specific purposes. Official Development Assistance is declining, and the funds under Global Environmental Facility (GEF) and other sources are inadequate to meet the needs of developing countries; there is a need for finding new and additional resources. Further, the issue of asymmetry in property rights—IPR protection for industrial innovations and weak property rights for biological resources and traditional knowledge—must be addressed.

IV. INDIGENOUS EST DEVELOPMENT, EST ADOPTION AND CAPACITY BUILDING

(a) Institutional Arrangements for EST Adoption

In India, the Department of Science and Technology with a network of research institutions under the Council of Scientific and Industrial Research, and Indian Institute of Technology at 4 cities are the principal agencies for research in industrial technologies. The International Technology Programme of the Department of Scientific and Industrial Research aims at (a) documentation of technology export performance and capabilities, (b) showcasing and documentation of technology export capabilities, and (c) facilitation of technology transfer and trade at the firm level.

NEP 2006 notes three barriers to the adoption of clean technologies. They are: (a) many of them are proprietary and protected by strong patent regimes held abroad; (b) lack of capacity in development financial institutions for appraisal of proposals for switching existing production facilities to clean technologies; and (c) lack of coordination in R&D efforts aimed at developing a shelf of commercially viable clean technologies. The Action Plan aims at removing the barriers. It also encourages industry associations to adopt ISO-14000 giving purchase preference in government procurement, formulation of "good practice guidelines" for ecolabels, and promotion of "good practice norms" to conserve natural resources and mitigate adverse environmental impacts. UNIDO's Country Service Framework: India aimed at contributing to achieving sustainable development in India by fostering skills, capabilities, and technologies for SMEs to keep space with the fast growing Indian economy and the demands of globalization. The five year programme (2002-07) envisaged strengthening the competitiveness of SMEs through technology-led intervention; promoting FDI, JV and equity participation; promoting cleaner and environment-friendly technologies and policies; and alleviating poverty and industrial development programmes in less developed areas.

In a few instances, India intervened both on the supply and demand sides to foster ESTs. To support commercialization of wind power and solar PV technologies in the 1990s, on the supply side it strengthened the capabilities of the Indian Renewable

Energy Department to promote and finance private sector investments in wind farms, raised funds from the World Bank, International Development Association and the Danish government, and gave special tax incentives for small independent power producers. On the demand side, it campaigned to raise consumer awareness for the clean energy and provided credit facilities and subsidies to rural consumers to purchase solar systems. The announcement of Semi-conductor Policy by the Government of India in 2007 with capital subsidy encouraged two foreign firms, Moser Baer and Signet Solar, establishing a thin film solar fab and thin film silicon solar photovoltaic modules in Special Economic Zones in India.

India has a number of bilateral cooperation programmes on technology and development with 12 countries including USA, Canada, Germany, UK, and China.

(b) Capacity Building

India is known for its vast pool of indigenous and traditional knowledge. This knowledge is being used by farmers in agriculture, tribals and locals in forestry, indigenous doctors in medicines and rural people in cottage and village industries. This knowledge is time tested and is in harmony with the ecosystem. Some of this knowledge is available not in scientific form in Indian languages and some knowledge are communicated orally from one generation to another generation among members of ethnic/ social groups. The Government of India has provided basic taxonomic support in terms of preparing inventories of plant species, their taxonomic characterization, occurrence, etc. in different ecosystems. The government also helped in creating the Traditional Knowledge Digital Library for preservation of traditional knowledge and prevention of misappropriation of traditional knowledge. This knowledge system is available to patent examiners in five languages—English, French, German, Spanish and Japanese—for establishing the prior art. The National Biodiversity Authority of India has initiated the process of preparing biodiversity registers at village levels for implementing the "access and benefit sharing regime" for biological resources and traditional knowledge. India has created Honey Bee Database of indigenous innovations and traditional knowledge at Indian Institute of Management at Ahmedabad.

India has a vast pool of scientific manpower and enabling technologies in areas such as information technology, remote sensing (RS), geographical information system (GIS) and biotechnologies necessary for sustainable use and management of natural resources. RS and GIS tools are being used in developing natural resource inventories, water resources assessment, and mapping. RS techniques are being used in monitoring land use, forest cover, pollution and ozone layer. Satellite technology serves as an important tool in developing an early warning system for disaster management as well as undertaking mitigation efforts (See *Rao*, 1996). The advantages of satellite technology are that they have synoptic coverage, multi-spectral capability, multi-temporal capability and the data are in digital form. There are significant cost and time savings as well as the benefit of getting early information. For recent Indian applications in meteorology and remote sensing (see *Raghavan and Sankar*, 2007 and *Rao and Sankar*, 2007 respectively).

The National Action Plan on Climate Change (NAPCC) notes that climate change may alter the distribution and quality of India's natural resources and adversely affect the livelihood of its people. India has no obligation for reduction of greenhouse gases but the NAPCC identifies measures that promote our development objectives while also yielding co-benefits for addressing climate change effectively. The NAPCC hinges on the development and use of new technologies. The eight national missions are on solar energy, sustainable habitat, enhanced energy efficiency, water, Himalayan ecosystem, green India, sustainable agriculture, and strategic knowledge for climate change (*Government of India, Prime Minister's Council on Climate Change*, 2008)]

Biotechnology has the potential for cleaner and more efficient alternatives to many existing processes and products and treatment of solid wastes and liquid wastes. India's National Biotechnology Development Strategy, 2007 recognizes biotechnology as a sunshine sector and lays a strong foundation for discovery and innovation, effectively utilizing novel technology platforms with potential to contribute to long-term benefits in agriculture, animal productivity, human health, environmental security and sustainable industrial growth. (*Goyernment of India, Department of Biotechnology*, 2007). However, some biotechnological processes and products may generate economic and environmental risks e.g. genetically modified products and processes. The government plans to create a National Biodiversity Regulatory Authority, an independent, autonomous and professionally led body as a single window mechanism for biosafety clearance of genetically modified products and processes.

India is a mega biodiversity country. It has biological resources and traditional and indigenous knowledge. As India's efforts in amending the TRIPS Agreement for inclusion of country of origin and mutually agreed terms for benefit sharing in applications for patents based on biological resources and traditional knowledge meet resistance, it must explore the feasibility of developing joint ventures or/and technology development programmes with foreign firms who possess modern biotechnologies for adoption/ adaptation in India to prevent biopiracy.

V. CONCLUDING REMARKS

The argument that a developing country must concentrate on growth first and after it has reached a stage of development, it must pay attention to improvement in environmental quality is based on the assumption that environmental quality is a luxury good. This assumption is no longer true as empirical evidence shows the greater dependence of the poor on environmental resources than the rich for their livelihood (See for example, *Dasgupta*, 1993/2000). Further, the poor cannot afford to spend money on the averting expenses, when pollution load exceeds carrying capacity of a region or rate of harvesting of a natural resource exceeds its renewal rate, irreversible damage may occur. A precautionary approach can prevent ecological insecurity. As India aims at an annual GDP growth rate of 10 percent now, it is time that equal weight is given to economic growth and environmental protection so that its growth is economically, socially and environmentally sustainable.

ESTs are desirable because they pollute less, recycle wastes and cause less harm to the environment. As adoption of ESTs also save materials and energy, and often result in "better" and "safer" products they are preferred. A major driver for EST domestically is compliance with domestic environmental standards. This will occur only when prices of environmental resources equal their social marginal costs and the cost of non-compliance with the standards is higher than the cost of compliance. In India environmental resources are priced below their social costs. India has not yet introduced economic instruments for pollution control and prices of many natural resources are below their social costs. Our accounting/costing practices are such that they ignore or underestimate the environmental costs to society. For example, if all external costs of using fossil fuels are taken into account in pricing of conventional energy sources, energy from renewable sources will be relatively more attractive. Similarly, a holistic approach to solid waste treatment problem may yield higher net social net benefit than viewing it simply a solid waste disposal problem. It is a good augury that the terms of reference of the Thirteenth Finance Commission contain the following: 'the need to manage ecology, environment and climate change consistent with sustainable development'.

Environmental policy also must change with liberalization and globalization. Environmental requirements in export markets necessitate demand for ESTs. India must play an active role in the WTO and MEA negotiations to articulate its concerns and trade-offs at the time of standard setting, and negotiations on positive measures like transfer of ESTs and technical assistance and S&DT. It must also play a proactive role in anticipating the changes in the global trading and environmental regimes and adjusting to the changes quickly. The role of government in the switch-over to ESTs by SMEs must be that of a facilitator rather than that of regulator.

There is a case for indigenous development of ESTs. The need arises because some foreign ESTs come under IPR and at monopoly prices. Some ESTs developed abroad may not meet the local requirements. In order to overcome the scale and marketing problems, India must play a catalytic role in fostering South-South cooperation in generation, adaptation and diffusion of ESTs. India must spend more on environmental R&D and environmental infrastructures. India has the necessary scientific and technological expertise in developing ESTs to promote the export of environmental goods and services and to comply with domestic and global environmental requirements. Shift from criminal liability to civil liability with economic instruments, elimination of perverse incentives and pricing of natural resources based on their social costs, fiscal incentives for development of ESTs, and incorporation of economic, social and environmental objectives in policy-making at all levels will trigger demand for ESTs and achieve sustainable development.

REFERENCES

Dasgupta, P. (1993/2000): Poverty and the Environmental Resource Base, *An Enquiry into Weil-Being and Destitution*, Oxford University, UK and in U. Sankar (ed.) (2000).

Government of India (Department of Biotechnology) (2007): *National Biotechnology Development Strategy*, New Delhi.

Government of India (Department of Science and Technology) (2003): *Science and Technology Policy*, 2003, http://dst.gov.in/stsyindia/stp/2003.htm.

Government of India (Ministry of Environment and Forests) (2006): *National Environment Policy*, 2006, New Delhi.

Government of India (Prime Minister's Council on Climate Change) (2008): *National Action Plan on Climate Change*, New Delhi.

Less, C. and S. McMillan (2005): Achieving the Successful Transfer of Environmentally Sound Technologies: Trade-related Aspects, OECD Trade and Environment Working Papers, 2005/2, OECD, Paris.

Maskus, K.E. (2004): Encouraging International Technology Transfer, International Centre for Trade and Sustainable Development and UNCTAD, Issue Paper No. 7. http://www.iprsonline.org/unctad ictsd/docs/cs pdf.

Porter, M.E. and C. Van der Linde (1995): Towards a New Conception of the Environment Competitiveness Relationship, *Journal of Economic Perspectives*, Vol. 9, No. 4, pp. 97-11.

Raghavan, S. and U. Sankar (2007): Meteorology, U. Sankar (ed.), *The Economics of India's Space Programme*, Oxford University Press, New Delhi

Rao, D.P. and U. Sankar (2007): Indian Remote Sensing Programme, U. Sankar, *The Economics of India's Space Programme*, Oxford University Press, New Delhi.

Rao, U.R. (1996): *Space Technology for Sustainable Development*, Tata-McGraw Hill, New Delhi.

Sahasranamam, A. (2006): Global Environmental Requirements, U. Sankar (ed.), *Trade and Environment: A Study of India's Leather Exports*, Oxford University Press, Delhi.

Sankar, U. (ed.) (2000): *Environmental Economics*, Oxford University Press, Delhi.

Sankar, U. (2006): *Trade and Environment: A Study of India's Leather Exports*, Oxford University Press, Delhi.

Solow, R. (1991/2000): 'Sustainability: An Economists' Perspective', Eighteenth J. Seward Johnson Lecture to the Marine Policy Centre, at

Woods Hole, Mass. U. Sankar (ed.) (2000): *Environmental Economics*, Oxford University Press, New Delhi.

United Nations Conference on Environment and Development (UNCED), (1992): *Agenda 21*, Rio de Janeiro.

United Nations Commission on Trade and Development (UNCTAD) (2003): *Transfer of Technology for Successful Integration into the Global Economy*, New York.

United Nations Environment Programme (2003): *Environmentally Sound Technologies for Sustainable Development*, 21 September. http://www.unep.or.jp/itec/techTran/focus/SustDev_EST_background.pdf.

United Nations Industrial Development Organization (UNIDO)(2002): *Country Service Framework: India*, http://www.unido.Org/doc/1932/

World Commission on Environment and Development (WCED) (1987): *Our Common Future*, Oxford University Press, Oxford.

World Bank (2007): *Warming up to Trade? Harnessing International Trade to Support Climate Change Objectives*, Washington D.C.

World Trade Organization (2001): *Doha Ministerial Declaration*, WT/MIN/01/ Dec. 17.

World Trade Organization (Working Group on Trade and Environment) (2002): *A Taxonomy on Country Experiences on International Technology Transfers*, Note by the Secretariat, WT/WGTTT/W4.

—— (2002): *Provisions Relating to Transfer of Technology in WTO Agreements*, Communication from Cuba, Egypt, Honduras, India, Indonesia, Kenya and Zimbabwe, WT/WG777/3.

World Trade Organization, (Committee on Trade and Environment Special Session) (2005). *An Alternative Approach for Negotiations under Paragraph 31(iii), Submission by India*, TN/TE/W/51 and Structural Dimensions of the Environment Project Approach, Submission by India, TN/TE/W/ 54.

Websites

http://www.basel.int
http://www, cbd.int/
http://ozone.unep.org
http://unfccc.int/kyotoprotocol
http://www/wto.ore.in

Ecosystem Accounts for Resource Allocation: A Framework for Sustainable Development

GOPAL K. KADEKODI

If human welfare include sustainability of resources as natural welfare we have solved the problem of defining sustainable development. One step in this direction is to define Green GDP. This in turn asks for green investment and savings.

This paper addresses to this issue of estimating green incomes, investments and savings from data on state level income, investment and savings, and values of natural resource endowments and changes in them. Treating eco-systems as the base for all natural resource flows, values of changes in the ecosystems are estimated at the state levels in India. They are compared with investments on ecosystem sustainability. The inference on balances then follows.

1. INTRODUCTION

There are several ways to understand sustainable development. To any simplistic mind, it is a process of sustaining a growth process against possible stationary state (Mill, 1848), or getting around several odds (*Solow*, 1974; *Sen*, 1989; *Atkinson et. al.*,

1997; *Dasgupta*, 2007 and 2001), dealing with irreversibilities (*Krutilla and Fisher*, 1985), building resilience powers (*Perrings*, 2006; *Kadekodi*, 2005), adding dignity, empowerment, freedom and quality of life (*Atkinson et al.*, 1997; *Dasgupta*, 2007 and 2001; *Krutilla and Rafael*, 2002; *Sen*, 1985, 1989b).

Today, from being driven by a narrowly defined 'welfare' framework of thought as *equating well-being with consumption*, synonymous to sustainable development', economists are talking about it in an inter-generational framework. For instance, the World Commission on Environment and Development (WCED) in 1987 defined sustainable development as: *'Sustainable development is development that meets the needs of the present without comprising the ability of future generations to meet their own needs.'* However, the report also adds a rider subsequently to say that *'In essence, sustainable development is a process of change, in which exploitation of resources, the direction of investments, the orientation of technological development, and institutional change are all in harmony and enhance both current and future potential to meet human needs and aspirations'*. In other words, it is necessary to link resource use and investments on resource developments as an intergenerational balancing act.

During the last fifty years, within the framework of economic development two major transitions took place in economic thoughts on welfare. First, starting with the writings of Sen (1984, 1989a, 1989b,) we have moved away from income growth narrowly viewed as *GDP Growth* to *'Well-being'* (*Sen*, 1970) as an indicator of development.[1] Second, the concept of income itself has been redefined as *' Green Income'* (*Maler*, 1991). The first diversion led to define welfare to include empowerment, functioning, capabilities, dignity and gender balance. Such a major conceptual shift has led to measure well-being in terms of, not only GDP but also by Human and Gender Development Indices (HDI and GDI, respectively). The other stream of thought on redefining GDP as Green was the result of the concern on depletion and degradation of natural resources like air, water, soil and land, and to account for all the good and bad externalities emerging from the use of natural and man-made resources (*Arrow et al.*, 2004; *Dasgupta*, 2001; *Hartwick*, 1990). A whole new concept of 'genuine rate of investment leading to welfare' was introduced by Hamilton and Clemens (1999); genuine investment to include net capital formation (as a flow of investments on man-made capital) plus, investments on human capital formation (viewed as addition to capability and net flows or changes in different forms of natural capital stocks, broadly observed as: (a) appreciation/degradation, (b) depletion of natural and ecological resources. Measures on these can be (a) the changes in carbon stock in plants and in soils, loss/gains in values of eco-system services and values of soil, forests, water, etc., and biodiversity values of forests, and (b) depletion of forests, agricultural and mining lands and resources. Associated with this genuine investment is Green GDP.

The basis for generating income, welfare or well-being is the wealths of the society. By now, several components of wealth are being talked about. The major ones are accumulation of man-made capital, human capital and natural capital. Maintaining a rate of investment on all these three types of wealth is a necessary condition for sustaining growth. That is the concept of *'Genuine investment'*, consistent with *'Green Growth'*.

This paper takes a mid-way between linking genuine investment to green growth. For this, contributions of natural resources for such a green growth and well-being are linked with budgetary investments on resource developments. Recall that contribution of man-made capital is normally accounted as capital formation (and its depreciation) or investments to derive strategies of economic development (*Rosenstein Rodan*, 1964). Likewise, human capital is analysed as inputs and accounted as value-added in GDP (*Hicks*, 1971). On the same lines, it is logically necessary to account for contributions, depletions and degradations from natural capital within the framework of income accounting which includes investments on natural resources management (*Howarth*, 1999; *Hartwick*, 1992). Only then, it can provide clues on a complete concept of Green GDP, as a measure of well-being (*Hartwick*, 1990; *Maler*, 1991).

The organization of the paper is as follows: Section II provides a brief on accounting for natural resources within the framework of income accountings. The next section makes an attempt to compare contributions from environmental and ecological resources with public investments on them for the Indian states for a recent year with comments. The final section draws some policies and investment strategies for the development of natural capital with some conclusions.

II. ACCOUNTING FOR NATURAL REOURCES: FROM GROWTH TO INCLUSIVE GROWTH

Sustainable development requires a complete understanding of the role of three major forms of wealths mentioned above, in both its static and inter-generational framework. It makes demands on their measures, flows and accounting of their contributions towards well-being. Therefore, as much as *'consumption'* the traditional indicator of welfare (*Ramsey*, 1928), *'ecosystem services'* from environmental and natural resources (*Kumar et al.*, 2006; *MEA*, 2005), and 'capability, dignity and empowerment in human capital' have emerged as other indicators of well-being (*MEA*, 2005; *Sen*, 1993/1999). Therefore, there is a need to integrate their contributions in a form similar to accounting for contributions of man-made capital in National Income Accounts (*Atkinson et al*, 1997; *Maler*, 1991; *Dasgupta*, 2001, 2007).

Contributions of natural resource ecosystems are many. They emerge from forests, agricultural lands, water resources, mineral resources and biodiversity. The notable ones are direct forest benefits or mineral benefits. They include timber, small timbers, fuelwood, fodder, medicinal materials, flowers, bark, leaf biomass, fossil oils or coal, etc. These are having enormous 'use values', as revealed through labour time inputs (and in some situations even capital inputs) in collection, transportation, processing, storing, marketing and pricing. Apart from these, 'non-use' and indirect benefits are derivable from forest resources or terrestrial eco-systems. They reflect complementary benefits and association with the entire eco-system. Some examples are soil retention and remediation, support for micro-organisms, carbon sequestration, waste assimilation, stream hydrology, climate moderation, and above all are the support for biodiversity having 'existence values'. While some of the 'use values' can be easily estimated, a large number of non-marketed and 'non-use values' are difficult to estimate (*Kadekodi*, 2004)

As far as agricultural lands are concerned, their contributions in terms of value added from agriculture are normally accounted in national income or GDP accounts. But if there are any changes in the soils due to use of lands either because of augmenting soil fertility through the use of chemical fertilizers and pesticides, or because of over-exploitation of lands, there would be changes in the soil wealth characteristics (*Parikh and Ghosh*, 1995). They are not accounted normally in GDP accounts. Accounting for all such natural resources changes is in order.

Likewise, the use of surface and ground waters for the welfare of the society are accounted in their contributions as inputs in production processes, be it in agriculture or in industry. However, depletion and degradation of all waters in terms of added pollution, and unsustainable use would amount to imbalanced inter-generational equity (*Bandyopadhyay*, 2009, *Murty et al.*, 1999). Hence their accounting for all such changes is necessary.

III. ECO-SYSTEM CONTRIBUTIONS AND BUDGETORY ALLOCATIONS

An attempt is made here to put across the values of eco-system services from land, forest and water resources as compared to the budgetary investment and expenditures on forest and environmental management at the state levels. Three steps are followed here.

First, recently a series of studies, commissioned by Green India States Trust (*www.Gistindia.org*), carried out by Haripriya Gundimeda, Pushpam Kumar among many others, have provided some detailed estimates of values for several of these ecosystem services and their annual changes from Indian forests, agricultural lands, and water resources. They cover the estimates of eco-system stocks and changes for the year 2002-03.

The eco-system value changes are measured in terms of (a) **Depletions:** Agricultural and pastures lands; changes in availability of timber, fuelwood, NTFPs, biodiversity; (b) **Degradations:** Soil retention, ground water recharge, flood control, carbon sequestration. Values of their annual stocks, and changes have been estimated using available/estimated data on respective accounting prices.[2] Using a year to year accounting framework the net annual changes in them are deduced as indicators of either depletion or degradation. Annual contributions, depletions and values of degradations are thus estimated for most of the Indian states for the year 2002-03, as shown in Table 1.[3] Here, values of depletion and degradation in agricultural and pasture lands (Column 3) and those of fresh water (Column 6) are treated as indirectly connected to forestry and wildlife management. By and large all the categories of eco-system contributions refer to changes in eco-system values from Indian forest and biodiversity resources.[4]

Second, the annual expenditures by the Ministry of Environment and Forests (both directly and through the states) on forest and wildlife in the year 2002-03 are taken as indicators of state level investments on eco-system regeneration, maintenance and growth. The annual expenditures include allocation of resources on forestry and wild life, allocated as Revenue and Capital Expenditures. The major expenditures are on Development of national parks and sanctuaries, Biosphere reserves, Conservation of mangroves, coral reefs and wetlands, Project Tiger and Elephants, National Afforestation Scheme and Integrated Forest Protection Schemes. These are shown in Table 2.

Third, a comparative analysis of these two series at the state levels can then provide some clues on state level links or mismatches between Eco-system contributions from forests and wildlife as compared to the levels of investments on them.

As can be seen from Table 1, a large number of states in India are losing their biodiversity, agricultural and pasture land capacities, resulting at the all India level, a net loss of biodiversity valued to a tune of Rs. 14746 Crores, and depletion of livelihood resources (NTFPs, timber, fuelwood etc.) to a tune of Rs. 7254 Crores. Even soil losses of agricultural and pasture lands leading to productivity losses have been valued as Rs. 949 Crores. Clearly, there are strong indications of unsustainable use of this important eco-system wealth and natural capital.

At the individual state levels, some states are showing extreme losses, while few others have registered some positive contributions. As far as Soil and Erosion Controls are concerned (Column 2), most of the states have been contributing positively (barring for states like Manipur, Meghalaya, Nagaland, Orissa and Tripura), with an all India gains in the eco-system values by Rs. 19040 Crores. In the cases of Agricultural and Pasture Lands (Column 3), all the states are losing their eco-system values. Even the Biodiversity Changes (Column 4) are negative for almost all

TABLE 1

Accounting for Contributions from Environmental Services and their Changes: 2002-03

(*Rs. Crores*)

Estimates for 2002-03	*Value of ecological services—water augmentation, soil erosion control, flood prevention*	*Value of depletion and degradation of agricultural and pasture land*	*Gain/Loss in biodiversity values of forests*	*Value of depletion of timber, fuelwood, NTFP and Carbon*	*Values of Freshwater gain/losses*	*Total eco-system values*
1	2	3	4	5	6	7
Andhra Pradesh	1007.106	-1772.062	-739.21	-809.407	-1351.18	-2313.57
Arunachal Pradesh	302.3165	-52.757	5098.19	613.484	0	5961.23
Assam	2162.405	-498.048	-17610.43	-74.718	-429.42	-16020.79
Bihar	328.6895	-1205.412	14490.88	-3780.955	-4275.48	- 9833.20
Jharkhand	0.00	0.00	0.00	0.00	0	NA
Goa	342.4355	-24.371	-26.52	32.753	-186.361	324.30
Gujarat	1704.559	-1735.993	-1205.83	-434.323	-868.84	-1671.59
Haryana	402.424	-593.415	-88.00	-218.786	-487.23	-497.78
Himachal Pradesh	1047.024	-113.538	-2209.05	-280.931	-1380.78	-1556.50
Jammu and Kashmir	874.896	-139.085	-325.21	100.757	0	511.36
Karnataka	2584.059	-1867.981	-7540.63	69.8	-1708.47	-6754.75
Kerala	1722.035	-383.954	-8544.11	-194.365	0	-7400.39
Madhya Pradesh	1062.655	-3468.128	5834.28	375.657	-1602.63	3804.46

Chhattisgarh	0.00	0.00	0.00	0.00	NA	NA
Maharashtra	1773.575	-3206.084	-2262.60	-373.203	-3638.08	-4068.31
Manipur	-599.348	-63.077	2828.69	-56.5	NA	2109.77
Meghalaya	-592.442	-53.988	3837.66	-24.532	NA	3166.70
Mizoram	1048.426	-22.949	-2406.16	63.415	NA	-1317.27
Nagaland	-226.028	-56.032	2002.14	599.494	NA	2319.57
Orissa	-135.926	-1125.077	3655.80	57.051	-1483.97	2451.85
Punjab	530.649	-691.453	-178.84	-570.036	-322.3	-909.68
Rajasthan	1252.231	-3103.237	-4207.39	-495.645	-1.9	-6554.04
Sikkim	0.00	0.00	0.00	0.00	-392.4	NA
Tamilnadu	346.6625	-1027.882	-425.53	-192.126	-766.65	-1298.88
Tripura	-1135.3	-80.322	8046.32	-192.126	NA	6638.57
Uttar Pradesh	2800.237	-2897.025	-12698.58	-60.674	-27536.09	-12856.04
Uttaranchal	0.00	0.00	0.00	0.00	NA	NA
West Bengal	214.3655	-949.035	3571.59	-1201.519	-11081	1635.40
Andaman and Nicobar Islands	0.00	0.00	-124.25	-7254.905	NA	NA
Chandigarh	0.00	0.00	0.00	361.688	NA	NA
Delhi	0.00	0.00	0.00	0	NA	NA
Pondicherry	0.00	0.00	0.00	0	NA	NA
India	19040.28	-949.035	-14746.00	-7254.905	-58658.61	-3909.66

NA = not available; State figures may not add to All India totals, as some Union Territories are not shown.

Source: www.gistindia.org.

TABLE 2

Resource Allocations on Forests and Wildlife: 2002-03

(*Rs. Lakhs*)

States	*Forest-wildlife-Revenue Exp.*	*Forest-wildlife Cap. Exp*	*Total Exp. on forest and wildlife*
Andhra Pradesh	20052	484	20536
Arunachal Pradesh	842	32	3874
Assam	9583	0	9583
Bihar	4466	0	4466
Jharkhand	28293	0	28293
Goa	900	17	917
Gujarat	12323	8407	20730
Haryana	7251	0	7251
Himachal Pradesh	32820	244	33064
Jammu and Kashmir	15177	1901	17078
Karnataka	24968	357	25325
Kerala	14088	333	14421
Madhya Pradesh	48543	173	48716
Chattisgarh	25302	340	25642
Maharashtra	28919	1166	30085
Manipur	1280	0	1280
Meghalaya	2818	0	2818
Mizoram	2112	619	2731
Nagaland	2555	178	2733
Orissa	9055	3275	12330
Punjab	8334	1746	10080
Rajasthan	13004	153	13157
Sikkim	1994	39	2033
Tamilnadu	8666	8474	17140
Tripura	2598	282	2880
Uttar Pradesh	11812	4076	15888
Uttaranchal	14118	21	14139
West Bengal	13011	1343	14354
Andaman and Nicobar Islands		NA	
Chandigarh	340	243	583
Delhi	921	700	1621
Pondicherry		NA	
India	389855	41495	431350

Source: RBI: Handbook of Statistics on State Govt. Finances

the states, except for Arunachal Pradesh, Bihar, Madhya Pradesh, Manipur, Meghalaya, Nagaland, Orissa, Tripura and West Bengal. Values of Depletion of Timber, Fuelwood, NTFP and Carbon (Column 5) are also invariably negative barring 3-4 states. The column 7 shows that majority of the states in India, on the whole, are losing their eco-system values annually. The total eco-system values are going down for almost all states, except for the north-eastern states like Arunachal Pradesh, Manipur, Meghalaya, Nagaland, Orissa, Tripura and West Bengal.

A logical way to analyse the links between eco-system contributions and budgetary efforts to restore and maintain them is to compare the two series of data on: (a) per sq. km. of *forest area* terms, or (b) per sq. km. of *forest cover* basis. While forest area is defined in legal terms as having at least 10% tree cover in a patch of 0.5 hectare of land, and notified under Indian Forest Act of 1927, forest cover is defined based on satellite imagery data covering at least one hectare of forest and tree areas irrespective of land ownership.

In Table 3, such a comparative data is shown for all the states of India on a sq. km. forest cover basis. Figure 1 depicts the same. As can be seen from the per sq. km. forest cover basis, considerable amount of mis-match (i.e., negative) is observable between the eco-system services as contributions and investment on forest and wildlife. The correlation between these two is of the order of –0.30. This itself suggests of no policy linkage between them. Likewise from Table 4 and the Figure 2, it can be seen that the link between these two series on forest area basis is also extremely poor, negative in most situations. However, the correlation between positive eco-system values and the corresponding allocation for forest and wildlife with forest cover as the basis is of the order of 0.40. This happens only among the north-eastern states of India (except for Madhya Pradesh included). In other words, there seems to be some considerations (though very minimal) on linking investment budget allocations on forestry and wildlife management in these states. One major observation can be made at this stage. A system of resource allocations should frame the basis for all those states where biodiversity, forest, water and wildlife resources are significant contributors to well-being.

TABLE 3

Eco-system Contributions on per Sq Km² of Forest Cover basis as against Budget Expenditures on Forest and Wildlife (Rs. 000, 2002-03)

States	*Eco-system value*	*Budget exp. on States Forest+wildlife*
Andhra Pradesh	-5.208521128	46.23246809
Arunachal Pradesh	8.764071068	5.695467443
Assam	-57.57489758	34.43901387
Bihar	176.9198003	80.35264484
Jharkhand	NA	124.5509773
Goa	15.04162801	42.53246753
Gujarat	-11.18417637	138.6993175
Haryana	-32.81324984	477.9828609
Himachal Pradesh	-10.84438793	230.3629903
Jammu and Kashmir	2.404467015	80.30281657
Karnataka	-18.53206398	69.48064419
Kerala	-47.50846761	92.57880208
Madhya Pradesh	4.977775452	63.74020333
Chhattisgarh	NA	45.7909211
Maharashtra	-8.680917529	64.19502827
Manipur	12.2525408	7.433648876
Meghalaya	18.80573668	16.73496051
Mizoram	-7.147411829	14.81823114
Nagaland	17.04441179	20.08229848
Orissa	5.069362776	25.493115
Punjab	-57.57468354	637.9746835
Rajasthan	-41.41312397	83'.1353469
Sikkim	NA	62.32372777
Tamil Nadu	-5.736322484	75.6966833
Tripura	82.0285679	35.58630916
Uttar Pradesh	-91.0613543	112.5371866
Uttaranchal	NA	57.79276517
West Bengal	13.24962732	116.2926355
Andaman and Nicobar Islands	NA	NA
Chandigarh	NA	3886.666667
Delhi	NA	953L?294 IT8
Pondicherry	NA	NA
India	-0.576362937	63.58971184
Corr. Coeff. with only positive eco-system		-0.30904
Corr. Coeff. with Values		0.3979

www.Indiastat.org; RBI: Handbook of Statistics on State Govt. Finances.

Figure 1: Eco-system Contributions and Budget Allocations

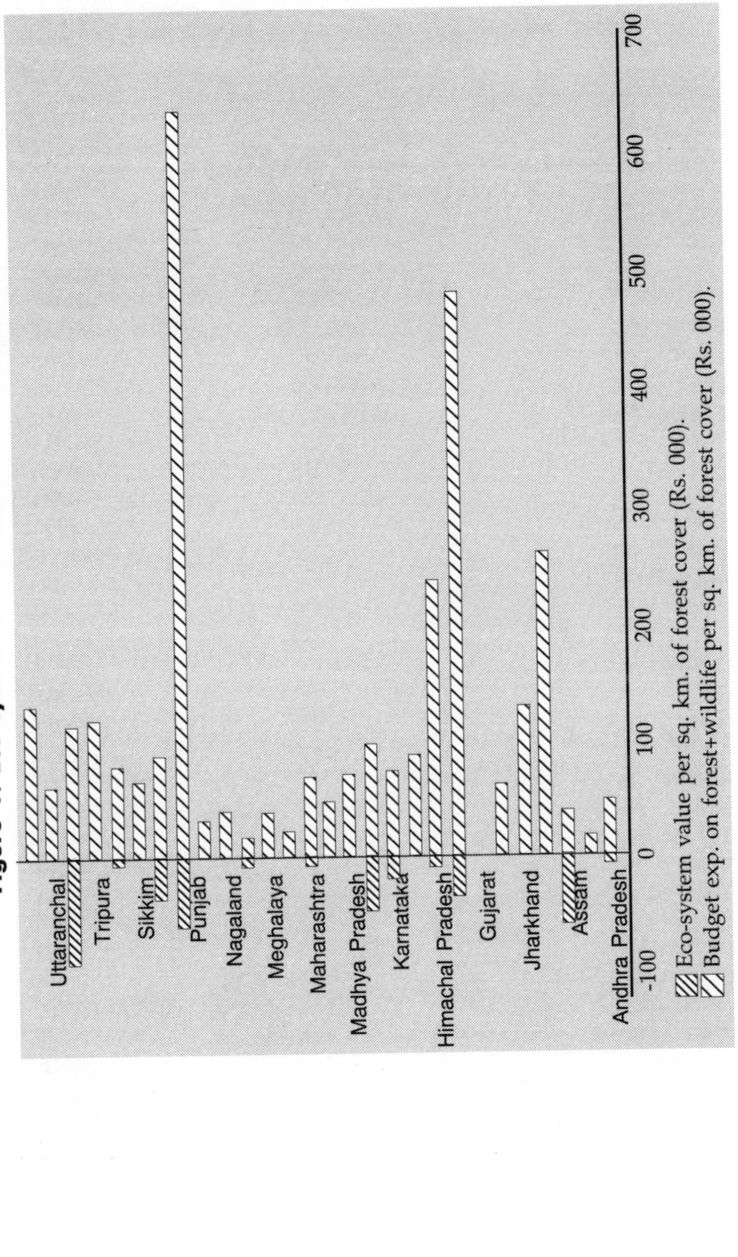

Uttaranchal
Tripura
Sikkim
Punjab
Nagaland
Meghalaya
Maharashtra
Madhya Pradesh
Karnataka
Himachal Pradesh
Gujarat
Jharkhand
Assam
Andhra Pradesh

-100 0 100 200 300 400 500 600 700

Eco-system value per sq. km. of forest cover (Rs. 000).

Budget exp. on forest+wildlife per sq. km. of forest cover (Rs. 000).

TABLE 4

Eco-system Contributions on per Sq Km² of Forest Area basis as against Budget Expenditures on Forest and Wildlife (Rs. 000, 2002-03)

States	*Eco-system value*	*Budget exp. on forest+wildlife*
Andhra Pradesh	-3.625096755	32.17749644
Arunachal Pradesh	11.5662272	7.516492045
Assam	-59.29673181	35.46894663
Bihar	151.9110536	68.99428395
Jharkhand	NA	119.8601991
Goa	26.49489379	74~91830065
Gujarat	-8.745811751	108.4602103
Haryana	-31.94974326	465.4043646
Himachal Pradesh	-4.202994626	892825318
Jammu and Kashmir	2.527721206	84.41917944
Karnataka	-15.6780986	58.78052177
Kerala	-65.67619808	127 9818956
Madhya Pradesh	3.995404375	51.1609834
Chhattisgarh	NA	42.89968547
Maharashtra	-6.568255865	48157198211
Manipur	12.11255598	7.348719715
Meghalaya	33.3477043	29.67565291
Mizoram	-7.879810971	16.33666328
Nagaland	26.88114498	3167226793
Orissa	4.21743498	21.2088895
Punjab	-29.49675746	326.848249
Rajasthan	-20.17372876	40.49803004
Sikkim	NA	34.80568396
Tamil Nadu	-5.677647856	74.92241116
Tripura	105.4913714	45.76513587
Uttar Pradesh	76.40581243	94.42529419
Uttaranchal	NA	40.79106803
West Bengal	1376716474	120.8350871
Andaman and Nicobar Islands	NA	NA
Chandigarh	NA	1714.705882
Delhi	NA	1976.829268
Pondicherry	NA	NA
India	-0.504641557	55.67674317
Corr. Coeff. with only positive eco-system		-0.25866
Corr. Coeff. with values		0.123

RBI: Handbook of Statistics on State Govt. Finances. www.lndiastat.org.

Figure 2: Eco-system Contributions Vs. Budget Allocations

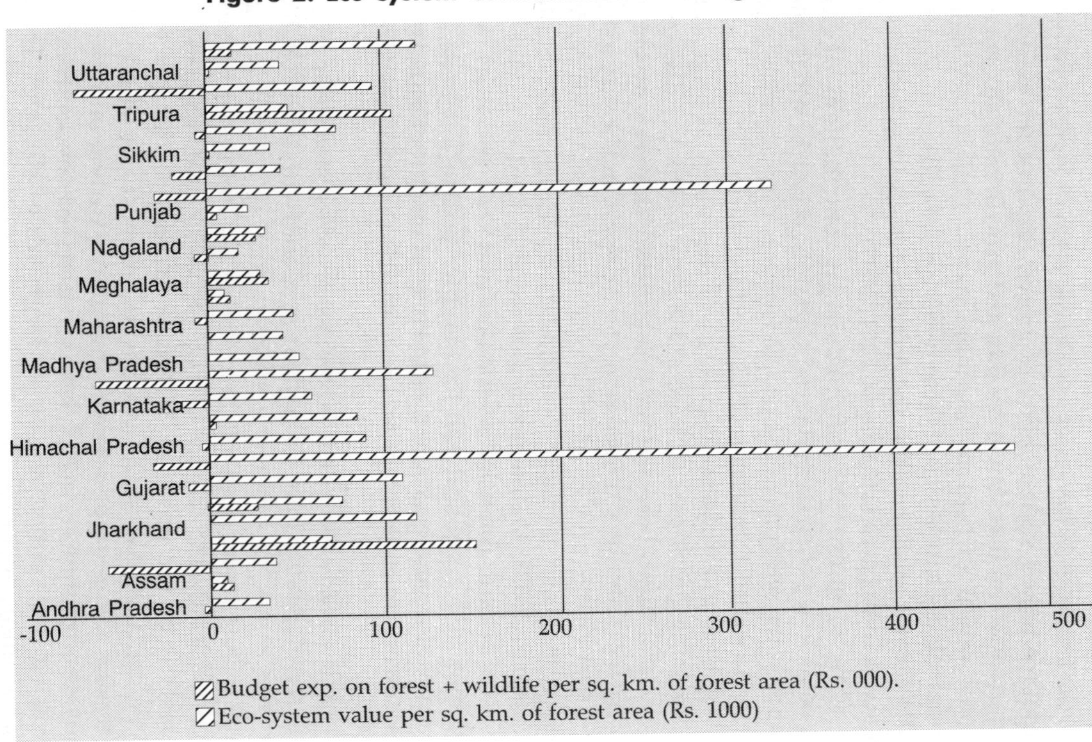

IV. TOWARDS BETTER DESIGN OF STATE LEVEL DEVELOPMENT

As analysed in the previous section, when it comes to natural resource linked sustainability of growth, against the perceived information on investment profiles and growth rates etc., several states reveal critical to warning status. Unless, ecological sustainability conditions of these resources are addressed together with income sustainability, the process of analysing 'well-being' remains only partial (*Dasgupta*, 2001, 2007).

How to internalize information on contributions of Eco-systems into policy formulation? Certainly, all such values enter either in the welfares of the people (some as direct consumption, more as indirect benefits), or as contributing to climate change mitigation and abatement policies of the world at large, and sustainable development.[5] Recent literature and policy dialogues have accordingly been shifting to addressing this issue by setting a case for claims on Compensation for Eco-system Services (CES). The first charge on CES should come from the state and central governments in terms of investments on forests and wildlife (*Kadekodi*, 2007). Maintenance and enhancement of ecosystem services require financial investments and well governed fiscal regimes, and a political will to introduce policies on trade and conservation, and creation of right kinds of institutions and legal framework to implement and govern the programmes (*Stern*, 2006).[6]

India already has a rich experience on eco-system restoration and development. Joint Forest Management (with over 700 JFM projects across the country) has shown the way with an average project investment costs of the order of Rs. 16,469 per hectare. Considering the fact that the average carbon sequestered in Indian forests is of the order of 37 ton of carbon per ha per year (*Gundimeda*, 2006a), such investments are most cost efficient in restoring the degraded forests, mitigating carbon and also to provide ecosystem services. Likewise, watershed development has revealed the potentials on a large scale all over India (*Vaidyanathan*, 2006).

Secondly, economic instruments of charging user fees, taxes, cess and entry fees for the use of forest, water and biodiversity resources should be introduced. Even in the parks and irrigation systems where entry fees, or user charges exist, studies show that the same can be increased further (*Kadekodi*, 2004). Water made available to cities, industries or to coal mine areas can be better charged. Even the PPP mode can be considered. Finally, using CDM/JI and other international payment mechanisms, the states should bid projects on forestry and biodiversity conservation. So far, under CDM hardly 1% of projects are approved under forestry and wildlife development (*Kadekodi*, 2007).

As a closing remark, it should be stressed that in order to provide more accurate designs of investment policies, there is a need for obtaining state level valuation of natural and human resources on a regular basis as part of National Green Income Acountings (*Kadekodi*, 2004).

Notes and References

1. Sen and several other welfare economists talk of 'functionings and capabilities' as additions to utility as a measure of welfare. For example: A person may be in vulnerable situation and still be contended with life if she has never known differently. A utilitarian evaluation will only assess her satisfaction and will not differentiate between a happy, healthy, well-sheltered person, and an equally happy, but unhealthy and badly sheltered person who has mentally adapted to her situation.
2. For details of estimating the values, shadow prices, etc., see Monographs pasted on www.gistindia.org
3. Annex 1 shows the same at the all India level, categories under various eco-systems, for two different years.
4. Similar changes in mineral resources are also needed to examine their rates of resources exploitation and their contribution to income and investment rates on their developments. But such data are still not available.
5. Carbon sequestration, water retention, flood control, soil-moisture management, climate remediation, temperature control, etc., essentially the global benefits, much more than local or regional benefits.
6. Stern report makes a reference to a needed just one percent of GDP as investment rates on ecology and environment

References

Arrow, Kenneth, Partha Dasgupta, Lawrence Goulder, Gretchen Daily, Paul Ehrlich, Geofrey Heal, Simon Levin, Karl-Goran Maler, Stephen Schneider, David Starrett and Brain Walker (2004): 'Are we consuming too much?', *Journal of Economic Perspectives*, Vol. 18, No. 3, pp.147-72

Atkinson, Giles, Richard Dubourg, Kirk Hamilton, Mohan Munasinghe, David Pearce and Carlos Young (1997): *Measuring sustainable development: Macroeconomics and the environment*, Cheltenham: Edward Elgar Pub.

Bandyopadhyay, Jayanta (2009): *Water, Ecosystems and Society*, Sage Publications, New Delhi.

Dasgupata, Partha (2001): *Human Well-Being and the Natural Environment*, Oxford University Press, New Delhi.

Dasgupta, Partha (2007): 'Measuring Sustainable Development: Theory and Application', Text of the Annual Distinguished Lecture, Asian Development Bank, Manila, 3 October 2007.

Dasgupta, Partha and Karl-Goran Maler *(2004): Environmental and Resource Economics: Some recent developments*, SANDEE Working Paper No. 7.

Hamilton, Kirk and Michael Clemens (1999): "Genuine Savings Rates in Developing Countries", *The World Bank Economic Review*, Vol. 13(2), pp. 333-56

Haripriya, Gundimeda, Sanjay Sanyal, Rajiv Sinha and Pavan Sukhdev (2007): *Estimating the Value of Educational Capital Formation in India*, Green Accounting for Indian States Project, Monograph 5, Green Indian States Trust, Chennai.

Hartwick, J.M. (1977): "Inter-generational Equity and Investing of Rents from Exhaustible Resources", *American Economic Review*, Vol. 67, No. 5, pp. 972-74.

Hartwick, J.M. (1990): "Natural Resources, National Income, Accounting and Economic Depreciation", *Journal of Public Economics*, Vol. 43, pp. 291-304.

Hartwick, J.M. (1992): 'Deforestation and National Accounting', *Environmental Resource Economics*, 2(5), pp. 513-22.

Howarth, R.B. (1991): "Inter-generational Equilibria and Exhaustible Resources: an Overlapping Generational Approach", *Ecological Economics*, Vol. 4 (3), p. 237.

Howarth, R.B. and R.B. Norgaard (1993): " Intergenerational transfers and the social discount rate", *Environmental and Resource Economics*, Vol. 3(4), pp. 337-58.

Kadekodi, Gopal K. (2004): *Environmental Economics in Practice*, Oxford University Press, New Delhi.

Kadekodi, Gopal K. (2005): "Linking biodiversity with quality of life: Issues of assessment, resilience and model integration", Sengupta, Nirmal and Jayanta Bandyopadhyay (Eds.): *Biodiversity and Quality of Life*, McMillan Publication, New Delhi.

Kadekodi, Gopal K. (2007): "Payment for ecosystem services to mitigation of climate change", paper presented at 17th AASSREC Conference, 27-30 September 2007, Nagoya.

Kumar, Pushpam, Sanjeev Sanyal, Rajiv Sinha and Pavan Sukhdev (2006): *Accounting for the Ecological Services of Indian's Forests*, Green Accounting for Indian States, Projects Monograph 7, Green India Status Trust, Chennai.

Krutilla, K.V. and A.C. Fisher (1985): "Irreversibility and the Optimal Use of Natural Environment".

Krutilla, K.V. and A.C. Fisher (Eds): *The Economics of Natural Environments*, Resources for the Future, Washington DC, pp. 39-59.

Krutilla, K.V. and Rafael Reuveny (2002): "The quality of life in the dynamics of economic development", *Environment and Development Economics*, Vol. 7(2), pp. 23-46.

Maler, Karl Goran (1991): "National accounts and environmental resources", *Environmental and Resource Economics*, Vol. 1, pp. 1-15.

Millennium Ecosystem Assessment *(2005): Ecosystems and Human Well-being: Synthesis*, World Resources Institute, Island Press, Washington, DC.

Munasinghe, Mohan, Osvaldo Sunkel, Carlos de Miguel (2001): *The Sustainability of Long-term Growth*, Edward Elgar Publication, Cheltenham, USA.

Murty, M.N., A.J. James, and Smitha Mishra (1999): *The Economic of Water Pollution: The Indian Experience*, Oxford University Press, New Delhi.

Parikh, K.S. and Utpal Ghosh (1995): 'Natural resource accounting for soils: Towards an empirical estimate of costs of soil degradation for India', IGIDR Discussion Paper No. 48, Indira Gandhi Institute of Development Research, Mumbai.

Perrings, Charles (2006): "Resilience and Sustainable Development", *Environmental and Development Economics*, Vol. 11, Part 4, pp. 417-27.

Ramsey, F.P. (1928): "A mathematical theory of savings", *Economic Journal*, Vol. 38, p. 543-59.

Rosenstein Rodan, P.N. (Ed.) (1964): *Capital Formation and Economic Development*, MIT Press, Cambridge.

Sen, Amartya (Ed.) (1970): *Growth Economics*, Penguin Books, Middlesex, UK.

Sen, Amartya (1984): 'Well-being, Agency and Freedom', the Deway Lecture in 1984, *Journal of Philosophy*, Vol. 82.

Sen, Amartya (1989a): 'The concept of development', Chenery, H.B. and T.N. Srinivasan (Eds): *Handbook of Development Economics*, Volume 1, Book 1, Amsterdam, Elsevier Science, pp. 9-26.

Sen, Amartya (1989b): *Development as Freedom*, Oxford Clarendon Press, New York.

Sen, Amartya Kumar (1993/1999): ' Capability and Well-being', Nussbaum, M.C. and A.K. Sen (eds.), *The Quality of Life*, Oxford University Press, New Delhi.

Solow, R.M. (1974): "The Economics of Resources or the Resource Economics?", *American Economic Review*, Vol. 64, No. 2, pp. 1-14.

Stern, N. (2006): The Economics of Climate Change, organised by the Foundation for Science and Technology at the Royal Society, London.

Vaidyanathan, A. (2006): 'Restructuring Watershed Development Programmes', *Economic and Political Weekly*, Vol. 41, Nos. 27-28, pp. 8-15.

Weitzman, M.L. (1976): "On the Welfare Significance of National Product in a Dynamic Economy", *Quarterly Journal of Economics,* Vol. 90, pp. 156-62.

WWW.gistindia.org (for data on environmental degradation, depletion etc!) WWW.mospi.nic.in (for data on state domestic products etc.).

World Bank (2003): *Sustainable Development in a Dynamic World: Transforming Institutions, Growth, and Quality of Life,* Washington DC.

World Commission on Environment and Development (1987): *Our Common Future,* Oxford University Press, New York.

Worldwatch Institute (2002): *State of the World 2002: Progress Towards a Sustainable Society,* London: Earthscan Pub.

ANNEX 1

Eco-system Services form Indian Forests: Some Estimates

Ecosystem services or changes	*2001*	*2003*	*Changes between two years*
Soil retention function			
Soil loss prevented by dense forests per year: million tonnes	(-)514.69	(-)482.20	Annual 'Soil losses' have come down
Loss of nutrients due to soil losses per year: Rs. Million	(-)50244	(-)47072	Annual 'Nutrient losses' have also reduced.
On ground recharge function			
Value of ground water recharge per year: Rs. million	1325	1238	Role as 'Ground Recharges' have gone down
On flood control function			
Effective avoided flood damage per year: Rs. Million	118510	111030	Role as 'Flood control' function has gone down
On carbon sequestration function			
Stock of carbon in a year: thousand tonnes of carbon in 2001	2473346 (opening stock)	2380128 (closing stock)	Carbon stocks have gone down
Monetary value of carbon stock: Rs. Billion	22260	21421	Carbon values of the stocks gone down
On Biodiversity conservation functions			
'Net total present value' of eco-tourism from forests:	Rs. 4.3 million	Rs. 4.3 million	
'Net present value' of bio-prospecting attributable to forests: Rs. million	1064400	997400	Declined due to reduction in forest cover.
Non-Use 'Net present value' of biodiversity flagship species: Rs. Million	322026	322026	

Source: www.gistindia.org: (2007).

SECTION III

NATURAL RESOURCES AND SUSTAINABLE DEVELOPMENT

Agricultural Sustainability and the Introduction of Genetically Modified Organisms (GMOs)

CLEM TISDELL

In order to cater for the predicted growth in global population and aspirations for increased living standards, the world needs to increase substantially its level of agricultural production and sustain agriculture's increased productivity. New technologies may enable this to occur but they also bring with them increased sustainability problems. There are many complex dimensions to achieving agricultural sustainability such as deciding on what agricultural attributes are worth sustaining and considering what trade-offs in objectives are required. These issues are discussed from a conceptual point of view. It is also shown using economic theory that market-based agriculture limits the opportunity for individual farmers to adopt sustainable agricultural techniques because of competitive economic pressures. It is argued that while modern agricultural methods and increased inter-regional trade have substantially increased agricultural supplies, they have also exacerbated the problem of sustaining agricultural production and yields and have had a disequilibrating effect on rural communities. Although genetic engineering is seen by some as a way forward for increasing agricultural production, it is shown that GMOs do not ensure sustainability of agricultural production and that they can be a source of rural disharmony and can threaten the sustainability of farming communities. Extension of intellectual property rights in new genetic material in recent times, particularly the granting of patents not only on techniques for producing GMOs but on the organisms themselves, have added to sustainability problems faced by modern agriculture.

1. INTRODUCTION

Global population is expected to increase by about 30% between now and 2050, and most of this increase will occur in developing countries. This means that in order to just maintain food and fibre supplies obtained from agriculture at present per capita levels, agricultural production needs also to rise by 30% in this time period. However, the demands on agriculture to increase its level of production may be even greater than this. As global stocks of oil decline, agriculture might be called in to supply more fuel in the form of ethanol and biodiesel and to make a larger proportionate contribution to the supply of fibres because most artificial fibres (such as nylon and polyester) are derived from oil. Is it possible to expand agriculture production sufficiently to meet these challenges? If so, how can this higher level of agricultural production be sustained?

The application of modern technologies to agriculture and continuing agricultural innovations have resulted in huge increases in global agricultural output. The question, however, arises of whether this process can continue unabated. Furthermore, are the contemplated increased yields of agriculture able to be sustained?

Again, we may ask what type of sustainability issues does modern agriculture face? Therefore, this article considers first what sustainability attributes of agriculture appear to be valued by societies and then outlines a series of potential threats to the sustainability of those attributes. Then the particular case of the introduction of genetically modified organisms (GMOs) to agriculture is considered. Genetic engineering is a relatively novel technique, the results of which are increasingly applied to agricultural production. It is believed by most of its proponents to be the key to substantially increasing agricultural production (see for example, *Shapiro*, 1999). However, the introduction of GMOs raises several types of sustainability issues, many of which are outlined in this article. Some of these sustainability issues are of an ecological nature whereas others have an economic basis. Particularly worrying is the nature of property rights bestowed on owners of GMOs by patents. This is because these patents can be used to limit the rights of farmers and can have negative effects on agricultural sustainability, for example, on the sustainability of future agricultural yields and on the desired characteristics of agricultural communities.

2. ATTRIBUTES OF AGRICULTURE THAT SOCIETIES MAY WISH TO SUSTAIN

In itself the word 'sustainability' only takes on meaning when it is related to an object(s) or to an attribute(s) of things. The social desirability of sustaining objects or attributes varies. Sustainability may be desirable or undesirable depending on the object to which it relates. For example, few would claim that it is desirable to sustain poverty although some dictators might want this if it helped to sustain their political power. On the other hand, most individuals would agree that is desirable to achieve and sustain a reasonable standard of living for all.

What type of sustainability attributes associated with agriculture are likely to be valued? One wish might be that agricultural output could be sustained without a large increase in effort, or that it could be increased and sustained so that there is not a fall in the per capita availability of agricultural produce. For these involved in the supply of agricultural produce to markets, this would require that their economic returns be maintained. Economic sustainability is required. However, sustainability of agricultural production will, amongst other things, depend on the continuing availability of important materials used in modern agriculture, such as chemical fertilizers many of which are derived from depletable non-renewable natural resources. Furthermore, sustainability of agricultural production will depend on the long-term ecological viability of agricultural systems and the ability of agriculture to adapt to environmental changes, such as climate change.

Another attribute of agriculture judged by some societies as important is sustaining an agricultural way of life and rural communities. For example, the European Union partly provides economic support to agriculture as a means of maintaining this way of life. To some extent, this attribute is treated as if it is a merit good. Even in the United States, some see virtue in an agrarian way of life involving independent family farms and closely knit local communities. They regret the disappearance of these features in American agriculture which is becoming more commercialized, industrialized and increasingly dominated by companies.

Often trade-offs are required between the sustainability of attributes. For example, society might want to sustain a high level of agricultural yields or economic returns as well as maintain a close-knit agricultural community or some other desirable attributes of this community. However, a compromise between these sustainability objectives is required if a curve like the ABCD in Figure 1 relates sustainable levels of agricultural yield or returns to a measure of desirable community attributes. For the set of possibilities in the segment CD of this curve, there is no conflict between raising yields or returns and securing a more desirable rural community but in the segment ABC, there is conflict. Higher agricultural yields or returns require a reduction in the perceived quality of the rural community. While the socially most desirable possibility occurs in the segment ABC, finding the socially optimal combination of possibilities is not easy in practice. Perhaps a social welfare function could be considered as way out of this problem. However, such an approach is problematic unless there is widespread agreement about the type of social welfare function that is appropriate. If the social indifference curves indicated by W_1W_1 and W_2W_2 apply, then the combination at B is the socially optimal choice. This means that in order to obtain higher agricultural returns, some reduction in the desired quality of the local community is required. However, individual self-interest may propel the agricultural system to point A because communal relationships are a product of externalities as far as individual farmers are concerned. This means that the social optimum corresponding to point B does not prevail but an inferior result. Individual self-interest is unlikely to promote the collective good in this case due to the presence of social externalities.

Figure 1: Achieving desired economic objectives and desired attributes for the nature of rural communities often requires trade-offs. As illustrated in this figure, it may be necessary to forgo desirable attributes of a rural community in order to achieve higher yields or returns from agriculture. Achieving and sustaining a socially desirable balance between these objectives is not easy because the nature of societies is an external consequence of individual decisions.

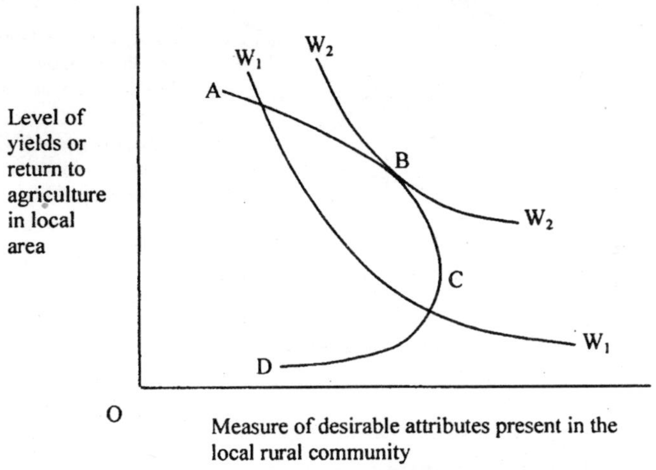

III. FARMERS WHO WANT TO ADOPT AGRICULTURAL PRACTICES TO SUSTAIN AGRICULTURAL PRODUCTION AND YIELDS MAY BE POWERLESS TO DO THIS

Farmers who want to adopt agricultural techniques to sustain agricultural production and yields may be powerless (because of economic competition) to do so. If enough other farmers are more myopic or discount the future more heavily (have a high time-preference) than those farmers who wish to be 'virtuous' by adopting sustainable techniques, the latter may be forced by economic competition not to adopt sustainable techniques. However, if all farmers adopt sustainable techniques, the choice of sustainable techniques may be profitable and the extent of current economic sacrifice by those wanting to switch to sustainable techniques may become manageable (compare for example, *Tisdell,* 1999; *Wilson and Tisdell,* 2001).

Figure 2: Market competition can prevent those who wish to use sustainable agricultural techniques for doing so because of the economic pressures generated in the short-term.

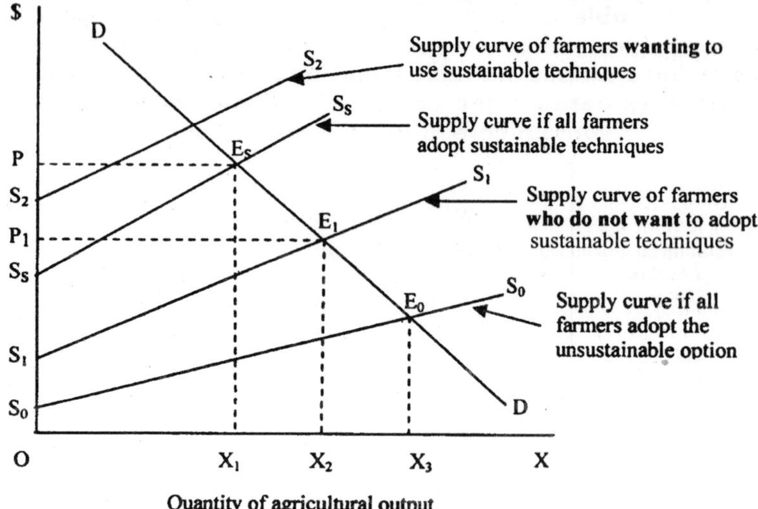

This can be illustrated by Figure 2 assuming that buyers are unwilling to pay a premium for sustainably grown agricultural produce. For simplicity, suppose that farmers can be divided into two groups. Group I is relatively myopic and favours the use of techniques that yield high profits and high yields in the short-term but reduced levels of these in the longer-term whereas Group II consists of farmers who favour techniques that result in lower profits in the short-term but higher yields and profits in the long-term. The supply curve of product X of Group I farmers in the initial period might be as represented by the line marked S_1S_1. If they happen to be the only suppliers, the equilibrium market price would be P_1 and they would supply X_2 of the product. The supply curve for Group II farmers in the initial period might be as shown by line S_2S_2 if they were to adopt sustainable techniques. However, by adopting these techniques, they are unable to make a profit. Hence, farmers in Group II are forced by liquidity and profit considerations to join farmers in Group I and adopt unsustainable techniques even though they could record a profit in the long-run by adopting sustainable techniques. In the short-run, the market supply curve will therefore, correspond to line S_0S_0 with market equilibrium established at E_0.

On the other hand, if all farmers adopt the sustainable technique, the market supply curve in the short-run might correspond to S_SS_S with market equilibrium corresponding to E_S. Use of the sustainable technique is now profitable even though supply of X in the short-term is lower and its price is higher than if the less sustainable technique is adopted. In the long-term, the opposite relationship should hold. Some economies from expansion of the market based on sustainable techniques may also be obtained of a Marshallian type. For example, economies of specialization in supplying inputs for farmers using the sustainable technique may occur. Consequently, the collective per unit cost of switching to the sustainable technique may be lower than appears initially to be the case for switching by an individual farmer.

IV. TO WHAT EXTENT HAVE INCREASED AGRICULTURAL YIELDS AND PRODUCTION BEEN OBTAINED AT THE EXPENSE OF THEIR SUSTAINABILITY?

Research and scientific advances have resulted in large increases in yields per hectare of agricultural land and have facilitated the extension of agriculture. Furthermore, growing international and inter-regional trade has contributed to increased agricultural output by encouraging greater specialisation in agricultural production by regions (as is predicted by the theory of comparative advantage) and many inputs or resources used in modern agriculture are now traded over greater geographical distances than in the past. The latter development makes agricultural production less dependent on local resources.

In addition, new agricultural methods have made agricultural yields less dependent on local natural environmental conditions than in the past. These methods have enabled humans to regulate (to a considerable extent) the actual environmental conditions experienced by crops and domesticated animals. Both new methods of agriculture production and increased ability to import agricultural inputs to regions that are deficient in these inputs have made agricultural production less dependent on local natural resources and environments than previously. For example, irrigation methods make agriculture less dependent on local rainfall, and chemical fertilizers can be imported to compensate for local soil deficiencies. As a result, there is greater control of agricultural micro-environments and increased agricultural yields. However, such developments are not without their risks because the high levels of agricultural production associated with these developments may not be sustainable. There are several reasons for concern.

First, many of the inputs used in modern agriculture are derived from depletable, non-renewable material resources, for example, oil. As these become scarcer, it will be more difficult to maintain agricultural production. At the very least, new agricultural technologies will be required to sustain agricultural production.

Secondly, the developments mentioned above reduce the genetic resources available to agriculture (*Tisdell*, 2003). This is because agricultural varieties that give high yields or returns under controlled environmental conditions replace those that give lower yields or returns under natural environmental conditions. However, these high yields depend on the ability of farmers to maintain desirable environmental conditions. In the long-term, this may prove to be impossible because resources used for environmental control may be exhausted or disappear due to natural causes. Two cases can be used to illustrate this matter.

Suppose that in a region two varieties of a crop are available. Variety I is a local variety and is well adapted to local environmental conditions. The magnitude of a relevant environmental condition is indicated by a variable, x. This might be water availability or soil fertility, for example. The production from variety I (yield per ha.) is assumed to be as indicated by curves ABCD. If the natural environmental condition is x_1, yield will correspond to B in the absence of any effort by farmers to alter this environmental condition. Suppose also that an improved variety, variety II, is available and that this has the yield relationship indicated by curves EFGH. This technique can give higher yields but only if natural environmental conditions are sufficiently controlled. Suppose that it is profitable to regulate the environmental conditions if variety II is adopted so that the artificial environmental conditions experienced by the crop are x_3. Yields then correspond to point F and variety I can be expected to disappear because it is less profitable than variety II.

Figure 3: Under natural conditions, variety I of a crop gives the highest yields but if environmental conditions can be regulated economically, variety II gives the highest yields and the highest economic returns. There is however, a problem if environmental conditions cannot be regulated in the future or if this cannot be done economically.

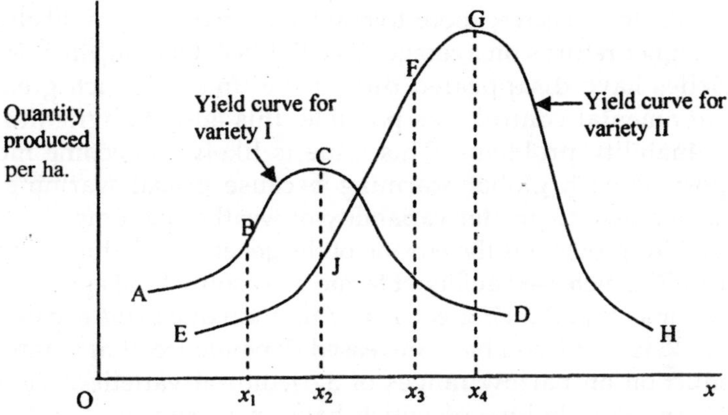

However, this situation can give rise to sustainability problems because the resources that allow the local agricultural environment to be regulated may not always be available, or may become very costly due to their increasing scarcity. For example, climate change may result in irrigation water no longer being available or supplies of artificial fertilizer may start to run out. Consequently, farmers may have to rely on natural environmental conditions again or may have to do so to a considerable extent. Therefore, yields using the improved variety fall drastically. For example, it may only be economic to regulate the environmental condition to x_2 and yield then falls to a level corresponding to J.

In addition, it is likely that variety I will have disappeared during the time interval in which variety II was the superior economic choice. Thus, it is impossible to revert to the use of Variety I even though it would be the superior possibility in the conditions that have eventuated. In this case, genetic loss adds to the agricultural sustainability problem.

A closely related aspect is that some local varieties of crops (or breeds of livestock) may be more tolerant to variations in environmental conditions than improved varieties. Consequently, improved varieties only turn out to be commercially superior if variations in environmental conditions can be sufficiently regulated. If the resources for such regulation should become unavailable or scarce, more tolerant local varieties are likely to give higher returns on average (*Tisdell*, 1983). Once again, if local varieties have disappeared during the time in which greater environmental control was possible, this adds to agricultural sustainability problems. This issue is likely to become more important with global warming because global warming is predicted lead to greater variability of weather patterns.

A third problem is the erosion of the genetic stock due to social causes. The increased ability of farmers to control local agricultural environments and their greater specialisation due to the expansion of markets and trade have increased dependence of agricultural production on narrow ranges of agricultural varieties, (*Tisdell*, 2003) the populations of which have increased in abundance because they are favoured by humans for agriculture. Their increased abundance raises the exposure of these varieties to diseases and pests and makes them more susceptible to these and in the longer-term, can be expected to reduce their ecological fitness. The presence of a greater diversity of crops and breeds of livestock reduces this sustainability problem.

Fourth, the yields from some crops and livestock depend on the use of pesticides. The effectiveness of these pesticides tends to decline over time as targeted pests develop biological resistance as a result of evolutionary processes. The maintenance of yields in such cases depends on effective new pesticides being developed to replace those that have lost their effectiveness. How long this process can be maintained is unknown.

While many modern agricultural innovations have added to concerns about agricultural sustainability (*Tisdell*, 2007) it would be wrong to believe that all agricultural innovations have reduced agricultural sustainability. Sustainable crop rotations, green manuring and some types of intercropping and polyculture can add to agricultural sustainability. However, the availability of artificial fertilizers often curtails these practices. In many cases, excessive use of artificial fertilizer is encouraged by government subsidies on their supply. Because the use of such fertilizer usually results in negative environmental spillovers, it would be more appropriate for governments to restrict their use rather than encourage it.

V. GENETICALLY MODIFIED ORGANISMS (GMOS), AGRICULTURAL PRODUCTION, AND ECOLOGICAL SUSTAINABILITY

In the last 25 years or so, spectacular advances have been made in the genetic engineering of organisms. These have made possible significant advances in medicine and more debatable progress in agriculture. It is sobering to realize that the first GM crops were only released in 1996 and that their rate and extent of adoption has been so rapid (*Kinderlerer*, 2008, p. 14).

Advocates of genetic engineering believe that it holds out the promise of greater agricultural yields, high economic returns, and greater environmental sustainability. Skeptics and critics of the genetic engineering revolution argue that the advantages of genetic engineering are overstated, that the environmental risks associated with GMOs are considerable and that yields from GMOs are likely to be unsustainable in the long-run, (*Wolfenberger. Engels and Phifer*, 2000; *Batie and Ervin*, 2001: *Andow and Zweblen*, 2006). In addition, it should be kept in mind that the potential for the creation of GMOs with particular attributes is limited by biological and physical constraints—the possibilities for genetic engineering are not unlimited. Even though Engels (1959) once triumphantly declared in criticizing Thomas Malthus that nothing is impossible to science, we know that this is not so.

To date there have been two principle types of genetic engineering introduced into agriculture and both are associated with the control of pests of crops. The first technique is the genetic engineering of crops to make them more tolerant of the application of particular herbicides, for example, glyphosate sold under the trade mark of 'Roundup'. This involves the insertion of genetic material into crops from plants that have shown themselves to be resistant in the field to the herbicide. The second innovation in the genetic engineering of crops is to incorporate within them toxins fatal to insect pests, mostly the larvae of moths and butterflies and some beetle species. For this purpose, genetic material from a bacterium *(Bacillus thuringiensis*, shortened usually to Bt) has been widely used. This bacterium is naturally fatal to several types of insects and occurs in some soils.

Crops that have been modified for herbicide resistance include soya beans and canola (rape). Crops that have been Bt modified include maize and cotton. Progress has been made in genetically modifying rice so that it is herbicide resistant as well as toxic to a range of insect pests but this rice has not been released for general cultivation.

Consider now some of the sustainability issues that can arise from the introduction of GMOs. If they actually give higher returns than traditional varieties (or farmers believe they do), they are likely to replace traditional varieties thereby reducing the biodiversity of organisms used in agriculture. Therefore, the types of problems mentioned in the previous section are likely to be exacerbated. Furthermore, for ecological reasons, the yields from GMOs are unlikely to be sustained.

In the case of herbicide-resistant crops, they are likely to cross-pollinate with their weedy relatives over a period of time. If this occurs, some of the targeted weeds in crops become resistant to the herbicide and the effectiveness of the genetic engineering is reduced.

Reduced sustainability of pest control is likely to occur more quickly for genetic engineering of crops that introduce toxins into plants to kill insect pests. This is mainly due to the rapidity with which new generations of insects occur. This accelerates evolutionary processes and the selection of populations of insect pests that are resistant to the toxins. This problem is now widely recognized by ecologists and policy-makers. In some countries, such as the USA and Australia, growers of Bt cotton are, for example, required to grow areas of non-Bt cotton to help sustain populations of insects that are not Bt resistant. The purpose of this is to slow the rate at which the total population of the pest becomes resistant to Bt. This, however, merely slows the process of the erosion of the effectiveness of the genetic engineering in raising agricultural yields. In the end, its effectiveness is likely to be completely undermined and the genetically modified crop varieties may give lower returns than traditional varieties.

We can conclude that ecological forces make it unlikely that increased agricultural yields obtained in the short to medium-term as a result of advances in genetic engineering can be sustained in the long-run (*Botie and Ervins*, 2001). The ecological forces involved seem to differ little from those that come into play when chemical pesticides are used to control pests. In such circumstances, the maintenance of increased agricultural yields is dependent on a continuing stream of innovations that enables new biological advances to replace earlier techniques that have lost their effectiveness. Whether or not such continuing scientific and technological momentum can be maintained is uncertain. A treadmill-type of phenomena is involved with the sustainability of agricultural production highly dependent on the ability of science to provide a stream of new advances. Once this flow stops or declines, lack of agricultural sustainability is liable to become a major problem. However, social sustainability problems are also raised by the use of GMOs in agriculture.

VI. CONCERNS ABOUT SOCIAL SUSTAINABILITY AND THE INTRODUCTION OF GMOS TO AGRICULTURE

Norgaard (1994) has argued that agricultural technologies and social relationships should evolve in relative harmony by a process of steady non-rapid co-evolution and Tisdell (2000) has elaborated on this theme. The type of co-evolution that Norgaard had in mind was achieved in the past when agricultural (or more generally rural) innovations originated in local communities. For example, in the past, genetic improvements in crops and domesticated livestock were achieved by human selection of lines that showed superior traits in daily use.

Today, this pattern of agricultural innovation has largely been replaced by the development of agricultural techniques by large firms and companies (many of which are multinationals) having no (or only limited) contact with local rural communities. Consequently, major changes in agricultural technologies can occur rapidly and cause social distress and disequilibrium in rural communities as these communities try to adjust to the new situation. This may be one reason why human illnesses such as hypertension (high blood pressure) associated with psychological stress are becoming more common amongst farmers. Adjustment to rapid technological and economic change can be stressful and the problem is exacerbated if social structures and relationships fail to adjust at a sufficiently fast rate to cope with these changes, as seems increasingly to be the case.

The separation of agricultural innovation from local rural communities was partly a result of the Industrial Revolution but has been reinforced by the extension of intellectual property rights for inventions. Governments have extended the types of inventions for which patents can be granted or similar types of entitlement given. The most recent extensions include the granting of Plant Variety Rights for new varieties of plants obtained by selective breeding, and of greater social consequence, the granting of patents covering not only techniques to produce GMOs but also in several countries, the organisms produced by applying these methods. Both types of monopoly rights of patents apply in most developed countries, e.g. the United States and Canada, but in some developing countries, such as China, only the techniques for producing GMOs can be patented. The United States in particular has been very active in its political lobbying for the recognition and enforcement of intellectual property rights internationally (*Phillips*, 2007). This is because the United States has been the source of many innovations in current use and stands to gain economically from the international recognition and enforcement of such rights.

As a rule, it seems that only large companies are in a position to develop new GMOs (because of the costs and risks involved), to effectively market these and to defend the intellectual property rights conferred on them by patents (*Tisdell*, 2008). The transaction costs involved in defending intellectual property rights can be very high. However, from a social point of view, transaction costs involve an economic waste because they are not productive—society would be economically better off if they could be avoided. Yet, given the type of social system adopted, they cannot be avoided. The potential reward for those who develop new GMOs, patent and market these are monopoly profits. If these are very high, they are likely to generate social criticism on the basis that there is inadequate sharing of the economic benefits of the innovation with farmers and consumers.

If a new GMO proves to be economically superior to traditional varieties, traditional varieties of crops are likely to disappear and farmers then become highly dependent on suppliers of GM seed for their future crops, especially if farmers are not permitted legally to save their GM seed or trade in it. The latter is the case in several countries (*Phillips*, 2007). Farmers may become hostile towards suppliers of GM seed if they become highly dependent and locked into this supply.

This economic dependence could be fostered by some suppliers of GM seed—they might engage in monopolisation. For example, a supplier of GM seed could initially keep its price low to encourage its adoption with the consequence that traditional varieties are no longer grown and are lost permanently. Once this has occurred, the supplier of GM seed would have a monopoly or near monopoly and be able to raise the price of GM seed to the detriment of farmers and consumers.

It has been said that some producers of GM seed are endeavouring to introduce a 'terminator' gene into their seed (*Phillips*, 2007). The seed obtained from crops grown from this seed might be infertile (or only have inferior quality) compared to the original GM seed. Therefore, farmers would have no incentive to save their seed or trade in it and the supplier of the GM seed would avoid many of the transaction costs involved in enforcing its intellectual property rights. This could have social economic advantages even though there is likely to be social opposition to the introduction of GM seed containing a terminator gene.

VII. CONCLUDING COMMENTS

A major global challenge is how to increase the level of agricultural production and sustain it while taking into account the environmental impacts of agricultural production. Between now and the middle of this century, approximately a 30 per cent increase in agricultural production will be needed to maintain the current availability of agricultural products. Unless there is income redistribution in favour of the poor, an even greater increase will be needed to overcome food poverty. Agricultural production needs to be increased and the increased production needs to be sustained.

The concept of agricultural sustainability was shown to be complex. This is because it is desirable to sustain some attributes of agriculture but not others. Value judgments are needed to decide which attributes should be sustained these. Sustainability is by no means an absolute virtue and it is often necessary to trade-off desirable sustainability objectives (to some extent) to achieve other objectives, or to forgo one sustainability objective to achieve another. Sustainability objectives are subject to the economic principle of opportunity costs. This should always be kept in mind in order to avoid fantasy.

It was shown that when farmers are dependent on the market system for their survival or economic welfare, they are often unable to adopt techniques which would sustain agricultural production and yields even though they may wish to do this. If some farmers go against the tide by adopting sustainable techniques, they may fail to make a profit in the short- to medium-term and suffer liquidity problems. In many cases, a collective approach is needed to ensure the adoption of sustainable agricultural techniques.

While scientific advances in agriculture have increased agricultural production and yields and while increased inter-regional trade has helped raise agricultural supplies, both of these developments have increased the risks of agricultural production not being sustained. Several different reasons for this were outlined. For example, loss of agricultural biodiversity as a result of these developments was identified as a factor that is likely to have negative sustainability consequences for agricultural production.

An important development in recent years has been the development of GMOs and their use in agriculture. It was argued that these developments add to sustainability problems in agriculture. Ecological responses to the introduction of GMOs in agriculture may make it impossible to sustain the initial increase in agricultural production obtained by the adoption of GMOs. Secondly, the introduction of GMOs to agriculture can lead to social conflict and disharmony. Various mechanisms were identified that may interfere with the sustainability of rural communities as a result of the adoption of GMOs in agriculture. It seems likely that the use of GMOs in agriculture will reinforce the agricultural sustainability problem created by modern commercial and industrial agriculture and the sustainability of agricultural production will come to depend even more heavily on continuing scientific and technological advances than in the past. It is uncertain whether such progress can or will be sustained.

REFERENCES

Andrew, D.A. and Zwahlen, C. (2006). 'Assessing Environmental Risks of Transgenic Plants,' *Ecology Letters*, 9, 196-214.

Batie, S.S. and Ervin, D.E. (2001). 'Transgenic Crops and the Environment: Missing Markets and Public Roles,' *Environment and Development Economics*, 6, pp. 435-57.

Engels, F. (1959). 'Outline of a Critique of Political Economy,' K Marx, *Economic and Philosophic Manuscripts of 1844*, Foreign Language Publishing House, Moscow.

Kinderlerer, J. (2008). 'The Cartagena Protocol on Biosafety,' *Collection of Biosafety Reviews*, 4, 12-65.

Norgaard, R.B. (1994). *Development Betrayed*. Routledge, London.

Phillips, P.W.B. (2007). 'Farmers' Privilege and Patented seeds,' pp. 49-64. P.W.B. Phillips and C.B. Onweukwe, *Accessing and Sharing the Benefits of the Genomics Revolution*. Springer, Dordrecht, The Netherlands.

Shapiro, R.B. (1999). 'How Genetic Engineering will save our Planet,' *The Futurist*, April, 28-29.

Tisdell, C. (1983). 'The Biological Law of Tolerance, Average Biomass and Production in a variable Uncontrolled Environment,' *International Journal of Ecology and Environmental Sciences*. 9(12), 99-109. Reprinted in C. Tisdell (2003), *Economics and Ecology in Agriculture and Marine Production*. Edward Elgar, Cheltenham, UK and Northampton, MA, USA.

Tisdell, C. (1999). 'Economics Aspects of Ecology and Sustainable Agricultural Production,' pp. 37-56, A.K. Dragan and C. Tisdell (eds.) *Sustainable Agriculture and Environment*. Edward Elgar, Cheltenham, UK and Northampton, MA, USA.

Tisdell, C. (2000), 'Coevolution, Agricultural Practices and Sustainability: Some major Social and Ecological Issues,' *International Journal of Agricultural Resources, Governance Ecology*, 1, 6-16. Reprinted in Tisdell (2003), *Ecological and Environmental Economics*. Edward Elgar, Cheltenham, UK and Northampton, MA, USA.

Tisdell, C. (2003). 'Socio-economic Causes of Loss of Animal Genetic Diversity: Analysis and Assessment,' *Ecological Economics*, 48, pp. 365-78.

Tisdell, C. (2007). 'Sustainable Agriculture', pp. 362-74, G. Atkinson, D. Dietz and E. Neumayer (eds). *Handbook of Sustainable Development*. Edward Elgar, Cheltenham, UK and Northampton, MA, USA.

Tisdell, C. (2008). 'Economics, Ecology and the Development and Use of GMOs: General Considerations and Biosafety Issues,' *Economics, Ecology and the Environment*. Working Paper No. 153, School of Economics, The University of Queensland, Brisbane, 4072.

Wilson, C. and Tisdell, C. (2001). 'Why Farmers Continue to Use Pesticides Despite Environmental Health and Sustainability Costs,' *Ecological Economics*, 39, pp. 449-62.

Wolfenberger, L.L. and Phifer, P.R. (2000). 'The Ecological Risks and Benefits of Genetically Engineered Plants,' *Science*, 290, pp. 2088-93.

Managing Forests for Biodiversity Conservation: The Case of West Bengal

DEBAL RAY

The relatively modest forest cover of West Bengal is spread over five major floristic zones. Correspondingly, a rich diversity of flora and fauna could be found in the state. In particular, the forests of Darjeeling, Duars and Sundarbans harbour large number of plant and animal taxa, which are either monotypic or endemic or endangered or a combination of above two/three categories. Consequently, biodiversity conservation should be a prime objective of forestry management in West Bengal.

The causes of biodiversity loss range from deforestation to habitat fragmentation, inappropriate silvicultural practices of past, species invasion, grazing by cattle, forest fire, soil erosion and lastly climate change. These forces influence biodiversity loss either through quantitative change in forest (deforestation) or through impoverisation of forest (inappropriate silvicultural practice, fire, species invasion) or through both (habitat fragmentation).

Strategies for biodiversity conservation go beyond eliminating/abating the forces that cause biodiversity loss.

Thus, both the National Biodiversity Action Plan (2008) and West Bengal State Biodiversity Strategy and Action Plan (2005) suggest novel approaches like captive breeding, reintroduction of species beside the traditional ones.

FORESTS OF WEST BENGAL

The recorded forest area of West Bengal is 11879 sq. km. which is 13.4% of state's geographical area. The forest areas of West Bengal can be classified into five broad floristic zones as per Champion and Seth (1968) classification.

I. Moist Tropical Forest

1. Tropical Semi-evergreen Forest

Extends from foothills to an elevation of 1000 metres in the heavy rainfall tracts of North Bengal. Top canopy of this forest is closed and mainly made up of evergreen species. Middle storey is dense. Depending on altitudinal variation, species combinations are also varied.

2. Tropical Moist Deciduous Forest

(i) *Moist Sal Forest:* This type of forest is present from Terai to an elevation of 650 metre or more. Dominant species is *Shorea robusta* in association with species of *Terminalia* and *Garuga* on mountain slopes.

(ii) *Mixed Moist Deciduous Forest:* Occurs in outer Himalayan ranges upto an elevation of 500-650 metre where rainfall is comparatively high. The forest is characterized by absence of sal trees. The dominant tree species are *Terminalia bellerica, Lagerstroemia parviflora, Schima wallichii,* etc.

3. Littoral and Swamp Forest

It is found in the adjoining areas of Sundarbans. The principal species are *Hibiscus tiliaceus, Thespesia populnea, Vitex negundo,* etc.

4. Tidal Swamp Forest

This forest is in the delta of Sundarbans. Mangrove species like *Heritierafomes, Sonneratia apetala, Bruguiera gymnorhiza,*

Nipafruticans are common. Trees with stilt roots, pneumatophores, and viviparous germination are usual in occurrence.

II. Dry Tropical Forest

1. Dry Deciduous Forest

Occurs in laterite tract of Purulia, Bankura, Birbhum and partly in West Midnapur districts. The main tree species include *Shorea robusta, Madhuca indica, Buchanania lanzan, Schleichera oleosa, Terminalia chebula,* etc. The shrub layer comprises of *Holarrhena antidysenterica, Zizyphus mauritiana,* etc.

2. Mixed Deciduous Forest

Occurs in Teesta river valley and Jaldapara area. The forest is generally called Khair *(Accacia catechu)—Sisso (Dalbergia sisso).* Grasses like *Saccharum procerum, Phragmites karaka* are common on the forest floor.

III. Sub-tropical Forest

This forest is mainly noticed at elevation from 1000-2000 metres in Darjeeling Himalaya with rainfall between 200-400 cm. Forest vegetation is dominated by *Schima-Castanopsis-Phobe* association in lower region and *Engelhardtia-Castanopsis-Schima-Betula* association in upper elevation.

IV. Temperate Forest

Occurs in elevation from 1800-3500 metres in Darjeeling Himalaya. Species composition varies depending on elevation. *Michelia-Machilus* association at lower ranges gives way to predominantly Oak *(Quercus sp)* in middle reaches. At higher elevation *Rhododendron-Conifer* forest is seen.

V. Grassland

Occur in riverian areas. Tall grasses like *Saccharum procerum, S. spontaneum, Themeda gigantean,* etc. grows luxuriantly.

BIODIVERSITY OF FORESTS OF WEST BENGAL

The flora of West Bengal is very rich in biodiversity, especially in the forests areas of Terai, Duars, Darjeeling Himalayas and Sundarbans. The flora comprises of 3580 species (21.33%)

belonging to 1333 genera (44.64%) and 200 families (78.74%) of Angiosperms out of 16779 species under 2986 genera and 254 families recorded in India. (*Chakraverty et al.*, 1999). The family Garminae shows maximum diversity represented by 433 species followed by Leguminosae with 324 species, Compositae with 133 species and so on. Total number of flowering and non-flowering plants comprise of 6545 species.

The fauna of West Bengal comprise of 8037 species which is 9% of faunal species of India. Of these, vast majority are insects with over 4770 species. The last number must be a gross underestimate as large majority of insect species are still not known to science. The state boasts of its vertebrate fauna which is 29% of all India figure. The faunal diversity is highest in Darjeeling; in case of mammalian species more than 50% of the species recorded in India could be found in Darjeeling.

Forests of West Bengal harbour a large number of **monotypic genera and families**. Hippocastanaceae *(Aesculus assamica)*, Stachyuraceae *(Stachyrus himalaicus)*, Rhizophoraceae (*Caralia integmmd)*, Datiscaceae *(Tetrameles nudiflora)*, Sonneretiaceae *(Duabanga grandiflora)*, Scrophulariaceae *(Wrightia giganted)*, Proleaceae *(Helicia erratica)*, Hamamelidaceae *(Exbucklandia populnea)* are few monotypic families of the state. At least 517 dicot and 171 monocot monotypic genera are also represented in the region. A large number of monotypic faunal genera such as *Anathana, Scotozous, Cuon, Melursus, Ailurus, Arctonyx, Mellivora; Arctogalidia, Paguma, Lutrogale, Neofelis, Hyaena, Pardofelis, Elephas, Cannomys, Nesokia, Caprolagus* (all mammals), *Netta, Butastur, Hydrophasianus, Metopidius, Philomachus* (all birds), *Catla, Rhinomugil* (Fish), *Oxyphyllum, Melanogryllus, Condronotulus, Meristopteryx* (Orthoptera), *Nevadne* (Cnidaria) and many others are also found. As there are no closely related genomes of these genera anywhere in the world, their conservation is of special significance. (*Alfred*, 2005)

A large number of plant species of Sundarbans are considered endangered. The names of the plants and the factors responsible for its endangered status are given below. (*Banerjee, L.K.*, 2002): *Amoora cucullata* (environmental change and alteration of habitat), *Cynometra iripa* (change of environmental conditions), *Heritiera fames* (change of environmental conditions and biotic pressure), *Intsia bijuga* (over-exploitation for its highly valuable furniture wood), *Kandelia candel* (environmental factors), *Merope angulata* (environmental change and alteration of habitat), *Rhizophora apiculata* (change of habitat and biotic pressure), *Sarcolobus carinatus* (due to its medicinal properties), *Sonneratia grifflthii* (over-exploitation and change of habitat)

The rich flora of Darjeeling has always attracted the tourists and the botanists alike and tempted them to collect plant parts for decoration and study respectively. However, this seemingly benign practice by a large number of people has created havoc. Botanical Survey of India notes that "tourist activities and large scale collection of the class room materials by the students and teachers from all over the country and by the material suppliers have almost fully denuded the vegetation of Darjeeling and suburbs. As a result, many species have become rare and threatened." (*Chakraverty, R.K. et al.*, 1999) Some of the endangered species of Darjeeling hills are: *Acer hookeri* var. *major, Acer osmastonii, Aconitum ferox, Begonia satrapis, Begonia rubella, Bulleyia yunnanensis, Calamus inermis, Christella clarkia, Codonopsis affinis, Cymbidium eburneum, Diplomeris hirsuta, Metathelypteris decipiens, Panax pseudoginseng, Phoenix rupicola, Pimpinella tongloensis, Polypodiodes wattii, Rhododendron edgeworthii, Tricarpelema gigantenum.*

In other areas of West Bengal following endangered plants are found: *Arundinella decempadalis, Cissus spectabilis, Calotropis filipes* var. *trichocarpa, Commelina appendiculata, Cymbopogon gidarba, Dimeria mooneyi, Hedyotis scabra, H. brunonis, Ischaemum duthiei, Ischaemum hirtum, Pandanus unguifer, Picrorhiza scrophulari flora, Pseudoraphis minuta,* etc. The factors responsible for their endangered status are often biotic pressure.

The occurrences of endangered taxa among faunal elements is even higher. The Zoological Survey of India has listed the following endangered vertebrates in West Bengal: *Petaurista magnificus, P. nobilis, Ratufa bicolor, Myotis annectans, M. mystacinus, Rhinolophus trifoliatus, Manis crass icaudata, Canis lupus, Cuon alpinus, Melurnus ursinus, Ailurus fulgens, Lutra lutra, Aonyx cinerea, Herpestes palustris, Hyaena hyaena, Prionailurus bengalensis, P. viverrinus, Neofelis nebulosa, Panthera pardus, Panthera tigris, Elephas maximus, Capricornis sumatraenis, Rhinoceros unicornis, Bos frontalis, Platanista gangetica, Orcaella brevirostris* (Mammals), *Ardea goliath, Ciconia ciconia, Leptoptilos dubius, L. javanicus, Platalea leucorodia,*

Dendrocygna bicolor, Threskiornis aethiopica, Aviceda jerdoni, A. leuphotes, Accipiter nisus, A. virgatus, Haliaectus leucogaster, Sarcogyps calvus, Gyps indicus, G. bengalensis, Pandion haliaetus, Falco peregrinus, Polyplectron bicalcaratum, Ithaginis cruentus, Lophurus leucomelana, Pavo cristatus, Grus nigricollis, Tyto alba, Aceros nipalensis, Anthracoceros malabaricus (Aves), *Crocodylus porosus, Lepidochelys olivacea, Batagur buska, Chelonia mydas, Eretmochelys imbricate, Lissemys punctata, Varanus bengalensis, V. flavescens, V. salvator, Python molurus, P. reticultus, Elachistodon westermanni, Ptyas mucosus, Naja naja* (Reptiles), *Trilototriton verrucosus* (Ambhibia), *Ompok pabo, O. bimaculatus, Ailia bengalensis, Bagrius bagarius, Eutropichthys vacha, Puntius sarana, Semiplolus semiplolus, Osphronemus nobilis, Labeo diacanthys, L. flmbriatus, L. gonius, Anabas testudineus, Notopterus notopterus, N. chitala, Pangasius pangasius,* Balitora brucci, *Gadusia chapra, Meastacembelus armatus, Mystas tangra, M. aor, Rasbora rasbora, Setipinna phasa, Bengala elonga, Wallago attu, Nandus nandus, Amblypharyngodon mola, Tor putitora, T. tor, Raiamas bola, Barilius vagra, Odontamblyopus rubicondus* (Pisces).

The causes of endangerment of certain important taxa are given in the table [modified from *Ajith Kumar et al* (2000) in *'Setting Biodiversity Conservation Priorities for India'*]

There are a number of faunal species which were not sighted within the state for a long period and may have become locally extinct. Among the vertebrates following species have not been recorded from the state for last few decades. (Alffred *et al*, 2005)

Mammals: Marbled Cat—*Pardofelis marmorata,* Golden Cat—*Catopuma temmincki,* Three-banded palm Civet—*Arctogalidia trivirgata.*

Reptiles: *Zaocys nigromarginatus,* Gore's Bronze Back—*Dendrelaphis gorei, Ahaetulla prosina.*

Amphibians: *Bufo abatus, Megophrys robusta, Philautus jerdonii, Occidozyga tima.*

There are some species which are surviving by a very small population in limited areas and only occasionally sighted or reported. A number of mammalian species such as Himalayan Tahr *(Hemitragus jemlahicus),* Pygmy Hog *(Sus salvanius),* Hispid Hare *(Caprolagus hispidus),* Asiatic Black Bear *(Selenarctos thibetanus),* Three Banded Palm Civet *(Arctogalidia trivirgata),* Hog

Sl. No.	*Plant/Animal Group*	*Cause of Endangermentl*
1.	Amphibians	Population fragmentation of almost all species and reduction in habitat quality. The latter results from degradation of forests, excessive use of insecticides in agricultural field, changes in soil pH due to use of lime, excessive use of pesticides and fertilizers in tea estates etc. Some species are caught in large number for alleged medicinal value (e.g. *Paa leibigii* from Darjeeling). The factors responsible for global decline of amphibian population like increased UV radiation, fungal infection of skin are also a matter of concern.
2.	Reptiles	Most species are considered threatened due to restricted distribution (e.g. *Oligodonjuglandifer),* fragmented population and declining habitat quality. Trade is considered a major factor for a limited number of species (e.g. *Python morulus, Naja naja, Geochelone elegans).* Harvesting for food (tortoise eggs, *Varanus bengalensis* meat) is another reason for endangerment.
3.	Mammals	Major reason for the threatened status of mammals are highly restricted distribution (e.g. most small mammals like shrews, bats and rodents), small distribution both fragmented or declining population and habitat degradation (e.g. most carnivores) and small declining population size (e.g. most artiodactyls). The decline in population may be attributed to trade of animal parts (e.g. Horn of *Rhinoceros unicornis,* ivory of *Elephas maximus*) and hunting (e.g.
4.	Lepidopterans	Butterflies and moths are traded as dead and live specimen. Dead specimens are mainly for collectors, for research and sometimes for exotic uses such as textiles designing in Japan. Live ones are for butterfly houses. Darjeeling is one of the focal point of illegal Lepidoptera collection. Families like Papilionidae, Danidae, Lycaenidae, etc. are special targets of collectors.
5.	Medicinal Plants	The high threatened status of medicinal plants is due to population decline, with over harvesting of the wild population being the major reason.

Badger (*Arctonyx collaris*), Burmese Ferret Badger (*Melogale personata*), Ratel (*Mellivora capensis*) belong to this category. Among birds, Bengal Florican *(Eupoditis bengalensis)* is only sporadically reported from the state.

Endemism of plants in the tidal forest of Sundarbans is very low. The species like *Sonneratia apetala, Heritierafomes, Phoenix paludosa* are main endemic species of Sundarbans (*Banerjee,* 2002). In the rest of the Bengal too, the representation of endemics are poor. However, Botanical Survey of India has identified the following endemic taxa: *Cardenthera uliginosa var. birbhumensis* from Birbhum district, *Cuscuta sharmanum* from Midnapur district, *Hydrocotyle himalaica from Darjeeling district, Hypericum assamcum from Darjeeling and Dalbergia duarensis from Alipurduar. Other endemic species are Acer osmastonii, Bulbophyllum roxburghii, etc.* (*Chakraverty, R.K. et al.,* 1999). Faunal elements of West Bengal exhibit a high degree of endemism. Among the vertebrates, the endemic taxa restricted to West Bengal include *Herpestes palustris* (Mammal) *Oligodon juglandifer* (Reptile), *Bufo abatus, Megophryus robusta, Rana senchalensis, R. annandalii, Rhacophorus jerdonii, R. dubius,* (Amphibia), *Puntius dukai* (Pisces). Some endemic fauna of India also occur in West Bengal along with some other states. The vertebrate elements of such endemic fauna included: *Anathana ellioti* (Mammals), *Perdicula manipurensis, Galloperdix lunulata* (Aves), *Sitana ponticeriana, Psammophilus blanfordanus, Japalura variegate* (Reptiles), *Ichthyophis sikkimensis, Rhacophorus tuberculatus, Limnonectus mawphlangensis* (Amphibia), *Labeo gonius, Noemacheilus devdevi, N. multifascialus, Balitora brucei* (Pisces)? (*Alfred et al,* 2005). Beside these, there are a large number of invertebrate endemic taxa. For a complete list please refer the publication *'Status of Biodiversity of West Bengal,* Vol. 1'.

CAUSES OF BIODIVERSITY LOSS

The **loss of forest** in last one and half century, particularly in last fifty years or so following independence, has been spectacular. Forests have been cleared for human settlement, for industrialization, for construction of dams and highways, for defence purposes and so on. As a result, once extensive forest tracts in south and north of Bengal was lost. Recent instances of such large scale clearing include those conducted for establishment of Durgapur Steel Plant and the township in south Bengal and for establishment of numerous military cantonments in north Bengal. Many conservationists believe that such unthoughtful destruction of forest would have continued till date but for timely enacted Forest Conservation Act in 1980. As a result of such deforestation, once extensive forest tract shrank in size and more importantly got fragmented. This can be illustrated using the example of forests of Birbhum district. The name of the district is derived from the words *'bir'* and *'bhumi'*. The former word means forest in tribal language whereas the later is a Sanskrit word meaning land. Thus, the name signifies that Birbhum was once a heavily forested land. Even at the time of Hunter's account we find that this land had extensive forest and was a part of *Junglemahal.* This forest too lost much of its spread and what remains today is a relic of the past. This, too, is fragmented into a number of small patches that struggle to keep their identity as forest. The effect of loss of forest cover and its fragmentation on biodiversity of West Bengal was automatic and severe.

Deforestation affects biodiversity through three effects: (a) habitat loss, (b) habitat fragmentation, and (c) edge effect at the boundary zone between forested and deforested areas.

It is generally argued that 'to reduce the area of a habitat is to lower the number of species that can live sustainably within it' (*Wilson*, 2002). The relationship between species richness and area is commonly approximated by the relationship given below.

$$S = cA^z$$
$$\log S = \log c + z \log A$$

where, S = number of species, A = area, c and z are constants

This is known as Arrhenius relationship. The slope of the equation (z) commonly varies from 0.25 to 0.3. This implies that a ten-fold (90%) reduction of habitat will result in loss of 50% of the species. A common example cited in support of this principle is the number of species of amphibians and reptiles in the West Indian islands of Cuba, Puerto Rico, Montserrat, Saba and Redonda. A frightening conclusion of this principle is that while removal of 90% of the forest cover still allows 50% of the species to hang on, final removal of remaining 10% of forest will wipe away reminder 50% of the species. The number of natural habitats reduced to fragments of this size or smaller is increasing (*Wilson*, 2002).

Fragmentation of forest generates a landscape consisting of remnant vegetation trapped in natural reserves that have become islands in a sea of cropland and suburban sprawl. Fragmentation results in change in the physical environment within the patches because the size of areas of vegetation influences local climate through, changes in microclimate, viz. wind turbulence, fluxes of radiation, etc. Fragmented forest patches also have a greater edge to area ratio. Smaller fragments contains proportionately more edge habitat and fragments particularly those under 10 ha. can effectively consist entirely of edge habitat. Fragment edge are generally inhospitable to a majority of native forest species. Fragments can also be bombarded with diasporas of exotic or weedy species that may be incorporated into remaining plant community. Rates of mortality and gap formation also increases near the edge after fragmentation (*Raghubangshi and Tripathy,* 2009).

In a fragmented landscape of forest, most species stay in a number of metapopulations. 'This is a network of local populations occupying discontinuous habitats, but partly connected to one another by occasional dispersal' (*Mooney et al,* 1995). Frequently, these metapopulations comprise one or more big populations and a number of small populations. In this 'mainland-island' pattern of species distribution, the population is relatively stable in the 'main land' whereas in 'islands' local population may go extinct frequently owing to disturbances, change in habitat or natural catastrophe. Such 'islands' are recolonized by immigration from the mainland.

So long as dispersal is not blocked, the species will persist in these metapopulations. The stability of species in these metapopulations depend on a number of factors like number and proximity of metapopulations, ability of the species to disperse, size of metapopulations, etc. Thus, the top predators or species with large body size and large area requirement are first to go extinct in a fragmented habitat. This is followed by extinction of the climax species which have very limited ability to disperse and colonize habitat patches. Conversely, the early successional species with their ability to disperse well and colonize patchy disturbed habitats survive well in a fragmented habitat. It has been observed that even if outright extinctions do not happen, fragmentation change the relative abundance of species in favour of early successional species and at expense of climax species. Although no study has been conducted, one can observe this pattern in the fragmented forests of south Bengal clearly.

Excessive fragmentation of forest land has also resulted in loss of critical animal corridors in north Bengal. Assessment made in 'Biodiversity Action Plan' (2002) shows that about 150 km long elephant corridor is lost in north Bengal due to diversion of forest land for rail, road or defence purposes. Earlier, an average of 4 elephants were killed per year on the railway track between Siliguri and Binnaguri. After gauge conversion, the speed of train on this route has gone up resulting in more elephant death than earlier.

Logging affects biodiversity both directly and indirectly. The former is through direct removal of the species in the logging process and the later through the disturbance that logging creates. Reduced impact logging is being advocated now-a-days to minimize its impact particularly on non-target trees; but it has limited acceptance in India. Logging practices in forests of south-west Bengal and north Bengal is such that it causes substantial damage to biodiversity. More serious are:

1. Selective removal of valuable timer species that sometimes pushes endemic or poorly represented species in the brink of extinction.
2. Logging practices that result in failure of the cut over site to regenerate (e.g., because of severe damage to soil, biotic pressure).
3. The coincident harvest of extensive areas, so that most of the landscape is in a single stage of forest stand development.
4. Maintaining stand on short rotation.

The last practice is primarily responsible for low biodiversity of forest in laterite tract of West Bengal.

Illegal logging is more damaging to the forest because it selectively removes valuable species from the forest. Moreover, the resultant gaps are often left as such owing to their small size; these blank areas may or may not regenerate depending on a number of climatic and biotic factors. There are, on the average, 7000 detected illegal tree felling cases per annum with seizure of 10000 m^3 timber. At least, an equal number of cases go undetected. Therefore, annual loss of 20000 m^3 timber takes place mainly from north Bengal forests. In addition, about 5 million m^3 fuelwood in green form is removed from the forest every year by the villagers—about 60% of this in south western Bengal and the balance in north Bengal.

Plant and animal taxas differ in their response to logging. Some animal taxas are sensitive to disturbance (amphibians, termites) and either disappear altogether or show reduced species abundance in a logged area. Birds, particularly specialized feeders, also show reduction in diversity. Conversely, some animal taxa can survive well in a logged forest (some primates). Plant diversity in a logged forest generally follows a specific pattern. Pioneer species tend to establish in open areas created by logging. These species are sun-loving, have efficient propagules (pollen, seeds), fast growth rate and high tolerance to a wide variety of environmental conditions. Hence, they are favoured in light-rich harsh microclimate created by opening of canopy. This pioneer guild is relatively homogeneous in species composition over large regions. Over time, logged forest tend to be increasingly homogeneous

Some **management practices** also caused considerable damage to biodiversity. The practice of cutting down natural forest and replanting the area with a single valuable species (commonly known as conversion to uniformity) was introduced in India by European foresters. The aim of this practice was to maximize timber production and simplify cultural operations. While this practice may not be so harmful in less diverse temperate forests, in tropical forests of India it spelled doom of biodiversity. Extensive teak plantation along Teesta valley in north Bengal was raised by cutting down species rich Sal forest. The resultant forest even after fifty years of creation do not show any sign of recovery of its original biodiversity.

Plantation creates a homogeneous forest comprising of one or a few species that are similar in age, size, etc. If the plantations use native species, the resultant stand will retain some of the original biodiversity like the parasites, symbionts and grazers of the tree species. But compared to original forest, the plantation will simplify the other components of ecosystem, not least the structure, fauna and flora of the soil. Where the plantation is raised using non-native species, as is done in industrial and social forestry plantations in West Bengal, the loss of native biodiversity is more complete through suppression of native undergrowth, parasites, etc. (*McNeely, et al,* 1995). The *Eucalyptus* and *Acacia auriculiformis* plantation raised in south Bengal over 259000 ha. area primarily to cater the need of paper mills is an example.

Grazing of cattle in forest create conditions unfavourable for retention of biodiversity. About 2/3rd of the forest, i.e. 8900 sq. km. are visited by 7 million cattle annually, causing severe damage to 10,000 ha. forest area every year. The causes of this practice may be traced to loss of traditional common lands, uneconomic returns for the development of pasture, retention of unproductive cattle for slaughter and uncontrolled cattle trade across the border. The cattle compacts the forest soil through its hoofs; this makes regeneration difficult. The palatable tree species in a new regeneration area may be lost through grazing. The cattle are often carrier of deadly diseases like anthrax and transmit them to the wildlife resulting in mass mortality. Finally, presence of large number of cattle creates disturbance in the forest making the habitat less than suitable for many disturbance-sensitive animals.

Controlled burning of different patches of the landscape at different times may help to increase biodiversity, whereas wildfires may decrease it. The long-term cumulative effect of burning can be substantial. Repeated burning of large areas of vegetation over long periods would eventually significantly modify the plant community and consequently also the associated animal community. In many areas a pyrosere is created, a biotic community resistant or adapted to fire that is prevented from further ecological succession or development by repeated burning. Recurrent ground fire in forests of south-west Bengal and hills has lead the selection process in favour of only fire-hardy species. These not only improvise the herbaceous vegetation through direct burning but also prevent regeneration of tree species.

Loss of tree cover often permits the recruitment of naturalized exotics. Establishment of *Acacia auriculiformis* over large areas in Ranibandh area of Bankura district is an example. This area was earlier covered with mixed dry deciduous forest which was subsequently cleared by illicit felling. The open area rapidly deteriorated in terms of soil quality and microclimate and the native species lost its competitive advantage in the changed condition. The exotic *Acacia* species which had source of seed in nearby areas colonized the open areas. Thus, over large areas exotic Acacia has homogenized the habitat and improvised the biodiversity.

A far more invasive species affecting the forests is maling bamboo (*Bambusa malingensis*). This temperate species is a strong light demander and colonizes open spaces and gaps in high forest. In Neora Valley National Park, West Bengal this species occupies all available floor space wherever light reaches. All gaps in canopy created by tree fall are quickly colonized by maling bamboo and new regeneration is not allowed to establish. As the rhizomes form a thick mat over the ground, no herb or shrub can grow in association with it. Availability of palatable species for the fauna is greatly reduced in the park. Thus, this species transforms the very nature of forest viz. composition, structure, etc. but most importantly the biodiversity of the area.

Another agent of ecosystem degradation is **soil erosion**. Although soil erosion is a natural process, the problem is greatly accelerated by human use of forests. Overgrazing by livestock, timber harvesting construction of forest roads, movement of vehicles are the proximate causes of soil erosion in forest land. In forest areas of Purulia, Bankura, Paschim Medinipur and Birbhum erosion is accelerated by presence of loose soil with high sand and low organic matter content. The undulating topography of the land also speeds up water movement and creates gullies.

As the forest ecosystem loses soil, its productivity is diminished. This reduces forest biomass of the area but biodiversity may remain unaffected at least in short-term. There is no simple relationship between productivity and biodiversity. Some highly productive ecosystems support very diverse biota (tropical rain forest) and some support relatively few species (salt marshes). In long-term however, diminishing productivity of forest for several centuries could be one more stressor that pushes a species that is dependent on that type of ecosystem a bit closer to extinction.

Climate change is comparatively recent addition of stressors that contribute to biodiversity loss. Range shift of species, early arrival of migratory birds, early onset of flowering and bud breaking, increasing salinization of esturine forest are some of the consequences of climate change. It is widely believed that worldwide mass mortality of amphibian caused by Chytrid fungus is triggered by warming of the planet making the fungus more virulent. Northward migration of range of many species has been detected in temperate forests of Europe and North America (*Parmesanand Yohe*, 2003). However, we have no such information about India's forests, because of paucity of studies. The occurrence of a large number of endemic species, presence of climatically vulnerable Sundarbans ecosystem, presence of preexisting stressors signify that the forests of West Bengal suffer from high degree of vulnerability from climate change.

STRATEGIES FOR CONSERVATION OF BIODIVERSITY

Removal of root causes of degradation of biodiversity in forest, theoretically speaking, is likely to restore biodiversity. However, this is difficult to implement. Given the high dependency of people residing in forest fringe areas on the forest resources, it is often not possible to restrict collection of fuel wood, NTFP or grazing of cattle. However, through the system of Joint Forest Management, access to the forest resources is sought to be regulated. In certain areas, like the laterite tract of West Bengal, this Joint Forest Management has brought about significant improvement of forest health and restoration of biodiversity. Consolidation of forest is often argued to be a solution to patchy and fragmented distribution of forests. Some success in this direction has indeed been achieved through translocation of forest villages from core to fringes of Protected Areas (PAs). But a full-fledged consolidation of forest areas is not feasible in the present socio-political environment. Ground fires in forest areas are mostly anthropogenic in origin and therefore controllable. Very often these are created by careless throwing of a burning cigarette or deliberate lighting to clear the ground of debris so as to facilitate *mohua* collection. Greater vigil on part of the Forest Protection Committees can reduce the fire incidence. Ministry of Environment and Forests, GOI, through implementation of Integrated Forest Protection scheme is trying to reduce the occurrence of fire in forests. Certain changes in forest management practices can create a positive impact on biodiversity. If plantations are raised using multiple native species and exotics are totally avoided, the resultant plantation can harbour greater biodiversity. Practicing reduced impact logging also helps in minimizing biodiversity loss during logging. It is often noticed that Sacred

Groves and Preservation Plots are like island, rich in biodiversity, in an otherwise depauperised forest. This is due to high degree of protection given to such plots by local inhabitants and forest administration. Mainstreaming such efforts of biodiversity conservation through incorporation in Working Plan may yield good result. In addition to these, certain generic measures exist for conservation of biodiversity in wilderness areas. The National Biodiversity Action Plan (2008) brought out by Ministry of Environment and Forests, Government of India gives a detailed account of such measures for conservation of biodiversity in all ecosystems found in India. The 'action points' applicable for forest areas of West Bengal include, *inter alia,* the following:

- Ensuring that human activities on the fringe areas of PAs do not degrade the habitat.
- Mitigating man-animal conflict, (e.g. elephant depredation of forest fringe villages in south and north Bengal forests).
- Conservation of forest preservation plots.
- Protecting areas of high endemism of genetic resources (biodiversity hotspots) while providing alternative livelihoods and access of resources to the local communities who may be affected thereby.
- Captive breeding and release into the wild of identified endangered species, (e.g. Red Panda breeding and reintroduction programme in P.N. Himalayan Zoological Park, Darjeeling, Crocodile breeding and reintroduction programme at Bhagabatipur, Sundarbans).
- Reintroduction of viable populations of threatened plant species.
- Promoting ecological and socially sensitive tourism and pilgrimage activities through adoption of best practice norms, (e.g. trekking in Nanda Devi Biosphere Reserve, Uttarakhand).
- Formulating and implementing programmes for conservation of endangered species outside PAs.
- Supporting capacity building for managing invasive alien species at different levels with priority on local area activities.
- Promoting restorative measures of degraded ecosystems

(invaded by Invasive Alien Species) using locally adapted native species.

- Promoting decentralized management of biological resources with emphasis on community participation, (e.g. the system of managing biodiversity at the grass-root level through Biodiversity Management Committees/ Forest Protection Committees/Eco-Development Committees).
- Promote sustainable use of biological resources.
- Integrating biodiversity concerns across development sectors (such as industry, infrastructure, power, mining etc.) and promote use of clean technologies.
- According priority to the potential impacts of development projects on biodiversity resources and natural heritage while undertaking EIA. In particular, ancient sacred groves and biodiversity hotspots should be treated as possessing incomparable values.
- Ensuring that in all cases of diversion of forest land, the essential minimum needed land for the project or activity is permitted. Restrict the diversion of dense natural forests, particularly areas of high endemism of genetic resources, to non-forest purpose, only to site specific cases of vital national interest.

References

Alfred, J.R.B., A.K. Sanyal, S. Tiwari and S. Mitra (2005): *Status of Biodiversity of West Bengal,* Final Technical Report, Vols. 1 & 2. Unpublished.

Banerjee, L.K. (2002): 'Sundarbans Biosphere Reserve'. *Floristic Diversity and Conservation Strategies in India,* Vol. V: *in situ* and *ex situ* Conservation, (eds), N.P. Singh and K.P. Singh, Botanical Survey of India, Kolkata, India

Bhattacharyya, U.C. (1997): 'Introduction' *Flora of West Bengal,* Vol. 1, Botanical Survey of India, Kolkata, India.

Chakraberty, R.K., R.C. Srivastava, S. Mitra, S. Bandopadhyay and S. Bandopadhyay (1999): 'West Bengal' *Floristic Diversity and Conservation Strategies in India,* Vol. III: In the Context of States and Union Territories, (eds.) V. Mudgal and P.K. Hazra, Botanical Survey of India, Kolkata, India

Champion, H.G. and S.K. Seth (1968): *A Revised Survey of Forest Types of India.* Manager of Publications, Delhi.

Daniel, J.C. (2002): *The Book of Indian Reptiles and Amphibians*, Bombay Natural History Society, Oxford University Press, India.

Dept. of Environment and Ramakrishna Mission, Narendrapur (2002): *West Bengal State Biodiversity Strategy and Action Plan.*

Gaston, K.J and J.I. Spicer (2004): *Biodiversity: An Introduction,* 2nd Ed., Blackwell Publishing, Oxford.

Halliday, T. (2001): 'Endangered Reptiles and Amphibians', *Encyclopedia of Biodiversity,* Vol. 2 (ed.) S.A. Levin, Academic Press, California, USA.

Hunter, M.L. Jr. (2002): *Fundamentals of Conservation Biology,* 2nd ed., Blackwell Science.

Hunter, W.W. (1875-77): *A Statistical Account of Bengal,* BiblioBazaar, LLC.

Kumar, A., S. Walker and S. Molur (2000): 'Prioritisation of Endangered Species', *Setting Biodiversity Conservation Priorities for India* (eds.) S. Singh, A.R.K. Singh, R. Mehta and V. Uppal, WWF—India, New Delhi, India.

Macdonald, D.W., C.M. King and R. Strachan (2007): 'Introduced Species and the Line between Biodiversity Conservation and Naturalistic Eugenics', *Key Topics in Conservation Biology* (eds.) D. Macdonald and K. Service, Blackwell Publishing, Oxford.

McNeely, J.A., M. Gadgil, C. Leveque, C. Padoch, K. Redford (1995): 'Human Influences on Biodiversity', *Global Biodiversity Assessment* (ed.) V.H. Heywood, Cambridge University Press.

Menon, V. and A. Kumar (1998): *Wildlife Crime: An Enforcement Guide,* 2nd Ed., Wildlife Protection Society of India, New Delhi.

Messmer, T.A. (2000): The Emergence of Human-Wildlife Conflict Management: Turning Challenges into Opportunities, *International Biodeterioration & Biodegradation,* Vol. 45.

Millenium Ecosystem Assessment (2005): *Ecosystem and Human Well-Being: Synthesis,* Island Press, Washington, DC.

Ministry of Environment and Forests, Government of India (2008): *National Biodiversity Action Plan.*

O'Malley, L.S.S. (1787): *Bengal District Gazetteers—Birbhum,* 1st Reprint: October 1996, Govt. of West Bengal.

Parmesan, C. and G. Yohe (2003): 'A Globally Coherent Fingerprint of Climate Change: Impacts Across Natural Systems', *Nature,* 421: (37-42).

Raghubanshi and Tripathi (2009): 'Effect of Disturbance, Habitat Fragmentation and alien Invasive Plants on Floral Diversity in Dry Tropical Forests of Vindhyan Highland: a Review', *Tropical Ecology,* Vol. 50, No. 1.

Singh, A.K., R.R. Singh and S. Chowdhury (2002): 'Human-Elephant Conflicts in Changed Landscapes of South West Bengal, India,' *Indian Forester,* India.

Wilson, E.O. (2002): *The Future of Life,* Abacus, U.K.

Biodiversity and Sustainable Development in an Indian Tribal Village Ecosystem

N.C. Sahu, C.D. Panda and L.P. Panda

Biodiversity is the most valuable and basic natural capital for sustainable development of human society. It has salutary interface with cultural and human-made capital. The biological resources promote and maintain quality of life through several ways. Two aspects of the contributions of biodiversity to the quality of life and sustainable development of the tribals are addressed in this paper. The first relates to a low cost healthy balanced diet, which a tribal family ensures from the surrounding environment. The second is the diversity of shifting and settled cultivation, and forest-related activities, which prevents a tribal economy to become vulnerable to the uncertainty and unsustainability associated with monoculture. These issues are examined through a case study of a Lanjia Saura tribal village ecosystem, namely, Gadiabanga, located five kms. away from Gunupur town in Rayagada district of Orissa, India. The households produce 14 types of crops, of which a major part comes from *Podu* (shifting) cultivation. They collect 15 types of products from the surrounding forests. An analysis of the systems of production, consumption, exports and imports in terms of physical, monetary and energy flows in a modified Keynesian framework shows that the Gidabanga tribals not only protect themselves by producing a large variety of commodities, but also export biological resources for promotion of the quality of life elsewhere.

I. INTRODUCTION

Biodiversity refers to wealth of life on earth. Loss of biodiversity affects the very basis of life in many ways. Being the most important component of natural capital of a human economy, it has very close interface with cultural and human-made capital. Through these interactive influences biodiversity fosters sustainable development. The biological resources promote and maintain quality of life in several ways such as food security, coping with uncertainty, ecological balance, outdoor recreation, high option and existence values and so on. This paper addresses the first two aspects in the context of the quality of life of the tribals in India. The objectives are to assess and estimate how a tribal family ensures a low cost healthy balanced diet, which comes from the surrounding environment. Then it critically appreciates an important function of biodiversity. It relates to the process through which diversity of shifting and settled cultivation, and forest-related activities prevent a tribal economy to become vulnerable to the uncertainties associated with monoculture. The problem is addressed through a case study of a Lanjia Saura tribal village ecosystem, namely Gadiabanga, located five kms. away from Gunupur town in Rayagada district of south Orissa, India.

II. IMPLICATIONS OF SUSTAINABLE DEVELOPMENT FOR BIODIVERSITY

Sustainable development (SD) has been a challenge to the humanity. In terms of public passion and intellectual engagement it hardly has any parallel. By its very nature, it keeps evolving and adapting to the ever-changing world. Its true appreciation can occur only through a trans-disciplinary framework. There is a consensus now that SD is open to several interpretations. It is a contestable concept like democracy, truth, honesty, peace or justice. It is not possible to define SD in the same way as one can define a standard measuring meter. But the very pluralistic basis of the concept is its strength. All great ideas are usually simple ideas, and SD is no exception. The first step to articulate the sustainability process is to recognize that it is essentially a management or an organizing principle. The pursuit of SD is the facilitation of a dynamic socio-economic process that maintains harmony with nature.

One implication is that the conditions for SD are to be identified through the interdependent ecological and economic approaches. Under both, constancy of the ecological state or capital stock is the fundamental requirement. The capital stock of an economy, which has to remain constant over time, comprises of the following three components.

- ***Natural capital:*** *Nature's dowry to humans* (Non-renewable resources, Renewable resources and Environmental services).
- ***Cultural capital:*** *Factors that provide means and adaptations to deal with nature* (World view, Environmental ethics, TEK, Social/Political institutions, and so on).
- ***Human-made capital:*** *Produced means of production* (Provisions generated via economic activity through human ingenuity and technological change).

Operationalisation of sustainability is guided by theories of SD. Given the widely accepted formulation that it implies non-declining per capita human well-being, two main theories have been proposed with reference to the capital theory in economics. The fundamental condition of sustainability is the maintenance of capital stock, which yields a flow of goods and services into the future. The overall capital stock at any point of time comprises of *natural capital* (K_n), *human-made capital* (K_m), the overlapping category of *cultivated natural capital* (K_{mn}), which include agriculture, aquaculture, plantation forestry and so on, and *cultural capital* (K_c) that occurs at the interface between K_m and K_n. One can, however, decompose K_{mn} into its K_n and K_m components. For example, a plantation forest has K_n component of sunlight, rainfall and soil nutrients; and K_m component of management services of planting, spacing, control of diseases, and so on.

There are two ways to maintain total capital constant over time. The *sum* of K_m and K_n can be maintained constant in some aggregate sense; or *each* component can be maintained constant separately, again in some aggregate value sense. In the latter case there is aggregation only within the two categories and not across them. The first way is reasonable if K_m and K_n are believed as substitutes. According to this view it is acceptable to divest K_n as long as one creates K_m of equivalent value by investment. The second way is reasonable if one believes that K_m and K_n are complements. The complements must each be maintained constant, separately or jointly in fixed proportion because the productivity of one depends on the availability of the other. The first case is called *week* sustainability (WS) and the second case *strong* sustainability (SS) (*Daly*, 2005).

In a large part of mainstream economics, K_m and K_n are considered as mainly substitutes. But ecological economists believe that the two are fundamentally complements and only marginally substitutes. Had they been substitutes, why did we bother to accumulate K_m in the first place, as we were already rich by nature with a perfect substitute? Further, K_m is a physical transformation of K_n, and production of the former requires the latter as an input. K_n is the material cause of production and K_m is the efficient cause of production. The material cause and efficient cause are complements, not substitutes (*Daly*, 1991).

In the ultimate analysis, SD implies that every future generation must have the option of being as well-off as its predecessor. In order to maintain a constant potential for wealth creation, the economy must maintain a constant means of production. This includes human-made capital, human capital (the level of learning), natural resources and technology. A sustainable path implies that along it the overall productive capacity is not reduced. As per the Solow-Hartwick approach, which comes under WS paradigm, what is necessary to know and monitor at each moment in time is how much of this productive base we can use up. This is given by environmentally adjusted net national product (ENNP) or '*green* NNP' (*Hanley et al.*, 1997), which is a measure of the total income earned by the economy in any year, less an allowance for the depreciation of K_M and K_N. This is the annual *pay-off* from the total capital ($K_N + K_M$) stock of an economy. In this paper an attempt is made to measure the Gross Village Income of Gadiabanga, which can be monitored over time for any such tribal village.

III. MATERIALS AND METHODS

This paper involves processing of a vast mass of secondary and primary materials. While the secondary information help us to build the detailed socio-economic and ecological profile of the village, the central theme is addressed with a large amount of field data. The primary information gathered from the village hovers around the annual product flows, first in physical terms, and then in terms of economic values and energy contents. After preliminary survey of the village, a questionnaire-*cum*-schedule was used during 2001. A census approach was followed to collect the data from each of the sixty households of Gadiabanga.

During the process of data collection, information on production, consumption, exports and imports of each of the item were maintained in local measures. Conversion factors were developed by physical weighing of most of the items to make quantitative analysis with standardized data. The prices of the different commodities and items were ascertained from Gadiabanga, Gunupur and Brahmani weekly market (*Hata*). Later, after thorough discussion with the tribals the ex-village price set was finalised. The local rates and conversion factors are used to construct a constant price set at standard units of weights and measures. For the purpose of understanding the process of shifting cultivation and other production activities and finalisation of prices, a series of PRA (Participatory Rural Appraisal) type surveys (*Mukherjee*, 1995) were conducted in the village.

The collected data were collated through several stages of tabulation. At the stage of primary tabulation, datasets were prepared for all the households, separately for twelve major aspects of the tribal life in the village. These include information on the particulars of the family, property, shifting cultivation, agriculture, home garden, miscellanies crops, livestock production, forest-related activities, labour inputs to each production sector, daily wage income, loan and debt, and the links with the market.

In order to appreciate the activities of the people in ecological terms, and analyse the energy flows through the ecosystem, energy contents of the different items are used. The set of inanimate and animate energy contents of the different items are taken from several published works including Dash and Misra (2001); Nayak *et al* (1993); Misra and Dash (2000); Nisanka and Misra (1990a and b).

The total value of property is estimated as the sum of the money value of land, house and cattle owned by a household. The value of annual production, income, consumption, exports and imports were determined from the weekly and monthly diary records maintained in physical terms by using the final price set. For each family these variables were estimated as, the sum of the value of the output from *Podu* (local name of shifting cultivation), agriculture, home garden, miscellanies crops, forests, livestock and daily wage sectors. Human energy inputs were recorded in terms of the hours of work devoted to a particular process of activity. Then for estimating employment, a human day is taken as 8 and 12 hours of work for the adults and children respectively.

IV. THE STUDY VILLAGE

The hamlet village, Gadiabanga is located at 83° 50' to 83° 53' 24" East longitude and 19° 5' to 19° 6' North latitude. The village is bounded by Pedakonda reserve forest in the South, which stretches towards the East. There exists the Rangamati reserve forest to the North and Gunupur town to the West. The village appears as a small compact patch on the foothills of large mountains.

The settlement area has a T-shape. The houses stretch through two rows. The houses are constructed with mud and bamboo. The roof is made of thatch grass collected from the forest. Typically there are no windows looking outwards. Verandah is meant for keeping their cot and by-cycle. The cowsheds are not adjacent to their houses. They occur on either ends of the *basti*. Cooking is generally done in the courtyards. The houses are neat and clean. Cow dung is used for cementing the floors. The women use the *basti* road for drying their podu crops.

The village comes under the Eastern Ghat agro-climatic zone of the state. The temperature varies between a minimum of 17.18° in winter to a maximum of 36.58° Celsius in summer (Sub-Collectorate, Gunupur). The climate of the area is of tropical monsoon type with pronounced summer. Rainfall is quite uncertain and erratic in nature. The average annual rainfall in the block is about 1228 mm. It has been seen that 70% to 80% rainfall is recorded normally during the monsoon months.

As per the 1991 census, the village consisted of 60 households with a population of 216, whereas in the 2001 census, the number of households increased to 69 with a population 350 (Tehsil Office, Gunupur). The people of the village belong to the *'Saura'* or *'Savaras'* tribe. The Savaras are the second largest tribal community in Orissa, after the Kondhs (*GOO*, 1989). It is one of the ancient aboriginal tribes of this country. It is believed that ten years ago the tribes of Gadiabang were recognized as *Lanjia Saura* but the characteristics and the identity of this seems to have been lost since long, especially after the operation of the Christian missionaries. The occupational pattern of the people in the village is predominantly agricultural (both hill and plain cultivation) and its allied activities. All the households of the village are practicing shifting *(podu)* cultivation.

The educational profile of the village shows that only 11% of the population is literate, which is much lower than the district and State literacy rates of 21.46 percent and 36.78 percent respectively (*GOO*, 2001). Male literacy is 9 percent, which is far higher than the female literacy rate of only 2 percent. There is a Sevashram primary school in the village.

The people are accustomed to taking food thrice a day. Gruel prepared from great millet flour serves as the breakfast. Rice and red gram are taken during the lunchtime in the *podu* field or inside the forest. During evening, mohua liquor or sago palm (salap) sap is consumed by all, irrespective of age and sex. Tobacco leaves are rolled inside sal leaves and smoked as *pika* by the males.

The Gadiabanga Savaras no more use their traditional clothes since the last two decades. They now wear simple dress. The men use half pant and a banyan during their work in the field. The women wear *langa* and blouse. The health of the men is characterized by strength and symmetry. The muscles of the limbs and body are clean and well developed. The skin is clean and glossy and the foot is relatively larger. The women are short, robust and sturdy. They are simple and frank, and naive in nature. The entire tract is very much malaria prone.

The Savaras observe a number of festivals and ceremonies at different stages of *podu* cultivation. The villagers celebrate different festivals in the name of the crops, such as Kandula Parab, Jana Parab, Kangu Parab and Dhana Parab. All the Savaras of the village are converted to Christians during the last 10 years. 'Badadina' is the main festival of the village people.

V. USES OF BIODIVERSITY: A MACRO FRAMEWORK

This section looks at the village Gadiabanga as an integrated economic and ecological system. There occurs flows of consumable products, non-consumable (from the point of view of human economy) biomass, money, and animate and inanimate energy through the system. Thus the flows of commodities are analysed in physical, value and energy terms. The processes of income, consumption, exports, imports, employment, inequality and poverty are critically examined.

From settled cultivation only vegetables like brinjal, chilly and tomato are exported. The *podu* products like castor, cowpea and niger flow out from the system. Red gram and horse gram are produced under both settled and shifting cultivation. Thus as many as 17 diverse items provide subsistence and nutrition to the tribals of the village. Quantitatively the forest sector contributes significantly to exports. The export items are firewood, bamboo, thatch grass, mohua flower, tooth stick and cashew nuts in the order of quantitative importance. Chicken is the only livestock output exported from Gadiabanga. The food items which are imported to Gadiabanga from the market are finger millet, meat, dry fish, sugar and gur, karamanga (vegetable), maize, milk powder, mohua liquor, rice, salt and tobacco.

The value of annual commodity flows in the Gadiabanga economy is presented in Table 1. In a macro sense, the open economy is viewed in the form of a modified Keynesian equation, such as $Y = P = C + (X - M)$. The aggregate Gross Domestic product of the village is estimated at Rs. 6.89 lakhs. The consumption, exports and imports are respectively Rs. 6.23 lakhs, Rs. 3.02 lakhs and Rs. 2.36 lakhs. The element of self-sufficiency of Gadiabanga system, being contributed and fostered by biological resources, is significantly visible from these figures. While comparing the physical and monetary flows it can be noted that the services of the bullock pairs are not transformed in money form. The village exports daily wage work service worth about Rs. 73,000 which is added to the income, though its physical dimension is not shown in Table 1. The village imports education, health care and transport services. One missing link in the modified Keynesian open economy equation relates to saving and

TABLE 1

Value of Annual Commodity Flows in Gadiabanga Economy

Sl. No.		*Aggregate (Rs. × 10³)*			*Per capita (Rs.)*		
		P	*C*	*X*	*M*	*P*	*C*
1	*2*	*3*	*4*	*5*	*6*	*7*	*8*
Settled Cultivation							
1.	Paddy	64.20	64.20	—	—	222.14	222.14
2.	Brinjal	11.00	2.30	8.70	—	38.05	7.96
3.	Carpet legume	2.07	2.07	—	—	7.17	7.17
4.	Chilli (Dry)	8.96	7.86	1.10	—	31.00	27.20
5.	Tomato	2.87	2.85	0.02	—	9.92	9.87
6.	Bottle gourd	4.72	4.72	—	—	16.33	16.33
7.	Papaya	1.06	1.06	—	—	3.67	3.67
8.	Plantain (Dozen)	3.51	3.51	—	—	12.15	12.15
9.	Red Pumpkin	3.85	3.85	—	—	13.34	13.34
10.	Ridged gourd	0.97	0.97	—	—	3.36	3.36
Shifting Cultivation							
11.	Castor	14.56	—	14.56	—	50.38	—
12.	Cow pea	2.37	1.59	0.78	—	8.19	5.51
13.	Fox tail millet	6.07	4.12	1.95	—	21.00	14.26
14.	Great millet	31.64	31.64	—	—	109.47	109.47
15.	Horsegram[1]	14.21	14.10	0.11	—	49.16	48.79
16.	Redgram[1]	48.64	34.01	14.63	—	168.29	117.67
17.	Niger	1.28	0.55	0.73	—	4.44	1.91
Forest							
18.	Bamboo	18.49	2.93	15.56	—	63.99	10.15
19.	Cashew apple[2]	0.43	0.43	—	—	1.50	1.50
20.	Cashew nuts	44.00	—	44.00	—	152.25	—
21.	Firewood	79.30	40.38	38.93	—	274.39	139.71
22.	Hill broom	0.82	0.82	—	—	2.84	2.84
23.	Housewood	5.96	5.96	—	—	20.64	20.64
24.	Jackfruit[2]	0.55	0.55	—	—	1.89	1.89
25.	Mango	12.45	12.45	—	—	43.06	43.06
26.	Mohua flower	63.20	—	63.20	—	218.69	—
27.	Sap of Sago Palm[2]	56.00	56.00	—	—	193.77	193.77
28.	Tamarind pulp[2]	0.95	0.95	—	—	3.27	3.27

1 2	3	4	5	6	7	8
29. Thatch grass	30.50	11.92	18.58	—	105.54	41.25
30. Tooth stick	4.57	1.52	3.05	—	15.81	5.27
31. Bird (Gunduri)[2]	6.55	6.55	—	—	22.66	22.66
Livestock						
32 Chicken[2]	5.13	1.88	3.25	—	17.75	6.51
33. Cow dung[3]	59.79	59.79	—	—	206.89	206.89
34. Egg	5.38	5.38	—	—	18.61	18.61
35. Meat[2]	—	44.00	—	44.00	—	152.25
Other items						
36. Bamboo basket	—	2.40	—	2.40	—	8.30
37. Clothes	—	16.24	—	16.24	—	56.19
38. Dry fish	—	9.31	—	9.31	—	32.21
39. Finger millet	—	10.42	—	10.42	—	36.06
40. Gur	—	1.73	—	1.73	—	5.99
41. Karamanga	—	0.69	—	0.69	—	2.39
42. Kerosene	—	1.16	—	1.16	—	4.01
43. Maize	—	1.37	—	1.37	—	4.74
44. Milk powder	—	5.90	—	5.90	—	20.42
45. Mohua liquor	—	75.45	—	75.45	—	261.07
46. Rice (FFW)	—	13.18	—	13.18	—	45.61
47. Salt	—	4.25	—	4.25	—	14.70
48. Sugar	—	2.91	—	2.91	—	10.07
49. Thatch rope	—	0.24	—	0.24	—	0.83
50. Tobacco	—	5.20	—	5.20	—	17.99
51. Wage/service	73.11	—	73.11	0.00	0.25	0.00
52. Education	—	4.05	—	4.05	—	0.01
53. Medicine	—	4.25	—	4.25	—	0.01
54. Festivals	—	11.42	—	11.42	—	0.04
55. Miscellaneous	—	21.43	—	21.43	—	0.07
Total	689.15	622.51	302.24	235.60	2131.88	2011.78

Note: P = Production, C = Consumption, X = Export and M = Import.

1. Includes the production under both settled and shifting cultivation.
2. Not included in the income of the individual households, as family specific production data could not be obtained.
3. Cow dung is a waste in the commercial sense, but it is left in the environment for recycling and consumed in the ecosystem through the natural ecological process of decomposition.

investment. The Savaras of Gadiabanga do not have savings worth the name in any institutionalized form except those mobilized through the Self-Help Group. The so-called investments come from the land development loans. It is to be appreciated that the saving-investment identity is a less visible process through the income-consumption system. Yet another invisible item relates to a type of savings in the form of storage of seeds. As it could not be possible to obtain appropriate information with the proper weights and measures at the family level, seeds are to be seen as parts of both production and consumption.

The economic value of cow dung has a unique position in the system. The livestock of the village generate about 60 tons of cow dung, whose money value comes to about Rs. 60,000. In a commercial sense, the dung is a waste. Even though, the Savaras do not take specific care to make compost, cow dung can be viewed as a material left in the ecosystem for recycling through the natural ecological process of decomposition. Thus, cow dung is considered as an ecological consumption of the system. Another set of similar items like the crop straws and residues could have been shown in the production and consumption of the system. Because of lack of information of prices these are estimated only in physical and energy terms.

Like cow dung, there are some other products which could not be considered as income of the individual households. Such items mostly derived from the forests include cashew apple, jackfruit, sap of sago palm (locally known as *Salap tadi* widely used as a mild intoxicating drink), tamarind pulp and wild birds. In the livestock sector chicken and meat also are not added to family income and consumption. The main reason, why it could not be included in the family incomes is non-availability of family specific production/collection data. The per-capita income and consumption are estimated at Rs. 2,132 and Rs. 2012 respectively. The net disposable incomes available to the individual families will, of course, be less because of the considerations such as those related to animal dung as noted here.

The ecosystem of Gadiabanga is an integrated entity in terms of energy transfers among the sectors. There occur transfers inside the system and exchanges across the other systems. Notwithstanding the usual critical view that economics represent 'monetary reductionism' and ecology involves 'energy reductionism' (*Soderbaum*, 1989), there are advantages in the articulation of the flows through money and energy. Just as it is not easily possible to express some type of service flows, such as tribal festivals in physical terms, it is difficult to articulate the value of crop straws and residues in economic terms. Consideration of flows in terms of energetic is relatively more comprehensive, even though willy nilly, we have to leave energy of inorganic materials like salt, chemical and drugs. After taking into account several additional features and a few left outs, the components of Keynesian modified equation such as production, consumption, export and import are respectively (in terms of GJ per year) estimated at about 4838, 3809, 1217 and 188. The per capita production and consumption per day are estimated at 45.86 and 36.11 MJ respectively. From the biomass composition of various types of settled and shifting cultivation crops, it has been found that the straw and residue components, which are ecologically consumed in the system, are much larger varying between 40.5% and 80.5%, than the grains and seeds, consumable by the humans (based on *Dash and Misra*, 2001; and *Nayak et al.*, 1993)

VI. COMPLEMENTARITY AND COMPETITIVENESS AMONG SECTORS

The Savaras households of Gadiabanga derive around 13% to 22% of income from *podu*. It has been observed that *podu* income is more stable and secure than the same from daily wage and paddy. Moreover, it is complementary to other activities and capable of meeting the resilience condition of the system. Because of simultaneous sowing and sequential harvesting, the *podu* crops are an insurance against uncertainty. This is the most important reason behind the continuation of the age old practice of shifting cultivation.

However, element of competitiveness among sectors is also found in terms of the claims of different activities on human labour. In other words, all activities compete for the human energy inputs of a family. So far as demand on human labour is concerned, the claim of *podu* sector is very high (about 45%). The forest sector takes the 3rd position after agriculture. The forests, which generate the highest income particularly because of the returns from plantations, require less than half the human energy required for shifting cultivation. The clue for intensifying investment in natural capital so as to promote ecological health for sustainable development of a system lies here.

VII. CONCLUSIONS

This paper examines how diversity of biological resources at the command of a tribal village ecosystem promotes quality of life by providing nutritious food, relative self-sufficiency of economic life and a coping mechanism against uncertainty. In Gadiabanga, the Savara households derive the bulk of their food requirements from a diverse of items produced through shifting and settled cultivation, and collection of forest produce. The macro-economic analysis indicates that the village is capable of generating surplus of biological resources. The process of simultaneous sowing and sequential harvesting of *podu* crops is a traditional natural insurance against uncertainty. Moreover, *podu* crops are complementary to the available other economic activities. But the element of competitiveness observed in respect of the demand on human energy shows that the tribal economy would gain and achieve sustainable development if the forest resources are protected and promoted.

The Gross Village Income estimated in this paper is a rough parallel of ENNP suggested in the Solow-Hartwick approach. By deducting the depreciation of natural capital over time, one can estimate environmentally-adjusted net village product. This can be used as an indicator of sustainable development of a tribal village ecosystem like Gadiabanga, which requires a sound accounting framework at the micro-level. Soil erosion is a fundamental outcome of tribal agriculture, which implies depletion of a natural capital. However, shifting cultivation is a resilient system. Therefore, the trade-off should be dealt through a careful strategy, for which a nation-wide machinery of *Micro-Planning for Sustainable Development* is necessary in India.

REFERENCES

Daly, H.E. (1991), 'Ecological Economics and Sustainable Development', C. Rossi and E. Tiezzi (Editors), *Ecological Physical Chemistry*, Elsevier, Amsterdam, pp. 185-201.

Daly, H.E. (2005), 'Operationalizing sustainable development by investing in natural capital', N.C. Sahu and A.K. Choudhury (ed.), *Dimensions of Environmental and Ecological Economics*, Universities Press/Orient Longman, pp. 481-94.

Dash, S.S. and M.K. Misra (2001), "Studies on hill agro-ecosystems of the tribal villages on the Eastern Ghat of Orissa, India," *Agriculture, Ecosystems and Environment*, Vol. 86, pp. 287-302.

GOO (1989), *Working Plan for the Reserved and Rayagada Forest Division, 1989-90 to 1998-99 for ten years*, District Forest Office, Rayagada.

GOO (2001), *Economic Survey*, Director of Economics and Statistics, Planning and Coordination Department, Bhubaneswar.

Hanley, N., J. Shogren, and B. White (1997), *Environmental Economics in Theory and Practice*, Macmillan Press, p. 464.

Misra, M.K. and S.S. Dash (2000), "Biomass and energetic of non-timber forest resource in a cluster of tribal village on the Eastern Ghat of Orissa, India," *Biomass and Bioenergy*, 1.8, pp. 229-47.

Mukherjee, N. (1995), *Participatory Rural Appraisal and Questionnaire Survey: Comparative Field Experience and Methodological Innovations*, Concept Publishing Company, New Delhi, p. 163.

Nayak, S.P., S.K. Nisanka and M.K. Misra (1993), "Biomass and energy dynamics in a tribal village ecosystem of Orissa, India," *Biomass and Energy*, Vol. 4, No. 1, pp. 23-34.

Nisanka, S.K and M.K. Misra (1990a), "Ecological study of an Indian village ecosystem; biomass production and consumption," *Biomass*, 23, Elsevier Science Publishers Ltd., England, pp. 117-36.

Nisanka, S.K and Misra (1990b), "Ecological study of an Indian Village Ecosystem: Energetics," *Biomass*, 23, Elsevier Science Publishers Ltd., England, pp. 165-78.

Soderbaum, P. (1989), "Paradigms and Environmental Economics," A Dubgaard and A.H. Nielsen (Editors), Economic Aspects of Environmental Regulations in Agriculture, Proceedings of the Symposium of the European Association of Agricultural Economists, 1-4 November, Tune, Copenhagen, Denmark, Wissenschaftverlag Vauk, Kiel, pp. 309-24.

Degrading the Development or Developing the Degradation?: A Case of Soil Salinity in Sugarcane Belt of Maharashtra

V.B. JUGALE

The human interaction with land, water, minerals, air and ecosystem are alarming with the red signals. The ecological values along with socio-cultural and ethical values have put moral "limits to the growth". Soil salinity in a very fertile land area is one of the most serious disorders of ecology and environment. The micro-organisms helpful for the growth of crops lessen due to improper use of chemical fertilizers and unscientific application of irrigation water during the cultivation of certain crops like sugarcane in western Maharashtra. An attempt has been made here to exhibit the economic problems of soil salinisation and to find out the remedial techniques. Normally, the farmers are blamed for their mismanagement of water resources and mis-priorities of cultivation of sugarcane in western Maharashtra. There is an immediate need to concentrate on the institutional and state efforts to ameliorate the salinity and alkalinity in the sugarcane belt. This will not only reward the farmers but also help to attain a standard level of sustainable agricultural development, which is urged on the eve of structural adjustments in the economy.

Key Words: soil salinity, sugarcane belt, water logging.

INTRODUCTION

The natural resources are either misused or extensively exploited for the selfish motives of the public. The carelessness in such resource use is consequential to the ecological and environmental disorders. Resource degradation and resource recycling are becoming the burning issues of the governance. The human interaction with land, water, minerals, air and cco-system are alarming with the red signals. The ecological values along with socio-cultural and ethical values have put moral "limits to the growth."

Soil is being degraded or exploited exhaustively without maintaining the original organic structure of the carbon, which is essential for earth's eco-system. In fact, earth's original structure consists of the carbon. The inorganic components have dismantled the organic structure of the soil through human interaction with the nature. So, it is one of the causes of ecological and environmental disorder. The use of resources for growth or regeneration or recycling of the resources is in fact a matter of economics; hence, the resource economics, bio-economics, ecological economics and environmental economics are becoming important issues of the governance.

The neo-classical capital (resources as capital) theory necessitates the private ownership for the rational use of natural resources. But the modern economists advocate the need of the joint management of the common resources as an effective media of reinstating the natural resources.

SOIL SALINITY IN SUGARCANE BELT: A CURSE ON THE HUMAN INTERACTION

Land is a traditional input to the production, and the influence of both land area and land qualities on economic scarcity have long been the subject of debate. Analysis of the role of land quantity on output has involved classic applications of the production function. But analysis of the role of land quality and land characteristics is more recent and has proved less straight forward. Soil salinity *vis-a-vis* various other types of soil degradation is caused by an increase of salts in the soil; build-up of free salts; (also called alkalization), the development of dominance of the exchange complex by sodium. As human-induced processes, these occur mainly through incorrect planning and management of irrigation schemes, saline intrusion, and incursion of sea water into coastal soils arising from over-abstraction of groundwater.*

Agriculture sector under the Green Revolution programmes has seen considerable transformation during the post-GR period. An increase in fertilizer use, pesticides, irrigation. HYVP seeds were accounted for better agriculture. However, the use of such biotechnology often have damaged the off-farm effects like quality of water, soil quality, ground water potebility, salinity and alkalinity, human health and biodiversity in a long period of time than the short-run on-farm benefits. Use of inorganic fertilizers supplemented the soil with loss of nutrients due to lack of organic matters, thereby lowering of water retention capacity, which again leads to compaction, increased run-off and loss of soil. Besides, fertilizer use causes leakages/run-off into surface water and groundwater. It has serious environmental consequences such as erophication (nitrogen and phosphorous over-concentration due to fertilizer run-off/leaching). This in reverse leads to explosive growth of algae, oxygen depletion, and death of fish and loss of biodiversity. The health and ecological impact of pesticides cannot be neglected. Similarly, irrigation results in water logging, salinisation, erosion, etc. the downstream land is degraded by salts, agrochemicals and toxic leacharts.

Soil salinity in a very fertile land area is one of the most serious disorders of ecology and environment. The micro organisms helpful for the growth of crops lessen due to improper use of chemical fertilizers and unscientific application of irrigation water during the cultivation of certain crops like sugarcane in western Maharashtra. In some parts of the western Maharashtra salinity

Note: * A complete classification of soil degradation is given in Oldeman (1991), quoted in Fourth Sub-regional Training Workshop on Environment Statistics, Bangkok, 1-12 October 2001, Agri-environmental Statistics, Soil Degradation prepared by: Statistics Division, FAO.

has assumed serious proportions warranting all our efforts towards its amelioration. Soil salinisation has caused the deterioration of the soil texture, soil structure and productive contents of the soils, resulting to a constant decrease in the crop yield since last 20 years. Soil salinity generally is developed as a result of the accumulation of chlorides, sulphates, phosphates, carbonates and bicarbonates of Calcium, Magnesium and Sodium. Generally, about 20 per cent of the basal dose of synthetic fertilisers applied to a crop is utilised by the crops through absorption and assimilation, the rest of it leaching down and sedimenting on the sub-soils, only re-rise to the surface soil resulting in soil salinity or in extreme cases even alkalinity. A constant use of brackish irrigation water and the blocking of natural trenches and free flowing rivulets in greedy pursuit to avail of more cultivable land and water by farmers also resulted in spoiling cultivable lands. Chemical ameliorants like gypsum (calcium sulphate) are generally useful as soil correctives, although it needs to be considered in addition of gypsum as desirable in soils having excess calcium or sulphates. Sulphur could be used in soils having excessive calcium.

The salinity affected area in the sugarcane belt of Maharashtra was well known for its fertile land area, which had a guarantee of crop yield even during the scanty rainfall. Unfortunately, neither the farmers nor the government or semi-government organizations have initiated to check further deterioration of soil fertility caused by improper agricultural input management, which should be adhered to mass movement for land reclamation and soil protection in sugarcane belt of Western Maharashtra.

The lift irrigation commands are generally seen in western Maharashtra. The salinity in water logging areas is caused by perennial irrigation water in the command area. But the salinity in fertile cultivable land area is caused by land topography, lack of drainage and misuse of irrigation water and chemical fertilizers for the commercial crops like sugarcane in western Maharashtra. Except the land topography, rest other factors are caused by collective actions of the farmers. Mismanagement of the water at the level of lift irrigation schemes is the major cause of action in developing the salinity in the belt.

An attempt has been made here to exhibit the economic problems of soil salinisation and to find out the remedial techniques. Normally, the farmers arc blamed for their mismanagement of water resources and mispriorities of cultivation of sugarcane in western Maharashtra. The location of co-operative sugar factories in western Maharashtra is obviously compelling the farmers by providing incentives to undertake sugarcane cultivation for the basic cause of survival of the industry. The co-operative lift irrigation schemes on river basins though managed by the group of farmers are also installed and inspired for the benefit of the sugar co-operatives. But now the cane farming is becoming more uneconomical and less rewarding due to declining yield of cane crop and increasing costs of cultivation because of the soil salinisation in the region. The loss-amelioration study has been conducted with an intention to protect the land resources from the infection of the salinity. Moreover, an attempt has been made to develop the awareness among the farmers about the sustainable agricultural development. The major cause of the salinisation in western Maharashtra is the unscientific use of chemical fertilizers and heavy doses of irrigation water to the sugarcane crop and lack of drainage since the natural trenches have been closed for better irrigation purposes

When a resource base is managed for private benefit, the decision process is relatively straightforward, because private resource use decisions are generally based on market goods and services that are sold to the consumers for a money price. Money price is usually assumed to measure the value of a market good or service to the people, and the contribution of market goods and services are supplemented to the well-being.

Businesses in the private sector generally make choices using formal rationality. It is one that gives the largest money profit. Money profits (money receipts minus money costs), are calculated for each choice. Money receipts are the amounts of market goods and services produced during the time for respective market prices. Money costs are the amounts of inputs needed for the production of the goods and services during the time for the respective money prices. When choices are based on profit, the decision process is simple, because only market goods and services are included in the process. Care must be taken in equating money price with value. Money prices can be based on forces other than demand and supply. In such cases, the money price is not the market price and may not provide a measure of value. For example, public utilities providing goods and services such as electricity, telephone, and water have an overseeing authority to set money prices based on costs rather than value.

Two different approaches to valuing resource extraction are compared. The depreciation approach and the wealth-based approach provide very different projections of net income. We demonstrate that when a renewable resource is subject to risk, the wealth-based approach provides a more appropriate measure of the influence of resource use on future consumption possibilities and the sustainability of net income.

The western Maharashtra is not topographically suitable for canal irrigation except some commands. The Co-operative Lift Irrigation Schemes are sponsored by the premier institutions like sugar co-operatives. Soil salinisation in canal command is caused by water logging, which is different from that of salinisation in lift irrigation command. The State Government, under Command Area Development Act (CADA) can undertake desalinization programmes in canal command on its own expenses, whereas CADA is not applicable to lift irrigation command. So, the seriousness of soil salinisation has spread throughout the lift irrigation command in western Maharashtra. Particularly, the area in low altitude around the closed run-offs is totally lying barren due to soil salinity. Before installation of irrigation schemes in 1970s, the land was well known for its deep black fertile soil with high yielding capabilities. Jowar, tobacco, pulses and other food crops were qualitatively grown in the area. There were natural drains through run-offs for excess water in the land areas. Such a very productive land area is now laying barren and salinity is encroaching in the nearby fertile uplands. Therefore, the seriousness of the problem attracts an attention to assess the problem in an economic framework.

SOIL SALINISATION: VARYING ISSUES AND CAUSES

Naturally, salts are observed more or less in almost all types of soils. All soils, even those formed in humid climates contain some amount of water soluble salts. The non-saline soils in humid climates also contains calcium and magnesium salts. Their content seldom exceeds 4 grams per litre of soil moisture. The arid and non-saline soils contain much larger amounts and varieties of salts and have a high percentage of exchangeable sodium. Such soils often have salt efflorescence or salt crusts on the surface particularly during the dry and desiccating period (March to June) and especially in the mansoonic climate.

Soil salinity in land irrigation commands is caused by water logging, which is again different from soil salinity in sugarcane belt. Water-logging lowers the land productivity through the rise in groundwater close to the soil surface. For sugarcane crop the minimum average water table depths (i.e. m below soil surface) is indicated at 1.0 for clay soils. 0.9 for loam/silt soils and 0.8 for sandy soils. In the water logging areas water table rises above the surface. Heightening the water table near to the surface through an excess of infiltrated water is environmental disorder. Water logging undermines the equilibrium of infiltration and discharge through evaporation, transpiration and ground water streams. With reduced drainage capacity, greater evaporation results in accumulation of salts in the upper soil horizons. On the other hand, insufficient application will also lead to salinity, as salts are not leached down. Water-logging is linked with salinity, both being brought about by incorrect irrigation management. The National Commission on Agriculture assessed (in 1976) that, an area of about 6.0 million hectare was waterlogged in the country. Out of this, an area of 3.4 million hectare was estimated to be suffering from surface water stagnation and 2.6 million hectare through rise in water table. The Ministry of Agriculture estimated (in 1984-85) that an area of 8.53 million hectare was suffering from the problem of water logging including both irrigated and non-irrigated areas. The Working Group constituted by the Ministry of Water Resources estimated in 1991 that an area of 2.46 million hectare was suffering from the problem of water logging under irrigation commands. State-wise break up of the areas affected by water logging as assessed from time to time is presented in the Table 1.

Similarly, the soil salinity in non-irrigated area is caused by drought climate. The fertile black deep cotton soil, which is found in sugarcane growing lands in western Maharashtra, turns to saline and alkaline due to heavy doses of water and unscientific use of chemical fertilizer. However, if the excess water (saline) from the undergrounds of saline fields is drained out the fertility

TABLE 1

Water Logging Area in Irrigated and Non-irrigated Areas

State	*Area Affected by water logging (both irrigated and non-irrigated) (National Commission on Agriculture, 1976)*	*Waterlogged Area (both irrigated and non-irrigated areas) (Ministry of Agriculture, 1984-85)*	*Area Estimated by the Working Group of MoWR-1991 (under irrigated commands)*
Andhra Pradesh	3.39	3.39	2.66
Assam	N.R.	4.50	N.R.
Bihar	1.17	7.07	6.20
Gujarat	4.84	4.84	1.72
Haryana	6.20	6.20	2.49
ammu & Kashmir	0.10	1.10	0.01
Karnataka	0.10	0.10	0.24
Kerala	0.61	0.61	0.12
Madhya Pradesh	0.57	0.57	0.73
Maharashtra	1.11	1.11	0.15
Orissa	0.60	0.60	1.96
Punjab	10.90	1090	2.00
Rajasthan	3.48	3.48	1.80
Tamilnadu	0.18	0.18	0.16
Uttar Pradesh	8.10	19.80	4.30
West Bengal	18.50	21.80	N.R.
Delhi	0.01	0.01	N.R.
Total (lakh ha.)	59.86	85.26	24.56
Total (Million ha.)	6.0	8.53	2.46

of the soil can be reinstated and productivity of the soil can be restored by some measures other than mere drain out of saline water.

The problematic soils are generally observed more or less in almost all parts of the Maharashtra. Besides, there are varieties of differences in their characteristics. The soil salinity in sugarcane belt is different from that of water logging in Akola, Amaravati and Buldhana districts of Maharashtra. The salinisation in sugarcane belt is man-made and attributes to unscientific use of inputs to the sugarcane crop. The soil and water testing reports discloses the different characteristics of saline soils in sugarcane belt. Salinity is also growing in the states of Punjab and Haryana, where large amount of basmati rice is grown on commercial purpose.

The land that has gone saline in India is roughly estimated to around 6 million hectares, out of which in Maharashtra alone, the area of saline land is estimated to 5.04 lakh hectares. The problem of salinisation is very grave in 12 states of India. (See Table 2). Out of irrigated area in 1991-92, India possess 11.80% of saline area. Almost 99.70% of saline area is observed only in 12 states of the country where 90.3% of land area is irrigated. Gujarat has highest saline land area of 45.66% to NIA.

TABLE 2

Saline Land in India (in lakh hectares)—1991-92

Sl. No.	*States*	*Net irrigated area*	*Saline land*	*% to NIA*
1.	Andhra Pradesh	43.51	2.94	6.76
2.	Bihar	33.54	8.44	25.16
3.	Gujarat	23.72	10.83	45.66
4.	Haryana	26.66	4.46	16.73
5.	Karnataka	23.08	0.75	3.25
6.	Madhya Pradesh	46.27	1.08	2.33
7.	Maharashtra	21.65	0.21	0.97
8.	Orissa	11.93	1.96	16.43
9.	Punjab	39.40	6.90	17.51
10.	Rajasthan	43.43	2.49	5.73
11.	Tamil Nadu	26.05	1.56	5.99
12.	Uttar Pradesh	105.42	15.81	15.0
	Total (1+12)	440.00	57.43	13.03
	All India Total	488.00	37.60	11.80
	% to All India	90.3	99.70	

Sources: 1. CMIE, September, 1995.
2. GOI, Ministry of Water Resources, 1991.

The state-wise figures of excess salt concentration worked out by the Working Group of Ministry of Water Resources are given in Table 3.

TABLE 3

State-wise Salt Affected Areas in India

State	*Excess salt concentration area (000 ha)*		
	Saline	*Alkali*	*Total*
Andhra Pradesh	5.00	22.80	27.80
Assam	—	—	—
Bihar	224.30	—	224.30
Gujarat	911.00	—	911.00
Haryana	125.20	72.00	197.20
Himachal Pradesh	—	—	—
Jammu & Kashmir	—	—	—
Karnataka	34.23	17.12	51.35
Kerala	—	—	—
Madhya Pradesh	—	35.79	35.79
Maharashtra	5.35	—	5.35
Orissa	—	—	—
Punjab	490.00	—	490.0
Rajasthan	70.00		70.00
Tamil Nadu	48.00	92.30	140.30
Uttar Pradesh	1150.00	—	1150.80
Total			
(a) in thousand ha.	3063.88	240.01	3303.89
(b) in million ha.	3.06	0.24	3.30

Source: Government of India (October, 2006), Report of Sub-Committee on More Crop and Income per Drop of Water, Advisory Council on Artificial Recharge of Ground Water, Ministry of Water Resources.

Gujarat Ecological Commission conducted a study covering some 10 per cent of the area of Gujarat; found that the extent of salt affected areas around the Gulf of Cambay went up from 7.4 percent in 1960 to 64 per cent in a little less than three decades since. Further the trend seems to have continued. Bhargav, G.P. (1989) estimated the salt affected soils in India to 9826 thousand (or 10 million) hectares. Maharashtra possesses salt affected area of 614 thousand hectares in 1997-98.

Use of excess water to crops is normally observed throughout the world. The Ganges is also drying up from overuse for irrigation and with over pumping of ground water threatens India with World's largest annual water shortage, which will affect food supply for the near billions of population (*ET*, 3.8.1999). Natural sources of water are being overused in all major food producing regions of the world—India, US and China. Irrigation projects in South Asia are cheapest at under $1500 (Rs. 60,000) per hectare as compared to around $ 4000 (Rs. 1,60,000) globally. Sandra Postal, Director, Global Water Policy Project (Massachusetts) and World Watch Senior Fellow, in her book, "Pillar of Sandican the Irrigation Miracle Last?" says; history has shown that most irrigation-based civilisations fail, unless resource management is planned to perfection. In India and China, which are dependent on agriculture, could pose a serious problem (*ET*, 3.8.1999).

The Maharashtra has gathered the data related to salt affected areas in the irrigated areas of the state in 1996. (Table 4). Akola district has 34.78 per cent of saline area followed by Amaravati district (16.57%) and Buldhana district (11.30%), Pune (4.2%), Satara (3.26%), Kolhapur (6.3%) and Solapur (9.20%) were hastily falling into the belt of salinity. This region has a very fertile land with perennial irrigation in the river basins.

TABLE 4

Salt Affected Area in Maharashtra (March, 1996)

Sl. No.	*Districts*	*Soil Survey Area (Hectares)*	*Salt Affected Area (Hectares)*
1	2	3	4
1.	Pune	8,29,098	15.027
2.	Satara	7,83,890	11,455
3.	Sangli	5,47,713	6,949
4.	Kolhapur	1,88,164	22,201
5.	Thane	7,86,350	6,605
6.	Raigad	6,16,795	7,695
7.	Ratnagiri	7,61,375	8,000
8.	Sindudurg	4,24,941	2.056
9.	Ahmadnagar	7,70,940	7,242
10.	Solapur	8,02,881	32.356
11.	Nasik	7,96,386	—
12.	Dhule	6,95,877	207
13.	Jalgaon	8,28,476	—
14 .	Aurangabad	8,11,118	126

(Contd.)

1	2	3	4
15.	Beed	7,49,972	655
16.	Jalana	3,78,269	424
17.	Parbhani	8,37,474	3,293
18.	Nanded	8.23.320	940
19.	Osmanabad	4,68,572	2.075
20.	Latur	3,75,927	4,174
21.	Akola	5,35,478	1,22,074
22.	Buldhana	8.38,305	39,733
23.	Amaravati	7,30,384	58.247
24.	Yavatmal	5,87,182	—
25.	Nagpur	3,60,026	—
26.	Vardha	4,49,950	—
27.	Bhandara	4,42,715	—
28.	Chandrapur	4,98,275	—
29.	Gadchiroli	2,06,037	—

Tables 5 and 6 explains the intensity of soil salinity in non-irrigated and irrigated areas in Maharashtra surveyed during the years 2000 and 1999 respectively.

TABLE 5

District-wise Distribution of Saline Soil in Non-irrigated Area in Maharashtra by the End of 2000

Sl. No.	*District*	*Total Geographical Area*	*Surveyed Area*	*Saline soil*	*% of Surveyed Area*
1	2	3	4	5	6
1.	Pune	1,607,269	905,674	31,776	3.51
2.	Ahmadnagar	1,681,801	855,508	12,298	1.44
3.	Solapur	1,484,534	868,615	60,182	6.93
4.	Kolhapur	773,680	268,481	3,010	1.12
5.	Satara	1,039,534	827,236	3,669	0.44
6.	Sangli	852,570	586,210	16,710	2.85
7.	Thane	949,528	828,281	15,171	1.83
8.	Raigad	686,475	647,073	18,485	2.86
9.	Ratnagiri	780,552	798,450	77,874	9.75
10.	Sindudurg	460,778	461,784	706	0.15
11.	Aurangabad	1,059,598	679,384	126	0.02
12.	Jalana	806,159	413,459	424	0.10

(Contd.)

1	2	3	4	5	6
13.	Beed	1,104,832	817,010	755	0.09
14.	Latur	704,873	276,314	4,300	1.56
15.	Parbhani	1,079,870	655,850	3,293	0.50
16.	Nanded	1,079,905	624,783	1,040	0.17
17.	Usmanabad	951,195	492,661	2,416	0.49
18.	Nasik	1,539,691	745,197	23	0.00
19.	Dhule	1,290,152	720,431	207	0.03
20.	Jalgaon	1,186,938	605,789	0	0.00
21.	Amaravati	1,201,854	864,097	53,562	6.20
22.	Akola	1,052,337	665,319	95,391	14.34
23.	Buldhana	1,034,942	873,051	1,262	0.14
24.	Yavatmal	1,363,280	648,082	0	0.00
25.	Nagpur	963,902	447,236	0	0.00
26.	Bhandara	934,647	587,485	0	0.00
27.	Vardha	630,549	455,276	0	0.00
28.	Chandrapur	1,174,917	722,839	0	0.00
29.	Gadchiroli	1,431,379	277,311	0	0.00
	Total	30,797,693	18,618,886	403,410	2.17

Source: Agricultural Commissionerate, Maharashtra State, Pune.

TABLE 6

District-wise Distribution of Saline Soil in Irrigated Area in Maharashtra by the End of 1999

Sl. No.	*Division*	*Districts*	*Total saline soil (in hectares)*
1	2	3	4
1.	Pune	Pune	5803
		Satara	2877
		Sangli	2578
		Solapur	6189
		Kolhapur	—
		Total	17447
2.	North Maharashtra	Ahmadnagar	3133
		Nasik	391
		Jalgaon	211
		Dhule	—
		Total	3735

(Contd.)

1	*2*	*3*	*4*
3.	Aurangabad	Aurangabad	101
		Beed	1764
		Usmanabad	47
		Latur	368
		Jalana	512
		Nanded	542
		Parbhani	767
		Hingoli	550
		Total	4651
4.	Nagpur	Nagpur	851
		Bhandara	—
		Vardha	25
		Chandrapur	—
		Gadchiroli	—
		Total	876
5.	Amaravati	Amaravati	—
		Yavatmal	249
		Akola	192
		Buldhana	26
		Total	467
6	Kokan	—	—
		Grant Total	27976

Source: Irrigation Research and Development Directorate, Pune.

The salinity in non-irrigated areas is a natural hazard created out of heavy rain and water logging in some of the commands in Maharashtra. The hot temperature and the topography are the responsible factors for salinisation in such zones. If the irrigation schemes are introduced in such areas, the salinisation processes get activated speedily. Salinisation in irrigated areas is of two types, viz. the water logging area and the actual saline barren lands. Water logging is normally caused by canals. Saline barren patch is created due to man-made mismanagement of water resources and the mispriorities of inorganic fertilizers. We surveyed such land area in western Maharashtra for five districts, which fall under the sugarcane crop. The causes of such salinisation process are indicated below after going through field visits and discussions with the farmers and the officials of Agricultural Department of GoM.

CAUSES OF SALINISATION

1. Scanty rainfall and tropical climate results to speedy evaporation in irrigated area. The underground salts climb up as a result of evaporation and the land becomes saline and alkaline.
2. The rate of water percolation in black-cotton deep clay soil is slow. The process of drain-out of excess water get thwarted due to land levelling efforts made by the farmers during the post-irrigation schemes causing a closure of natural drains. Construction of dams in the uplands, barrages and bridges on trenches and rivers, etc. An impeded drainage condition in heavy deep black soils is another cause of salinisation.
3. Use of indiscriminate, improper and imbalanced doses of chemical fertilizers and unscientific and irregular use of water resources for sugarcane crop is another cause of salinisation. The use of chemical fertilizer e.g. in Kolhapur-Sangli region went up to 217.6 kg and 123.3 kg. per hectare which is highest in the state in 1994-95. This has again gone up to 497 kg. per hectare in Sangli district and 817 kg. in Kolhapur district during the year 1998-99. Urea is the main chemical fertilizer applied to the sugarcane belt (66,800 and 42,000 M.T. in 1999-2000 was proposed). More or less this is the case of all districts falling under the sugarcane crop in western Maharashtra.
4 Low lying lands are receiving salt washes from uplands.
5. There is no change in the cropping pattern since 1970s.
6. The typography is also responsible for inadequate drain out of excess water.
7. Growth of lift irrigation schemes in the river basins is enhanced and encouraged by sugar co-operatives in the region. The use of irrigation water is not proper and economical.

RECLAMATION MEASURES FOR SALT-AFFECTED AREAS

The following measures are normally recommended for reclamation of salt-affected areas.

(a) Establishment of proper drainage systems in the problem areas.

(b) Leaching, i.e. the transporting of soluble salts by downward movement of water through soil combined with flushing, i.e. the washing out of salts in the run-off of the water at the lower end of fields.

(c) Application of inorganic (chemical) amendments, either soluble calcium salts like calcium chloride and gypsum or relatively less soluble ground limestone and lime sludge from sugar factories or acids and acid forms like sulphuric acid, sulphur, aluminium sulphate, etc. in addition to leaching and flushing in case of alkaline soils; and

(d) Proper crop management and selection of crops depending upon their suitability to different salt levels and addition of organic amendments like cattle manure, molasses, crop residues as a source of organic matter to the soil.

Various methods are being used for soil reclamation. They can be conveniently grouped into: (i) Chemical method, (ii) Agro-technical method, (iii) Biological method, and (iv) Hydro-technical method. The last group includes engineering aspects of soil drainage and relates mainly to reclamation of saline in water-logged soils (*Bhargav*, 1989). The details of the amelioration through these methods are given below.

A. Chemical Treatments

The chemical methods for alkali soil reclamation, many inorganic amendments are used. Some contains calcium, such as gypsum calcium chloride, phospho-gypsum, rock phosphate and basic sag, while others are either acids or acid forming material, like sulphuric acid, sulphur, iron, pyrites, iron sulphate, aluminium sulphate, etc. Some other industrial waste materials like press mud are also used on a limited scale.

B. Agro-technical Treatments

This technique basically includes steps in the process of alkali soil reclamation through proper land levelling, bunding, amendment application (preferably prior to the onset of the Monsoon) and other fertilizer uses.

This method covers the following ways and means to

overcome alkalinity:

(i) Proper management of crops and fertilizer application.
(ii) Effects of mulch in alkali soil reclamation (e.g. use of rice husk).

C. Biological Methods

Biological methods are also enhanced if suitable for reclamation processes in amelioration of alkali soils. Chemical amendments often remain transitory in the absence of biological methods. Under this method green manuring, tree plantation, silviplasturing, in addition of organic materials are normally used.

D. Hydro-technical Methods

This envisages lowering of water table and application of amendments for neutralisation of alkanity in alkali soils with solid ground waters. Black soils affected with alkali problem also need similar management techniques. Saline soil invariably requires surface or sub-surface drainage or both for reclamation (*Bhargav,* 1989).

The agencies and the factors responsible for the salinisation process in the belt is due to the installation of sugar factories and the irrigation facilities, consequently, huge amount of NPK was applied to the sugarcane crop. The subsidiary activities and their linkages with other co-operatives have bees motivated the farmers to go for cane cultivation consistently, without crop rotation and crop combination techniques. The region is having vertical and horizontal linkages (credit linkages to production and marketing) with various development activities centred around the co-operative sugar factories. The sugar factories are the growth centres in the region. The political leadership is very much interested in the co-operatives. Chougule, B.A. *et al.* have introduced the abnormal conditions in the soil quality caused by high doses of irrigation water and unscientific application of chemical fertilizers. Such conditions are not suitable for the growth of crops, following are some of the causes of low productivity of crops in such lands: (1) Poor aeration of crop root zone, (2) Reduction in the activity of soil originations, (3) Obstruction to seed germination and seeding growth, (4) Excessive weed growth, (5) Hindrances to farm operations, (6) Upsetting salt and water balance leading to development of salinity, (7) Damage to building roads etc., (8) Frost action in soil.

When pH remain around 8.5 and Ece around 13 to 15, the drain of excess water from the grounds be removed towards the slopes, but the slopes have been closed by the farmers for irrigation purposes, soon after the installation of LIS. After a post irrigation gap of 10-15 years, the undrained land area started salting.

TABLE 7

Characteristics of Problematic Soils in Sugarcane Belt

Soil groups	*pH*	*Electric conductivity Ece d Sm-1*	*Exchangeable sodium %*
Saline	< 8.5	< 4.0	> 15
Sodic or *chopan*	> 8.5	< 4.0	> 15
Saline sodic	< 8.5	> 4.0	> 15

CONCLUSIONS

In conclusion it can be said that, the salinisation in sugarcane belt is a man-made *vis-a-vis* natural discourse, which can be ameliorated through the human efforts. It requires a wide range of changes to be brought in the institutional and organisational set-up so far located in the region as growth drivers. Government support for this endeavour is decidedly indispensable. If not the resource degradation may cause to drive out the habitats from their localisations. Saline soil normally is observed in arid, semi-arid, sub-humid or humid climate, which needs salt leaching to make the root zone free of excess from salts so as to keep the reclaimed soil at optimum level of solute concentration, so, that the crops do not suffer in future. Leaching requirement is defined as the fraction of water entering into the soil must pass through the root zone in order to prevent soil salinity from exceeding a specific value needs to be worked out. Soil porosity influences leaching requirements, which depends on texture, structure and clay mineralogy of the soil. However, various types of saline soils require different kinds of drainage treatments. It's planning, designing and implementation of a drainage scheme requires information on rainfall and run-off characteristics, data on annual groundwater cycle, data on tidal and lake level fluctuations in case of coastal, deltaic and lacustrine saline soils and geological investigations on channel stability.

Soil salinity has become an acute problem resulting a fall in. Irrigation is thus, both bane and boon to its users. Irrigation has engendered many unfavourable environmental impacts on land and men. The State Governments in India have now realised the seriousness of the problem. The salt affected area in the sugarcane districts has been burdened by varieties of losses excluding the value of land. The salinity is encroaching at the rate of 10 per cent every year. The cost of amelioration is essential; consequently it is burden on the state treasury. The loss due to salinisation and cost of amelioration are going beyond imagination. The State Government is also initiated in moving away the problem of salinity through institutional efforts, immediately after the request from the farmers of the locality.

Following recommendations are suggested for permanent desalinisation:

(i) Amelioration of soil salinity at an individual level is inadequate. It should be properly designed collectively on the basis of the watershed and slope *of* the area. The farmer beneficiaries in the command area should come together and form the self-help group with an intention to implement the amelioration programmes.

(ii) Technical help should be taken up from the authorised consulting agencies or government departments. Phase-wise programme with time bound efforts should be enlisted and followed accordingly.

(iii) There should be a proper monitoring of the work done and the results of it. District level monitoring and supervision and advisory committee can be set-up.

(iv) Farmer's training programmes should be designed under a crash scheme. The crash scheme may be entitled as *"Jal Saksharata Abhiyan"* means education to the resource users. In this *"Abhiyan,"* training in the use of irrigation water and chemical fertilizer, land tilling, crop cultivation and overall farm management techniques may be imparted to the farmers. The post-amelioration follow up should also be taught to the farmers.

(v) There should be a group financing to the specially established SHGs from the upper agencies, for amelioration programme at the concessional rate of interest. One-third of the total fund can be collected from the farmers in equal instalments. Another 2/3rd amount can be financed by the Government out of its budgetary provision or from the Rural Infrastructural Development Fund of NABARD.

(vi) While installing the irrigation projects henceforth, proper care should taken to facilitate by proper drainage network. Lack of drainage network is the main problem that the farmers in perennial irrigation areas are facing. The individual efforts go futile, if there is no proper common drainage facility.

(vii) NGOs may be encouraged and assisted for their interest in ameliorating the soil salinity and alkalinity. Some efforts of this kind are in progress in Sangli district. Foreign funds are being used for amelioration programme. Such efforts are inadequate and obstructs, in case of non-availability of adequate funds. In fact the activities of the NGOs are more economical and efficient than any government sponsored activities.

(viii) Water management techniques of co-operative lift irrigation scheme operating at the village levels should improve their functioning. The management of co-operative lift irrigation schemes to a greater extent are responsible for soil salinity and alkalinity in sugarcane belt. Most of the lift irrigation schemes are managed by co-operative sugar factories.

(ix) Use of micro-irrigation techniques (Drip and Sprinkling) should be encouraged and supported by state assistance. The percentage of micro-irrigation to total irrigation in India and China is less than 0.1 percent; whereas in Cyprus it is 71.4 percent; in Israel it is 48.7 percent. State Government is allocating irrigation subsidies to such micro-irrigation techniques.

There is an immediate need to concentrate on the institutional and state efforts to ameliorate the salinity and alkalinity in the sugarcane belt. This will not only reward the farmers but also help to attain a standard level of sustainable agricultural development, which is urged on the eve of structural adjustments in the economy. Protection of ecology and environment, no doubt is more accessible and essential rather than hap hazardous process of economic development, however, development at any stage must not be hurdled. So, what is required is to protect the eco-system and ecological balance through strategies of sustained development. In this regard, the rote of institutions and government should be enhancing and encouraging. The *"Jal Saksharata Abhiyan"* may be instituted to educate the farmers.

REFERENCES

Bhargav, G.P., *Salt Affected Soils in India: A Source Book.*

Chougule, B.A., Kamble, B.M.. Shahare P.U., Rathod, S.D. and Yadav, B.S. (Bulletin No. 68). *Reclamation of Water Logged Saline Black Soils in Irrigated Commands,* Agricultural Research Station, Digraj, Mahatma Phule Krishi Vidyapith, Rahuri.

CMIE (1995). *Agriculture Sector in India,* Sept.

Deosthali Vrishali, Akmanchi Anand and Chavan, Manoj (2005), *Prioritization of Villages for Reclamation of Salt-affected Areas in Irrigated Tracts of Sangli District. A GIS and Remote Sensing Approach,* Technical Report, GR 01/05 Department of Geography, University of Pune, Pune.

GOI (1991), *Water logging. Soil Salinity and Alkalinity Report of the Working Group on Problems Identification in Irrigated Area with suggested Remedial Measures.* Ministry of Water Resources. December, New Delhi.

Government of India (October, 2006), *Report of Sub-Committee on More crop and Income per Drop of Water,* Advisory Council on Artificial Recharge of Ground Water.

Jugale, V.B. (1998), *An Economic Analysis of Problems of Soil Salinity in Sugarcane Belt of Maharashtra,* Monograph No. 5, Department of Economics. Shivaji University, Kolhapur.

Jugale, V.B. (1997), *Financing for Desalinization of Soils in Maharashtra,* NABARD, Chair Occasional Paper-1, VAMNICOM. Pune.

Parikh, Kirit and Ghosh, Upal (1995), *Natural Resource Accounting for Soils: Towards an Empirical Estimate of Costs of Soil Degradation for India,* IGIDR, Goregaon, East Mumbai.

Tradable Water Rights for Sustainable Water Management in India: Problems and Prospects

L. VENKATACHALAM

Appropriate institutions do matter for efficient, equitable and sustainable water management. However, issues related to 'asymmetric information' and 'bounded rationality' prevent us from identifying these appropriate institutions. Given the institutional diversity in the water sector where governments, markets and other non-governmental organizations could potentially play a 'collective role' in order to achieve efficiency, formulating water policy with the 'right combination' of these institutions is always a challenging task. As economic theory suggests, it is the transaction cost that determines the right combination of institutions. Since the market as an institution plays a major role in minimizing the transaction costs, the analogy is that water policies giving emphasis on 'market-based instruments' (MBIs) for water allocation are capable of achieving Pareto-efficient outcomes in the water sector. Among all the MBIs, the 'tradable water rights' (TWR) is found to be most efficient in allocating water, as demonstrated by many empirical studies across the world. In this paper, we highlight the importance of introducing the TWR in the water sector and potential problems encountered under the TWR regime; we also provide some policy prescriptions to make the TWR work successfully in future.

INTRODUCTION

The problem of ever increasing water scarcity lays a substantial amount of constraints on achieving the normative goal of efficient, equitable and sustainable agricultural development in India. One of the major challenges faced by development economists, planners and water managers has always been to address the problems associated with acute water scarcity in our country where the scarcity induced social costs impose additional burden on the already distressed agriculture sector. In recent years, the institutional issues of water management assume paramount importance in the development discourse because of the fact that those institutions that are supposed to mitigate the social costs by way of assuaging the water scarcity had indeed failed to do so; in many cases, these institutions are either weak or do not exist at all. The accumulation of social costs due to what is being described as 'institutional failure' has been an ever increasing phenomenon in recent years, as demonstrated by Brandon and Homman (1995), which contributes to the declining agricultural growth and increased food insecurity at regional level. For example, studies dealing with government failure in water sector have clearly demonstrated how such a failure and its resulting negative impacts has adversely affected the regional sustainable development of agricultural sector in the Indian context (e.g. *Venkatachalam*, 2004). Due to inherent government failure in the water sector, 'informal water markets' have emerged in many different parts of the country and the emerging empirical evidences suggest that the size of these markets is also expanding rapidly. It is found that these informal water markets have generated considerable beneficial effects in certain regions in India (*Shah*, 1993). However, these markets have also intensified water scarcity in many other regions since the private market operations led to problems such as, over-exploitation of groundwater (*Janakarjan and Moench*, 2006). The negative externality generated by these markets and the resulting economic and environmental costs have become irreversible and pervasive in many of the Indian river basins (see *Venkatachalam*, 2005). Therefore, the combined effects of government failure and market failure warrant for 'institutional reforms' (*Saleth and Dinar*, 2004) in water sector in general and irrigation sector in particular.

The early reforms in the water sector were based on the slogan of 'getting the price right'. The major aim of this approach has been to generate revenue, apart from providing appropriate incentives and disincentives to the farmers *not* to over-use the water resources. Real world experiences suggest that 'pricing' of irrigation water runs into many different problems that are both economic and political in nature. On the economic front, the current practices of pricing are not based on the 'true value' or the 'true opportunity cost' of water use. As pointed out by many, this can be attributed to the general inability of the centralized authority to process 'all relevant' information for fixing the 'right' price that reflects the true value so that the allocation of water can be Pareto optimal. Improper pricing may generate counter productive outcomes. For example, pricing water below its true value will lead to over-use of it. Moreover, in most of the cases the price fixed is not based on the farmers' willingness to pay for it and therefore, mis-use of water becomes a common phenomenon. When the pricing is based on the preferences of the farmers, then one could expect the farmers to use their share of water more efficiently based on the incentives and dis-incentives structure embedded in the pricing mechanism. Besides, mere pricing alone is not sufficient to yield expected results in the water sector because the outcomes under the pricing regimes are determined by various other complex economic factors—such as, market uncertainty—that are beyond the control of the decision-makers. The expected outcomes of water pricing depend mainly on how effectively the incentives and disincentives are being utilised by the farmers. So, it was realized that unless or until these important factors are adequately taken into account in the pricing mechanism, the objectives of water pricing would become futile. On the political front, the water pricing is always opposed by the farmers' lobbies and therefore, the indented objectives of pricing—such as, revenue generation are not being met with. The politicians and bureaucrats also prefer to maintain the *status-quo* regime, creating a 'path dependency' in water pricing policy. The end result is a Prisoner's dilemma type non-Pareto optimal outcome where every one knows that overall efficiency in water use could have been brought about 'collectively' by increasing the price equivalent to true value but nobody wants to do so.

Another approach that was adopted in the irrigation reforms was, 'getting the property rights right'. The public goods nature of the irrigation water was found to be instrumental in encouraging the farmers to over-use it; so, a 'tragedy of the commons' problem became imminent especially in the groundwater sector. Similarly, using the public goods nature of the irrigation water the farmers were also found to adopt 'free-riding' behaviour thereby adversely affecting the revenue generation. As a result, reform measures were aimed at defining the property rights 'right' in the area of irrigation management. Measures such as, irrigation management transfer, etc. are considered to fall within this broader approach. However, this approach has also been not effective; empirical evidences have shown that even those resources (e.g. land) with well-defined property rights are not free from experiencing negative externality problem. This implies that defining property rights alone is not sufficient for ensuring efficient water allocation. Results of many empirical studies that looked at the performance of irrigation management transfer schemes in many of the canal systems in India have also supported this conclusion.

Since many experiments attempted with narrow approaches have failed in the past, an institutional approach with a slogan of 'getting the institutions right' is being attempted in the water sector in recent years. Under this approach, apart from the governments and markets, other institutions such as, water users associations (WUAs), non-governmental organizations and other civil society organizations are supposed to play a collective role in achieving efficiency in water use as well as increase in revenue. One of the important questions to be answered in the 'institutional approach' is to decide which organisation has to play what role—if at all these organizations will have to play a collective role in achieving the underlying objectives of water policy. At theoretical level, the answer for this question comes from the transaction cost analysis within 'new institutional economics' literature; the transaction costs analysis suggests that *ceteris paribus,* the size of the transaction cost determines the role of each institution in an organization structure. As many theoretical and empirical studies have demonstrated, the market within a given organizational structure is found to be relatively more efficient in reducing the transaction cost (*Thobani*, 1998) in water allocation. This being the case, the institutional approach at present prescribes largely the 'market-based instruments' (MBIs) for surface water allocation, provided a specific supporting role is being played by other institutions such as, the government.

It should be noted that both India's Water Policy, 2002 and the National Environment Policy, 2006 prescribe introducing MBIs in the water sector for effectively addressing the scarcity problem in the coming years. The problem with these policies is that they do not clearly spell out what kind of MBIs will have to be introduced in the water sector and what role that a chosen MBI (or combination of MBIs) will have to play in a given institutional environment. There are also Indian researchers who are skeptical about the role of MBIs in addressing the water scarcity in the Indian context (e.g. *Shah and Koppen*, 2006). However, empirical evidences from different parts of the world—especially, from developing countries—suggest that out of all MBIs, the 'tradable water rights' are found to be more efficient in allocating the scarce water resources among competing uses (*Griffin*, 1998; *Thobani*, 1998). They are more 'incentive-based' ones and do reflect the preferences of the farmers that are dynamic in nature, according to changing external environment. Since the exchange of water between users takes place on the basis of 'true value' of the water, the allocation of water is Pareto-efficient at any given point in time. Tradable water rights approach is nothing but a 'regulated market' for water. It should be noted that this approach, if properly implemented, provides sufficient incentives for the farmers to make use of the water more efficiently, develop efficient infrastructure on their own, and explore innovative technologies to sustain water use efficiency on a long-term basis. In the following section, we will critically evaluate the theoretical and empirical studies dealing with the tradable water rights.

ADVANTAGES WITH TRADABLE WATER RIGHTS

The fundamental principle underlying the tradable water rights system is that inefficient allocation of water and the problems associated with it do arise due to ill-defined property rights over water use. Assigning water rights to water buyers implies that these rights could be appropriated at a cost, reflected in terms of their WTP (willingness to pay) for acquiring the rights. The WTP value, which reflects the true scarcity value of water at the existing level of scarcity, would automatically compensate the sellers of water, provided that WTA (willingness to accept) compensation by the sellers is at least equivalent to the WTP value of the buyers. On the other hand, the water rights to the sellers imply that they could sell the water to the potential buyers with high value uses, based on the opportunity cost of their water use. As economic theory suggests, the market exchange brings equilibrium between demand for and supply of water irrespective of who owns the initial property rights provided a conducive, competitive environment is created for minimizing the cost of transaction of exchange. Therefore, the concept of water rights fundamentally recognizes that acquiring property rights over water involves a considerable amount of opportunity cost of resource transfer in terms of its alternative uses. Any alteration of quantity or quality of the stock of the water due to transfer would cause different levels of scarcity, altering the distribution of costs and benefits experienced by the users. Once the tradable rights are introduced, the production system is expected to automatically adjust to the new scarcity regime. With the new efficiency level in the water use system, the economic system also settles down at a new, efficient level of equilibrium. Similarly, the system would adjust to different levels of scarcity when it moves on the time scale as well. Therefore, economists insist on the importance of assigning tradable water rights (*Easter*, 2008; *Thobani*, 1998) to the users so that the formal market mechanism can ensure efficient utilization of scarce water on the basis of opportunity cost of water use.

In a world of absolute water scarcity, property rights-based approach to water use is justified from a pure economic point of view. Many economists argue that water is an economic commodity[1] (*Rogers et al.* 2002) and therefore, it is argued that the market can be a more efficient institution to allocate this scarce resource to its optimum use. Many economists put-forward different types of economic arguments to support this normative stand. One of the arguments is based on the 'big-bills theory'—one of the fundamental principles of mainstream economics. If the big-bills theory is extended to the water sector, it implies that under the command and control regime where the property rights over water use are ill-defined, the farmers have no incentive to utilize the unexploited benefits in the water sector; once the tradable rights are assigned, the incentive structure changes in such a way that all these unutilized benefits would be appropriately exploited by the 'rational' farmers. The enhanced benefits under the new tradable regime is realized in terms of increased producer surplus and reduced transaction cost due to efficient use of water; a win-win situation arises where not only the farmers could exploit considerable amount of previously unexploited benefits but also the governments could garner larger amount of benefits through enhanced revenue. As we have already seen, many empirical studies on farmers' WTP for improvements in irrigation water supply has also provided strong evidence to strengthen the big-bills theory argument in the water sector. Moreover, studies on informal water markets in the agriculture sector reveals that farmers are already incurring a substantial amount of their farm income on water-related activities and therefore, introducing tradable water rights system is assumed to transfer a major part of this income to the government sector and at the same time, it would also reduce the transaction cost incurred by the farmers in the informal water markets.

ISSUES IN MEASUREMENT OF TRANSACTION COSTS

Transaction cost analysis of moving towards MBIs is a special case in the economic analysis of water management. Analysis of transaction cost is an integral part of institutional change—from a government dominated one to a market dominated one—because institutions without transaction cost do not matter much in any economic analysis (*Coase*, 1992) of water scarcity. Saleth and Dinar (2004), based on their stage-based perspective, classify stages of institutional change into four major categories: the first stage where change in the mind set takes place; the second stage with political agreement for change; the third stage where institutional supply occurs; and the forth one with behavioural changes to cause desirable changes in the water allocation and management. All these stages are associated with different levels of transaction costs. A movement from one stage to another stage would be possible only if the benefits exceed the transaction costs of the move. This warrants for quantifying the transaction costs and efficiency gains in monetary terms. However, there are certain difficulties in measuring the transaction cost of institutional changes. One such difficulty arises from the fact that the users of enhanced water availability resulting from alternative institutional arrangements may not always be able to quantify the transaction cost involved in those arrangements because of their inability to perceive it. This implies that such decisions are constrained mainly by the availability of information; if additional information about the transaction cost is made available to the farmers, then the decision on water use will be efficient. However, when asymmetric information about the transaction cost is inherent, sub-optimal decisions will become imminent. This being the case, the studies aims at measuring the transaction cost that rely mainly on farmers' information may provide biased results for policy-making.

The second type of difficulty arises from 'bounded rationality' of the farmers whose cognitive constraints affect their decision to minimize the transaction costs (*Williamson*, 2000). Under this bounded rationality assumption, it is found that even if full information on the transaction cost is made available, the farmers may not be able to minimize the same due to cognitive constraints in processing the information. While errors in measurement due to asymmetric information can be corrected by adopting a methodology in which one can look at the nature of the causal relationship between changes in decision-making caused by changes in the information made available, the error coming from the bounded rationality cannot be corrected or can be corrected only with a substantial amount of transaction cost on removing the cognitive constraints. Moreover, if the researchers measuring the transaction cost are also boundedly rational, then the error in predictions will be robust. Therefore, it is argued that more bounded rationality-based economic models will have to be used for measuring the transaction cost (*Conlisk*, 1996) in water sector in coming years. Despite these theoretical difficulties, it should be noted that work in measuring the transaction cost in the water sector is progressing with the assumption that the transaction cost can be measurable with minimum error.

Measurement of transaction cost at empirical level is a challenging task (*Williamson*, 2000). First of all, what constitutes transaction cost itself is a controversial issue (see *McCann et al.* 2005). The existing literature provides various kinds of definitions of transaction costs. They are: cost of exchanging ownership titles; cost of effecting exchange; expenses of organizing or participating in a market or implementing a government policy; cost of carrying out market transactions; administrative cost of transaction; costs incurred to establish and maintain property rights; and so on. To avoid confusion, Saleth and Dinar (2004) define transaction cost in water sector as follows: 'The transaction costs cover both the real and monetary costs of altering the regulatory, monitoring and enforcement mechanisms related to water development, allocation and management' (p. 5). *McCann et al.* (2005) provide a detailed typology of transaction costs to be measured in the water sector. It includes costs on: (1) Research and Information; (2) Enactment or Litigation; (3) Design and Implementation; (4) Support and Administration; (5) Contracting; and (6) Monitoring and Detection. These costs are borne by the legislators, courts, water agencies and other stakeholders and the magnitude of the incidence differs across these organizations and individuals. While the typology makes the task of identifying the transaction cost easier, the next issue that arises in measurement of transaction cost is nothing but collecting detailed data on these costs. This is because the nature of the transaction costs differs widely across different entities. For example, it can be both *implicit* and *explicit;* it can be both *ex-ante* and *ex-post* and so on. Some empirical studies have attempted to measure the transaction costs in the water sector, which we discuss in the next section.

Empirical studies estimating the transaction cost of market transfer of water are limited, though there exists a bulky literature on the theoretical side. Colby (2000 and 1990) tried to estimate the 'policy induced transaction cost (PITC)' arising from obtaining 'legal approval' for a proposed water transfer—to transfer water from agricultural to non-agricultural uses—especially in the US context. The PITC is incurred both by 'gainers' and 'losers' and it includes attorney's fee, costs on engineering and hydrological studies, court costs and fees paid to state agencies. The opportunity cost of waiting for obtaining approvals and costs incurred to challenge the transfer of water also constitute substantial part of the transaction costs. The PITCs operates as Pigouvian solution in addressing the externalities of water transfer and therefore, the author suggests that the government should increase the transaction costs for those activities that generate negative externalities and reduce it for those activities which generate positive externalities.

Colby (2000) found that in water markets in USA, larger water transfers reduces the transaction costs substantially because of economies of scale. Studies found that the 'efficiency gains' in transferring water from agriculture to other areas (to improve water quality) in Central California are also substantial. Apart from this, the cost of establishing market transfer has been comparatively lower than other policy measures to improve the quality of water. Colby (2000) points out that though gains from water trades are significant (average annual net benefit of US$ 185/acre foot in urban use compared to US$ 10-30/acre foot in agriculture), resistance to transfer of water is still a main problem in different parts of the California state. According to McCann and Easter (2004) and McCann *et al.* (2005), many empirical studies try to measure only the *ex-post* transaction cost, i.e. the costs on transaction of water after the formal markets have emerged in the water sector. However, it should be noted that the transaction cost incurred by the water users prior to market regime (i.e. *ex-ante)* has not yet been estimated properly. This is an important area of future research.

CASE FOR TRADABLE WATER RIGHTS IN INDIA

It should be noted that the problem of water scarcity in India has reached such an extent where it imposes greater constraints—both directly and indirectly—on the economic development in general and agriculture development in particular. India adopted economic reform measures in the middle of 1980s and subsequently, some amount of reform measures was initiated in the water sector during the 90s (see *Gulati and Narayanan*, 2001). The initial reform measures focused mainly on the financial reforms in the irrigation sector in order to eliminate huge amount of subsidies given to the agriculture sector, which was identified to contribute to negative consequences such as, over-exploitation of groundwater (*Dubash*, 2008; *Gulati and Narayanan*, 2001). The reform measures included pricing of irrigation water in such a way that inefficient water use could be discouraged. These measures gradually moved onto other institutional measures such as, introducing water user associations under the umbrella of Participatory Irrigation Management System (PIMS) (*Marothia*, 2005). It should be noted that the institutional reforms carried out so far are indeed vague and are not adequate to manage India's scarce water resources; rather, it is argued by Shah *et al.* (2004a) that India's water sector is still crying for 'real' institutional reforms.

A meaningful institutional reform to address acute water scarcity in different parts of the regions in India comes in the form of introducing 'formal markets' in managing water in an efficient manner. Like many other countries in South Asia, one of the unique features of India's water sector is characterized by the existence of informal water markets at a large scale (*Shah*, 1991; *Saleth*, 1996; see *Meinzen-Dick*, 1998) especially in the groundwater sector. These informal groundwater markets emerged as a strong institution to address the increased level of water scarcity in different pockets of India (*Saleth*, 1996). A good summary about the economics and institutional aspects of these informal water markets in India is available in Saleth (1998). A rough estimate of monetary value of groundwater sales in the informal water markets stands at US$ 1.38 billion per year (*Saleth*, 1998). Since the informal water markets are very strong in the scarce regions of India, introducing formal markets should not pose any major problem in terms of transaction costs, as suggested by Easter *et al.* (1998). However, the existing informal water markets in different regions of India suggest that they are indeed inefficient in terms of minimizing the transaction cost and therefore, the existing institutional set-up under the informal markets may not be conducive to introducing formal markets in the water sector. The informal markets, for example, are not competitive because of monopoly power of sellers who indulge in price discrimination and non-price discriminations such as, irregularities practiced in supplying quality and reliability of irrigation water. It is localized and highly fragmented in nature; characteristics such as, monopoly power of the seller, trade on the basis of surplus supply, trade being influenced by social factors, variation in payment place to place and time to time and inefficient use and over-exploitation of groundwater (*Mohanty and Gupta*, 2002) contribute largely to increased transaction cost, than reducing it. Since the tariff prevailing in these markets is usually greater than the competitive tariff, exploitation of consumer surplus becomes a predominant strategy of the sellers. Moreover, unregulated, informal markets lead to over-exploitation of groundwater, causing environmental problems that increase the social cost in the regional economy; availability of free electricity in different parts of the country intensify the existing adverse impacts arising from over-exploitation of groundwater (see *Dubash*, 2000).

It should be noted that huge amount of private investment on tube-wells and bore-wells to augment groundwater suggests that the farmers have already appropriated the water rights 'indirectly' through their legal right over private land. In other words, the private water rights are being established 'informally' through investment on groundwater augmenting measures, linked to the land rights (see *Kumar*, 2007). As demonstrated by many earlier studies on water markets, the 'contract' farmers who do not have land rights could not acquire water rights and part of their producer surplus is being exploited by those land owners from whom they purchase water. The argument against the exploitation thesis is that if the exploitative informal water markets had not come into being in the water scenario, even the existing level of producer surplus enjoyed by the 'agents' would not have been generated; the end result would be nothing but more farmers' distress in the country. The negative consequences of informal water markets imply that these water markets indeed increase the transaction cost in the water economy and therefore, introducing formal water markets would reduce both the visible and invisible transaction cost in a substantial manner (see *Saleth*, 1998). The important questions that arise in this context are: Why an inefficient institution, namely, the informal market, emerged strongly and sustained itself in the water sector? If the formal water markets are efficient in minimizing transaction cost, then why these institutions have not emerged in the water sector at all? Is it due to initial burden imposed by additional transaction costs involved in moving from the present regime to a more market-based regime? It is due to the information constraint at the farmers' level that prevents them from switching over to formal trade? Is it due to the existing policy and institutions that facilitate trading activity at individual level informally but impose constraints on large scale formal trading of water? Is it due to physical constraints emanating from the hydrological features of the water related dynamics at river basin level? One of the major lacunae in the water market studies in the Indian context is that these studies give more emphasize on the groundwater markets, neglecting completely the role of markets in surface water allocation. As we know, introducing formal markets in the groundwater sector is a difficult task whereas such a measure can be relative easy in surface water sector. Since the groundwater is indirectly priced (in terms of cost of extraction embedded in the water used), the pricing of currently freely available surface water is warranted for addressing the efficiency and equity issues in water resources management. The latter is possible once we introduce tradable water rights in the surface water sector.

As far as India is concerned, no concrete policy exists to facilitate formal markets (*Mohanty and Gupta*, 2002) in the water sector. Rather, the existing polices dealing with water allocation are highly fragmented, embedded in piecemeal approach and highly *ad hoc* in nature. The Integrated Water Resource Management (IWRM) approach adopted in India's Water Policy 2002 prescribes introducing water rights for managing water resources at the river basin level (see *Shah and van Koppen*, 2006). However, very few states in India have adopted this IWRM approach and that also, only partially. The approach is also subject to various criticisms. For example, Shah and van Koppen (2006) argue that implementing the withdrawal permits for augmenting groundwater prescribed in the IWRM requires effective monitoring; the very presence of informal groundwater markets at large scale makes the monitoring part more difficult and economically costly. But this does not tell us whether we will encounter with same problems in case the withdrawal permits are introduced for surface irrigation. It is argued that the IWRM will work in those areas where the primary water diverters are large in size, corporate bodies are few in number, most water users are supplied by organized water providers and capital accumulation in terms of infrastructure creation is already high (*Shah and van Koppen*, 2006). Effective implementation of IWRM in the Indian context is hindered by existence of a large number of households who are the primary water divertors who self-supply water from the natural sources and generate very low level of capital accumulation in the water sector (*Shah and van Koppen*, 2006). Another major issue with the IWRM approach relates to pricing of irrigation water appropriately so that the formal markets could function efficiently. However, no proper institutional mechanism is available for generating information that could be used for 'proper' pricing. Dharmadhikary (2007) highlights some of the problems with the IWRM approach, especially in relation to institutions on water trading. For example, Maharashtra Water Resources Regulatory Authority (MWRRA) has been created to implement IWRM in Maharashtra and this authority has been assigned with the task of creating 'trading water entitlements'. The MWRRA is responsible for distributing the entitlements between various users so that these entitlements can be transferred, bartered, bought or sold on annual or seasonal basis within a market system. However, due to lack of information and guidance the prospect of the authority to effectively regulate the water markets has become grim. Also, many fear that tradable water rights suggested in the IWRM approach will lead to allocation of water to economically powerful people (*Dharmadhikary*, 2007) and therefore, there will be stiff resistance especially from the resource poor users of water (*Kumar*, 2003 cited in *Kumar*, 2007). Similarly, implementation of IWRM requires local or regional level institutions such as, the Catchment Management Institutions (CMAs) existing in countries like South Africa where the IWRM is more effective. Formation of CMAs, involving water user associations and developing appropriate technologies are some of the challenges in implementing the IWRM in the Indian context (*Shah and van Koppen*, 2006).

From the above analysis, one could get an impression that introducing formal markets in the Indian scenario is a difficult task, though not an impossible task. While discussing institutional options for water management in India, Saleth (1998) argues that '... a legally instituted and locally managed water quota system defined within an ecologically consistent overall withdrawal limit could eliminate the negative effects of markets and magnify their positive efficiency and conservation benefits. While the magnitude of benefits from observed water markets is tremendous, their contribution is only a fraction of the efficiency, equity, and sustainability gains possible from formal markets emerging within well-managed water quota system. The prevailing institutional vacuum thus makes the currently observed water markets only a distant second-best option' (*Saleth*, 1998).

MOVING TOWARDS 'FIRST BEST-OPTION'

How to make the distant, second-best option as a practicable, 'first best option' in the near future is an important question that we have to address here. As we have already discussed, the need for moving to the first-best option arises from the fact that water scarcity under the existing institutional and policy regime in India is becoming acute and generates huge social cost that is mainly 'invisible'. This being the case, the importance of establishing 'tradable water rights' in India has been already underlined by many researchers (e.g. *Kumar*, 2007; *Saleth*, 1996). However, we have no acceptable 'blue-print' on how to introduce formal markets in the water sector which is characterized by complexity and uncertainty; we also have no idea of what kind of the additional institutional arrangement is required for allowing formal markets so that water could be managed in an efficient, sustainable and equitable manner under the new market regime. Since 'bounded rationality' poses greater difficulty in understanding the required level of institutions, we need to do explorative empirical studies at more micro levels in the Indian context.

In the case of macro-level institutions, many countries have introduced various kinds of institutional and policy measures such as enacting and amending water laws, introducing regulatory authorities, reforming water pricing, etc. that provide conducive environment for water trade. However, the actual implementation of these measures at the ground level depends mainly on the institutions at micro-level that provide appropriate incentives and disincentives to the stakeholders—through change in the relative prices—to use water efficiently. In Texas, USA, for example, water districts or river authorities play an important role in allocating surface water by way of creating a market exchange through the tradable water rights. While partial ownership is exercised over the surface water, farmers enjoy absolute ownership over the groundwater in places like Texas. This means that the individual farmers having water rights are treated as the basic entities in the water markets. In Spain, trading of water takes place at community level. It has been demonstrated that in Spain, if the trade is allowed to take place across larger communities instead of individual communities the gains from water trade would be more (*Garrido*, 1998). In Canada, introducing water markets across sub-basins is found to result in increased benefits (*Horbulik and Lo*, 1998). In the developing country context, the institutional arrangements at regional and local level are somewhat different. In China, for example, the irrigation service providers play a major role in allocating water under the new regime, while the government has full right to water resources (*Shah et al.* 2004b). In Thailand, the basin working committees consisting of different stakeholders take up overall responsibility of managing water at the river basin level, while local water user associations control the allocation of water through market exchange (*Patamatamkul*, 2001).

In the Indian context, both the central and the state governments have taken a few steps at macro and micro-level to moot institutional reforms in the water sector. For example, the IWRM approach has been adopted in the national water policy, recognizing river basin as planning unit, water an economic commodity, etc. However, the IWRM approach is not being effectively implemented due various kinds of problems at the ground level. For instance, many issues such as, how to generate adequate information about the water use and values so that water could be allocated on economic principles, are not being properly spelt out in the approach. Moreover, there is no proper monitoring mechanism to control stealing of water taking place among the unorganized users in the scarce regions. The transaction cost of monitoring and controlling unauthorized use is extremely high and therefore, the resource-poor government agencies are not able to properly monitor and control these problems. On top of everything, electricity subsidy provided to the farmers also intensifies stealing of water in already scarce basins.

Some of the state governments like Maharashtra have established Regulatory Authorities in the water sector to guide water allocation (*Dharmathikary*, 2007). But these authorities are not effective because their roles and functions are not properly defined and they don't have access to required information for water allocation decisions. In some other states like Tamil Nadu, River Basin Boards have been created for some specific river basins.

These boards consist of various kinds of stakeholders and the major aim of these boards is to resolve water scarcity problem at the basin level through efficient conflict resolution mechanisms. However, these Boards are also not functioning well because of issues such as lack of political interest and lack of information available for decision-making. In many state governments, WUAs have been created for managing water at local level, under the umbrella of 'Participatory Irrigation Management System' (PIMS). However, the results are not satisfactory here as well (see *Marothia*, 2005). Apart from these bodies which are directly involved in managing water resources at regional level, other organizations at local level such as Village Panchayats and non-governmental organizations (NGOs) are also involved in water managements at river basin level. The outcomes of these arrangements are also not satisfactory, on an average. Altogether, it should be noted that the governments in India have established more than adequate level of institutions to manage water but the net result is not satisfactory. In the existing policies related to water sector, a piecemeal approach is glaring everywhere. Therefore, if at all water scarcity needs to be addressed properly in the Indian context, an integrated approach is warranted for. One of the important aspects that is completely missing in the existing institutional arrangements is that there is no proper guiding principle on the basis of which the institutions should function. One can bring in numerous institutional changes but if the overall policy guiding water allocation is still within the conventional regime, then the outcomes would be counterproductive. The existing fragmented institutions suggest that the transaction cost of creating and operationalizing these institutions are enormous and in the present form, all these institutions are scarcity inducing rather than scarcity minimizing. Keeping this in view, it is argued that there is a need for redesigning water policies in such a way that more MBIs such as tradable water rights can be introduced in the future so that the existing institutions can be systematically integrated for achieving the goal of efficient, equitable and sustainable water management.

Once the appropriate policy regime has been created, then other practical problems related to water trade may crop up in the scenario. For example, at what level the trade in water should take place, what kind of trade is transaction cost minimizing, who has to be responsible for regulating water trade, what kind of infrastructure is required for facilitating water trade, etc. are some of the questions which need to be answered. It should be noted that the answers for these questions will have to come from the regional and local level factors affecting water trade. For example, though water trading may not be possible between individual farmers or between individual farmers and urban buyers, such trading can be effective across sub-command areas or across WUAs in each canal within the sub-command. This is possible in the case of groundwater the groundwater resources are moved from the present 'open access regime' towards a 'common property regime' where the communities at local level will have more control over the groundwater resources (*Narain*, 1998). Similarly, trading may take place between WUAs and urban water supply authorities, rather than on individual to individual basis. However, when the markets mature water trade becomes a viable option at the farmer's level. In the case of groundwater, Kumar (2007) suggests that assignment of equal water rights to all farmers irrespective of the size of the land will lead to equitable allocation of water since the large farmers needing water over and above their own quota will end up buying water from small farmers who have got surplus water to sell; this mechanism will bring equity among the farmers. It may be noted that even if the small farmers do not have adequate infrastructure to pump their own share of water, the rationality of the farmers will lead to arrangements in such a way that the large farmers can pump water and share it with small farmers depending on the total costs and benefits of doing so. At local level, the individual tradable permits may be issued on the basis of the renewable amount of water so that over-exploitation of aquifers will be avoided, especially in the scarce regions. In case the water trade causes negative externality, the institutions such as village level institutions, watershed committees and aquifer management committees can be established exclusively for addressing these negative externalities (*Kumar*, 2007). The overall regulation of trading in order to avoid any conflict or negative externalities at regional or basin level, may lie with the Basin Boards or with the Regulatory Authority.

Sometimes, the standard economic prescriptions such as enacting efficient laws, introducing formal institutional arrangements, etc. under the broader model applied elsewhere may not be effective because of huge amount of uncertainties about appropriate institutions and the behaviour of the economic agents to be shaped by these prescriptions. At the rational and local level, the market operations are facilitated by non-conventional, behavioral factors such as, reciprocal behaviour and rule rationality. Adequate inputs on these aspects needs to be generated through scientific studies and should be incorporated in the design of instruments for water allocation. On top of everything, different types of institutional arrangements and their effectiveness need to be assessed in terms of the net gains achieved through transaction cost minimization. Studies within the new institutional economics frameworks—including bounded rationality framework—is warranted for at the river basin level in order to assess the net gains of market-based institutions for managing water, in the coming years.

Implementing tradable water rights system in a developing country context poses greater difficulty since it requires revamping the existing institutions and setting up new institutions which are both economically and politically highly costly. There are two issues to be addressed prior to implementing tradable water rights: (a) the supporting institutional arrangements combining the existing and new institutions to facilitate introduction of tradable water rights; and (b) estimation of transaction cost under the present institutional regime and that of under the new regime. It should be noted that empirical studies on measurement of transaction costs focus mainly on those types of transaction costs once the 'market' regime has been implemented. However, no attempt has been made to measure the transaction costs of moving from the present 'command and control regime' of water allocation to a market-based regime (*McCann and Easter*, 2004). Future research has to be directed towards this important area.*

*Acknowledgements: An earlier version of this paper has been presented in the IWMI-TATA 7th Annual Partners' Meet on Managing Water in the Face of Growing Scarcity, Inequality and Declining Returns: Exploring Fresh Approaches in Hyderabad during 2-4 April, 2008. The author thanks all the participants for their valuable comments. This paper forms part of a research study on Alternative Institutions for Water Management in India sponsored by the IWMI-TATA programme, Hyderbad. The author thanks the IWMI-TATA for its generous financial assistance.

Note and Reference

1. For an excellent critical review on water as an economic commodity, please see Hanemann (2006).

References

Brandon, Carter and Kirsten Hommann (1995). 'The Cost of Inaction: Valuing The Economy-wide Cost of Environmental Degradation in India', *Asia Environment Division*, The World Bank, Washington, DC.

Coase, Ronald H. (1992). 'The Institutional Structure of Production', *American Economic Review*, 82 (4): 713-19.

Colby, Bonnie G. (2000). 'Cap-and-Trade Policy Challenges: A Tale of Three Markets', *Land Economics*, 76 (4): 638-58.

Colby, Bennie G. (1990). 'Transaction Costs and Efficiency in Western Water Allocation', *American Journal of Agriculture Economics*, 72 (5): 1184 -92.

Conlisk, John, (1996). 'Why bounded rationality?' *Journal of Economic Literature*, 34 (2): 669-700.

Dharmadhikary, Shripad (2007). 'A Flawed Model for Water Regulation', *India Together*, www.indiatogether.org/2007/may/env-mwrra.htm.

Dubash, Navroz (2008). 'The Electricity-Groundwater Conundrum: Case for a Political Solution for a Political Problem, *Economic and Political Weekly*, 42 (52): 45-55.

Dubash, Navroz (2000). 'Ecologically and Socially Embedded Exchange: 'Gujarat Model' of Water Markets', *Economic and Political Weekly*, 35 (16): 1376-86.

Easter, Wiliam K., Ariel Dinar and Mark Rosegrant (1998). 'Water Markets: Transaction Costs and Institutional Options' In: K. William Easter, Mark W. Rosegrant and Ariel Dinar (Eds.) *Markets for Water: Potential and Performance*, Kluwer Academic Publishers, Boston, pp. 1-15.

Garrido, Alberto (1998). 'Economic Analysis of Water Markets in the Spanish Agriculture Sector: Can They Provide Substantial Benefits? In: K. William Easter, Mark W. Rosegrant and Ariel Dinar (Eds.) *Markets for Water: Potential and Performance*, Kluwer Academic Publishers, Boston, pp. 223-37.

Griffin, Charles W (1998). 'The Application of Water Market Doctrines in Texas', In: K. William Easter, Mark W. Rosegrant and Ariel Dinar (Eds.) *Markets for Water: Potential and Performance*, Kluwer Academic Publishers, Boston, pp. 51-64.

Gulati, Ashok and Sudha Narayanan (2001). 'Subsidies and Reforms in Indian Irrigation', In: Brennan, Donna (Ed.) *Water Policy Reform: Lessons from Asia and Australia, Proceedings of an International Workshop, Bangkok,* Thailand, pp. 131-48.

Horbulik, Theodre M. and Lynda J. Lo (1998).' Welfare Gains from Potential Water Markets in Alberta, Canada', In: K. William Easter, Mark W.

Rosegrant and Ariel Dinar (Eds.) *Markets for Water: Potential and Performance*, Kluwer Academic Publishers, Boston, 241-58.

Janakarajan, S. and Marcus Moench (2006). 'Are Wells a Potential Threat to Farmers' Well-being? Case of Deteriorating Groundwater Irrigation in Tamil Nadu', *Economic and Political Weekly*, 41 (37): 3977-87.

Kumar, Dinesh, M. (2007). 'Towards Evolving Institutional Arrangements for Managing Groundwater', In: M. Dinesh Kumar with O.P. Singh (Eds.) *Groundwater Management in India: Physical, Institutional and Policy Alternatives*, Sage Publications, New Delhi, pp. 288-320.

Kumar, Dinesh, M. (2003). 'Demand Management in the Face of Growing Water Scarcity and Conflicts in India: Institutional and Policy Alternatives for Future', In: Kanchan Chopra, C.H. Hanumantha Rao and Ram Prasad Sengupta (Eds.) *Water Resources, Sustainable Livelihoods and Ecosystem Services*, Concept Publishing Company, New Delhi.

Marothia, Dinesh (2005). 'Institutional Reforms in Canal Irrigation System', *Economic and Political Weekly*, 40 (28): 3074-84.

McCann, Laura and K. William Easter (2004). 'A Framework for Estimating the Transaction Costs of Alternative Mechanisms for Water Exchange and Allocation, *Water Resources Research*, 40, W09-S09.

McCann, Laura, Bonnie Colby, K. William Easter, Alexander Kasterined, K.V. Kuperan (2005). Transaction Cost Measurement for Evaluating Environmental Policies, *Ecological Economics*, 52 (4): 527-42.

Meinzen-Dick, Ruth (1998). 'Groundwater Markets in Pakistan: Institutional Development and Productivity Impacts', In: K. William Easter, Mark W. Rosegrant and Ariel Dinar (Eds.) *Markets for Water: Potential and Performance*, Kluwer Academic Publishers, Boston, 207-22.

Meinzen-Dick, Ruth (1996). *'Groundwater Markets in Pakistan: Participation and Productivity'*, International Food Policy Research Institute, Washington, D.C.

Mohanty, Nirmal and Shreekanth Gupta (2002). ' Breaking the Gridlock in Water Reforms through Water Markets: International Experience and Implementation Issues for India', *Working Paper Series, Julian L. Simon Centre for Policy Research.*

Narain, Vishal (1998). 'Toward a New Groundwater Institution for India', *Water Policy*, 1: 357-65.

Patamatamkul, Sanguan (2001). 'Integrated Water Resources Management for a Small Basin: Huai Yai Basin, North-eastern Thailand', In: Brennan, Donna (Ed.) *Water Policy Reform: Lessons from Asia and Australia, Proceedings of an International Workshop*, Bangkok, Thailand, pp. 177-88.

Rogers, Peter, Radika de Silva and Ramesh R. Bhatia (2002), 'Water is an Economic Good: How to Use Prices to Promote Equity, Efficiency and Sustainability', *Water Policy*, 4(1): 1-17.

Saleth, Maria (1998). 'Water Markets in India: Economic and Institutional Aspects', In: Easter, William K., Mark W. Rosegrant and Ariel Dinar

(Eds.). *Markets for Water: Potential and Performance*, Kluwer Academic Publishers, London, pp: 187-205.

Saleth, Maria R. (1996). *'Water Institutions in India: Economics, Law and Policy'*, Institute for Economic Growth, Commonwealth Publishers, New Delhi.

Saleth, Maria R. and Ariel Dinar (2004). *'The Institutional Economics of Water: A Crosscountry Analysis of Institutions and Performance'*, Edward Elgar, Cheltenham, UK.

Shah, Tushaar (1993). *Groundwater Markets and Irrigation Development*, Oxford University Press, New Delhi.

Shah, Tushaar and Barbara van Koppen (2006). 'Is India Ripe for Integrated Water Resources Management? Fitting Water Policy to National Development Context', *Economic and Political Weekly*, Vol. 41 (31): 3413-21.

Shah, Tushaar, Christopher Scott, Stephanie Buechler (2004a). 'Water Sector Reforms in Mexico, Lessons for India's New Water Policy', *Economic and Political Weekly*, 39 (4): 361-70.

Shah, Tushaar, Mark Giordano and Jinxia Wang (2004b). 'Irrigation Institutions in a Dynamic Economy: What Is China Doing Differently from India?' *Economic and Political Weekly*, 39 (31): 3452-61.

Thobani, Mateen (1998). 'Meeting Water needs in Developing Countries: Resolving Issues in Establishing Tradable Water Rights', In: Easter, William K., Mark W. Rosegrant and Ariel Dinar (Eds.). *Markets for Water: Potential and Performance*, Kluwer Academic Publishers, London, pp. 35-50.

Venkatachalam, L. (2005). Damage Assessment and Compensation to Farmers: Lessons from Verdict of Loss of Ecology Authority in Tamil Nadu, *Economic and Political Weekly, XL* (15): 1556-60.

Venkatachalam, L. (2004). 'Sources of Government Failure and the Environmental Externality: Analysis of Groundwater Pollution in Tamil Nadu, India', *Water Policy*, 6 (5): 413-26.

Williamson, Oliver E. (2000). 'The New Institutional Economics: Taking Stock, Looking Aheads', *Journal of Economic Literature*, 38 (3): 595-613.

Sustainability of Indian Fisheries: An Assessment

Pradeep K. Katiha and Sanchita Sarkar

Indian agriculture is witnessing slow growth rate during past one decade, but fisheries sector emerged as one of the fast growing enterprise. It also offers immense potential for rural development, food and nutritional security and employment generation through initialization of ancillary industries, reduction of gender inequality and rising export earnings. With rich aquatic diversity ranging from deep seas to high mountain lakes and over 10% of the world's fish biodiversity, India secured third position in global fisheries and second in aquaculture. Current fish production of the country reached over 7.13 million t from meager 0.75 million t in 1950-51. India's share is increasing gradually in global fish production. Such a turnaround in Indian fisheries reflected its brighter side. It has many contributory enterprises, whose sustainability and growth varied significantly over the years. An attempt has been made in present communication to investigate sustainability and growth drivers of Indian fisheries and suggest some of the measures for keep their pace on for development of the sector. The investigations are primarily based on analysis of secondary data collected from various sources.

The technological innovation and investment enhancements led to significant growth of marine fisheries till mid-nineties, but failed to sustain in this century due to overexploitation and diminishing commercial fish stocks. Since independence, Indian marine fisheries observed three phases. The phase I (1950 to 1968) was characterized by dominance of fishing by traditional fishing methods including non-mechanized crafts and gears. The mechanization and initiation of motorization of crafts and gears was the characteristic feature of phase II during 1969-88. The phase III since 1989 witnessed intensive mechanization and motorization of crafts and multiday fishing with extension of fishing grounds. It noticed unstable growth and finally the marine fish production became almost stagnant. The liberalization and globalization of fish trade opened new avenues for fish exports. Over the years, dependence on shrimp for seafood export is substituted by other frozen fish. Despite this diversification, marine fisheries may not be sustainable to meet the demands for domestic supply and export. The other sector of inland fisheries followed a constantly growing trend. It observed structural changes in composition of its fish production. Till mid-eighties, fisheries was the major contributor, which was replaced by aquaculture. Depleting fisheries resources, energy crisis and resultant high cost of fishing, etc. have led to realization of potential and versatility of aquaculture as a sustainable and cost-effective alternative to capture fisheries. It has over 80% share in inland fish production now. But, it must overcome several challenges to sustain growth.

For marine fisheries, deep sea fishing by targeting untapped high sea fish potential is probably the only option to enhance and sustain the contribution from this sector. It would require enhanced investment in mechanized vessels, capacity strengthening of artisanal and a proper institutional structure to share the benefits. In general, major drivers to sustain the growth of fisheries sector are technology, infrastructure and market apart from enhanced investments in research and development. Technology for quality seed production, formulation of low cost feed materials and fabrication of nets for efficient fishing; infrastructure such as construction of mini-harbours, jetties, landing centres, introduction of trawlers and mechanized vessels, etc. and market development through creation of institutional structures, storage, transportation and standardization facilities and market information are required for sustainable fisheries development in India.

INTRODUCTION

Indian agriculture has been witnessing slow growth rate for past one decade, but fisheries sector emerged as one of the fast growing enterprises. It also offers immense potential for rural development, food and nutritional security and employment generation through its ancillary industries, reduction of gender inequalities and rising export earnings. With rich aquatic diversity ranging from deep seas to high mountain lakes and over 10% of the world's fish biodiversity, India has third position in global fisheries and second in aquaculture. Current fish production of the country reached over 7.13 million t from meager 0.75 million t in 1950-51 (*Ayyappan*, 2009). The share of India is increasing gradually in global fish production. The sector witnessed increased knowledge, dynamism and technological advances. Such a turnaround in Indian fisheries though reflected its brighter side, but it may not be an indicator of sustainability of the sector. Sustainable growth generates income for poor people that means rural development: improving transport, development of market facilities and linkages, improving (access to) information, participation of the rural poor in decision-making, providing access to credit, and so on (*Rao*, 2007). In other words, sustainable growth of fisheries requires country's fishing operations and policies to be designed with a view to achieving long-term sustainable use of fisheries resources, as a means of assuring resource conservation, continued food supplies and alleviating poverty in fishing communities (*FAO*, 1997). The multiple use aquatic resources are although renewable but not infinite and need sustainable management towards fisheries and aquaculture to contribute significantly to nutrition, economic and social well-being of the growing population of the country. Indian fisheries have many contributory enterprises, whose sustainability and growth varied significantly over the years. An attempt has been made in present communication to investigate sustainability and growth drivers of Indian fisheries and suggest some of the measures for keep their pace on for development of the sector.

The investigations are primarily based on analysis of secondary data collected from various sources. These sources included Department of Animal Husbandry, Dairying and Fisheries (DAHD&F), Ministry of Agriculture (MoA), Government of India (GoI), New Delhi; Institutes of Fisheries Division, Indian Council of Agricultural Research (ICAR), New Delhi; Departments of Fisheries (DoFs) of Indian States; and XIth Five Year Plan Working Group Reports for Fisheries Sector submitted to The Planning Commission, Government of India, New Delhi.

RESULTS AND DISCUSSIONS

The results of the analysis done for aqua-resources of the country and the sustainability of fish production from marine and inland waters in India are presented in this section.

The Fisheries Resources

India is endowed with vast marine and inland aqua-resources. These waters have varied dimensions (Table 1) according to their expanse and ecological features across different states of the country. These waters harbour richest aquatic organisms diversity in the world.

TABLE 1

Indian Aqua-Resource for Fisheries and Aquaculture

Indian Aqua-resource	*The length/expanse*
Marine	
Coastline	8,118 km
EEZ	2.03 million km^2
Continental Self	0.53 million km^2
Inland	
Rivers & Canals	1,95,210 km
Reservoirs	3.17 million ha.
Ponds and Tanks	2.41 million ha.
Oxbow lakes & derelict waters	0.80 million ha.
Brackishwater	1.24 million ha.

Source: Katiha *et al*., 2009, Anon, 2006.

The marine resources include coastal line over 8,100 km with a continental shelf of 0.53 million km^2 and Exclusive Economic Zone (EEZ) with an expanse of 2.03 million km^2. The inland waters comprised of both large open and small closed waters, which are utilized for fisheries and aquaculture.

Marine Fisheries Resources

The marine fisheries waters (Table 2) in form of coastal line have maximum length around A&N islands followed by Gujarat, Tamil Nadu and Andhra Pradesh. The continental shelf has maximum area in Gujarat followed by Maharashtra.

The total area of EEZ of India is estimated at 2.03 million km^2 against its land area of about 3.2 million km^2. The continental shelf area between 0 and 50 m and between 0 and 200 m depth, is estimated at 1,91,972 km^2 and 3,62,060 km^2, respectively. There are general topo-hydrographical differences in the features of the coastline and adjacent seas, distribution and abundance pattern of the species and their fishery characteristics along the west and east coasts. Primary and secondary productivity is higher on the west coast compared to the east, mainly due to the strong upwelling process, which therefore supports a more abundant fishery. The northwest coast (15°-23°N Lat) has extensive fishing grounds and the sea bottom is generally muddy while the southwest coast (8°-15°N Lat) has a narrow continental shelf with less extensive fishing grounds. The southeast coast (10°-15°N Lat) is characterized by coral and rocky grounds while the sea bottom of the northeast coast (15°-21°N Lat) is predominantly muddy and suitable for bottom trawling.

TABLE 2

Marine Fisheries Resources of India

Sl. No.	*State/Union Territory*	*Length of coast line (km)*	*Continental shelf (000 sq. km.)*
1.	Andhra Pradesh	974	33
2.	Goa	104	10
3.	Gujarat	1,600	184
4.	Karnataka	300	27
5.	Kerala (P)	590	40
6.	Maharashtra	720	112
7.	Orissa	480	26
8.	Tamil Nadu	1,076	41
9.	West Bengal	158	17
10.	A & N Islands (P)	1,912	35
11.	Daman and Diu (P)	27	NA
12.	Lakshadweep (P)	132	4
13.	Pondicherry	45	1
	Total	8,118	530

P = Provisional.

Source: Anon (2007).

The northern Indian Ocean, together with its two major bays, the Arabian Sea and the Bay of Bengal, is landlocked in the north by the Asian continent which separates the northern Indian Ocean from the deep-reaching vertical convection areas of the Arctic seas and the cold climate regions of the northern hemisphere. The monsoon current which is towards west during the northeast monsoon period (October-December) and towards east during the south-west monsoon season (May-October) has significant impact on the coastal fisheries.

Inland Fisheries Resources

The inland fishery waters can be categorised into rivers and canals, reservoirs, aquacultural waters in form of ponds and tanks for fresh and brackish water and floodplain wetlands in form of *heels*, oxbow lakes and derelict water bodies and estuaries. The details of their expanse in different states are summarised in Table 3. The rivers and canals has maximum stretch in Uttar Pradesh followed by Jammu and Kashmir, Madhya Pradesh, Maharashtra, Punjab and Andhra Pradesh. The areas under reservoirs is maximum in Andhra Pradesh followed by Karnataka, Madhya Pradesh, Tamil Nadu, Uttar Pradesh, Gujarat, Maharashtra and Rajasthan. For freshwater aquaculture, the highest area is under the state of Andhra Pradesh followed by Tamil Nadu, Karnataka, West Bengal, Rajasthan and Uttar Pradesh. The brackish waters suitable for aquaculture were primarily restricted in coastal states of Orissa, West Bengal, Karnataka and Andman & Nicobar Islands. The floodplain wetlands and derelict waters were primarily confined to Kerela, Assam, Orissa, Bihar, etc. Inland waters are highly diverse in terms of their distribution, water quality, accessibility and productivity. Due to diverse in distribution and variation in their expanse because of rainfall, it is very difficult to give their exact magnitude. Different sources provide their varied expanse, particularly the reservoirs have high draw down over the year in different seasons. These constraints in their exact expanse also restrain the estimates for their potential and existing fish productivity. These factors have an influence on the sustainability of their fish productivity. The details of these resources are mentioned below.

TABLE 3
Inland Fishery Resources of India

Sl. No.	*States/UTs*	*Rivers & canals (km)*	*Reservoirs (million ha)*	*Ponds & Tanks (million ha)*	*Beels, Oxbow lakes and Derelict bodies (million ha)*	*Brackish water (million ha)*
1.	Andhra Pradesh	11,514	0.52631	0.52	—	0.06
2.	Assam	4,820	—	0.023	0.11	—
3.	Bihar	3,200	0.00662	0.10	0.01	—
4.	Goa	250	—	0.003	—	Neg
5.	Gujarat	3,865	0.28623	0.07	0.01	0.1
6.	Haryana	5,000	0.00028	0.01	0.01	—
7.	Himachal Pradesh	3,000	0.0418	0.001	—	—
8.	Jammu & Kashmir	27,781	0.0097	0.02	0.01	—
9.	Karnataka	9,000	0.43729	0.29	—	0.01
10.	Kerala	3092	0.02964	0.03	0.24	0.24
11.	Madhya Pradesh	17,088	0.37232	0.06	—	—
12.	Maharashtra	16,000	0.27375	0.06	—	0.01
13.	Manipur	3,360	—	0.01	0.004	—
14.	Meghalaya	5,600	—	0.002	Neg	—
15.	Nagaland	1,600	—	0.05	Neg	—
16.	Orissa	4,500	0.1982	0.11	0.18	0.43
17.	Punjab	15,270	—	0.04	—	—
18.	Rajasthan	*5290	0.15854	0.18	—	—
19.	Sikkim	900	—	—	0.003	—
20.	Tamil Nadu	7,420	0.35068	0.34	0.01	0.06
21.	Tripura	1,200	—	0.013	—	—
22.	Uttar Pradesh	28,500	0.31449	0.16	0.13	—
23.	West Bengal	2,526	0.01573	0.28	0.04	0.21
24.	Arunachal Pradesh	2,000	—	Neg	0.04	—
25.	Mizoram	1,395	—	0.002	—	—
26.	A & N Islands	115	—	0.003	—	0.12
27.	Chandigarh	2	—	Neg	Neg	—
28.	Delhi	150	—	—	—	—
29.	Lakshadweep	—	—	—	—	—
30.	Pondicherry	247	—	Neg	0.001	Neg
31.	Dadra & Nagar Haveli	54	—	—	—	—
32.	Daman & Diu	12	—	Neg	—	Neg
33.	Chhattisgarh	3,573	0.08807	0.06	—	—
34.	Uttaranchal	2,686	0.02035	0.001	—	—
35.	Jharkhand	4,200	0.04884	0.03	—	—
	Total	1,95,210	3.17221	2.407	0.797	1.24

Source: Sugunan, 1995, Katiha *et al*, 2009; Hand Book on Fisheries Statistics, 2005; Report of Working Group on Fisheries for Xth Five Year Plan, MoA, 2001.

The Rivers and Canals

For rivers and canals, canals are rarely utilized for fisheries or aquaculture in the country, although offer great scope for freshwater aquaculture and fisheries. The fishery of canals is mostly limited to fishing for natural fish species. The river systems of India may be classified into two major groups, namely, Himalayan or extra-peninsular rivers and peninsular rivers. Originating from the Himalayas to transverse great alluvial Indo-Gangatic plains, Himalayan snow and rainfed rivers are characterized by complicated flood regimes and seasonal variations in volume of flow. These rivers are categorised into three systems, the Ganga, the Brahamputra and the Indus. The Ganga river system has combined length of 12,500 kms and a catchment area of 97.6 million ha. The Ganga, Ghagra, Gomti, Ramganga, Kosi, Gandak, Yamuna, Chambal, Sone and Tons are the major rivers of this system. These rivers are spread over most of the north Indian states (except the hilly states) to extend upto West Bengal through Bihar. In the upland waters of system commercial fisheries is virtually absent, due to inaccessible terrain and other exploitation problems. The stretch of river Ganga from Haridwar to Lalgola is recognised as one of the richest source of capture fisheries in India, comprising highly priced major carps, hilsa and catfishes. Mid-September to June are peak months for fishing. The combined length of the Brahamputra river system is 4023 km. with catchment area of 51 million ha. Originating from Tibet the river flows through northern slopes of Himalayas to enter India at north-east corner of Arunachal Pradesh. It has 918 km stretch in India, including 730 km in Assam alone. Its northern tributaries Subansiri, Kameng and Manas are large with steep, shallow-braided channels, whereas those on the southern bank, Buri Dihing, Dhansiri and Kopilli are deeper with meandering channels and low gradient. The Brahamputra vally is marked for its abandoned river beds (beels) supporting rich fishery. Catfishes and major and minor carps dominate the commercial catches of upper middle and lower stretches, while the commercial catch in lower-middle stretch primarily composed of catfish and miscellaneous catch.

In case of the Indus river system, main Indus and its tributaries in upper, and Beas and Sutlej in the lower reaches are important from Indian fisheries viewpoint. Its headwaters in the states of

Jammu and Kashmir, Himachal Pradesh and Punjab mainly harbour mahaseer, snow trout, some cyprinids and exotic trouts. The rivers Beas and Sutlej contain indigenous carps and catfishes, which are commercially exploited.

The torrential and rain fed, peninsular rivers have well defined stable course. These include two river systems, the East Coast and the West Coast. The East Coast river system has vast expanse of water in the states of Orissa, Madhya Pradesh, Maharashtra, Andhra Pradesh, Karnataka and Tamil Nadu. This river system mainly has four constituent rivers, the Mahanadi, the Godavari, the Krishna and the Cauvery have a combined length of 6437 km and catchment area of 121 million ha. This system drains entire Peninsular India and east of Western Ghats in the west and south parts of central India. Besides its own fish fauna of several carps, catfishes, murrels, and prawn, the systen is repeatedly enriched by transplantation of Gangatic carps.

The combined length of rivers of West Coast river system and catchment area are 3380 km and 69.16 million ha, respectively. The Narmada and the Tapti are the longest rivers of system along with 600 small rivers. Its rivers are distributed in the states of Gujarat, Maharastra and Madhya Pradesh. The fish fauna of the system consists of carps, catfishes, mahaseers, prawns, etc.

The Reservoirs

During post-independence period, large number of river valley projects created a chain of impoundments, which are highly amenable for fishery activities. These man-made water bodies created by obstructing the surface flow, by erecting a dam of any description, on a river, stream or any water course are called reservoirs (*Sugunan*, 1995). These are generally classified into small (<1000 ha), medium (1000-5000 ha) and large (>5000 ha). The area under these water bodies is on a continuous increase by adopting more and more reservoirs for fisheries. At present in India total area under reservoirs is 3.17 million ha, out of which small reservoirs occupy 1.5 million ha followed by large 1.14 million ha and medium 0.53 million ha. Among the states, maximum percentage area under reservoirs is in Madhya Pradesh (14.6) followed by Andhra (14.54), Karnataka (13.87) and Tamil Nadu (11.38). Among different sized reservoirs, maximum annual production is from small reservoirs (49.9 kg/ha) followed by medium (12.3 kg/ha) and large (11.43 kg/ha) with overall average of 20.13 kg/ha.

The Aquaculture Waters

By virtue of its geographical situation in monsoon belt, India is endowed with good rainfall and consequently extensive aquacultural water bodies. The inland aquacultural water resources in the form of ponds and tanks have been distributed almost over all the states of India. Total expanse under ponds and tanks is over 2.4 million ha. The area under these waters is primarily concentrated in the states of Andhra Pradesh, Tamil Nadu, West Bengal and Karnataka. The total area brought under umbrella of aquaculture is about 0.85 million ha. In early seventies, with World Bank assistance, Fish Farmers Development Agency (FFDA) has been set-up, with the objectives of promotion of pond fish culture and adoption of modern aquacultural techniques to achieve high fish production. This agency has adopted over half of the area covered under fish culture. The maximum percentage of area covered by FFDA was in the states of Punjab and Haryana, where fish farmers were taking more than one crop, as evident from higher cropped area than the actual. The productivity was also highest for Punjab at 4085 kg/ha/year followed by Haryana at 3501 kg/ha/year. The national average productivity from FFDA supported ponds has increased from 50 kg/ha/year in 1974-75 to about 2135 kg/ha/year in 1994-95. Now, the national fish yield is estimated over 2.5 t/ha.

Oxbow Lakes

India has extensive floodplains in the form of oxbow lakes (mauns, beels, chaurs and jheels) especially in the states of Assam, Bihar and West Bengal. The total area under these waters is over 0.32 million ha. These are shallow, nutrient rich water bodies formed due to change in course of the river. Some of these retain connection with the main river, atleast in monsoons, while others have lost it permanently (*Sinha*, 1997). These water bodies has very high fish production potential varying from 2-3 t/ha against existing production of 0.5 to 1 t/ha.

Estuary

The estuarine capture fishery forms an important component

of inland fisheries (*Sinha*, 1997). The open estuarine system includes Hoogly-Matlah and Mahanadi estuarine systems (Table 8). Godavari estuary is the main estuary of peninsular India, with Adyar Mankanam and Mandovi as other estuaries and Chilka, Pulicat and Vembanad as important brackish water lagoons. These estuaries and lagoons are recognised as excellent sources of naturally occurring fish and prawn seed. The fisheries of the estuaries are considered as above the subsistence level. The average yield varies between 45-75 kg/ha.

Brackish Water

The data on concentration and distribution of area for brackish water across different states in India is given in Table 3. The area along the coastal line of India is suitable for brackish water shrimp culture. Only 12% area was covered by shrimp farms. Therefore, it has immense scope for expansion both horizontally and diversification with inclusion of different fish species under umbrella of brackish water aquaculture.

THE SUSTAINABILITY OF INDIAN FISH PRODUCTION

The sustainability of fish production was estimated in terms of temporal sustainability index (TSI) using the formula (*Katiha*, 1994)

$$TSI = \frac{Y_t - S_t}{Y_{tmax}}$$

where Y_t = Average fish production during study period,
S_t = Standard Deviation of fish production during study period, and
Y_{tmax} = Maximum fish production during study period.

Since independence, fish production of India has increased from 0.75 million t to 7.13 million t (Table 4).

The maximum increment in fish production was in the last three decades of eighties, nineties and after 2000. As mentioned earlier that India is endowed with both marine and inland sectors and under inland both natural waters and aquaculture water bodies. During these decades the fish production of the country increased for both marine and inland waters, the maximum increment was for inland aquaculture.

TABLE 4

The Trend of Indian Fish Production for Past Six Decades

Year	*Fish production (in million t)*	*Change in production*	*% change*
1950-51	0.75	—	—
1960-61	1.16	0.41	54.67
1970-71	1.76	0.60	51.72
1980-81	2.45	0.69	39.20
1990-91	3.84	1.39	56.73
2000-01	5.66	1.82	47.40
2007-08	7.13	1.47	25.97

The maximum increment in fish production was in the last three decades of eighties, nineties and after 2000. As mentioned earlier that India is endowed with both marine and inland sectors and under inland both natural waters and aquaculture water bodies. During these decades the fish production of the country increased for both marine and inland waters, the maximum increment was for inland aquaculture.

The estimates of temporal sustainability index for country's fish production lowest during late eighties (Table 5) due to higher annual increments during this period. Although, the standard deviation was maximum during the current decade, but the higher quantum of average and maximum annual fish production resulted in comparatively better sustainability indices.

TABLE 5

Temporal Sustainable Indices for Indian Fish Production

Period	*Average Production ('000 t)*	*Standard Deviation*	*TSI*
1980-81 to 1984-85	2512	151.07	0.84
1985-86 to 1989-90	3121	292.71	0.77
1990-91 to 1994-95	4358	340.73	0.84
1995-96 to 1999-00	5332	231.90	0.90
2000-01 to 2007-08	6365	425.18	0.83

The Sustainability of Fish Production in Marine Sector

The marine sector noticed unstable growth and finally its fish production became almost stagnant. The percentage change in marine fish production is shown in Table 6 indicated declining growth. The highest increment in fish production was during the decade of eighties when marine fish production increased by 0.74 million. Thereafter the increase was lower and during recent decade of after 2000 the fish production became almost stagnant.

TABLE 6

The Trend of Fish Production in Marine Sector for Past Six Decades

Year	*Marine production (in million t)*	*Change in production (marine)*	*% change*
1950-51	0.53	—	—
1960-61	0.88	0.35	66.04
1970-71	1.09	0.21	23.86
1980-81	1.56	0.47	43.12
1990-91	2.3	0.74	47.44
2000-01	2.81	0.51	22.17
2007-08	2.91	0.09	3.2

Source: Hand Book on Fisheries Statistics, 2005, Department of Animal Husbandry, Dairying and Fisheries, Ministry of Agriculture, Govt. of India & Ayyappan, 2009.

The temporal sustainability indices estimates were higher for past one and half decades due to less variation in fish production (Table 7).

TABLE 7

Temporal Sustainable Indices for Marine Fish Production

Period	*Average Production ('000 t)*	*Standard Deviation*	*TSI*
1980-81 to 1984-85	1529	96.74	0.84
1985-86 to 1989-90	1836	225.52	0.71
1990-91 to 1994-95	2533	143.02	0.89
1995-96 to 1999-00	2834	115.45	0.92
2000-01 to 2007-08	2872	68.52	0.94

The technological innovation and investment enhancements led to significant growth of marine fisheries till mid nineties, but failed to sustain in this century due to overexploitation and diminishing commercial fish stocks. Since independence, Indian marine fisheries observed three phases (Figure 1).

Figure 1: Marine Fish Production in India during Different Phases of Growth

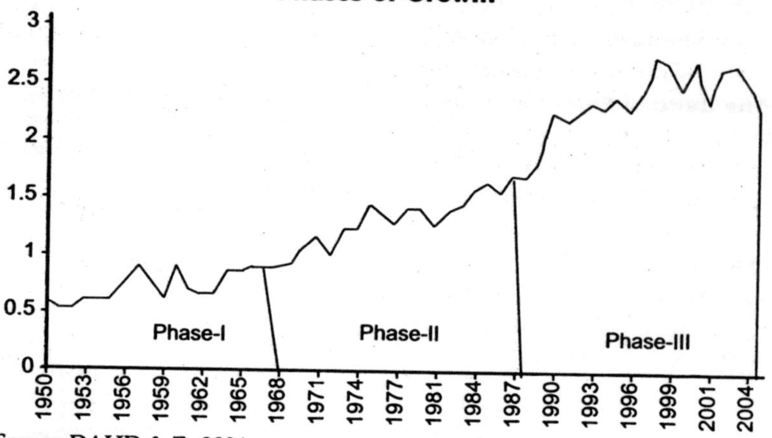

Source: DAHD & F., 2004.

The phase I (1950.to 1968) was characterized by dominance of fishing by traditional fishing methods including non-mechanized crafts and gears. The mechanization and initiation of motorization of crafts and gears was the characteristic feature of phase II during 1969-88. The phase III since 1989 witnessed intensive mechanization and motorization of crafts and multi-day fishing with extension of fishing grounds.

Issues such as unregulated open access fisheries, indiscriminate capture and downgrading of juveniles and sub adults, environmental degrading, biodiversity loss and ineffective regulatory measures, increased fishing costs and decreased profitability, poor infrastructure and linkages for domestic marking, underutilization of oceanic and deep sea resources and emerging inter and intra-sectoral conflicts are responsible factors for the stagnation of marine fisheries in India. Under such condition deep sea fishing by targeting untapped high sea fish potential is found to be the only option to enhance the contribution of this sector. To sustain the enhancement reduction of overcapacity in the mechanised sector is required. The strategies to be taken comprises changing over from an open access to a regulated regime, employing a fishery management regime supported by a multi-dimensional information platform, upgrading technologies and capabilities in the artisanal and small mechanized sector for diversification, reducing the excess capacity of fishing fleet, freezing the entry of new coastal mechanized fishing crafts, establishing an oceanic tuna and squid fishery, promoting mariculture for finfishes, edible bivalves, sea plants, and other commercially important species and sustain fish production through the effective enforcement of MFRAs. These in turn would require enhanced investment in this sector and proper institutional structure to share the benefits.

Declining marine capture fisheries which is mainly because of declining yields from pelagic finfishes along with conflicts of stakeholders and usage of large variety of fishing fleets necessitates effective management of the exploited stocks. Table 8 showed the status of pelagic fisheries in India.

TABLE 8

Comparison of Percentage Composition of Different Pelagic Fishes in Total Pelagic Catch

Groups	*1961-65*	*1990-2005*
Oil Sardine	42.40	18.02
Mackerel	9.44	13.14
Carangids	5.38	11.42
Ribbonfishes	5.90	10.39
Anchovies	5.57	9.31
Bombay Duck	20.62	8.88
Lesser sardines	7.17	7.80
Other clupeids		3.83
Tunas and bill fishes	1.03	3.69
Seerfishes	2.48	3.50
Hilsa shad		2.03
Wolf herrings		1.22
Barracudas		1.13
Other pelagics		5.64
Total pelagics	100.00	100.00

Source: Pillai and Katiha, 2005.

Sustainability for Inland Fish Production

The inland fish production is major source of fish for domestic consumption. It has contribution from fisheries and aquaculture activities. The fish production has become nearly 19 times during last six decades (Table 9). From independence to mid-eighties fisheries has the mainstay in inland fish production, but due to anthropogenic and other pressures on the natural inland waters, their fish production declined regularly. But, the technological interventions in inland aquaculture sector in form of induced breeding of Indian major carps and composite fish culture technologies increased its fish production manifold. It led to reversal of major contributing activity from capture fisheries to aquaculture. This trend is continuing till date. The inland aquaculture is recognized as one of the fastest growing enterprise in the country.

TABLE 9

The Trend of Inland Fish Production in India

Year	*Inland production (in million t)*	*Change in production*	*% change*
1950-51	0.22		
1960-61	0.28	0.06	27.27
1970-71	0.67	0.39	139.29
1980-81	0.89	0.22	32.84
1990-91	1.54	0.65	73.03
2000-01	2.85	1.31	85.06
2007-08	4.22	1.37	48.07

Source: Hand Book on Fisheries Statistics, 2006, Department of Animal Husbandry, Dairying and Fisheries, Ministry of Agriculture, Govt. of India.

The temporal sustainability indices also fluctuated due magnitude of these increments over different periods over past two and half decades. The index was at its lowest during early nineties, when the standard deviation was high due to larger annual increment in inland aquaculture. Similar observations were made during recent decade because of higher investments through number of developmental institutions in the country.

TABLE 10

Temporal Sustainable Indices for Inland Fish Production

Period	*Average Production ('000 t)*	*Standard Deviation*	*TSI*
1980-81 to 1984-85	983	71.75	0.83
1985-86 to 1989-90	1285	83.91	0.86
1990-91 to 1994-95	1825	200.46	0.77
1995-96 to 1999-00	2497	199.63	0.81
2000-01 to 2007-08	3492	407.84	0.73

Finally, it can be concluded that inland fisheries observed structural changes in composition of its fish production. Till mid eighties, capture fisheries was the major contributor, which was replaced by aquaculture afterwards. Depleting fisheries resources, energy crisis and resultant high cost of fishing, etc. have led to realization of potential and versatility of aquaculture as a sustainable and cost-effective alternative to capture fisheries. Consequently, thrusts were given on development of freshwater aquaculture, development of integrated coastal aquaculture, development of coldwater fisheries and aquaculture in hilly region, development of water logged areas into aquaculture estates, utilization of inland saline/alkaline soils for aquaculture and inland capture fisheries from unconventional and highly potential fisheries resources, i.e. reservoirs, floodplain wetland, etc. (*Anon*, 2006). Aquaculture, although now has over 80% share in inland fish production but, it must overcome several challenges to sustain growth. Despite immense efforts for horizontal expansion of this industry, only one third of the area could be brought under scientific fish culture. This untapped production potential can be harnessed through effective and intensive adoptions of available technologies, transfer of technical know-how and provision for material inputs. Flexibility in areas of operation and scales of investments, and compatibility of freshwater aquaculture practices with other farming systems coupled with high potentials of eco-restoration have provided congenial environment to establish it as a fast growing activity. Considering its potential and impressive annual growth rate of over 6%, Government of India is also emphasizing on aquaculture development. The national freshwater aquaculture development plan proposed to increase the area under aquaculture to 1.2 million ha (Table 4), with average productivity of 2762 kg ha^{-1} yr^{-1}. The state-wise distribution of area under ponds and tanks according to their production potential and projected productivity is estimated. The increase in area under different production levels as a percentage of total projected area (1.2 million ha) shows 3.67% for 8 t/ha/year, 0.50% for 6 t/ha/year, 16.51% for 5 t/ha/year, 34.33% for 3 t/ha/year, 17.48% for 2 t/ha/year, 19.17% for 1 t/ha/year and 8.34% for 0.5 t/ha/year. The major emphasis is to have a yield of 3 t or less with area over 79%. It seems to be a viable and realistic proposition. To achieve this goal, suitable strategies for enhancement of area coverage and productivity are needed considering components of horizontal and vertical expansion in concurrence with the potential and problems of different states.

CONCLUSIONS

In general, major drivers to sustain the growth of fisheries sector are technology, infrastructure and market apart from enhanced investments in research and development. The stress is on strengthening the technical wings and extension agencies of DoFs to assist fishers and fish farmers to adopt various improved package and practices of fisheries and aquaculture. It also emphasizes on expansion of prawn farming and setting up of medium sized fish feed units. Technology for quality seed production, formulation of low cost feed materials and fabrication of nets for efficient fishing; infrastructure such as construction of mini harbours, jetties, landing centres, introduction of trawlers and mechanized vessels, etc.; and market development through creation of institutional structures, storage, transportation and standardization facilities and market information are required for sustainable fisheries development in India.

REFERENCES

Anon, 2001. Report of Working Group on Fisheries for Xth Five Year Plan, Planning Commission, Government of India, New Delhi.

Anon, 2006. Hand Book on Fisheries Statistics, Department of Animal Husbandry, Dairying and Fisheries, Ministry of Agriculture, Govt. of India.

Anon, 2007. Report of the Working Group on Fisheries for the Eleventh Five Year Plan (2007-12), Planning Commission, Government of India, New Delhi.

Ayyappan, S., 2009. Presentation at National Conference of State Fisheries Ministers, 4-5 July, 2009, Bhubaneswar.

Food and Agriculture Organisation (1997). *FAO Technical Guidelines for Responsible Fisheries: Inland Fisheries.* FAO Fisheries Department, Rome, No. 6, p. 36.

Katiha, P.K., 1994. Natural Resource Management: A Case Study of Reservoir Fisheries in Himachal Pradesh. Ph.D. Thesis, Unpublished. Department of Social Sciences, Dr. Y.S. P armor University of Horticulture and Forestry, Nauni, Solan (H.P.), p. 192.

Katiha, P.K.; Vass, K.K.; Shrivastava, N.P. and Das, A.K., 2009. Improving Productivity of Reservoir Fisheries in India, Central Inland Fisheries Research Institute, Barrackpore.

Pillai, N.G.K. and Katiha, P.K., 2005. Evolution of fisheries and aquaculture in India. Central Marine Fisheries Research Institute, Kochi, Kerala, India.

Rao, V.M., 2007. Sustainability of Indian Agriculture: Towards an Assessment, eSS working paper/agriculture/Rao/August 2007.

Sinha, M., 1997. Inland Fisheries Resources of India and Their Utilisation. *In Fisheries Enhancement of Small Reservoirs and Floodplain Lakes in India,* edited by V.V. Sugunan and M. Sinha. Bulletin 75, Central Inland Capture Fisheries Research Institute, *Barrackpore.* pp. 167-174.

Sugunan, V.V., 1995. Reservoir Fisheries in India. FAO Fisheries Technical Paper No. 345, Food and Agriculture Organisation, Rome, pp. 6, 12.

Anon. 2007. Report of the Working Group on Fisheries for the Eleventh Five Year Plan (2007-12), Planning Commission, Government of India, New Delhi.

Ayyappan, S. 2009. Presentation at National Conference of State Fisheries Ministers, 4-5 July, 2009, Bhubaneswar.

Food and Agriculture Organisation. (1997). *FAO Technical Guidelines for Responsible Fisheries-Inland fisheries*. FAO Fisheries Department, Rome. No 6, p. 36.

Katiha, P.K. 1993. *Natural Resource Management: An Assessment of Reservoir Fisheries in Himachal Pradesh*. Ph.D. thesis, Unpublished. Department of Social Sciences, Dr. Y.S. Parmar University of Horticulture and Forestry, Nauni, Solan (H.P.), p 178.

Katiha, P.K., Vass, K.K., Shrivastava, N.P. and Das, A.K. 2009. *Improving Productivity of Reservoir Fisheries in India*. Central Inland Fisheries Research Institute, Barrackpore.

Pillai, N.G.K. and Katiha, P.K. 2007. *Evolution of Fisheries and Aquaculture in India*. Central Marine Fisheries Research Institute, Kochi, Kerala, India.

Rao, V.M. 2007. Sustainability of Indian Agriculture: [illegible] working paper, agriculture: [illegible]

Sinha, M. 1999. Inland fisheries resources of India and their utilisation. In: *Fisheries Enhancement of Small Reservoirs and Floodplain Lakes in India*, edited by V.V. Sugunan and M. Sinha. Bulletin 75, Central Inland Capture Fisheries Research Institute, Barrackpore, pp. [illegible]

Sugunan, V.V. 1995. *Reservoir Fisheries in India*. FAO Fisheries Technical Paper No. [illegible], Food and Agriculture Organisation [illegible]

SECTION IV

MITIGATING IMPACTS FOR CLIMATE CHANGE

Sectoral Approach for Negotiating Climate Change: What is in it for the Indian Economy?

JOYASHREE ROY, MOUMITA ROY AND SHREYA ROYCHOWDHURY

In any international negotiation on climate change close link among science, economics and politics can hardly be ignored. The argument for mitigation in case of long lived stock pollutants can never be rationally based on current growth level. It is a complex situation and any over simplified approach will further complicate rather than lead to any positive solution. Competitiveness argument, border adjustment, trade barriers on emission intensive goods and services of Annex I countries can hardly be justified even at the current market share in trade, production, consumption. The best way to approach the problem can be to combine domestic and international actions judiciously. Need for transition to globally low carbon economy by the end of the century is least contested today. Common responsibility of attaining decarbonised growth path for global human welfare is uncontested but much contested is the differentiated responsibility design mechanism. Differentiated responsibility is a dynamic notion. So who should do how much and when, in dynamic context, is still an unresolved research question.

But what is understood well is a fully functional global carbon market with global carbon price can provide a least cost solution with desired level of autonomy chosen by each country. Past attempts through CDM provide a small short term step towards that for flow of finance in niche investments and new technology, Sectoral Approach (SA) can provide a second level of stepping stone towards fully functional carbon market through financial flow into non niche market such as energy efficiency type of investment. India today is one of the leader among Non-Annex I countries in CDM, and with first layer of capacity building it can be the natural leaders in SA.

I. BACKGROUND

Need for transition to low Green House Gas (GHG) economy by the end of the century is least contested today. Least contested is also the scientific assessment based on wide variety of information from rigorous research studies that the production and consumption path of the diverse economies followed since industrial revolution till date across the world do not guarantee low GHG future. Global pollutant character and long resident time (decades to centuries) of GHGs emitted from economic activities make it a special challenge in nationally governed world (*Roy*, 2007) to achieve low carbon future. Multiple gases can be expressed in single unit of carbon equivalent so low carbon can be synonymously used for low GHG. GHGs produced by human actions are not primary products rather by products of consumption and production. Various institutions manage production and consumption activities across world where both price mechanism and regulatory mechanism have roles to play. Major challenge is how can these institutions (defined by price and regulations) be redesigned to drive the production and consumption activity decisions towards low carbon future. Hope has been raised by the various global assessments over past years (*IPCC*, 2007; *Stern*, 2007, *IEA*, 2008) that given the global pool of technology and knowledge it is achievable through ideally designed and followed well coordinated global action. However, to deliver this "global good" in the form of low carbon involves costs and investment decisions. Globally efficient solution is possible through co-operation as nationally acceptable "global deal" can deliver a price and regulatory mechanism which can deliver least cost solution to achieve low GHG transition. However this transition can not happen overnight so the path to transition needs to be worked out. This involves inter-temporal decision and investment allocation. Multiple time horizons, multiple countries, and multiple players, multiple goals are creating complexity in a world nationally defined, divided, governed and managed (*Roy*, 2008). However, apparent complexity should not work as a barrier towards solution. So far human society has solved sharing of global goods by defining national boundaries and national endowment of resources. Initial difference in endowments have been solved through creation of market exchange and price has played an important role to allocate across multiple players. Same market-price mechanism has been applied across nations in the form of trade relations. To correct any perceived inequality regulatory mechanisms and various social, economic and political adjustment processes have been tried. It is most logical and possible to show that similar known and much practiced market-price and regulatory mechanisms can be applied to share the 'new global good' as well. So crux of the problem is how do we define the size of the 'new global good' or the natural resource and how the total endowment can be shared initially and then how can trade as a vehicle both intra- and inter-nationally can lead to redistribution of the initial endowment given the demand for it. This implies in macro sense adding to our list of markets like labour market, commodity market, money market, bond market, capital market, a fully functional 'carbon market'. However, this new "carbon market" will have some unique features due to its global public good character. So it is important to design this new market in such a way that it does not distort the current resource allocation, income distribution and political autonomy of the nations. So it is crucial to adopt a systems approach so that additional features introduced through carbon market in the global economic system has a smooth linkages with other markets without creating disruptions in the globally linked national markets. Besides this macro aspect of the transition, micro aspect is can this market generate enough market signals for relevant players. Real challenge is how to make this transition smooth and faster. Sooner we decide the global deal on this carbon market size, initial allocation of the total carbon rights and initial carbon price, better we manage the transition path. Finding the shortest route (time and cost wise) to this ultimate goal is the real challenge today. Major hurdle in the way is to answer this complexity arising out of lack of information on whether least cost solution will produce Pareto efficient solution. Any Pareto inefficient solution i.e., that makes any country worse off than today in the global deal will not be acceptable. It is the distributive impact of transition pathway least understood and most contested. Given the stock pollutant nature historical burden sharing and distributive justice question was attempted to be resolved through common but differentiated responsibility criterion. However, differentiated responsibility is not a static deal it is inherently dynamic. Over time responsibility of various countries will continue to change depending on their contributions to GHG stock.

In this paper we try to analyse how this reality is changing over time for India. How transition towards the global carbon market is emerging and how nations are responding to global deal and what are the forces that might distort emergence of global deal and how national strategies need to be revised in keeping with the changing realities.

II. CHANGING REALITY

The reality is changing fast for Five Large Developing countries (FLDCs): China, Brazil, India, Mexico and South Africa, among Non annex I countries. In absolute terms carbon emissions is rising for Non annex I countries. The absolute emission rose for Small Developing Countries in the 2000-2005 period, from 4925 million metric tonnes in 2000 to 6031 million metric tonnes in 2005. It is interesting to note that over the same period the carbon dioxide emission of the five large developing countries increased from 4292 million metric tonnes to 7671 million metric tonnes in 2005. The CO_2 emission of FLDC increased by 78% in the span of five years (2000-05). The percentage contribution of FLDCs in world emissions increased from 18% to 27%. In the same period the carbon dioxide emission of India increased form 1012 million metric tonnes in 2000 to 1914 million metric tonnes in 2005. The percentage contribution of India in world emission increased from 4.2% in 2000 to 4.5% in 2005.These trends are to be kept into consideration in implementation of low carbon intensive growth policies.

Figure 1: Regional CO_2 Emissions in 2000 and 2005

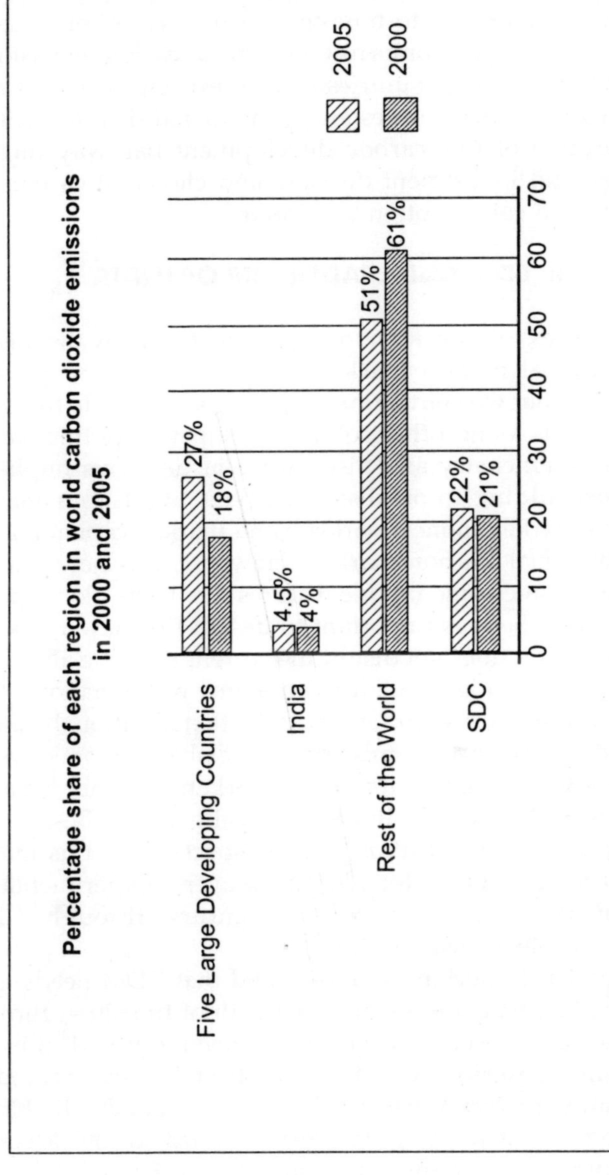

Data Source: http://www.eia.doe.gov/pub/international/iealf/tablehIco2.xls (Authors' estimates).

It is true that still developed nations account for most of the historic emissions but the emerging economies are fast catching up too. It is interesting to note that today's emission becomes historical contribution tomorrow in term of carbon emission so among the developing countries FLDCs, especially India has an important role to play in designing the global deal to facilitate faster adoption of low carbon development pathway through technology and investment decision and choice of carbon free production and consumption behaviour.

III. CDM AND LEADERSHIP OF INDIA

In the process of transition to low carbon economy the missing link is a global carbon market with global carbon price as facilitator. Sooner we start on moving to this inevitable transition path better it is as no other solution is superior to this both in terms of cost efficiency and distributive justice. This implies in macro sense adding to our list of markets like labour market, commodity market, money market, bond market, capital market, a fully functional 'carbon market'. However, this new "carbon market" will have some unique features due to its global public good character. So it is important to design this new market in such a way that it does not distort the current resource allocation, income distribution and political autonomy of the nations. So it is crucial to adopt a systems approach so that additional features introduced through carbon market in the global economic system has a smooth linkages with other markets without creating disruptions in the globally linked national markets. Besides this macro aspect of the transition, micro aspect is can this market generate enough signals for relevant players. Experimentation started at the beginning of this century through Clean Development Mechanism (CDM).

Upfront it is important to understand that CDM needs to be looked into as first experiment in the path of transition through certain niche markets. Niches have been defined through additionality criterion. CDM can at best be understood as demonstration project. Carbon reduction as a 'good', eligible for trading, pricing, marketing has been established and accepted today through CDM demonstration projects. Economic agents have an idea now who can be a buyer and who can be a seller.

Figure 2 shows how India has become market leader in CDM. As first mover India has participated and gained in terms of major share in carbon market through new economic activity generation by carbon projects and trading of CERs. India currently accounts for 29% of total CDM projects registered by host country. Almost one third of all the CDM projects (registered by host country) belong to India. But it is interesting to and important to note that compared to China India accounts for 24% of the total CERs generated. It is the CERs which show financial flow and not the number of projects *per se*.

Figure 2: Number of Projects Activities Registered by Host Country

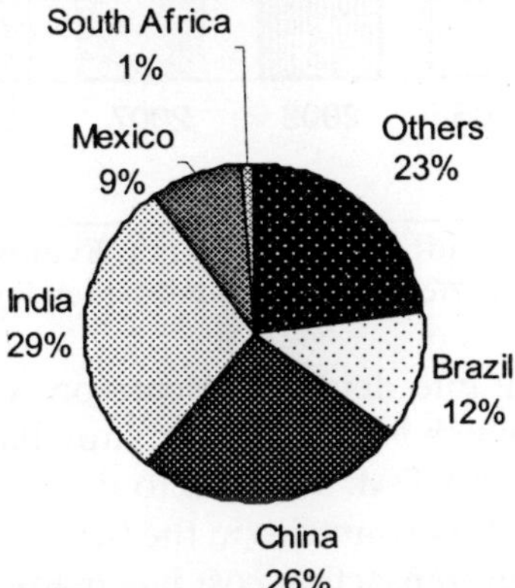

Source: Authors' estimate based on http://cdm.unfccc.int/Statistics/index.html

Figure 3: CERs Issued by Host Party

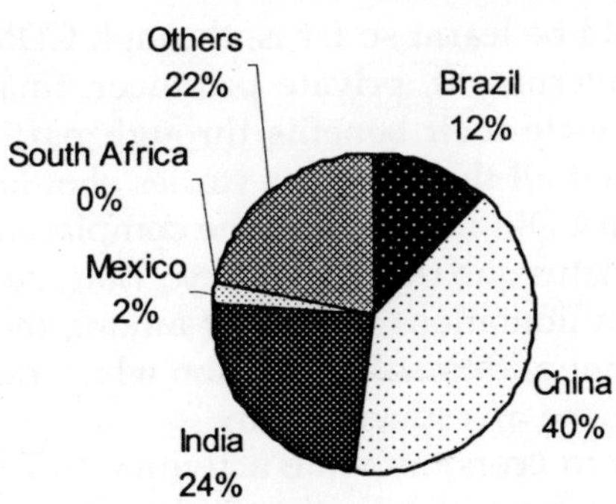

Source: Authors' estimate based on http://cdm.unfccc.int/Statistics/Issuance/

Figure 4: Value of Carbon Credits Traded

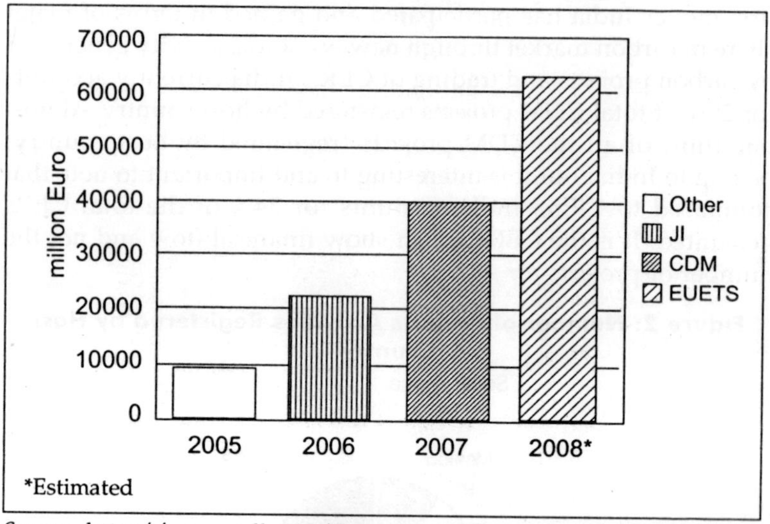

Source: http://www.adb.org/Documents/Events/2008/CDM-Project-Development-Workshop/Carbon-Market-Toru-Kubo.pdf.

Without going into detailed discussion we want to state that EU ETS system which is regional in nature has generated a much bigger market than CDM. This has to do with non-participation of few larger emitting countries in the buyers market, knowledge intensity and high transaction cost has made seller market small as well. In the sellers market for carbon credit China is the leader (62%) and the buyers market for carbon credit is dominated by United Kingdom (46%).

But what could be learnt so far is, through CDM all kinds of stakeholders: government, private producer, financial market players all can relate their benefits through participation in a carbon market. But all these success stories should not lead the current players in CDM market with the complacence or bias for maintaining the status quo (*Roy, Roy, Gueye, Fang*, 2008). However, CDM has its own limitations. The chief among them is scale of operation due to the additionality criterion which makes it a good instrument for 'niche investments' only.

So scaling up to economy wide activities and investment is necessary both to achieve stabilisation goal and participation from

Figure 5

Buyers of Carbon Credit

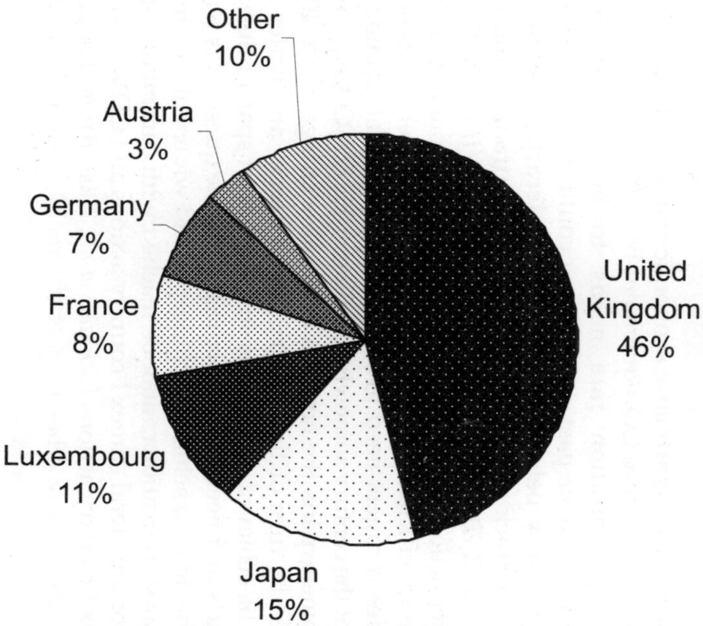

United Kingdom 46%
Japan 15%
Luxembourg 11%
France 8%
Germany 7%
Austria 3%
Other 10%

Sellers of Carbon credit

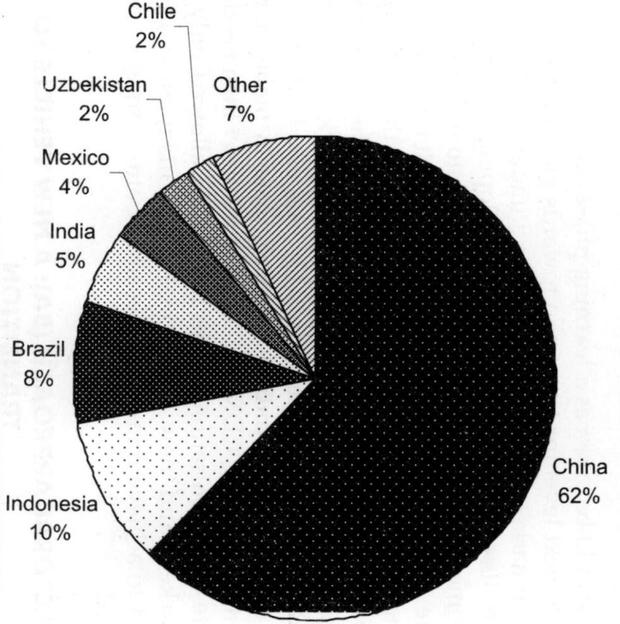

China 62%
Indonesia 10%
Brazil 8%
India 5%
Mexico 4%
Uzbekistan 2%
Chile 2%
Other 7%

Source: Energy, Transport and Water Division, Regional & Sustainable Development Department, Asian Development Bank (accessed 30th Nov. 2008).

all. CDM should be taken as a learning phase and now need is to move up to next level for transition towards global carbon price and carbon market. The capacity building under CDM phase in fact puts India one step ahead of other developing countries who are late comers or who have not yet jumped into the business of CDM due to lack of enough knowledge, understanding and capacity to make CDM markets functional. India through South-South Cooperation can indeed act as leader for other developing countries in post-2012 phase for CDM markets in non-participating developing countries for capacity building and Annex I countries can continue to participate in niche market investments. However, CDM has long-term impact than need for immediate decarbonisation target and can be allowed only for niche markets and new additional mechanism need to be developed to achieve immediate decarbonisation target in post-2012 period.

IV. SECTORAL APPROACH (SA): A NEW VEHICLE TO TRANSITION

Target is to decarbonise economic activities globally at such a rate so as to reduce CO_2 equivalent by 50% by 2050. This means the decarbonisation rate needs to be between 0.6-2.5%. Historically, over past decades we could decarbonise by 0.3% which is way below desired rate of decarbonisation. Global collective track record so far has been far from satisfactory. We have added 70% more GHGs over 1970-2004 (*IPCC*, 2007) despite 33% reduction in energy intensity globally. Doubling or trebling of energy efficiency improvement for fossil fuel use in next two decades is urgent need to achieve the target stabilization by the turn of the century somewhere between 450-550 CO_2 eq. However, for some experts the target is even more stringent like 400 ppm CO_2 eq by turn of the century. Much deeper and wider actions must be achieved collectively in a very short span of time. These are facts and need to be accepted. Now the question is what can then be done to achieve such deeper and wider cuts in emission? The target transition cannot be reached with current or enhanced level of unilateral Annex I country actions and CDM driven non-Annex I country actions (*Schmidt et al.*, 2006; *Baron et al.*, 2006).

In case of any other market (financial, commodity, etc.) in a fully functional global carbon market each player has the autonomy to select level of emission reduction (supply of carbon credits) and generation (demand for carbon credit). The only difference is total credit or size of the market will be globally managed through negotiation across nations starting from an initial allocation of total endowment across nations. CDM is far of from this final market size and extent. National preparedness also do not show readiness towards that due to lack of enough information, capacity and knowledge. SA is an intermediate step between CDM and global carbon market.

Though not a new concept in climate negotiation literature, sectoral approaches (SAs) have gained prominence in post-2007 and after publication of Intergovernmental Panel on Climate Change (IPCC) assessment of sectoral mitigation potential and in post-2007 Bali Convention. While there are conflicting interpretations of what SAs may bring about but one thing is clear that SA need to target at broad-based participation in mitigation action, widening of options and opportunities in mitigation action compared to current additionality driven narrow coverage of Clean Development Mechanism (CDM), increased financial flow in mitigation activities, making technology diffusion faster in sectors with high mitigation potential, bridge the gap between now and future globally active carbon market without creating distortions through early actions.

Sceptics argue SA is designed to address leakage and/or competitiveness argument of current carbon constrained developed countries. It is important to understand that it is neither a time for scepticism, nor of blame game nor of non-cooperation. Rather it is time to put forward national priorities with clear goal oriented targets and to find out of the box solutions to help in evolving a globally functional carbon market through information generational and negotiation. SAs is not a closed chapter rather it provides a platform for global discussion and opens up scope for designing mechanism for each country/group of countries to choose a win-win kind of interim solution in post-2012 period. This paper focuses on the concerns of India and how India can play an integral role in SA negotiations, ensuring that SAs reflect their interests and long-term development goals. With voluntary participation, they can realise the potential gains of sectoral approaches that can facilitate technology transfer, utilise carbon trading mechanism for broader development goals, enhance existing capacity and pave the way for global carbon market participation.

V. COMPETITIVENESS ARGUMENT BASED SA AND TRADE INSTRUMENTS: A WEAK ARGUMENT TO TRIGGER PARTICIPATION

Competitiveness argument in sectoral approach focus on large developing countries Brazil, China, India, Mexico and South Africa. Because of their low historic emissions, FLDCs do not face mandatory emissions cuts under the Kyoto Protocol, given the principle of "common but differentiated responsibilities" and they have not been actively engaged in the "universal" sectoral approaches negotiating process. Producers of steel, cement, aluminium, pulp and paper and agrochemicals and other energy-intensive goods in the developed nations allege that such climate change policies would put them at a disadvantage compared to developing nations as far as international trade in the energy intensive goods sector is concerned. They argue that by introducing a price for carbon, the cost of production in the energy intensive sectors in developed countries would rise compared to developing nations and that would cause them to lose market share to foreign competitors that do not face similar costs at home. Many of these industries are facing tough competition in the global market from large emerging economies such as China, India, and Brazil that are not bound to have emission cuts under the current international climate regime. The developed countries propose to either limit the price of carbon these producers face or impose similar costs on imports of carbon-intensive goods from their competitors in developing countries.

In Figure 6 rest of the world is Annex I countries and the small island countries whose share is almost negligible. Annex I countries dominate with disproportionately high share in world export, import as well as GDP barring population which gives them market power, competitive edge and more responsible. (*Roy, Roy, Gueye, Fang*, 2008)

As of now, Annex I countries clearly dominate in both the export and import of energy-intensive goods (Figure 6). India and other FLDCs could barely make their presence felt in indicators

Figure 6: Regional Shares in Global Total 2000, 2006

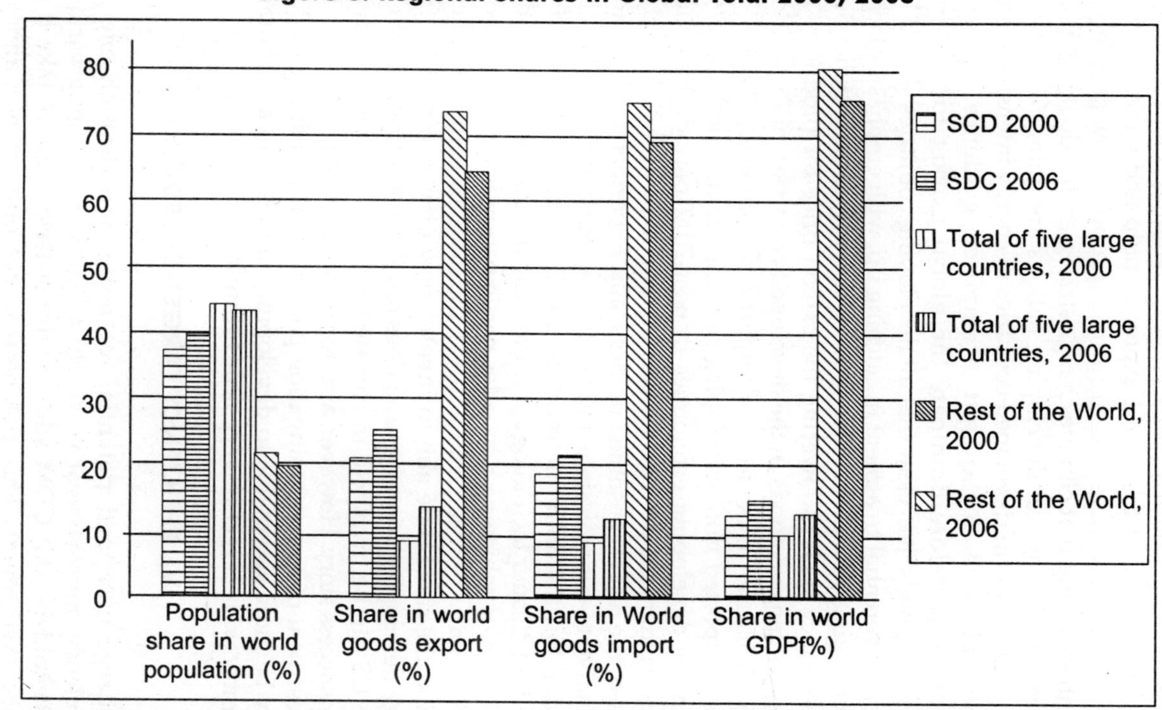

Source: Authors' estimate based on http://stat.wto.org/CountryProfile/WSDBCountryPFReporter

and sectors. Pulp and paper, aluminium and fertilisers exports are almost entirely dominated by Annex I nations. Annex I nations account for 80% of the world export of pulp and paper in 2006. Thus the competitiveness argument proposed by developed countries saying that climate change strategies that do not impose carbon constraints on developing nations are going to hurt the competitiveness of developed countries in energy intensive sector is not validated in the light of empirical evidence. Annex I countries therefore dominate the global market for energy-intensive goods, it is clear that all developing countries should be given preferential treatment in catching up, with emphasis placed on emerging economies like India. Thus any climate policy led trade policy such as lowering the carbon price for producers of energy intensive goods in the developed countries, or imposition of trade barrier in the form of import tariffs on energy intensive goods imported from developing countries cannot find approval from the developing economies in post-2012 period. Also such trade barriers are not efficient as only one third of India's steel is traded, the rest is consumed domestically. Exporters will have any incentive to cut emissions in case their goods are checked at the border. But the domestic producers will not have any incentive to adopt cleaner technology if trade instruments are used. So the basic aim of achieving a broader participation is not addressed.

Sectoral Approach that address the issue of competitiveness and at the same time aim to involve new players especially the large developing countries and does not show how large emitters like US can be involved, in climate change framework will find low success story. However, a sector wide approach based on self-assessment of sectoral mitigation potential with crediting facility may be more acceptable to developing nations than an arbitrary country wide target in very near future.

VI. EFFICIENCY TARGET-BASED SA

Large untapped potential for mitigation through energy efficiency improvement is widely accepted fact among various stakeholders. But CDM additionally criterion cannot take it as niche investment. This potential is not only in non-annex I countries but exist in developed countries as well though this is not obvious from aggregate metrics as emissions GHG intensity

Figure 7: Share in Global total exports of Iron and Steel, Pulp and Paper, Aluminium, Fertilisers, 2002 and 2006

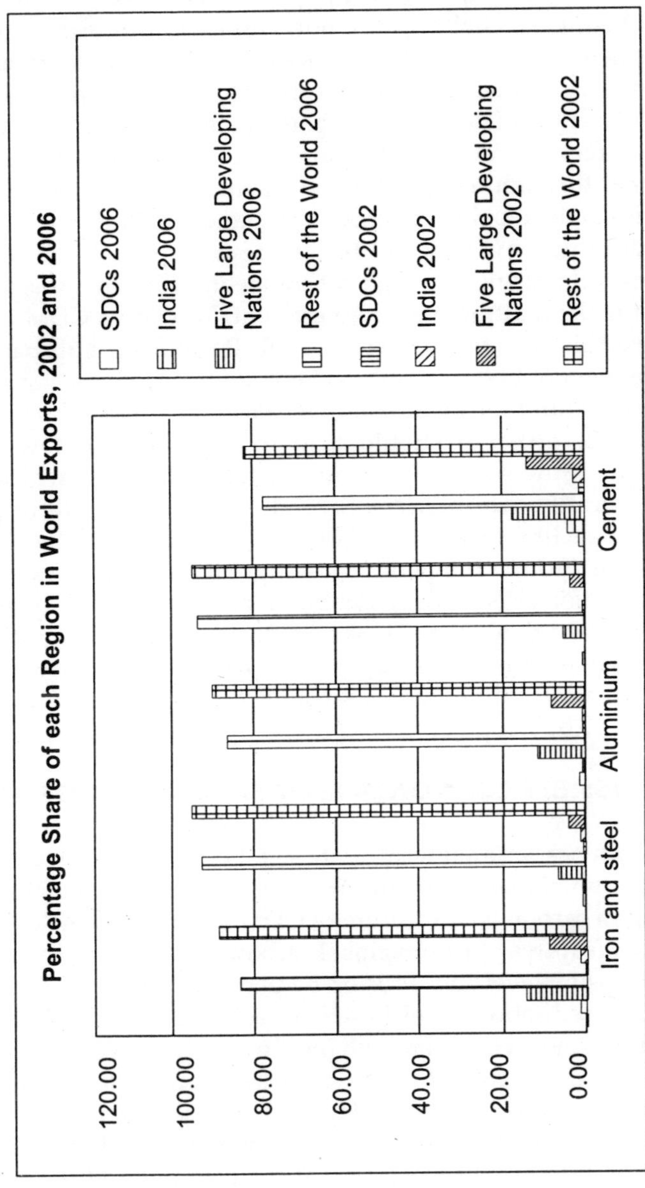

Source: Authors' estimate based on http://stat.wto.org/StatisticalProgram/WSDBViewData.aspx

as it is 0.68 kg CO_2eq/US$ GDPppp for Annex I countries and 1.06 kg CO_2eq/US$ GDPppp for non-Annex-I countries. Sectoral assessment across various countries can yield accurate mitigation potential assessment and market size. How sectoral potential can be achieved through all country participation through trading will be an effective vehicle to enhance the market and realise the potential through technology and financial flow. Although new facilities in developing countries in major energy intensive sectors are adopting new efficient technologies replacement need of existing technologies are high but competition for investment fund do not make it attractive for investment. Top down CDM cannot achieve this due to its specific goal. Bottom up approach for Deployment of best available technology (BAT) in a sector across countries sound idealistic solution (*Roy, Roy, Gueye, Fang,* 2008). In practice either it should lead to monopoly or few firms dominating the sectors with multinational character which will face several known barriers. Second option will be diffusion of technology liberally across companies which may be facing hindrance through competitiveness argument and business ethics. So transnational sectoral standard or deployment of BAT both may fail to succeed though may look attractive upfront. Who owns BAT to be used as standard is highly controversial due to asymmetry of information. Moreover, this may act as disincentive for new technology development.

VII. POSSIBLE COMPONENTS OF SA AND ROLE OF INDIA

SA can best be an intermediate step between CDM world and globally functional carbon market world. It needs to maintain the trading in carbon credit feature of CDM and need to include two essential features of future global carbon market: one, negotiated total emission level and decision by players to select their chosen emission reduction level based on self-assessment. This will honour business ethics and will incentivise the players for correct reporting. In practice these two market features for SA will be negotiating among sectoral players. For example, it may be for emission reduction level in 2012-20 period and declaration of reduction targets by each player at the beginning of the period. These two need to match through negotiation among the players. Through out the commited period players will get chances to trade among themselves. Carbon price will be determined through demand and supply within the market or on a pre-negotiated price. Price will act as incentive. Defaulters will need to pay the price of commited but unrealised reduction and any reduction beyond committed reduction will fetch revenue at the carbon price. If there is over supply for good practices by each player in the sector a pool of carbon credit can be created that can be auctioned and money be redistributed among the players and if there is default that will fetch in pool of finance from the defaulters at carbon price at the sectoral level and through sectoral action money can be ploughed back. Ideally in a macro-economy wide functional market these will be traded across sectors and macro-balance will be maintained through price mechanism.

To be broad-based SA must have wider coverage by allowing any measurable carbon reduction strategy starting from energy efficiency. It avoids political apathy for commitment due to enough information, but allows the direct stakeholders to participate in the negotiation process. However, the players need to consider national circumstances and macro-goals. They need to be consistent and players cannot commit with private motive alone. So there is need for close interaction among national government and sectoral players as the sectoral players' commitments need to be consistent with country's development goals. This may need some enabling policy support as well. This sector wide participation of investors in carbon trading and market generation with third party investor's role will help in capacity building towards smooth transition to global carbon market. Therefore, in order for sectoral approaches to be effective both government and business needs to build mutually acceptable incentives to be a reliable partner in the process.

To encourage both developing country objective of development and new investment and Annex I country problem of lock in through high emission intensive investment due to past decisions but ownership of efficient technology can be solved if voluntary target emission reduction declaration by industry players are allowed and trading is allowed in carbon with third party investment possibility as well then all players across nations get incentive to reduce efficiency. The trading can be within one group of industry players as well as between industry players and third party investor. Carbon price will be determined by size of the market. This SA arrangement can continue with CDM for investments in niche areas as well as mandatory target for Annex I countries. There is no need for country wide commitment for Non-annex I countries. Emerging economies due to sheer size of their market and economic activity can take leadership in SA and gain much through financial flow and technology transfer in non-CDM covered markets and build additional capacity and preparedness for next beyond 2020 period. CDM with niche character will be shrinking in India and will be finding new locations in unattended markets so far and SA can play much larger role in India. This will help India to monitor emissions in it's high growth path with ultimate aim of decoupling emissions from growth and will allow on carbon neutral growth path.

In the global economic transition India is bound to play important role with second largest global population. Human welfare at global scale will be determined by how fast India and other developing nations can generate and distribute economic benefits. So anticipated growth rates in the range of 5-10% is inevitable. So how to manage this global economic transition on a low GHG pathway is the challenge which is a global responsibility in a very idealistic situation. But as soon as national interests and national autonomy creeps in aligning national goals with global goals becomes a major challenge. The conflict of global and national goal becomes explicit when goods cross-borders. When it does not then issue is much simpler. Best strategy for countries in SA will be to select major emitting sectors like power, steel, alumimum, cement, transport and buildings, etc. and allow each country players to come up with nationally consistent strategies. It makes next few month very crucial in terms of information generation. Unless such intermediate step is followed in post-2012 period the stabilization process will be delayed leading to more adaptation and steep mitigation cost burden on developing economies in near future. Additionally wide capacity building through practical experience will be delayed. Neither efficiency nor justice can be achieved by delaying the process of expansion of carbon market through SA especially when world is not ready for globally functional full scale carbon market. India with peaking economic activities in next one decade need to take lead role in design of SA to achieve low carbon growth path in next decade and to avoid high adaptation and mitigation cost a decade later and gain in 2012-20 period from historical advantageous position due to low share in global GHG pool.

VIII. CONCLUDING REMARKS

Sectoral Approach (SA) needs to be clearly defined keeping mind its role as stepping stone towards fully functional carbon market. It need to go beyond CDM and replicate global carbon characteristics at a sectoral scale. India today is the leader among Non-Annex I countries in CDM and with first layer of capacity building they can be the natural leaders in SA and by assuming an active role can enhance the financial and technology flow from the very beginning by expression of interest consistent with national advantage. In global deal for 2012 period India can bargain for much broad and target flow of finance and technology as per national developmental need assessment and very well play the role of Global deal maker in voicing their need in SA and in determination of carbon price and sector selection. How carbon price can be used as incentive for participation of low emitters and as payment vehicle for non delivery of commitment by large emitters for ploughing back into the system through enhanced investment are some of the bargaining points for India in post-2012 period. In CDM, China needs to push for more niche investments from Annex I countries and can become provider of knowledge and capacity building in underserved nations in CDM first phase. CDM and SA can scale up the experiments with newer carbon market concept and lead the way to fully functional carbon market through appropriate capacity building. Next few months for India before 2012 deal is made are very crucial in terms of information generation towards SA. Post-2012 period need to be devoted for knowledge sharing in design of initial endowment and carbon price that will prevail in future.

REFERENCES

Baron Richard (2006), Sectoral approaches to GHG mitigation: scenarios for integration, International Energy Agency.

Houser, Trevor, Rob Bradley, Britt Childs, Jacob Werksman, and Robert Heilmayr (2008), "Leveling the carbon playing field: international competition and US policy design." Peterson Institute for International Economics, World Resources Institute.

International Energy Agency (2008), *Energy Technology Perspectives, 2008*: Scenarios and Strategies to 2050, Paris.

IPCC (2007), Climate Change 2007: Mitigation of Climate Change, working Group III contribution to the Fourth Assessment Report of the Intergovernmental Panel on Climate Change. Summary for Policy-makers and Technical Summary, UNEP, WMO.

Roy, Joyashree (2007), IPCC WG I Report—Climate Change 2007, How does it matter us?, *Indian Express*, 14.2.2007, New Delhi.

Roy, Joyashree (2008a), "An Incentive for Tackling Climate Change", *Connecting*, April-May 2008, British Council India.

Roy, Joyashree (2008b), Climate Change Response and Action at Cross Roads: *Time to Revisit Clean Development Mechanism* http://www.tokyofoundation.org/en/sylff/voices-from-the-sylff-community/climate-change-response-at-a-crossroads

Roy, Joyashree (2008c), Climate Change: International Negotiations and Mitigation Policy, Accepted for Publication in Edited Volume "Hand Book on Environmental Economics in India" (ed.) Kanchan Chopra and Vikram Dayal, OUP (In press).

Roy, Joyashree, M. Roy, Moustapha Kamal Gueye and Samantha T. Fang (2008), Sectoral Approaches in Climate Change: Implications for Small Developing Countries Report Submitted to ICTSD International Centre for Trade and Sustainable Development.

Schmidt Jake, Helme Ned, Lee Jin, Houdashelt Mark (2006), "Sector-based Approach to the Post-2012 Climate Change Policy Architecture", Center For Clean Air Policy.

Stern, N. (2007), The Economics of Climate Change—The Stern Review, Cambridge University Press, UK, London.

World Bank (2008). Country Data. http://wwwr.worldbank.org/data/countrydata/countrydata/ (Accessed May 2008).

World Trade Organisation (2008), http://www.wto.org/english/res_e/statise/Statis_e.htm (Accessed May 2008).

Energy Information Administration, International Energy Annual 2006 http://www.eia.doe.gov/pub/international/iealf/tablehlco2.xls (Accessed May 2008)

United Nations Framework Convention on Climate Change http://unfccc.int/2860.php (Accessed June 2009)

Indo-Bangladesh Co-operation to Mitigate Climate Change: Impacts on Sunderbans

Raj Kumar Sen and Somnath Hazra

This paper attempts to address an important segment of the SAARC region namely, Bangladesh and India, the two most populous countries of SAARC and the prospects and problems of their co-operation and collaboration in identifying and financing the ways in mitigating the current and future impacts of climate change. For this purpose it has chosen an area where such problems are transformed into transboundary issues. The most important of such areas is the Sunderbans which is also one of the most vulnerable areas to climate change adverse impacts and which is extended over both India and Bangladesh, the later occupying 62% of the total area.

This paper is distributed over the following sections. In section I the general dangers and fallout of climate change are described with special reference to India and Bangladesh in particular and the SAARC countries in general. The special

Based on an earlier draft of the paper submitted for Presentation in the International Conference on "Financing for Climate Change—Challenges and Way Forward" (Theme: Climate Change—Current Regime), Aug. 2008, Dhaka, Bangladesh.

type of vulnerability of Bangladesh and some coastal areas of India due to their geographical locations are taken up in this section. How the human activities have further degraded these regions is also discussed in this context. The feature of vulnerability of the Sunderban regions in both countries and threat to its existence from submergence due to the impact of climate change is the focal theme of the section II of this paper. The importance of this region as the largest mangrove forest which protects the region from violent storms, etc. and one of the major areas of biodiversity in the world and the adverse impacts of climate change on it are discussed which are mostly common for the two parts of the Sunderbans belonging to India and Bangladesh. The similarities and differences of the current official responses in these two countries to meet the adverse impacts are also described briefly.

The last section of the paper tries to identify the gaps in the current official policies in both countries to mitigate the adverse impact of climate change on the Sunderbans and in this context highlights the prospects of collaboration and co-operation between them in various ways to meet the challenges in a more effective manner. This scope of mitigating climate change both globally (e.g. restriction in fossil fuel consumption without curtailing agriculture or construction of carbon sinks) and locally (e.g. disaster management strategies, afforestation for coastal protection, depopulation for environmentally fragile region, etc.) are also discussed under policy prescriptions at the end.

I. IMPACTS OF CLIMATE CHANGE ON INDIA AND BANGLADESH

There is strong evidence that largely due to human activities and overconsumption by the rich North, the concentration of green house gases in the earth's atmosphere is rapidly increasing which results in progressive global warming and climate change. However, though the rich countries are largely responsible for this phenomenon for this high level of fossil fuel consumption, due to their geographical location between the tropics, the developing countries usually suffer more disproportionately more from adverse effects of the climate change.

This paper concentrates on the impacts of climate change on India and Bangladesh, the two most populous countries of the SAARC region and both are most vulnerable to the danger of sea level rise and other impacts of global warming. For these two countries, we have chosen the Sunderban region, which is common to both countries and the existence of which is threatened due to global warming. In the next two sections of this paper, we try to show Sunderban's importance and vulnerability, and the potential of Indo-Bangladesh cooperation in effectively meeting the challenge of adverse impacts of climate change.

II. ABOUT SUNDARBANS AND ITS IMPORTANCE AND VULNERABILITY

Sundarbans is a region extending to two countries, viz. India and Bangladesh, while 62% of its area belongs to the smaller country (Fig. 1). It is stretched between the south-western Bangladesh and the adjoining state of West Bengal in India to the west and located on the northern limits of the Bay of Bengal and the old Ganges delta. It is world famous as the largest mangrove forest area covering more than 10,000 sq. km, seat of Royal Bengal tiger and a large number of flora and fauna, one of the important areas known for their bio-diversity, and now intensely discussed for its acute vulnerability in the face of adverse impacts of climate change which is the fall-out of the incidence of global warming, a feature which is the most recent concern of the world as it is no longer a possibility for the future but a reality for the present. It houses at least 69 species of flora, of which *sundari* (from which the forest derived its name) and *gewa* are the dominant ones that provide timber for paper and wood products. Apart from the majestic Royal Bengal tiger, 425 species of wildlife have been identified here. Considering the richness of bio-diversity of this region, UNESCO has declared Sundarbans in both India and Bangladesh as world heritage sites. The crucial ecological and environmental importance of the Sunderban is well known to all. Thus it helped the geology of the region through land formation by soil accumulation. It also helps to maintain the materiological and hydrological balance of the region by providing the forest cover. Further the dense forest provides effective protection to the habitats from the occasional storms and submergence from tidal waves. The Sunderbans have given birth to its own way of life for the people residing in it. The forests are also the depositories of renewable resources.

Figure 1: Sundarbans in India and Bangladesh

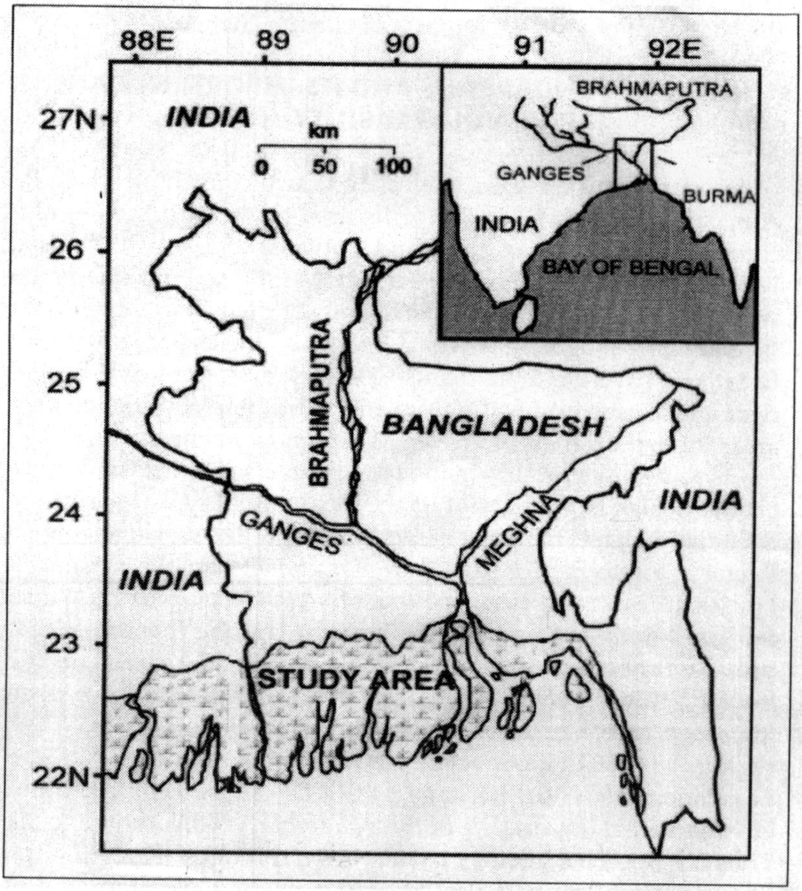

Source: Allison, M.A. and E.B. Kepple (2001).

Both parts of Sundarbans offer subsistence livelihood to a large number of people within and around the boundaries of the Bangladesh Sundarban Reserve Forest and the Indian sanctuary for the Tiger Project. Sundarbans consists of numerous creeks and rivulets (Fig. 2) through which a critical balance is maintained in this area between saline water ingress from the sea during tides and freshwater flows obtained from the rivers and rainfall. Naturally salinity levels are at the highest in the dry summer season and freshwater dominates during the monsoons. This area is prone to coastal flooding and natural disasters like cyclones, violent storms and tornadoes from the very beginning mainly due to its geographical location. The funnel shaped Bay of Bengal itself in the south is the breeding place of catastrophic cyclones. In fact the worst disasters in the world tend to concentrate between the two Tropics, which is coincidentally that part of the world which contains the poorer countries. This is particularly true for Bangladesh, which is one of the worst victims of recurring natural disasters and consequently the country is subjected to food shortages in spite of favourable climate, navigable rivers and fertile land conditions. The very high population density of the area under Sundarbans in both India and Bangladesh has enhanced many times the human losses of life and property due to coastal flooding and other natural disasters. However, over the years people had to settle in this fragile land not suitable for human habitat and became used to the unique characteristics of the Sundarbans. Thus the cultivators harvested seasonal salinity and flood-resistant rice with the help of temporary dykes and built their huts on raised platforms. In the dry season, the dykes were dismantled to allow the tidal movements to operate and the fishing of the salt tolerant varieties became the source of supplementary livelihood for a large number of people.

This satellite image (Fig. 2) shows the forest in the protected area. The Sundarbans appears deep green, surrounded to the north by a landscape of agricultural lands, which appear lighter green, towns, which appear tan, and streams, which are blue.

However, in recent times, this traditional interaction between the unique and fragile eco-system of the Sundarbans and the people living there have changed a lot due to human activities resulting from rapid population growth and migration between

Figure 2: Satellite Picture of Figure 1.

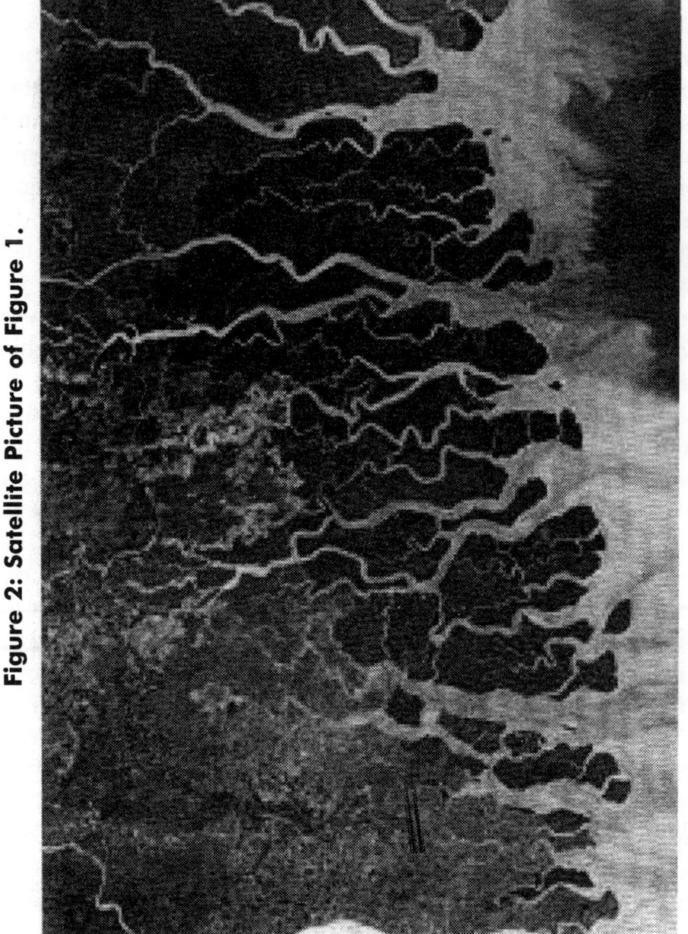

Source: http://en.wikipedia.org/wiki/Sundarbans.

two countries due to partition of India in 1947. Due to ever-growing population pressure on the same eco-system has led to serious threats to environment in the form of illegal felling of trees and wildlife poaching which already led to the extinction of several species. Growing trade through Sundarbans with the help of launches and establishment of industries in the fringe areas have increased the pressure on the environmental resources of the area including the pollution through the oil spill by the increasing traffic of barges aided by a lax enforcement of environmental laws due to lack of public awareness and corruption. As an adaptation to coastal flooding in Bangladesh and to protect the cultivated land from saline sea water in India, a series of coastal embankments were built in both parts of Sundarbans in the two neighbouring countries. Over time due to unscientific construction and unsatisfactory maintenance of these embankments, these led to drainage congestions and water logging problems in this area. The construction of the Farakka barrage in India over the river Ganges coupled with large scale withdrawal of freshwater in the upstream has adverse effects on the flow of water in the river system of the Sundarbans leading to large scale salinity in a number of places especially in the dry seasons. This enhanced salinity level has also adversely affected the agricultural production especially in Bangladesh. Compared with the pre-Farakka period, this salinity ingress has also caused increase in soil salinity in various places where irrigation of arable land used slightly saline surface water at the beginning of the dry season. Though the salinity increases and inundation of forest land have changed the Sundarbans eco-system and the livelihood of the dependent people, yet apparently they opened an ideal opportunity for shrimp farming in both parts of Sundarbans. This became an export-oriented cash industry leading to enhancing steeply the local incomes. This again motivated the shrimp farmers to artificially inundate lands with brackish water in the wet season also and this causes severe damage to the forest cover. This again increased pressure on other parts of Sundarbans for timber, fuelwood and other forest resources which further accelerated the rate of forest degradation and depletion. Shrimp farming also results in the depletion of the stock of other fish species as the thin wire mess used in this process leads to the capture and then destruction of the larvae of other fish species.

It is necessary to analyze the impacts of the recent problem of climate change due to global warming on Sundarbans in the perspective of the growing vulnerability of Sundarbans as described above. It may be mentioned that while even two decades back, people were not very sure about the gradual increase in the temperature of the world's surface; the scenario of climate change has taken a definite and certain shape by the turn of the century. There is now near unanimity that the climate is definitely changing throughout the globe and its impacts are now quite visible in various parts of different countries and Sundarbans is one of the regions which are likely to be most adversely affected. It is apprehended that climate change will make the sea level to rise inundating nearly one-tenth of the total land area along the total length of Sundarbans. As a consequence nearly 10 million people living in the coastal areas will have to migrate further inland putting enormous pressure on the already overpopulated regions of the two countries. The sea level rise (SLR) is feared to completely submerge the Maldives. So far as Sundarbans is concerned, the SLR will put the low-lying areas of Sundarbans under water thus reducing agricultural and forest lands and shrinking the land for human habitat. It is likely to accelerate coastal erosion and increase the risk of floods. Intrusion of salt waters can damage coastal embankments, destroy mangroves, beaches and farm lands and create drainage and irrigation problems. The main impacts of global warming induced climate change may be considered under the following categories, viz., agriculture, salinity intrusion, forests, fisheries and eco-system including bio-diversity.

So far as agriculture is concerned, it is likely that climate change will affect crop production as crop yields strongly depend on climate factors. It is further apprehended that climate change will increase the disparities between the rich and poor countries in terms of cereal production as the production in the former will increase while that in the second group of countries will fall. It is further presumed that there will be a net increase in soil salinity and it has been considered as a major constraint to foodgrain production in the coastal areas of Bangladesh where more than 30% of the arable land is located in coastal areas (some of which are not cultivated due to salinity.) The extent of increase in soil salinity due to climate change in the fringe areas of Sundarbans would determine the extent of crop loss. Of course all these are at the preliminary stage only which requires further investigations and observations at the field level. The salinity intrusion will also affect negatively particularly the winter crops depending on groundwater for irrigation in the coastal areas. The already endangered Sundarban forests due to various factors (e.g., increased consumption of forest products, human encroachment, deforestation, low flows in the Ganges distributaries in the dry season, natural disasters, etc.) inhibiting the growth and regeneration of different forest species, are expected to face further problems due to climate change impacts like SLR, lower availability of freshwater in the winter with increased evaporation causing moisture stress, increased inland intrusion of saline water, etc. The resulting shrinkage in the mangrove forests (for factors like extinction of many species less resistant to salinity, restriction on the forest area to expand due to densely populated fringe areas and others) will adversely affect the ecosystem and the overall economy. The shortage in the supply of forest resources will affect the dependent industries adversely creating unemployment and other problems. Climate change impacts will also adversely affect the rich Sundarban biodiversity (both flora and fauna) inviting more frequent and intense natural disasters. The fisheries sector, which is the inseparable part of the life, culture, employment and economy of the Bengali population living both in Bangladesh and West Bengal in India, will also be adversely affected by the reduction of the freshwater fishing area due to SLR and increased salinity. Thus the adverse impacts of the climate change due to SLR and increase in the global warming, may be considered as real threats not only to the mangrove forests of Sundarbans but also to the whole ecosystem and biodiversity of both Bangladesh and India.

III. INDO-BANGLADESH CO-OPERATION TO PROTECT SUNDARBANS

While economic co-operation among two or more countries has been a long established goal in the international arena, it has rarely highlighted so far on the transboundary environmental problems which are very common among the neighbouring countries as environment and ecology have always occupied low priority areas to the politicians and policy-makers in developing countries. Enormous potential lies there to reap both economic and social benefits from such co-operation between countries with common borders. This is especially true for large countries like India sharing her long border with so many countries in the Indian sub-continent. In fact, such cooperations are really important for the regional and global prosperity even in the present era when competition is the buzzword. In fact there has been a continuous trend towards international and regional environmental co-operation during the last three decades. Some of the existing treaties towards this objective where both India and Bangladesh are members are SACEP's Strategy and Programme (1992-96) and ICIMD established in 1986 in Nepal. The major areas of environmental co-operation between India and Bangladesh may be identified as: (i) optimum use of common rivers, (ii) mutual co-operation in the deep sea fishing in the Bay of Bengal, (iii) protection of the ecology and wildlife and development of Sundarbans and other forests which are spread over both the countries, (iv) joint adoption of steps against illegal poaching of wild animals, (v) jointly formulated steps to protect the people and rehabilitate them in case of natural hazards and the dangers of global warming, (vi) development of eco-tourism jointly in the northern and southern parts of Bangladesh and West Bengal of India, and (vii) optimum sharing of physical resources like natural gas, etc. between the two countries and similar other areas. Some of these areas are actually multilateral which involve Nepal and China as well. Out of these listed prospective areas, quite a few are especially relevant for the theme of this article, i.e., in the context of the protection of the Sundarbans from the adverse impacts of climate change. If we analyse the issues in more details, it is possible to identify more micro areas within Sundarbans where bilateral or multilateral cooperation will be possible in future.

The various policy options suggested to save Sundarbans from the adverse impacts of climate change are mainly: (i) to find out ways to enhance sedimentation on the forest floor by means of guided sedimentation techniques, if possible, to prevent permanent inundation due to SLR, and (ii) to reduce the threats of increasing salinity especially in the dry season by adopting a range of physical measures to increase freshwater flows. In both these cases Indo-Bangladesh co-operation is a pre-condition of success. The Ganges Water Sharing Treaty 1996 may be considered as a first step to enhance flow regime of the Ganges and its distributaries. One of the declared targets of the Farakka-Sundarban component of the interlinking of river project adopted by Government of India is to increase the flow of water to Sundarban forest area. This project however ran into rough weather as it neglected the international dimensions associated with it. At the individual country level of course there are a number of ongoing projects. The Govt. of Bangladesh took up the Gorai River Restoration Project—a project considered to be economically and technically justifiable—to restore the flow of the Gorai by dredging the mouth of river during 1999-2002. In 2001 the Bangladesh Water Development Board started a project called Re-excavation of the Kobadak River to restore its previous capacity to supply freshwater to the central part of the forest area currently lost due to gradual sedimentation and human encroachment over time. Re-excavation of the Betna river is also needed as it serves the same purpose like the Gorai to the western part of Sundarbans. Many other similar projects like Integrated Coastal Zone Management Plan, Study on Options for the Ganges Dependent Areas, Sundarbans Bio-Diversity Conservation Project, The Coastal Greenbelt Project and others are going on in Bangladesh with the aim to reduce the vulnerability of Sundarbans arising out of the climate change impacts. Similar activities on the Indian side of Sundarbans are not visible to this extent on a comparable basis. Moreover, while everyone realizes the need for bilateral or multilateral co-operation among the neighbouring countries to meet the challenges of the impact of climate change as most of them are of trans-boundary nature, yet the countries are miles to go before they can effectively tackle such issues.

Of course we cannot deny the existence of several difficulties existing on the way of full-fledged implementation of Indo-Bangladesh co-operation in a number of areas including the protection of the two Sundarbans in these two countries. While the political factors are no doubt playing havoc to the scope of such co-operation, the economic factors also are no less important in this area. The existence of widespread poverty in the SAARC region has actually sidelined the question of environmental degradation. In fact poverty may be said as the greatest polluter. Also the lack of data about environmental resources is a serious bottleneck in the area of formulating co-operative policies in practice. Proper exchange of information not only among neighbouring countries but also between the developing and developed countries is urgently needed to make such co-operation effective and successful. This is more true so far as the framing of appropriate policies to mitigate the adverse impacts of climate change as most of the research in this area are done in the developed countries only and the developing countries are dependent on the results of such research. Moreover, the conclusions are mostly based on small scale surveys conducted in the developed countries only where the environmental conditions are quite different from those in the developing countries. More objectionable are the prescribed policies like carbon financing which tries to bypass the main causes of global warming and puts the main burden on the poor countries. While it is well-known that excessive fossil fuel consumption by the rich countries to maintain their high level of standard of living is mainly responsible for global warming, such countries are quite unwilling to reduce their unsustainable and resource degrading level of consumption. Unless the poor countries can unite to change this situation, there cannot be any permanent solution of the adverse impacts of the climate change.

REFERENCES

Agarwala, S., *et al.* (2003): *Development and Climate Change in Bangladesh: Focus on Coastal Flooding and the Sundarbans.* OECD, France.

Allison, M.A. and E.B. Kepple (2001): Modern Sediment Supply to the Lower Delta Plain of the Ganges-Bramhaputra River in Bangladesh, *Geo-Marine Letters,* Springer-Verlag Publishers.

Govt. of Bangladesh (2002): *Bangladesh: State of the Environment, 2001. Dhaka.*

Hazra, Somnath and Raj Kumar Sen (2005): 'An Economic Analysis of Sundarbans and its Embankments'. Jana, D.P. (ed.) *Embankments of Sundarbans and Related Issues.* Institute of Educational Research and Evaluation, Kolkata.

Sen, Raj Kumar and Somnath Hazra (2007): 'Ecological Sustainability, Economic Development and Coastal Ecosystems in India and other Developing Countries'. *Rabindra Bharati University Journal of Economics,* Vol. 1, Economics Dept., Rabindra Bharati University, Kolkata.

Hazra, Somnath and Raj Kumar Sen (2008): 'Globalization, Deforestation and

Global Warming', Paper for presentation in the 15th World Congress of the International Economic Association, Istanbul, June.

Sen, Raj Kumar and Somnath Hazra (2003): 'Ecological Sustainability and Economic Development in Low Income Economies: A Case Study of Wetland and Mangrove Ecosystem in Sundarbans'. Misra, S.N. (ed.) *Indian Economy and Socio-Economic Transformation: Emerging Issues and Problems*. Deep & Deep Publications Pvt. Ltd., New Delhi.

Sen, Raj Kumar and Somnath Hazra (2007): 'Environmental Co-operation Between India and Her Neighbouring Countries'. Pal, P.K. (ed.): *Economic Co-operation and Asian Countries*. Regal Publishers, New Delhi.

SECTION V

INSTITUTIONS, MANAGEMENT PRACTICES AND SOCIAL RESPONSIBILITIES FOR SUSTAINABLE DEVELOPMENT

Institutions for Sustainable Development

The Role of Prices, Norms and Law in Global and National Policy Perspectives

KANCHAN CHOPRA

Growth of national economies, dominated by the following characteristics, continues to pervade the global picture, whether viewed from the 'southern' or the 'northern' perspectives: a preference for material well-being, pushing other aspects of well-being into the background; preference for technologies that address "scarcity alleviation" in the somewhat limited sense in which economics defines it; a limited concern for the global impacts of unmitigated growth and with the state of planet earth and not much attention to the issues raised by "over-consumption" by the rich everywhere, whether in the north or the south.

However, climate change has been brought into the mental horizon of stakeholders all over the world by successive IPCC reports. Other more 'local' environmental degradation issues are equally significant in developing countries. Feedbacks from land and water degradation, for instance, have in some regions begun to impact agricultural growth. Both global and local ecosystems need attention. Humans face an unfinished agenda of trying to device national and international processes through which they agree on how to ensure increases in human well-being without further impacting our common future negatively. It is important to link this ecosystem view to national, regional and local development issues. This paper attempts to amplify some of the issues through a focus on either missing or multiple institutions. To illustrate, we select two examples, the reduction of green house emissions by the world at large and the acceleration of agricultural growth in India.

1. GROWTH AND WELL-BEING: A FEW FACTUAL OBSERVATIONS

The global perspective is often pervaded by the extraordinary economic success of China and India as exemplified by high rates of growth. This has been tempered somewhat by the recessionary consequences of upheavals in financial markets and in mid-2009, the looming spectre of drought in India makes the short-term prognosis more pessimistic. The following characteristics, however, continue to pervade the larger picture, whether viewed from the 'southern' or the 'northern' perspectives:

1. A preference for material well-being, pushing other aspects of well-being into the background;
2. Preference for technologies that address "scarcity alleviation" in the somewhat limited sense in which economics defines it;
3. A limited concern for the global impacts of unmitigated growth and with the state of planet earth; and
4. Not much attention to the issues raised by "over-consumption" by the rich everywhere, whether in the north or the south.

Meanwhile, the different IPCC reports (most notably the Fourth) provide careful documentation of the impact that anthropogenic activity has had on the planet earth. While impending climate change is indeed on the mental horizon of stakeholders all over the world, we are far from implementing or even designing a slew of policy instruments to meet the challenge. Humans face an unfinished agenda of trying to device national and international processes through which they agree on how to ensure increases in human well-being without further impacting our common future negatively. Other more 'local' environmental degradation issues are equally significant in developing countries. Feedbacks from land and water degradation, for instance, have in some regions begun to impact agricultural growth. Both global and local ecosystems need attention.

It is important to link this 'ecosystem view' to national, regional and local development issues. The elements of a possible framework in which to do this lie in the twin concepts of *"ecosystem services" and "human well-being"* and their interrelation. Ecosystem services are similar to other goods and services in that they contribute to human well-being. Further, they can be of the provisioning, regulating or cultural kind and each of these to the well-being of humans, in particular when human well-being is viewed as a matter of multiple capabilities and access to different kinds of resources. The timely and uninterrupted availability of services from a wide variety of natural ecosystems (such as forests, marine and mountain ecosystems) enhances material welfare, health status, security and minimizes conflict. Finally, given appropriate time and spatial scales, there can exist a fair degree of compatibility between environmental and developmental concerns.

However, the emergence of this compatibility depends critically on the existence and evolution of appropriate institutional arrangements at international, national and even local levels. A large number of ecosystem services are provided outside the market and non-market institutions tend to be neglected, or else, overtaken by fast moving markets. Not enough attention is invested by decision-makers in their individual and collective capacities to investigate into the nature and efficiency of the appropriate arrangements within which ecosystem services accrue and add to welfare. Why does this happen and what can we do about it? This paper attempts to amplify some of the issues concerned with the relations between policy intent and its success through a focus on either missing or multiple institutions. To illustrate, we select two examples, the reduction of green house emissions by the world at large and the acceleration of agricultural growth in India.

2. WHY? ON THE ROLE OF MARKETS: EITHER 'ASYMMETRICALLY EMPOWERED' OR 'MISSING'?

Decisions taken at the individual, community or national levels by different agents get implemented through a diverse set of institutions. Some of these institutions are better linked with each other, and thereby impact choice between alternative uses of ecosystems faster and with greater impact. Foremost among these institutions are markets which often function well in ensuring provisioning services accruing from ecosystems for groups of stakeholders. Typically, regulating and cultural services of natural ecosystems are not mediated or even taken account of in these overly powerful market institutions. This results in asymmetrical significance to different kinds of services, often to the detriment of the well-being of some sections and definitely at the cost of future well-being of all.

Perceptive theoretical analysts have commented on this asymetry. Note, for instance, the following:

> "Markets for all sorts of commodities are missing in our world. Prominent among those assets that don't have markets, competitive or otherwise, are transnational watersheds, the atmosphere, and the resources of the open seas. As the world community remains unable to get governments to step in, prices of commodities relying substantially on global natural resources don't even approximately reflect their scarcity values. Turning to local resources, such assets as micro-watersheds and mangrove forests are vital to the rural poor. However, the ecological, services they provide to industry and fish farms are in many cases not paid for. But governments in poor countries all too often have no tax policies or regulations in place to eliminate the price distortions arising from an absence of markets for those services."[1]

In some cases, solutions can be found in extending and making imaginative use of markets. We know that globalization of the world economy implies that trade has a profound impact on local incomes as also use of resources such as land and water. By way of example, a few results from a study in eastern India provide important learnings.[2] We found that increased export of shrimp led to increased incomes both from production and processing for large number of people. However, full cost of using natural resources was not taken into account in the presence of short-run profit orientation and the simultaneous availability of cheap labour. In this region, the huge expansion in land under aquaculture did not lead to the establishment of hatcheries to provide prawn seed, as would have been expected. This was due to the presence of adjacent water-bodies populated with wild prawn seed together with the availability of cheap labour to collect these using crude methods of collection. Our study shows that these methods led to a decrease in biodiversity at several locations (as measured by an index based on time series data).

Further, results based on an econometric analysis of costs indicate that such a development was completely unwarranted, given the high price of shrimp in the international market. Even if a biodiversity loss cost were to be assigned and seed prices to aquaculturists were to rise as a consequence, farmers would be able to absorb the rise, given the structure of costs and the price levels for their output. The nature of the international demand in this case suggests that compensation for biodiversity loss could have been made or the cost of hatcheries could have been supported. Absence of awareness of the loss of ecological services results in this callous indifference. Pricing resources correctly and ensuring functioning markets for different kinds of services can take us *part of the way* towards an appropriate design of market-based interventions.

3. ON IGNORING THE ROLE OF INSTITUTIONS OTHER THAN THE MARKET: THE LAW AND SOCIAL NORMS

The right prices operating in well-functioning markets cannot provide all the answers. Even the most perfect of markets reflect individual preferences and in a large number of situations, "there is a wedge between the rates private investors use to discount their future earnings and the rates the world community ought to use to discount collective benefits in the future."[3]

It is because of this that instruments such as law and social norms, which reflect the larger ethical concerns of humans, have a significant role to play. Future progress in designing appropriate policy responses to the climate change issue will have to address these ethical underpinnings squarely. Stern (2006)[4] in fact starts by noting these ethical concerns, which at times have entered the literature through responses to the issue of appropriate social rates of discount He has called for immediate decisive action to stabilize greenhouse gases because "the benefits of strong early action on climate change outweigh the costs." The Stern Review, also points towards the danger of-extending the principles of economics to the analysis of problems of critical import for the existence of life on earth. While Stern does so in the context of a problem facing the global commons and the depletion of the global natural capital through the concentration of green house gases, the same conclusions could be reached through an analysis of critical ecosystem services and 'biodiversity'. More than a decade earlier, the NOAA Panel in the United States also opted for use of the precautionary principle in a large gamut of issues where the limits to human understanding posed significant questions. The limits of economic analysis are perhaps best understood by the most authentic of its practitioners.

Such limits are, in particular, relevant to issues such as biodiversity which need to be viewed from multiple perspectives, both within and outside the fold of ecosystem services. The existence of multiple species provides services of many kinds to humans. These can be valued but 'biodiversity' as a contributor to "life-on earth" is beyond narrow notions of value. This is a clear pointer to policy analysts to treat some issues as beyond the scope of prices and economic instruments not because they are unimportant but because they are invaluable.

It is in this vein that, in advising on valuation of forest land for non-forest use, the Expert Committee constituted by the Supreme Court of India[5] recommended that critical habitats and protected areas, embodying high levels of biodiversity, not be converted to non-forest use at any cost. Well-implemented law was recommended as the policy instrument to protect such habitat. Other non-critical habitats were to be valued using benefit-cost based net present values with discounting and other such principles as guideposts.. The dividing line between what can or should be valued by the market and what should not may vary from culture to culture as institutions and values differ.

Decision-making in the political context often does not give credence to this dividing line. A recent ruling by the Supreme

Court of India,[6] for instance says, "the use of forest land in National Parks/Wildlife sanctuaries will be permissible in totally unavoidable circumstances for public interests and after obtaining permission from the Honourable Court. Such permissions *may be considered on payment of an amount equal to ten times in case of national parks . . . of the NPV payable for such areas"*. Applying the principle of payment for conversion, (how-so-ever high) to the case of biodiversity conserving national parks is exhibits a dangerous level of economic fundamentalism. The appropriate route to biodiversity conservation is good implementation of legal impediments backed by precise scientific definition of critical habitats.

As another example, witness the current focus in urban contexts such as Delhi to expand built environments in particular for specific events such as the Commonwealth Games, to the utter disregard of the regulating services provided by spaces such as river beds where the expansion is to take place. The Yamuna floodplains augment ground water supply in a city where demand for water is increasing but that does not seem to impact decision-making in the short-run. How do we as a society, protect the water regulating service of a floodplain when urban construction is the boom sector driving employment and growth? This acquires more significance as chronic water scarcity and episodic flooding may be the lot of the same urban habitats a few years down the line.

4. REACHING THE APPROPRIATE MIX OF DIVERSE INSTITUTIONS

In some contexts, new institutional structures need to be designed. The issue, in essence, is: in a fast developing world, how do we create space for the non-market related aspects of well being created by ecosystems: in particular, provisioning services in the future, cultural services, regulating services and the contribution of biodiversity? The process needs more accurate knowledge and its transformation into policy relevant conclusions followed by a constant dialogue between stakeholders with differing interests, perceptions and power. We analyse and list a few overarching and critical requirements for such an institutional evolution below. Two significant issues are selected for illustration: the first the international context of climate change and the second the link between natural resources and implementation of agricultural policy in India.

4.1 Climate Change Policy, Incomplete and Missing International Institutions

In the area of climate change related policy, we see the beginnings of an international institutionalized structure. The successive IPCC assessments enabled a coming together on issues relating to knowledge creation and provision and the Conference of Parties (COP) enabled a coming together of stakeholders. It can of course be claimed that this structure has only highlighted differences between groups of nations. The Kyoto Protocol, the most widely accepted agreement reached on, has been critiqued for its faulty design. In retrospect, its quantitative obligations (which even most of the EU did not fulfil) did not reflect the complete market principle of charging each state for all emissions, past and current.[7] And we are aware of the pitfalls facing global negotiators as we think in terms of a post-2012 regime. The failure of global understanding in the light of national positions and interests is all too overwhelming as we move towards the Copenhagen meeting.[8]

New international institutions are needed for changing behaviour, to increase local appreciation of shared global concerns and to correct collective action failures that cause global-scale problems. For example, people sometimes reduce their energy use when made aware that they consume more than the social norm. Thus, changes in the way knowledge is communicated can amplify the effect of energy pricing on behavior. However, this change in behaviour assumes the acceptance of a common international norm of consumption.[9] While institutions are designed to impact behaviour, the emergence of a set of acceptable rules assumes the existence of acceptable common norms. Such a precondition becomes critical when it comes to consumption of global commons such as the atmosphere. In this case, no price measure exists which will ensure a rationing of use and non-price socially acceptable norms must be in place. This, in turn, is more likely to emerge with decreases in inequalities in distribution of income and power and more interaction across the globe. In other words, once the knowledge base is agreed on, the design of well-functioning institutions needs commonalities in norms and limits in unequal distribution of income and power.

As we pursue some of the above mentioned forward looking policy options, we need to ensure that the dialogue leading to the design of appropriate interventions is facilitated. This will happen if:

(a) developed countries pursue the goal of responsible development by accepting significant cuts in emission levels, to move towards an acceptable norm, and
(b) fast growing developing economies are seen internationally as nations which also view their commitments to the future of planet earth in a responsible fashion and put in place credible policies supporting low carbon growth (to stay within the same norm) through appropriate technology.

4.2 Designing Institutions: Use of Natural Resources for Agricultural Development in India in the Case of Multiple Institutions

Multiple or incorrectly designed institutions with overlapping mandates can at times become a constraint to development as well. Take, for instance, the deceleration in growth rates of agriculture seen in India since 1994-95 something which had not been witnessed for a long period.[11] Some would interpret this as the visible face of the long overseen and neglected issues with respect to institutions for the management of land and water in a sustainable manner. The Hanumantha Rao Committee (2008) identifies *degradation of the natural resource base, lack of adequate incentives and institutions, and rapid and widespread decline in ground water table threatening sustainability as causes for concern in the context of planning for agriculture in the Eleventh Plan.*We give below the policy response, the institutional lacunae and possible steps to fill the gaps.

One of the significant initiatives of the Eleventh Plan has been a focus on rainfed areas with watershed development as one of the focal points. The NREGA put in place in 2007 and 2008 stresses linkages with local water and land-based programmes. It found that a plethora of programmes and organizations existed at local levels. Each of these were the outcome of prior policy initiatives at different points of time. Consequently, convergence across institutions, including government departments in the interest of integrated management of land and water became one of the new challenges for increasing agricultural production in the next phase. This has led to focus on the adoption of local level approaches including the 'watershed' approach. What does this imply for new institutions for governance?

The focus on rainfed area development and extensive funding for watershed-based resource use creates the necessity to bring about institutional change which incorporates the learnings from earlier implementation efforts. This learning indicates that *in addition to watershed management there is need for watershed plus interventions such as input supply, value addition of crops, credit and market linkages, etc., integration of 'on-farm' and 'non-farm' activities. There is the heed to raise the watershed agenda in planning for subsistence livelihoods to a market linked inclusive growth. Such an agenda is indicated because* studies have shown that, in its absence, the traditional watershed development activities are good for drought mitigation, at most for two to three consecutive years. In drought or even semi-drought conditions for the fourth consecutive year there is hardly any difference between a watershed and a non-watershed village.

To be successful, such a Watershed Plus approach shall have to take on board all institutions existing within a certain local context. Here, we seem to be disadvantaged by the existence of a plethora of institutions. A variety of committees and organizations currently exist in different parts of the country. Some of these are: *watershed committees, community-based organisations and joint forest management committees.* Each of these committees has created its own power centres with access to funds of particular kinds. Integration would have to give a specific role to each of these institutions.

It is proposed that the process of planning for area development take on board all significant institutions in a certain locale. *These may function under the overall governance purview of the Panchayati Raj Institutions (PRIs), which have a constitutional mandate creating them.*

Experience has shown that *panchayat bodies have not always been efficient watershed managers largely because they are territorial units, not related to ecological entities and not technically equipped The proposed structure for institutional integration corrects for this and makes use of the comparative strengths of all institutions while placing the PRIs in the role of legally constituted governance structures.*

Another significant institution to be re-examined and which cannot be ignored under this institutional integration are the Joint Forest Management Committees (JFMCs). Since 1990, JFM Committees have been set-up in most states on the basis of different State Governments' Orders. By March 2005, 99,868 committees covering 28.17% of forest area in India had been constituted. There has been considerable criticism of the manner in which their constitution keeps power in the hands of the Forest Department while transferring responsibility to the people. These committees have only partly fulfilled their mandate of carrying forward the participatory forest management agenda. Community Based Organisations (CBOs) for forest management have performed better in many states. Further conflicts between PRIs and JFMCs are an emerging concern in some states.

The proposed institutional integration will link JFMCs to PRIs through common members and make them more accountable to representative bodies, rather than to Forest Departments. In other words, all institutions or organisations functioning within a certain Panchayat shall be held accountable to it. To deal with overlapping geographic jurisdiction issues, federations of panchayats need to be created as well so that this federation, if not one panchayat, deals with the watershed or the larger JFMC.

A suitable division of authority and responsibility between different institutions will need to be worked out for successful integration. For instance, the watershed committee can focus on programmes for:

- Enhancing rural livelihoods through—
  (a) on-farm interventions such as watershed management, productivity enhancement, etc. and
  (b) non-farm interventions such as value addition, dairying, market linkages, etc.
- Integrated planning of the catchment and command areas as per the drainage system. For this, the following steps shall be necessary an Intensive Base line survey of:
  1. Physical resources such as land, rainfall, water bodies, animal stock, etc.

2. *Issues*—problems faced by the community *vis-a-vis* water availability, agriculture, fodder availability, etc.
3. *Property rights*—actual ownership and user rights to all lands, forest produce, etc.
4. *Existing Institutions*—affinity groups, dairy co-operatives in addition to PRIs: links between the two.

The oversight role given to PRIs in the above mentioned schema is in line with the PESA (Panchayat Extension to Scheduled Areas Act) of 1996. However, PRIs need strengthening in order to make the above possible. Some of the ways in which this can be done are listed below:

1. *Devolution of Finances and Functionaries to PRIs is necessary*: Steps are being taken in this direction in some states. Kerala has shown the way to nearly 40% devolution of its Plan outlay to the Panchayats for planning and implementation. In Karnataka, financial devolution to the Panchayats is of the order of Rs. 7,500 crore per annum. There is reason to believe, in terms of commitments made by State Governments, that there will be a fair measure of devolution of functions, finances and functionaries all over the country by the end of the next fiscal year, 2007-08. Meanwhile, States that are already well advanced in respect of such devolution are undertaking reviews to further improve their patterns and content of devolution.
2. *Assignment of Functionaries:* The devolution of Functionaries to that level of the Panchayati Raj system to which any given activity has been assigned in the Activity Map is also called for to ensure that the devolution is meaningful.
3. *Panchayat Sector Windows in State Budgets:* Based on the Activity Map drawn up by Panchayats and in conformity with that pattern of devolution of functions, the opening of a Panchayat sector window through the insertion of an appropriate budget line in the budgets of relevant line departments of the State government to ensure the flow of funds for undertaking devolved activities to the panchayats at the level to which any given activity had been devolved.

Institutional Integration at local levels

The following guidance principles are to be followed:

- PRI as governance body.
- All other institutions, i.e. Watershed Committees, JFMCs, CBOs to have specified areas of work and to have Panchayat members on them.
- Overall coordination of Activities for rural livelihoods with PRI.
- Federations of PRIs to be created for watershed and any other relevant non-administrative unit levels so that activities in the entire area are covered.
- Stengthening of PRIs with funds, functionaries and budgets.

The direction taken by planning for agricultural growth at the national level necessitates a careful look at local issues from the perspective of existence of appropriate institutions for natural resource use. A strengthening of local governance is indicated by these developments. This reinforces its significance from parallel considerations of equity and stakeholders' interests, which have received attention earlier.

4. CONCLUDING REMARKS

A critical look at the issues facilitating and inhibiting the emergence of appropriate institutions in different contexts provides interesting insights. A good knowledge base with regard to constraints on resource availability both in the present and the future is a prior condition. In some situations, this can lead to an extension and imaginative use of markets and prices to achieve sustainable use. In other cases, non-market institutions need to be put in place. The existence of a shared norm for use is an essential ingredient in for making a credible beginning in such a process. Further, in the emergence of sustainable institutions for impacting human behaviour, issues of inequity between participants assume great significance, though an acceptable norm on degree of inequality permissible may exist and facilitate the process. Preexisting institutions and the sharing of power and responsibility with them will have to constitute an important part of the design.

While some of the above points have been made in the context of the local commons, this paper extends the analysis to the global commons and to the successful implementation of agricultural policy with respect to land and water at local levels. It is found that the design of successful institutions cannot be separated from issues of socially acceptable norms of consumption and of pre-existing institutions determining distribution of power. This constitutes the challenge, both at the international and the national level.

NOTES AND REFERENCES

1. Dasgupta (2005).
2. For full details, See Chopra, Kumar and Kapuria (2009).
3. See Dasgupta (2005).
4. See Stern (2006), The Stern Review on the Economics of Climate Change.
5. Chopra, Dasgupta, Eswaran and Kadekodi, *Report of the Expert Committee on Net Present Value of Forest Land (2006).*
6. Order of the Supreme Court of India dated March 28, 2008 in Writ Petition No. 826, etc.
7. For a succinct analysis arguing for charging for all, stock and flow emissions see Bhagwati (2008), talk on Global Warming at Florence, Italy, April.
8. See Walker, B., Barrett, S. *et al.* "Looming Global Scale Failures and Missing Institutions," forthcoming *Science.*
9. Basu, Kaushik, "Social Norms and Co-operative Behaviour, Notes from the Hinterland between Economics and Anthropology" in Bardhan, P. and Isha Ray (edited), "The Contested Commons, Conversations between Economists and Anthropologists," Blackwell Publishing (2008).
10. Report of the Steering Committee on Agriculture and Allied Sectors for formulation of the Eleventh Plan (2008).

REFERENCES

Basu, Kaushik, "Social Norms and Co-operative Behaviour, Notes from the Hinterland between Economics and Anthropology" in Bardhan, P. and Isha Ray (edited), "The Contested Commons, Conversations between Economists and Anthropologists," Blackwell Publishing (2008).

Bhagwati, Jagdish (2008), Talk on Global Warming at Florence, Italy, April.

Chopra, Kanchan, Kapuria, Preeti and Kumar, Pushpam (2009), Biodiversity, Land-Use Change and Human Well-being; a study of Aquaculture in the Indian Sundarbans, Oxford University Press, Delhi.

Chopra, Kanchan, Dasgupta, P., Eswaran, V.B. and Kadekodi, G.K. (2006), Report of the Expert Committee on Net Present Value of Forest Land, submitted to the Supreme Court of India

Dasgupta, Partha (2005), Nature and the economy, Three essays, Mimeographed.

Hanumantha Rao, C.H.H. *et al.* Report of the Steering Committee on Agriculture and Allied Sectors for formulation of the Eleventh Plan (2008).

Stern, N. (2006), The Stern Review on the Economics of Climate Change.

Walker, Brian, Barrett, Scott, *et al.* "Looming Global Scale Failures and Missing Institutions," forthcoming *Science*.

17

Design of Economic Instruments and Participatory Institutions for Environmental Management in India

M.N. Murty

This paper examines the possibilities of using economic instruments, especially pollution taxes and bargaining approaches resulting in people's participation for environmental management in India. It tries to provide an intuitive description of methods of designing economic instruments and bargaining approaches for environmental management. The bargaining methods providing incentives for all stakeholders of an environmental resource to participate in its management result in decentralized solutions and savings in the transaction costs. A case study describes the estimation of pollution taxes for controlling air pollution in thermal power generation in India. The discussion of how bargaining methods are already in force in India shows their usefulness in controlling industrial pollution.

1. INTRODUCTION

Environmental resources (air and water) have natural regenerative capacity and they can accept certain amounts of pollution loads from anthropogenic activities without affecting themselves. That means this natural regenerative capacity of air and water imposes a constraint on the supply of waste disposal services. Industry and households demand waste disposal services and if this demand exceeds the supply constrained by the natural regenerative capacity, the degradation of environment starts. Given the public good nature of waste disposal service,[1] market is absent for this service and the polluter takes it as a free service. Therefore, the demand for the waste disposal service may exceed the natural supply. The problem then is to look for instruments and institutions to reduce the demand for waste disposal services to their natural levels of supply.

This paper examines the possibilities of using economic instruments, especially pollution taxes and bargaining approaches resulting in people's participation in pollution control. Section II provides a brief and less technical account of the alternative instruments and institutions for pollution abatement. Sections III and IV describe respectively certain methods of designing pollution taxes and participatory institutions to control industrial pollution in India. Finally Section IV provides the conclusions.

2. ALTERNATIVE INSTRUMENTS AND INSTITUTIONS FOR POLLUTION ABATEMENT

Alternative institutions for the control of environmental pollution are (a) Market, (b) Government, and (c) Community or Associations of people. A practical policy may involve all these institutions.[2] Normally one does not come across a market with producers of waste and processors of waste acting with same price/cost arrangements to abate pollution. Therefore, it is generally stated that market forces fail to control environmental pollution. Government has been viewed as an alternative institution to deal or manage the environment. Community action or people's participation is now gaining prominence as an alternative to Governmental agencies for the management of environmental resources.[3]

Market, Government and Instruments for Pollution Control

Non-market policy instruments include command-and-controls (CAC). Market based instruments consist of pollution taxes (Pigou, 1920) and marketable pollution permits (Dales, 1968). These are often referred to as economic instruments. The choice between these instruments depends both on their efficacy in achieving the target level of emissions as well as on the relative size of welfare losses they produce (Baumol and Oates, 1988). Government can use either non-market policy instruments or market based or economic instruments or a combination of two.

Command and Controls (CAC)

The CAC instruments are in the form of fines, penalties and threats of legal' action for closure of the factories and imprisonment of the owners. They can be used either for facilitating the use of specific technologies for the environment management or for the realization of specific environmental standards. It can be shown that the cost of imposing and implementing compliance are generally higher when CAC instruments are used than with economic instruments. Furthermore, under CAC instruments, there can be no incentives for firms to innovate or invest in more efficient pollution control technologies or in cleaner process technologies.

Economic Instruments

Economic instruments can be divided in to three categories: price based instruments, quantity based instruments and hybrid instruments. These instruments are often called as market based instruments. Together with supply-demand forces of the market they achieve efficiency even with the presence of environmental externalities like air and water pollution.

Price-based Instruments

The price-based instruments are first suggested by Pigou in 1920 in the form of taxes and subsidies to deal with detrimental and beneficial environmental externalities in production and consumption. Instances are pollution taxes on a polluting commodity either through its production (paper, leather, electricity, etc.) or consumption (cigarette, packed food, etc.) or on a polluting input (fuel inputs, chemicals, etc.). It could be a tax on either polluting output or pollution load. Also, they can be subsidies on the commodities the production of which generate environmental benefits (e.g., neighbor's rose garden giving one the free benefit of beauty). The pollution tax or Pigouvian tax is a corrective instrument to realize the socially optimal level of economic activity generating pollution.

Pollution tax could be interpreted as the price the polluter has to pay for using the waste disposal services from the environmental media. Since the market is missing for the waste disposal service, this price could not be determined in the market. The supply and demand schedules for this service could not be observed in the market. However, given the property right to the environmental resource to the public or government, environmental regulation[4] by the government or public could make the polluter liable to pay a price for the waste disposal service. The polluter pays the price in the form of cost he incurs for complying with the environmental regulation. Therefore, the marginal cost of pollution abatement or the cost the polluter is willing to incur for reducing every successive unit of pollution abatement (MCA) could be interpreted as the demand price of waste disposal service. Figure 1 depicts the demand curve for the waste disposal service as the falling MCA or demand price with respect to the pollution load generated. Alternatively, it could be seen as the curve depicting the rising MCA with respect to the pollution load reduction.

There is an opportunity cost or health and other damages suffered by the public by allowing the pollution. The supply price of waste disposal service is the price charged to the polluter by the government or public for every unit disposal of waste in to the environmental media. Therefore, the marginal damages (MD) or damages from every successive unit of pollution that the public is willing to bear could be interpreted as the supply price of waste disposal service. Figure 1 describes the supply curve of waste disposal service as the rising marginal damages (MD) or supply price with respect to the pollution loads.

Let us illustrate the Pigouvian tax/subsidy framework diagrammatically. In Fig. 1, MCA, MD respectively represent the marginal cost of abatement and marginal damages from pollution. E^m, E^* stand respectively for pollution loads with and without tax instrument and 't' stands for the pollution tax. With the polluters using the pollution abatement technologies, the optimality or maximization of welfare requires that the pollution to be reduced up to the level at which the MCA equals the MD as shown in Fig. 1. If a tax equivalent to 't' on per unit of pollution is levied on the polluter based on the polluter pay principle, the polluter has an incentive to reduce pollution up to the optimal level, E* in the free market. The polluter has two choices: Pay tax equivalent to E^*ERE^m or reduce pollution load from E^m to E^* incurring the cost equal to E^*ESE^m. If he reduces the pollution, he will save cost equal to ERS as in Fig. 1. Therefore, given the tax rate equivalent to 't', he chooses to reduce pollution rather than paying the tax.

The damages from pollution are felt by a large number of people (more so with water pollution). Therefore, the damages from a unit of pollution at margin are the sum of marginal damages to all the affected people. Therefore, to design a Pigouvian tax, we require the information about abatement cost functions of polluting firms and damage functions for all the affected people. The cost of collecting the information to estimate these functions can be prohibitively high. For example, millions of people are affected from the pollution of a major river like Ganges and an urban air shed like Delhi and therefore it may not be economically feasible to design the Pigouvian tax.

Figure 1

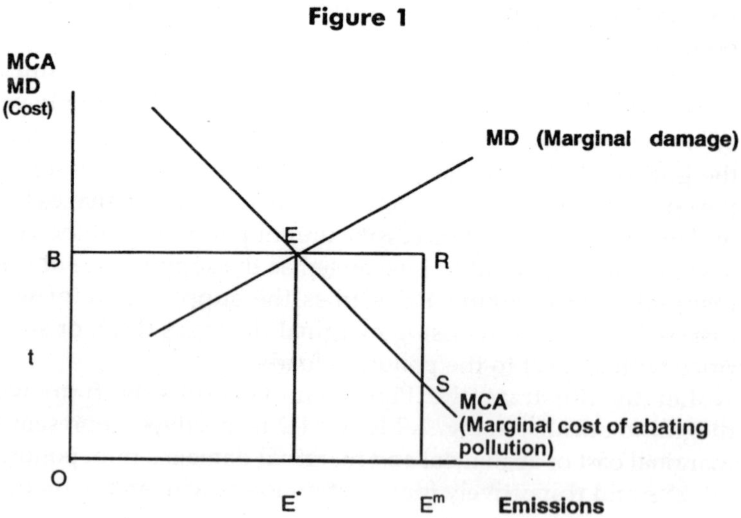

Quantity-based Instrument

D.H. Dales (1968) has suggested an alternative to the pollution tax, a system of tradable pollution rights for the management of environment. He has proposed that the property rights be defined to the use and abuse of environment and such entitlement be offered for sale to the highest bidder. This system is like a tax to achieve the specified environment target at a minimum cost. For example in the case of air pollution, this approach first determines the optimal level pollution in a given geographical area. This level of pollution to be tolerated is then divided in to a number of permits among the various polluting units within the area (either by free distribution or by auctioning). Firms which are already comparatively more efficient in controlling their wastes or pollution (the ones that face lower unit cost for pollution control) may continue their original level of production and emissions. But they will have some extra pollution permits (or entitlements) to spare. They can sell such extra permits to firms which are less efficient in controlling their wastes (the ones that face higher unit costs for pollution abatement). Provided monitoring is possible and effective, the net result is that total pollution is kept within the prescribed levels. The more efficient firms will sell their surplus permits to less efficient firms which require more permits in order to continue with original production plans. In this process, a market for pollution permits is created in which trading in permits takes place up to the point at which the aggregate supply of permits is equal to the aggregate demand for permits and the equilibrium permit price is equal to the marginal cost of abatement to each firm.

Mixed Instruments: A Practical Approach

In practice, we should have a mixture of both command and controls and economic instruments. Economic instruments alone may not be feasible because of high their imposition requires lot of information on firm level emission, technology, etc. which are not easy to come by. Command and control measures alone are inefficient measures (they may result even in the use of costly pollution abatement technologies by the firms). Similarly, the estimation of damages to affected people in the case of pollution tax, and knowing before the optimal level of pollution in the case of tradable permits pose practical problems for the design of economic instruments. Fixation of pollution standards by Pollution Control Boards and using either pollution tax or marketable permits instrument to induce the polluter industry to meet those standards is an hybrid method using regulatory and economic instruments. However, in this case the criteria of fixation of environmental standards are a subject of debate about whether they have to be decided on scientific basis or on the basis of referendum or political process. Scientifically, they have to be based on the evidence concerning the effects of air pollution on health or of polluted water on fish and human life. They can be alternatively decided through a political process by having referendum on the choice among alternative sets of pollution standards. Still, there are issues such as should they be at state levels or national, should the standards be a compromise between the industry and people and so on.

Once the environmental standards are given *apriori,* the difficult problem of estimating the damages to all the affected people from pollution can be avoided for designing the economic instruments. However, we need an estimate of pollution abatement cost. It is economically feasible to obtain an estimate of pollution abatement costs because (a) the polluters may normally be much less in number than the affected people, and (b) tangible information can be obtained about technologies used by the polluters, pollution loads and levels of production. Using the firm level data on pollution loads, costs of abatement and production levels the pollution abatement cost functions can be estimated using econometric techniques. Given the environmental standards and the estimated marginal abatement cost function, a rate of tax can be fixed such that the firms will automatically have an incentive to reduce pollution for meeting the standards. This is explained in Fig. 2.

Let the emission standard be OE. Let the current rate of the firms emission be OD. If the firm has to reduce pollution load from D to E as per the environmental standard, the rate of tax equivalent to OA will make the firm to do so. The firm has an incentive to do pollution abatement rather than paying tax because the cost of abatement given by the area BFDE in the figure is lower than the tax liability given by the area BCDE. Similarly, marketable pollution permits can be used to obtain the reduction

Figure 2

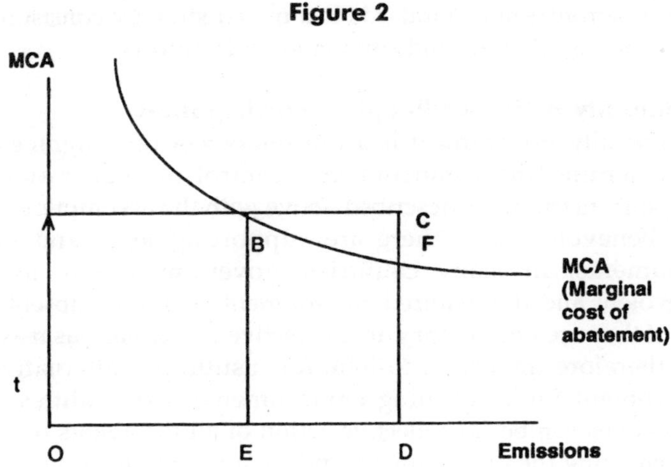

in pollution loads by the firms as required by the environmental standards. It can be shown that the taxes standards or tradable permits and standards method results in the adoption of least cost technologies by the firms.[5]

There can be many situations in which command and control instruments are unavoidable. In several cases, the social cost of a particular activity depends on factors beyond the control of those directly involved. For example, the effects of discharge of effluents into a river depend upon the conditions of the river at that particular point of time. Similarly, stagnant air can trap pollutants of air, perhaps even collecting them becomes hazardous. Therefore, exogenous meteorological conditions may contribute to occasional crisis requiring temporary emergency measures in the form of command and controls. Pollution tax rates cannot be changed on short notice to deal with emergencies and even if the changes are effected, polluters respond with a longer time lag. Marketable permits also result in long-run adjustments in environmental quality and are not suitable for emergencies. Command and control measures on the other hand can be quickly operated to deal with more than normal amount of emissions arising out of emergencies, since they do not require extra monitoring. Therefore, in practice neither economic instruments nor command and controls alone constitute an optimal environmental strategy. The cost minimizing strategy to realize given environmental standards is a mixed strategy consisting of economic instruments and command and controls.

Community Action or People's Participation

Generally, government is given the power of designing and implementing the command and control measures and the economic instruments described above with the assumptions that it is benevolent and there are supporting legal and other instruments. In many countries, government may not be benevolent and the required environmental laws are absent and even if they are present they are ineffective due to various reasons. It is therefore important to look for institutions alternative to government for controlling environmental externalities. The alternatives can be (a) collective action of all the agents relevant for managing the environment, and (b) a purely market option.

Coase (1960) has argued that many types of externalities can be optimally controlled by creating specific property rights among concerned agents. Property rights mean either rights to clean water and air to people or rights to pollute to the producers and consumers. This important finding of Coase, now known as Coase theorem, is stated as follows: Consider a situation of an externality (say pollution). These are two agents involved here namely the generator and the affected parts. Given the initial property rights to any resource either to the generator of the externality or to the affected party, and if the cost of bargaining is zero, the bargaining between the two parties results in the optimal control of externality. The final outcome of bargaining is invariant to the initial property rights (for example in the case of air pollution whether the right to clean air is vested in the affected people or whether the right to pollute is given to the polluter). This result is further explained in Fig. 3. In this figure, pollution load is measured along x-axis and the marginal cost of pollution abatement (MCA) and the marginal damages (MD) are measured along y-axis. The optimal pollution load is given as OE. For the pollution loads higher and lower than OE, there are incentives for gainful bargaining between the polluter and the affected party. If the polluter has the right to pollute beyond OE, then the MD is higher than MCA for the pollution loads, the affected party has an incentive to bribe the polluter at any rate lower than MD for a unit reduction in pollution and the polluter has an incentive to accept the bribe at any rate higher than the MCA. Therefore, bargaining between the two parties takes place until the pollution load is reduced to OE. Similarly, since MCA is higher than MD for the pollution loads lower than OE, the polluter has an incentive to offer bribe to the affected party at any rate lower than MCA and the affected party has an incentive to accept bribe at any rate higher than MD. Again, the bargaining between them leads to the optimal pollution load OE.

There are several practical problems for the Cosean bargaining to work in practice for controlling the environmental externalities. First of all, in reality, the transaction costs or costs of bargaining are not zero but positive. It can be shown that with positive costs of bargaining, the resulting pollution load through bargaining can be higher or lower than the optimal pollution load 'OE' depending on the initial property rights.

That means with the positive transaction costs, the final result will be no longer invariant to the initial property rights. Secondly, one of the key assumptions in the Coasean solution is that all the externalities are captured in the value of property rights and there are incentives for gainful bargaining. This can work well for the externalities on a smaller scale or local externalities of the type described by Coase (a building that blocks wind mill's air currents;

Figure 3

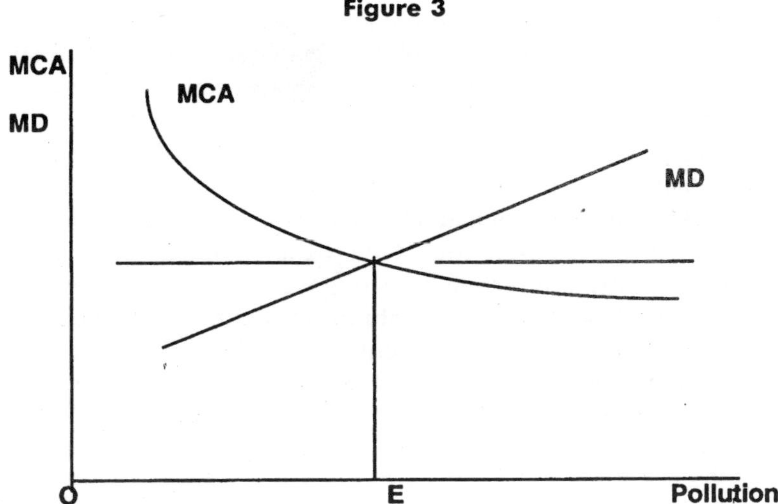

a confectioner's machine that disturbs doctor's quiet, etc.). However, many environmental externalities occur on a grander scale with a large number of receivers and many times a good number of generators (for example pollution of a river and the atmosphere) which makes defining property rights and facilitating bargaining difficult. One way of dealing with this problem is to create a common property right to the river for all the affected people as one group and have an association of polluters of the river so that the bargaining to reduce the river pollution can take place between the two parties. The third problem for Coasean bargaining arises again in the context of defining the property rights for an environmental resource. The environmental resource is a stock affecting the welfare of both present and future generations. Capitalization of future benefits from this resource is not possible because property rights to future generations of affected people can not be defined. One approach to take care of future generation is to consider the government as its representative. The government can compete in the market for environmental property rights of the future generation and pay for it by issuing a debt which has to be serviced by the future generation. Another approach is based on the assumption that the present generation has a bequest motive to the future and wants to bequeath to the future the preserved resources. However, both government intervention and bequest motive are outside the scope of Coases's property rights approach.

In the Coasean bargaining solution, government has a minimal role to play. Its role is only to create property rights and protect them and then the free market bargaining between the agents will optimally control the externality. Various institutional alternatives now considered for the control of environmental externalities contain some elements of market mechanism with the government playing only a limited role. Given the doubtful quality of government and transaction costs of government instruments, it is imperative to look for new institutions to define and implement property rights for the environmental externalities. The collective action by all the agents involved has been found to be one such new institution.

3. ESTIMATING POLLUTION TAXES FOR AIR POLLUTION ABATEMENT

Environment provides waste disposal services as productive inputs to industry. Given the environmental regulation, producers place a value on these inputs as they value other conventional inputs labour, man-made capital and materials. Environmental regulation meant for ensuring the environmentally sustainable industrial development imposes a cost on the industry. UN[6] methodology for the integrated environmental and economic accounting calls this cost as maintenance cost or the cost to the industry for maintaining the quality of environment at its natural regenerative level. As explained in Section 2, environmental regulation of pollution taxes or other instruments are needed for making the industry to internalize this cost. There is a need for estimates of shadow prices environmental inputs to estimate the maintenance cost to the industry and the estimates of pollution abatement cost functions for designing pollution taxes.

A model describing the technology of power generation as one of producing jointly good output, power and bad output, pollution load can be used for estimating the shadow prices and marginal pollution abatement cost functions of industrial pollutants. This model is known as output distance function in the theory of production. The processes of waste generation or material balance conditions are indirectly considered in the production relation expressed in the reduced form as output distance function[7]. The producer demand price for waste disposal services from environment could be defined as the opportunity cost in terms of good output foregone to reduce bad output in this model and this price may be regarded as the shadow price of pollution or marginal cost of pollution abatement. Using the estimate of this model, the estimates of marginal cost of abatement of industrial pollutants can be obtained. Appendix A describes the output distance function and its estimate for the thermal power generating industry in Andhra Pradesh (AP) state of India.[8] Table 1 provides estimates of shadow prices of pollutants SPM, SO_2, and NO_x for thermal power generation in AP.

TABLE 1

Shadow Prices of Pollutants

(*Rs. per tonne*)

Industrial Pollutants	*Mean*	*Standard Deviation*
SPM	1043	1067
SO_2	5867	8706
NO_X	11539	21153

Cost of Environmentally Sustainable Power Generation

Scientifically, the environmental standards, (Minimum National Standards (MINAS) in India or WHO standards) are supposed to be designed taking into account the natural regenerative capacity of environment media. Therefore, the cost of complying with these standards to the industry may be interpreted as cost of environmentally sustainable industrial development. This cost has to be accounted in the measurement of Green GDP or environmentally corrected net national product (ENNP). The ENNP could be defined as:[9]

$$ENNP = C + P_k \Delta K + P_n \Delta N \quad (1)$$

where C, ΔK, and ΔN represent respectively consumption, changes in manmade capital, and natural or environmental capital and P_k and P_n are prices of manmade and natural capital.

The first two terms in equation (1) constitute the conventional NNP while the last term accounts for the value of change in natural resource stock (change in environmental quality) due to various economic activities during the year. UN methodology suggests the development of physical and monetary accounts of natural capital as satellite accounts to conventional national accounts for estimating $P_n \Delta N$. Time series of physical accounts of ambient quality of atmosphere, and water resources and forest cover have to be developed to estimate ΔN. For example in the case of air pollution studied in this paper, ΔN could be measured as the excess of pollution load of SPM over the pollution load corresponding to safe ambient standards. In the case of CO_2, ΔN could be simply pollution load generated because it adds to the stock of CO_2 already present in the atmosphere.

Table 2 provides physical and monetary accounts of air pollution for a representative firm belonging to AP power generating industry during a year. The annual cost of reducing the pollution levels of SPM, SO_2, and NO_X from the current levels to zero in all thermal power generating plants in AP is estimated as Rs. 534 million. This cost could be interpreted as the cost of environmentally sustainable thermal power generation in AP.

TABLE 2

Physical and Monetary Accounts of Air Pollution for an Average Thermal Power Generating Firm in AP

	SPM	*SO_2*	*NO_X*
Load (Tonnes/yr.)	7836	10488	1668
Shadow Price (Rs.)	1043	5867	11539
Cost of Abatement (Rs. million)	8.173	61.533	19.247

Note: Row 2 of Table shows the data of observed emissions of SPM, NO_X, and SO_2.

Shadow Prices of Pollutants and Pollution Taxes

Estimation of pollution taxes using Taxes-Standards method requires the estimates of marginal cost of pollution abatement and the data about pollution standards. The shadow prices of pollutants reported in Table 1 could be also interpreted as marginal costs of pollution abatement. Using the estimated distance function in Appendix A for thermal power generation in AP, plant specific shadow prices could be calculated. The marginal cost of pollution abatement for each pollutant could be obtained by finding a relationship between the shadow price of pollutant and pollution load. The marginal cost of pollution abatement of a plant could depend on output, pollution and plant specific characteristics among others. Specifying this relationship as stochastic, marginal cost of pollution abatement function for thermal power generation in AP is estimated each for SPM, SO_2 and NO_X as given in equations 2, 3 and 4 respectively. In these equations, the dependent variables are shadow prices or marginal costs of pollutants (SPMS, SO_2S, NO_XS) and independent variables are electricity output, pollution concentrations (SPMC, SO_2C, NO_XC), plant specific dummy variables (D_i, i = 1 . . . 4) and time.

There is a rising marginal cost with respect to pollution reduction as expected.

SPM

$$\ln SPMP = 11.82 + 0.255^* \ln(OUT) - 1.02^* \ln(SPMC) + 0.705^*D1 + 0.308^*D2 - 0.57^*D3$$
(22.80) (2.92) (-13.71) (2.96) (1.00) (-3.31)

$$0.108^*D4 - 0.22^*TIME$$
(0.55) (13.71) (2)

Adjusted $R^2 = 0.7822$

Figure 4 depicts the marginal pollution abatement cost function for SPM. On y-axis marginal cost of abatement and on x-axis SPM concentration are measured.

SO_2

$$\ln SO_2P = 9.33 + 1.012^* \ln(OUT) - 0.835^* \ln(SO_2C) - 02.16^*D1 - 2.27^*D2 - 1.69^*D3$$
(27.24) (11.73) (-14.85) (-8.37) (-6.68) (-10.13)

$$- 0.352^*D4 - 0.073^*TIME$$
(-1.47) (-3.01) (2)

Adjusted $R^2 = 0.8196$

NO_X

$$\ln NO_XP = 4.94 + 1.21^* \ln(OUT) - 0.63^* \ln(NO_XC) - 3.88^*D1 - 2.41^*D2 - 0.93^*D3$$
(14.67) (13.48) (-10.67) (-16.58) (-7.50) (-5.23)

$$-1.38^*D4 - 0.27^*TIME$$
(-6.34) (10.8) (3)

Adjusted $R^2 = 0.8062$

Using the above abatement cost of functions and using MINAS Stack Emission Standards of 115, 80 and 80 milligrams per NM^3 respectively for SPM, SO_2 and NO_X, the tax rates are computed as Rs. 2099, 20519 and 5554 per tonne of emissions. If these taxes are levied on power generating company, the company has incentives to internalize the maintenance cost or cost of pollution abatement as discussed in Section 2.

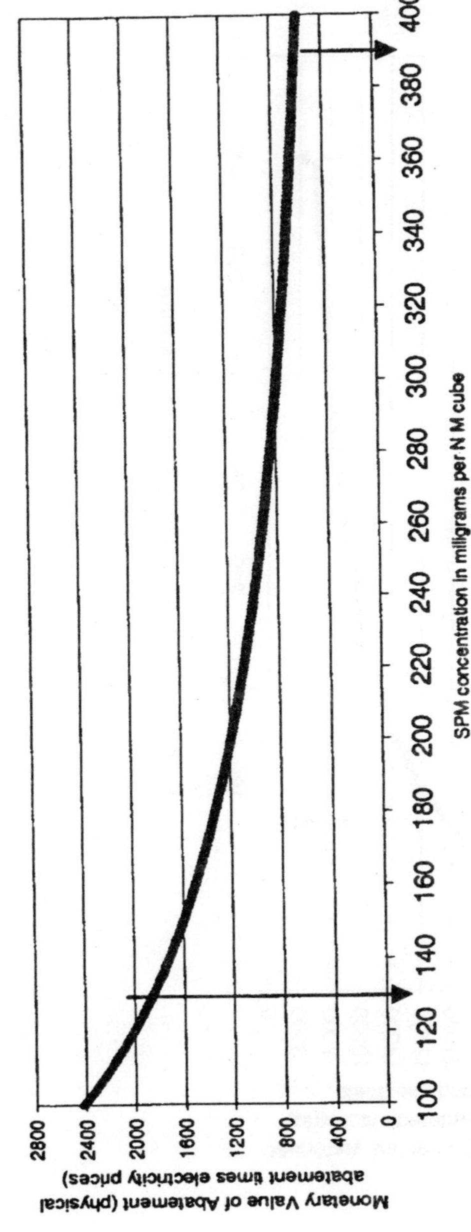

Figure 4: Abatement Function for SPM Concentration

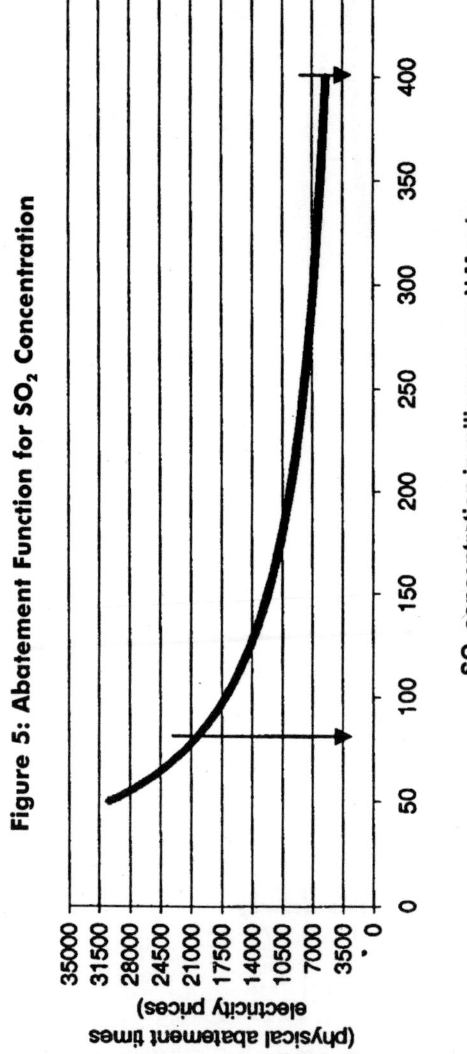

Figure 5: Abatement Function for SO_2 Concentration

Figure 6: Abatement Function for NOx Concentration

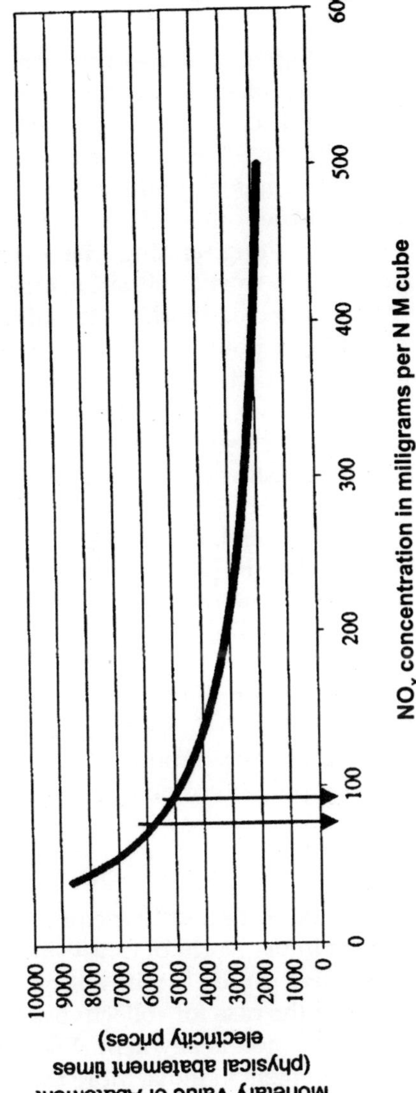

4. COLLECTIVE ACTION: A DETERRENT TO COLLUDING INDUSTRY AND CORRUPT BUREAUCRACY[10]

Governments of many developing countries and even some of developed countries are non-benevolent, so that the responsibility of dealing with market failure and achieving some developmental objectives cannot be completely left to them. In the case of control of externalities like the environmental pollution, the corrupt bureaucracy of developing countries often colludes with external diseconomy creating agents in augmenting the externality problem rather than controlling it. In such situations there is no other option left to the parties affected by the externality but to take recourse to collective action or political influence for dealing with the bureaucracy and the perpetrator of the externality. As already explained in Section 2, Coase (1960) argues that given the initial property rights to either the externality generator or the receivers, the costless bargaining between them in a free market will result in the optimal control of the externality, the final outcome being independent of the initial allocation of property rights. Becker (1983) has shown that the political influence exerted by pressure groups can have similar effects as having a benevolent government to deal with market failure. In his own words:

> 'The same analysis of competition among pressure groups, without the introduction of social welfare function or benevolent government, explains expenditures on defense and other public goods, taxes on pollution, and other government activities that raise efficiency, even when some groups are hurt by the activities (*Becker*, 1983)'.

However, bargaining cannot be costless as Coase proposes, and transaction costs are important in the world of Coase and Becker. Even with transaction costs, there can be significant net welfare gains from collective action, and the case for collective action will be reinforced if the government is non-benevolent. Take the case of industrial water pollution abatement in India. More than twenty years of environmental legislation in India has not produced a pollution tax and the CAC methods used so far by the Indian government have not made a dent in industrial pollution control. This has also been the case with many developing countries. One important reason of this is the absence of awareness among the people.about the extent of damage from pollution, and their inability to organize themselves as pressure groups for participating in the management of pollution abatement. In such a situation, industry and the non-benevolent bureaucracy have incentives to collude for violating environmental standards. Industry can bribe the regulator to over report its effluent quality or not report it at all. There are several agents involved in the political economy of industrial pollution abatement: affected people, elected representatives, bureaucracy and industry. Incentives exist for a sub-coalition of agents, like a coalition of affected people and elected representatives and another coalition of bureaucracy and industry. These conditions could constitute politically active pressure groups. Murty (1995b) has shown that the competition among these pressure groups may result in the optimal control of pollution.

Pollution Taxes, Corruption, Bribes and Penalties

In the case of non-benevolent government, as it may be the case in many developing countries, the mere enactment of environmental laws does not guarantee that they are actually executed. There can be several points of view about the way corruption takes place in bureaucracy. One view point is that in the pyramid cal structure of bureaucracy, corruption increases as one goes down the cadre while it is virtually zero at the highest level. Opportunities for corruption arise when principal officer delegates enforcement authority to lower-cadre officer Rose-Ackerman, 1978; Milgrom and Roberts, 1988. In such a system checks and balances operate to minimize corruption in bureaucracy since there is a probability that the bribe taking lower cadre officer is being caught and penalized by the superior officer. Mukherjee and Png (1994) have shown that in a pyramid cal structure of corruption, the penalty for bribe taking and the compensation for honesty behaviour of lower cadre officers affected by regulator have uncertain effects on pollution abatement. Another view point is that corruption is distributed (perhaps evenly) among all cadres of bureaucracy. There is tacit agreement among officers of all cadres to share the bribe collected so that a lower cadre officer, say an inspector, has the sanction of his superior to take bribe. It is this bureaucratic corruption of this form that manifests in many developing countries. In India it is a commonly held public belief that inspectors dealing with collection of taxes, monitoring industrial pollution, etc. have sanction of their bosses to take bribe. The third view point is that corruption provides incentives for both bureaucracy and politicians (the legislature or elected representatives) to collude. There may be collusion between bureaucracy and elected representatives with motive of rent seeking from the power constitutionally granted to them. This type of corruption can find a place in the societies where the public is not politically active or organized to deal with erring legislators as is the case with democracies in many developing countries. A check on later two types of bureaucracy can only come through politically active groups or people affected by industrial pollution.

Politically active groups of people affected by an externality can influence their elected representatives in a democracy to stem bureaucratic corruption. They can bring pressure on their elected representatives, say, a municipal committee in case of a local externality, to impose penalties on bribe taking bureaucracy. Alternatively, they organize themselves as pressure groups to take recourse to legal action against colluding elected representatives, bureaucracy and industry. Thus depending upon the way corruption actually takes place, there can be sub-coalition of agents relevant for industrial water pollution abatement: a coalition of affected people and elected representatives and a coalition of industry and bureaucracy in the second case; affected people alone and a coalition of industry, bureaucracy and elected representatives in the third case. Collective action of affected people has transaction costs in the form of time devoted and efforts made to organize for detecting violation of environmental standards by a coalition of bureaucracy and industry and for effecting legal action.

Public Perception of Damages and Penalties

Consider a situation in which four sets of agents are involved in the industrial pollution abatement: (a) affected public, (b) elected representatives of public (say a municipal committee), (c) bureaucracy (the executive implementing the environmental legislation), and (d) industry. In the absence of any checks from the affected public, there can be incentives to bureaucracy and industry to violate the environmental standards.[11] Given a pollution tax as per the environmental legislation, industry has an incentive to bribe the bureaucracy, at a rate less than the tax per unit of effluent, for over-reporting its effluent quality. A false certification of higher effluent quality by bureaucracy helps industry to shun its responsibility for meeting the standards. The extent to which the affected public can make bureaucracy and industry to comply with environmental standards depends upon its degree of perception of damages and influence it can exert either through either its political organization or elected representatives, or both. The degree or probability with which the affected people perceive their damage and are able to apprehend the bribe taking bureaucracy and non-complying industry depends upon the amount of time and effort devoted for politically organizing themselves. Politically active affected people can bring pressure on their elected representatives to impose penalties on bureaucracy and industry if they are caught colluding with each other for violating the standards. Probability with which they are caught depends upon the degree of political activity.

Non-benevolent Government and Strategic Behaviour of Active Groups in Water Pollution Abatement

There are incentives for the formation of sub-coalitions of various agents involved in industrial water pollution abetment if the bureaucracy or regulator is corrupt.[12] As explained earlier, it may be possible that affected people and municipal committee act in tandem. People need the help of their representatives to deal with industry and bureaucracy, and the representatives require people's support to get re-elected. Also it may be possible that industry and bureaucracy have incentives to collude for sharing the cost saved from non-compliance of environmental standards by industry. This simple bifurcation of politics into two sub-coalitions is made to highlight the effect of political activity of pressure groups on industrial water pollution abetment. However, in actuality, a few other sub-coalitions are possible and a similar analysis can be attempted with them. Thus we have two groups of agents: Group I Affected people and municipal committee with a strategy of time spent on political organization, W and cost function G^1 and Group II Industry and bureaucracy with a strategy of level of environmental quality, E and cost function G^2. The cost

Figure 7: Strategic Behaviour of Active Groups in Water Pollution Abatement

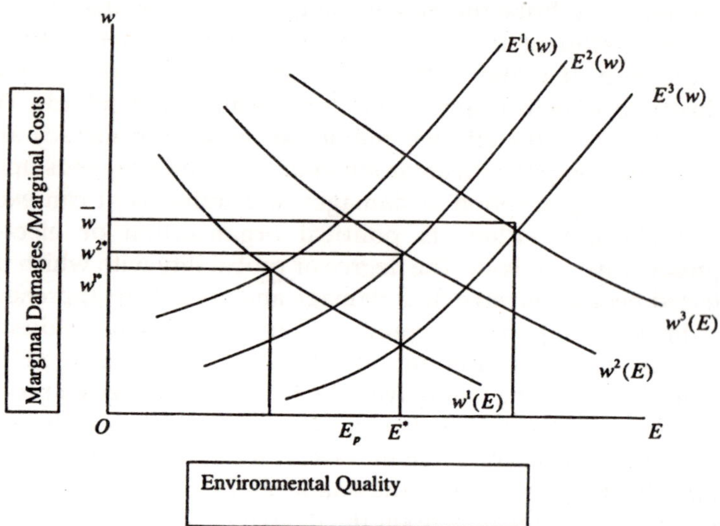

to each group depends on the W, E and penalties and bribes.[13] Given penalties and bribe, Group I minimizes G^1 with respect to W given E while group II minimizes G^2 with respect to E given W. The strategic behaviour of groups I and II yields the reaction functions $W(E) = \frac{\delta G^1}{\delta W}$, $W'(E) \leq 0$ and $E\,(W) = \frac{\delta G^2}{\delta E}$, $E'\,(W) \geq 0$.

The equilibrium strategies of two persons Nash non-cooperative game are defined as W* (E*), and E* (W*) which are given by the intersection of curves depicting the reaction functions of groups I and II as shown in Fig. 7. Increasing penalties on industry and bureaucracy have the effects of increasing environmental quality E, given W, and decreasing the time devoted to political activity W, given the environmental quality E. The equilibrium environmental quality of a two person Nash non-cooperative game increases as the penalties increase. Thus there are welfare gains of increasing penalties either in the form of decrease in damages due to the improvement in environmental quality, or in the form of saving in cost of political activity. Since there are costs to industry from increasing E, there can be net welfare gains from increasing penalties so long as incremental damage reductions to affected parties are higher than the incremental cost to industry. In fact the optimal rates of penalties and optimal environmental quality are determined by the condition that marginal cost of abatement to industry is equal to marginal reduction in damages. However, in the current framework, the optimal rates of penalties are determined by the statutorily fixed environmental standards. It could be shown that even if the government is non-benevolent, the statutorily fixed environmental quality could be achieved through political competition.[14]

Coase and Becker in Practice: Some Examples from India

Empirical findings of a survey of some industrial estates in India[15] provide an evidence for the presence of active pressure groups for the control of externality of industrial pollution. Data from this survey provides insights into empirical aspects of the economic and non-economic processes leading to collective action in industrial water pollution abatement. The data shows that collective action of various agents like people affected by water pollution, elected representatives, industries NGOs and the government is responsible for triggering the processes leading to control of industrial water pollution. It is observed that untreated waste waters from factories in the industrial estates surveyed have been deposited on the surface and in local streams, resulting in the degradation of cultivable lands and ground water contamination. Local people have suffered from crop and cattle losses and contracted a variety of water-born diseases. The government has failed to take cognizance of the damages, which may support the local people's view, that there is collusion between the factories and government officials for sharing the cost saved by factories from non-compliance with pollution standards.

Initial organized efforts by local people through persuasion and even with physical threats to factory owners have not yielded any results. An organized group of local people has had to take recourse to legal action by filling public litigation cases in courts. There are now a number of successful public litigation cases dealing with industrial water pollution abatement in India. In one such public litigation case (*Supreme Court*, 1990) concerning an industrial estate in Hyderabad in India, the Supreme Court of

India has ordered the constitution of an expert committee (*NEERI*, 1991) to study the problem of water pollution and to make recommendations about the extent of compensation to be paid to the affected people by industries and the remedial measure that the industries and the government have to take for preventing water pollution in future. After receiving the committee's recommendations, the supreme court has directed factories to pay compensation to the affected people and ask the government to take action as per existing environmental laws against factories so that, they comply with pollution standards. Political organization of affected people in this case also enlisted the active support of their elected representatives (members of local state assembly and union parliament) for the cause of industrial water pollution abatement. Elected representatives in turn have made local pollution control problems part of their election manifestos. There is therefore, a coalition of affected people and elected representative to deal with a coalition of factories and bureaucracy for controlling water pollution in this industrial area. Emergence of such an institutional setting, in which there is competition among pressure groups or interest groups have resulted in adoption of common effluent plant (CETP) technology by factories in each industrial estate. Collective action of affected people has induced factories to organize themselves as a club to construct and manage a CETP.[16] Also it is interesting to note that there are many instances now in India, in which the government plays a catalytic role rather than its conventional coercive role in environmental management, by providing financial and other incentives to a club of factories for having a CEPT.[17]

V. CONCLUSION

Economic instruments of pollution taxes and marketable permits and institutions facilitating people's participation are two efficient methods of controlling environmental pollution. Coase bargaining methods with participatory institutions result in the decentralized solutions with significant savings of transaction costs as opposed to Pigovian taxes. There is enough empirical evidence of environmental regulation through people's participation in the developing countries (*Murty et al.*, 1999; *World Bank*, 1999).

A method of estimating pollution taxes for thermal power generating industry in India described in this paper underscores the informational requirements for designing such taxes. There is a cost associated with the environmentally sustainable industrial development that is described by the UN methodology of Integrated Environmental and Economic Accounting as the maintenance cost. This cost could be considered as the cost to the industry of complying with the environmental standards fixed taking into account natural regenerative capacity of environmental media. A method in the theory of production describing pollution as a bad output jointly produced with the good output is used in this paper to estimate the maintenance cost. The panel data of 5 coal fired thermal power plants in Andhra Pradesh state of India for 8 years are used for the estimation.

The shadow prices of pollutants and cost of pollution abatement are estimated for AP GENCO. The pollution taxes to make the thermal power plants in AP to comply with the MINAS stack standards are estimated as Rs. 2099, 20519 and 5554 respectively for SPM, SO_2 and NO_X.

Political activity of people affected by an externality is measured in terms of a fraction or the number of people perceiving damages from the externality or the probability at which they can apprehend the colluding industry or the bureaucracy. There is a cost of political activity in terms of time devoted to it by the affected people. A sub-coalition of affected people and elected representatives can impose penalties on the bureaucracy and industry if the former is caught taking bribes and the later is found over stating the effluent quality.

The Nash non-cooperative game among the sub-coalitions of agents yields an equilibrium environmental quality which is superior to the environmental quality without political activity. As the rates of penalties increase, equilibrium environmental quality of the game increases. There can be rates of penalties and a level of political activity with respect to which statutorily fixed environmental standards can be achieved. Also, the rate of penalty required to achieve statutory environmental quality through competition between the pressure groups with non-benevolent government is the same as the rate of tax required, using the taxes standard approach with benevolent government.

NOTES AND REFERENCES

1. Waste disposal service of environmental resources is a public good with a property that the exclusion is not possible by charging a price for it.
2. See Murty *et al.* (1999) and World Bank (1999) for details.
3. This alternative is now becoming attractive because of high monitoring and enforcing costs to the Pollution Control Boards and other governmental agencies and the presence of corruption of government especially in many developing countries.
4. In the current literature, the regulation by the government and the public are respectively regarded as the formal and informal regulation. See World Bank (1999).
5. For more details, Baumol and Oates, 1988.
6. UN (1993).
7. Murty and Russell (2000) have shown that there could be problems in defining the shadow prices of pollution and finding the trade off between pollution and output along the production frontier in this model. However, they have shown that modelling abatement as an intermediary input does yield the positive trade-off and facilitate the definition of shadow prices of pollution.
8. See Murty and Gulati for details (2007).
9. See Witzman (1974), Dasgupta and Maler ( ), and Murty and Surender Kumar (2004).
10. This section is drawn mainly from Murty (1995b).
11. The second view point on corruption is chosen here for attempting a detailed analysis. A similar type of analysis can also be made with respect to the third view point on corruption.
12. The structure of corruption in bureaucracy assumed here is different from the one considered in some recent works in this area. It is assumed that the bribes taken by bureaucracy is shared by all cadres of officers, while some recent studies consider a pyramidical structure of corruption (corruption reduces as one climbs up the bureaucratic ladder, becoming virtually zero at the top).
13. See Appendix B.
14. See Murty (1995b) for proof.
15. A survey of seventeen highly water polluting industries in India conducted by the Institute of Economic Growth, Delhi in 1996.
16. Mr. Adun Roud of Centre for Development and Environment of University of Oslo, while commenting on an earlier version of this paper, has noted that a kind of collective action had actually taken place among people affected by industrial pollution along the Hoogly river in the southeren parts of Calcutta before a well known environmental lawyer Mr M.C. Mehta actually brought these cases to Supreme Court of India. The court rulings from 1994 urged several heavily water polluting units along Hooghly river to install required pollution control equipment.

Later the West Bengal Pollution Control Board insisted on implementing the court rulings by threating to close 12 major polluters unless significant steps were taken to reduce water pollution. Thus he feels this is the first instance where collective action succeeded. However, he observes that he political influence of the industrial lobby and relatively weak position of the environmental lobby significantly influences the speed of the environmental process.

17. Mishra and Murty, 1999.

REFERENCES

Aigner, D.J. and S.F. Chu (1968): Estimating the Industry Production Function, *American Economic Review*, Vol. 58, pp. 826-39.

Baik, K. and J.F. Shogren (1994): Reimbursments for Citizen Suits, *Journal of Environmental Economics and Management*, Vol. 27, No. 1, pp. 1-21.

Baumol, W.J. (1972): On Taxation and Control of Externalities, *American Economic Review*, Vol. 42, No. 3, 1972, pp. 307-322.

Baumal, W.J. and W. Oates (1988): *The Theory of Environmental Policy*, Second Edition, Cambridge University Press, Cambridge.

Becker, G.S. (1983): A Theory of Competition Among Pressure Groups for Political Influence, *Quarterly Journal of Economics*, Vol. 98, pp. 371-400.

Coggins, J.S. and J.R. Swinton (1996): The Price of Pollution: A Dual Approach to Valuing SO_2 Allowances, *Journal of Environmental Economics and Management*, Vol. 30, pp. 58-72.

Coase, R.H. (1960): The Problem of Social Cost, *Journal of Law and Economics*, Vol. 3, pp. 1-44.

O'Connor, D. (1992): The Use of Economic Instruments in Environmental Management: The Experience of East Asia, *Economic Instruments for Environmental Management in Developing Countries*, Proceedings of a workshop held at OECD Headquarters in Paris on 8 October 1992, Paris: OECD.

CPCB (1995): Standards for Pollutants, Central Pollution Control Board, New Delhi.

Dales, J.H. (1968): *Pollution, Property and Prices*. University of Toronto Press, Toronto.

Fare, R. (1988): *Fundamentals of Production Theory*, Springer-Verlag, Berlin.

Fare, R., *et al.* (1993): "Derivation of Shadow Prices for Undesirable Outputs: A Distance Function Approach", *Review of Economics and Statistics*, Vol. 75, pp. 375-80.

Fare, R., S. Grosskopf, and J. Nelson (1990): On Price Efficiency, *International Economic Review*, Vol. 31, pp. 709-20.

Fare, R., S. Grosskopf and C.A.K. Lovell (1994): *Production Frontiers*, Cambridge University Press, Cambridge.

Fare, R. and D. Primont (1995): *Multi-Output Production and Duality: Theory and Applications*, Kluwer Academic Publishers, Netherlands.

Gray, W.B. and S.J. Shadbegian (1993): Environmental Regulation and Manufacturing Productivity at a the Plant Level, Working Paper No. 4321, National Bureau of Economic Research, Washington.

Heyes, A.G. (1977): Environmental Regulation by Private Contest, *Journal of Public Economics*, Vol. 63, pp. 407-28.

James, A.J. and M.N. Murty (1996): Water Pollution Abatement: A Taxes-Standards Approach for Indian Industry, Working Paper No. E/177/96, Institute of Economic Growth, Delhi.

Konar, S. and M. Cohen (1997): Information as Regulation: The Effect of Community Right to Know Laws on Toxic Emissions, *Journal of Environmental Economics and Management*, Vol. 32, pp. 109-24.

Mehta, S., S. Mundle and U. Sankar (1995): *Controlling Water Pollution: Incentives and Regulation*, SAGE, New Delhi.

Milgrom, P. and J. Roberts (1988): An Economic Approach to Influence Activities in Organization, *American Journal of Sociology*, Vol. 94.

Mukherjee, D. and I. Png (1994): Corruptible Law Enforcers: How should they be Compensated?, Discussion Paper No. 94-07, Indian Statistical Institute, Delhi.

Murty, M.N. (1991), Management of Common Property Resources: Limits to Voluntary Collective Action, *Journal of Environmental & Resource Economics*, Vol. 4, pp. 581-94.

Murty, M.N. (1995a): Environmental Regulation in the Developing World: the Case of India, *Review of European Community and International Environmental Law*, Vol. 4, Issue 4, pp. 330-37.

Murty, M.N. (1995b): Collective Action: A Deterrent to Colluding Industry and Corrupt Bureaucracy, Working paper No. E/165/95, Institute of Economic Growth, Delhi. Also Printed in Murty, M.N., A.J. James and Smita Misra (1999).

Murty, M.N. (2009): Environment, Sustainable Development and Well-being: Valuation, Incentives and Taxes, Oxford University Press, Delhi, 2009.

Murty, M.N., A.J. James and Smita Misra (1999): *The Economics of Water Pollution: The Indian Experience*, Oxford University Press, New Delhi.

Murty, M.N. and U.R. Prasad (1999): Emission Reductions and Influence of Local Communities in India, in Murty, James and Misra (1999).

Murty, M.N. and Surender Kumar (2002): Measuring Cost of Environmentally Sustainable Industrial Development in India: A Distance Function Approach, Environmental and Development Economics, 467-86.

Murty, M.N., and Surendar Kumar (2003): *Environmental and Economic Accounting for Industry*, Oxford University Press, New Delhi.

Murty, M.N. and S.C. Gulati (2007): Measuring Cost of Environmentally Sustainable Industrial Development and Designing Pollution Taxes: A Case Study of Thermal Power Generation, February 2007, *Indian Economic Journal*.

Nandy, I., R.A. Daryapurkar and S.N. Kaul (1991): Common Effluent Treatment Plant—An Overview, National Environmental Engineering Research Institute (NEERI), Nagpur.

NEERI (1991): Report on Environmental Pollution Caused by Patancheru and Bollaram Industrial Estates in Nearby Villages of Medak District of Andhra Pradesh, India, Nagpur.

Pargal, S. and David Wheeler (1996): Informal Regulation of Industrial pollution in Developing Countries: Evidence from Indonesia, *Journal of Political Economy*, Vol. 104, No. 6, pp. 1814-27.

Pigue, A.C. (1920): *The Economics of Welfare,* MacMillan, London.

Porter, M.E. and C. van der Linde (1995): 'Towards a new conception of the environment competitiveness relationship', *Journal of Economic Perspectives*, Vol. 9, pp. 97-118.

Rose-Ackerman, S. (1978): Corruption: A Study in Political Economy. Academic Press, New York.

Shephard, R.W. (1970): *Theory of Cost and Production Functions*, Princeton University Press.

Sushama Murty and R.R. Russell (2002): *"On Modelling Pollution, Mimeograph, Department of Economics"*, University of California, Riverside, U.S.A.

UN (1993): *Integrated Environmental and Economic Accounting: Interim version* (Sales No. E93 XVII. 12), United Nations, New York.

World Bank (1999). Greening Industry: New Roles to Communities, Markets and Governments, Oxford University Press, New York.

APPENDIX A

Output Distance Function and Estimation for Thermal Power Generation in AP

Suppose that a firm employs a vector of inputs $x \in \Re^N_+$ to produce a vector of outputs $y \in \Re^M_+$, $\Re^N+$, $\Re^M+$, are non-negative N- and M-dimensional Euclidean spaces, respectively. Let P (x) be the feasible output set for the given input vector x and L (y) is the input requirement set for a given output vector y. Now the technology set is defined as

$$T = \{(y, x) \in \Re^{M+N}_+ \; y \in P(x)\}. \tag{A1}$$

The output distance function is defined as,

$$D_0 (x, y) = \min\{\lambda > 0 : (y/\lambda) \in P(x)\} \; \forall x \in \Re^N_+. \tag{A2}$$

Equation (A2) characterizes the output possibility set by the maximum equi-proportional expansion of all outputs consistent with the technology set (A1).

The assumptions about the disposability of outputs become very important in the context of a firm producing both good and bad outputs. The normal assumption of strong or free disposability about the technology implies,

if $(y_1, y_2) \in P(x)$ and $0 < y_1{}^* \leq y_1, 0 \leq y_2{}^* \leq y_2 \Rightarrow (y_1{}^*, y^*{}_2) \in P(x)$.

That means, we can reduce some outputs given the other outputs or without reducing them. This assumption may exclude important production processes, such as undesirable outputs like pollution. The assumption of weak disposability is relevant to describe such production processes. The assumption of weak disposability implies,

if $y \in P(x)$ and $0 \leq \lambda \leq 1 \Rightarrow \lambda y \in P(x)$. That means, a firm can reduce the bad output only by decreasing simultaneously the output of desirable produce.

The idea of deriving shadow prices using output and input distance functions and the duality results is originally from Shephard (1970). A study by Fare, Grosskopf and Nelson (1990) is the first in computing shadow prices using the distance function and non-parametric linear programming methods. Fare *et al.* (1993) is the first study deriving the shadow prices of undesirable outputs using the output distance function.

The derivation of absolute shadow prices for bad outputs using distance function requires the assumption that one observed output price is shadow price. Let y_1 denote the good output and assume that the observed good output price (r_1^0) equals its absolute shadow price (r_1^s) (i.e., for $m = 1$, $r_1^0 = r_1^s$). Fare *et al.* (1993) have shown that the absolute shadow prices for each observation of undesirable output ($m = 2, \ldots\ldots, M$) can be derived as,[1]

$$(r^s_m) = (r_1^0) \bullet \frac{\partial D_0(x, y)/\partial y_m}{\partial D_0(x, y)/\partial y_1}. \qquad \text{(A3)}$$

The shadow prices reflect the trade-off between desirable and undesirable outputs at the actual mix of outputs, which may or may not be consistent with the maximum allowable under regulation (*Fare et al.* 1993, p. 376). Further, the shadow prices do not require that the plants operate on the production frontier.

Estimation Procedure and Data

In order to estimate the shadow prices of pollutants (bad outputs) for the thermal power generation in Andhrapradesh using equation (A3), the parameters of output distance function have to be estimated. The trans-log functional form[2] used for estimating these functions is given as follows:

$$\ln D_0(x, y) = \alpha_0 + \Sigma\beta_n \ln x_n + \Sigma\, \alpha_m \ln y_m + 1/2\, \Sigma\Sigma\, \beta_{nn'} (\ln x_n)(\ln x_{n'}) + 1/2\, \Sigma\Sigma\, \alpha_{mm'} (\ln y_m)(y_{m'}) + \Sigma\Sigma\gamma_{nm} (\ln x_n)(\ln y_m) + \iota_1 d_1 + \iota_2 d_2 + \iota_3 d_3 + \iota_4 d_4 \qquad \text{(A4)}$$

where x and y are respectively, $N \times 1$ and $M \times 1$ vectors of inputs and outputs. There are three inputs: capital, labour, and energy and four outputs: good output, Electricity, and bad outputs, SPM, NO_X, and SO_2, and d_i is the dummy variable representing the plant. A linear programming technique is used to estimate the parameters of a deterministic translog output distance function

1. See Fare (1988) for derivation.
2. Many earlier studies for estimating shadow prices of pollutants have used the translog functional form for estimating the output distance function. These include Pitman (1981), Fare *et al.* (1990), and Coggins and Swinton (1996).

(*Aigner and Chu*, 1968). This is accomplished by solving the problem,

$$\max \Sigma\, [\ln D_0\, (x, y) - \ln 1], \tag{A5}$$

subject to:

(i) $\ln D_0\, (x, y) \leq 0$
(ii) $(\partial \ln D_0\, (x, y))/(\partial \ln y_1) \geq 0$
(iii) $(\partial \ln D_0\, (x, y))/(\partial \ln y_i) \leq 0$
(iv) $(\partial \ln D_0\, (x, y))/(\partial \ln x_i) \leq 0$
(v) $\Sigma\, \alpha_m = 1$
$\Sigma\, \alpha_{mm} = \Sigma\, \gamma_{mm} = 0$
(vi) $\alpha_{mm} = \alpha_{mm}$
$\beta_{nn} = \beta_{nn}$

Here the first output is desirable and the rest of (M – 1) outputs are undesirable. The objective function minimizes the sum of the deviations of individual observations from the frontier of technology. Since the distance function takes a value of less than or equal to one, the natural logarithm of the distance function is less than or equal to zero, and the deviation from the frontier is less than or equal to zero. Hence, the maximization of the objective function is done implying the minimization of sum of deviations of individual observations from the frontier of technology. The constraints in (i) restrict the individual observations to be on or below the frontier of the technology. The constraints in (ii) ensure that the desirable output have a non-negative shadow price. The constraints in (iv) restrict that the shadow prices of bad outputs are non-positive, i.e. weak disposability of bad outputs whereas the restrictions in (v) is the derivative property of output distance function with respect to inputs, i.e. the derivatives of output distance function with respect to inputs is non-increasing. The constraints in (v) impose homogeneity of degree +1 in outputs (which also ensures that technology satisfies weak disposability of outputs). Finally, constraints in (vi) impose symmetry. There is no constraint imposed to ensure non-negative values to the shadow prices of undesirable outputs.

Output distance function described above is estimated by

TABLE A1

Descriptive Statistics of Variables Used in Study

Variable	*Unit*	*Mean*	*Standard Dev.*	*Maximum*	*Minimum*
Electricity	Million Units	298.28	13.91	933.58	0.01
SPM	Tonnes	653	0.033	3.526	0.018
SO_2	Tonnes	874	0.049	4.268	0.004
NO_{xC}	Tonnes	139	0.013	1.984	0.001
Coal	Tonnes	223460	9.93	667.05	0.01
Capital	Rupees millions	1913.231	905.46	62395.28	148.59
Wage Bill	Rupees millions	255.628	111.03	9332.04	344.16

considering electricity as good output and pollution loads of SPM, NO_X, and SO_2 as bad outputs using data about thermal power generation by APGENCO in Andhra Pradesh state. Table A1 provides the descriptive statistic of variables used in the estimation of distance function. The estimates of parameters of distance function are reported in Table A2. Using the estimated distance function, the shadow price of a pollutant is estimated in

TABLE A2

Estimates of Parameters of Output Distance Function

Coefficients of the Output Distance Function Model						
Variables	*Description*	*Coefficients*	*Variables*	*Coefficients*	*Variables*	*Coefficients*
Y1	electricity	3.025	x33	-0.431	y3x1	0.167
Y2	SPM	1.297	y12	0.032	y3x2	-0.268
Y3	SO_2	1.330	y13	0.004	y3x3	-0.100
Y4	No_x	0.605	y14	0.163	y4x1	-0.085
X1	capital	-1.041	y1x1	-1.095	y4x2	0.669
X2	Wage	19.104	y1x2	0.820	y4x3	-0.290
X3	Coal	-0.408	y1x3	0.213	X12	-1.858
y11		-0.199	y23	0.069	X13	1.116
y22		-0.062	y24	-0.038	X23	0.402
y33		0.110	y2x1	0.199	Intercept	
y44		0.059	y2x2	-0.448		
X11		1.692	y2x3	0.051		
X22		7.411	y34	-0.183		

terms of units of good output foregone for one unit reduction in pollution. The computed shadow prices for a representative plant of APGENCO are Rupees 1043.688, 11539.15, and 5866.812 thousand units of electricity respectively per ton reduction of SPM, NO_X, and SO_2. The current electricity tariff for industries in AP is on the average Rs. 3.60 per unit. Using this price shadow prices of pollutants could be expressed in rupees as reported in Table A3.

Description of Variables in the Estimated Distance Function

TABLE A3

Names of Variables and their Identification

Output	Y1	coal2	x33	Socap	Y3x1
SPM	Y2	Outspm	y12	Sowage	Y3x2
SO_2	Y3	Outso	y13	Sofuel	Y3x3
NO_X	Y4	Outno	y14	wagecoal	X23
Capital	X1	Outcap	y1x1	Nocap	Y4x1
Wage	X2	Outwage	y1x2	Nowage	Y4x2
Coal	X3	Outcoal	y1x3	Nocoal	Y4x3
Output2	y11	Spmso	y23	Noother	Y4x4
spm2	y22	Spmno	y24	Capwage	X12
so2	y33	Spmcap	y2x1	Capfuel	X13
no2	y44	Spmwage	y2x2		
cap2	x11	Spmcoal	y2x3		
Wage2	x22	Sono	y34		

APPENDIX B

Coase-Becker Model of Collective Action

The following notation is used for developing a model of collective action in the industrial pollution abatement.

$\bar{E}$: Environmental quality corresponding to statutory level of pollution;[1]

$\hat{E}$: Actual environmental quality attained by industry;

E: Environmental quality reported by bureaucracy;

D (E): Actual damage received by affected people, $D^{I}(E) < 0$, $D^{II}(E) > 0$;

$A(E)$: Cost of treatment of effluent to the industry, $A^{I}(E) \geq 0$, $A^{II}(E) \geq 0$;

W: Time devoted by affected people for political organization;

V (W): Cost of political organization;

λ (W): Probability with which affected people (or a fraction thereof) perceive damages from degraded environment; $0 \leq \lambda \leq 1$;

t: Pollution tax per unit of effluent;

b: Bribe received by bureaucracy from industry per unit of over-reporting of environmental quality;

p: penalty on bureaucracy per unit of under-reporting of environmental quality; and

s: Penalty on industry per unit of non-discloser of effluent quality.

Now the cost and benefits to various agents involved in the industrial water pollution abetment can be identified as follows:

(a) Perceived damages of affected people

$$\phi\,(W, E) = \lambda\,(W)\,D\,(E) + (1 - \lambda\,(W))\,D\,(\bar{E}) + V\,(W) \quad \text{(B1)}$$

1. In case of an optimal pollution tax or Pigouvian tax liability of a firm is computed as tax rate multiplied by the difference between the actual pollution level and the pollution level with respect to which the marginal damage is zero. However, in case of the taxes-and-standards method (Boumol and Oates, 1988), the tax liability of a firm is computed as the tax rate multiplied by the difference between the actual and statutory level (level corresponding to pollution standards) of pollution.

(b) Income to municipal committee

$$M\ (W, E) = \lambda\ (W)\ (s + p)\ (\hat{E} - E) + t\ (\hat{E} - E) \quad \text{(B2)}$$

(c) Income to bureaucracy

$$R\ (W, E) = (b - \lambda\ (w)\ p)\ (\hat{E} - E) \quad \text{(B3)}$$

(d) Cost to factory

$$C\ (W, E) = A\ (E) + (b - s\lambda\ (W))\ (\hat{E} - E) + t\ (\hat{E} - \bar{E}) \quad \text{(B4)}$$

Net perceived cost to society can be defined as:

$$\pi\ (W, E) = \phi\ (W, E) + C\ (W, E) - R\ (W, E) - M\ (W, E)$$

$$= \lambda\ (W)\ D\ (E) + (1 - \lambda\ (W))\ D\ (\bar{E}) + V(W) + A\ (E) \quad \text{(B5)}$$

Net actual cost to society can be defined as

$$\phi\ (E, W) = D\ (E) + V\ (W) + A\ (E) \quad \text{(B6)}$$

Group I Affected people and municipal committee with a strategy W and cost function

$$G^1 = \lambda D\ (E) + (1 - \lambda)\ D\ (\bar{E}) + V(W) - \lambda\ (s + p)\ (\hat{E} - E) - t\ (\bar{E} - \hat{E}) \quad \text{(B7)}$$

Group II Industry and bureaucracy with a strategy E and cost function

$$G^2 = A\ (E) - \lambda\ (s + p)\ (\hat{E} - E) + t\ (E - E) \quad \text{(B8)}$$

Given penalties and bribe (p, s, b), Group I minimizes G^1 with respect to W given E while group II minimizes G^2 with respect to E given W. We have:

$$\frac{\delta G^1}{\delta W} = \lambda'\ [(s + p)\ (\hat{E} - E) - (D\ (E) - D\ (\bar{E}))\ I] - V'\ (W) = 0 \quad \text{(B9)}$$

$$(s + p)\ (\hat{E} - E) - (D\ (E) - D\ (\bar{E})) = \frac{V^I}{\lambda^I}$$

$$\frac{\delta G^2}{\delta E} = A'\ (E) - \lambda\ (s + p) = 0$$

$$A'\ (E) = \lambda\ (s + p) \quad \text{(B10)}$$

Equations (B9) and (B10) yield the reaction functions of groups I and II which are respectively given by (B11) and (B12)

$$W(E),\ W'(E) < 0 \tag{B11}$$
$$E(W),\ E'(W) > 0 \tag{B12}$$

The equilibrium strategies of two persons Nash non-cooperative game are defined as:

$$W^* = W(E^*)$$

and

$$E^* = E(W^*)$$

which are given by the intersection of curves depicting the reaction functions of group I and II in Fig. 4.

Proposition 1: Increasing penalties s and p on industry and bureaucracy have the effects of increasing environmental quality E, given W, and decreasing the time devoted to political activity W, given the environmental quality E. The equilibrium environmental quality of a two person Nash non-cooperative game increases as either at least one of s and p or both s and p increase.[2]

2. See Murty, 1995b for proof.

Impact of Environmental Management Practices on Profitability and Market Value of Indian Industrial Firms

Bishwanath Goldar

Using data for about 1600 corporate sector industrial firms in India, the impact of environmental management practices, or more specifically the adoption of ISO 14001 standards, on profitability and market value is econometrically investigated. The regression results show that the adoption of ISO 14001 standards raises profitability and market value of firms. These results are in agreement with the findings of a large number of previous studies broadly on the same subject, most undertaken for developed countries, and signify that improvements in environmental performance in corporate sector industrial firms may be financially advantageous even in developing countries.

Earlier versions of the paper were presented at the Ninth Biennial Conference of the International Society for Ecological Economics (ISEE) on "Ecological Sustainability and Human Well-Being", Delhi, 15-18 December 2006, and at the National Conference on "Expanding Freedom: Towards Social and Economic Transformation in a Globalising World", held at the Institute of Economic Growth, Delhi, April 11-13, 2007.

1. INTRODUCTION

There have been a large number of studies on the impact of corporate environmental performance on their financial performance (*Cohen, et al.*, 1995; *Cormier, et al.*, 1993; *Dowell, et al.*, 2000; *Feldman, et al.*, 1996; *Guenster et al.*, 2005; *Hamilton*, 1995; *Hart and Ahuja*, 1996; *Klassen and McLaughlin*, 1996; *Konar and Cohen*, 2001; *Mahoney and Roberts*, 2002; *Russo and Fouts*, 1997; *White*, 1995; among many others). A shared view emerging from a majority of the studies is that corporate environmental performance has a favourable effect on their financial performance; several studies find that better environmental performance leads to higher profitability, and several others find that better environmental performance augments stock prices or value of the firm.[1]

Most of the research on the impact of corporate environmental performance on their financial performance has been done in the context of developed countries, and there have been relatively much fewer studies for developing countries. To mention here some of the studies undertaken for developing countries, Dasgupta, Laplante and Mamingi (2001) have shown that capital markets in Argentina, Chile, Mexico and Philippines react to both positive and negative environmental news (favourably to positive news and unfavourably to negative news). They have used the event study methodology for their analysis, as done, for instance, by Hamilton (1995), Klassen and McLaughlin (1996), and Khanna *et al.* (1998). Applying the same methodology, Gupta and Goldar (2005) have analysed the impact of 'green rating' announcement for large pulp and paper and chlor alkali firms in India on their stock prices. They conclude that the market generally penalizes environmentally un-friendly behaviour in that announcement of weak environmental performance by a firm leads to negative abnormal returns of up to 30 percent. Also, they find a positive correlation between abnormal returns to a firm's stock and the level of its environmental performance. Grand and D'Elia (2005) have carried out a study of the impact of environmental news on stock market performance of firms in Argentina. They have used the event study methodology as done by Dasgupta *et al.* (2001) and Gupta and Goldar (2005). They find that positive environmental news have no impact, while negative news do have an adverse impact on the average rates of return a few days following its appearance. Examining the impact of different types of positive news, they find that the news of ISO certification in the 14000 family has no effect whatsoever, while news concerning environment-related investment decisions do have some positive significant influence on returns. As regards negative news, they find that the influence of such news on stock returns is particularly significant for events linked to citizen complaints and government rulings (confirming results of other studies) and for media coverage of oil company issues.

While the three studies mentioned above use the event study methodology to link environmental performance to stock market performance, Dowell *et al.* (2000) have used cross-firm regression analysis to link environmental performance with firm value. They consider a sample of US-based multinational enterprises investing in emerging and developing countries. They find that the firms adopting a single, stringent global environmental standard have much higher market values, as measured by Tobin's q, than the firms defaulting to less stringent, or poorly enforced host country standards.

The object of this paper is to analyse the impact of environmental management practices, particularly the adoption of ISO 14001 standards, in Indian corporate sector industrial firms on their financial performance. Two aspects of financial performance are considered: stock market performance measured by Tobin's q and profitability performance measure by the rate of return on assets. A comparison is made between the companies that have acquired ISO 14001 certification and those that have not done so, and this is taken as the basis for assessing the impact of environmental management practices. As mentioned above, the impact of environmental performance on stock market performance and profitability has extensively been studied for developed countries, but there have been very few such studies in the context of developing countries. This paper makes an attempt towards filling this gap in the literature.[2]

The finding of Grand and D'Elia (2005) that news of ISO certification in the 14000 family had no effect on the share prices of Argentine firms may give the impression that the stock markets in developing countries generally do not value the benefits of a good environmental management system much above the associated costs. It is important therefore to verify this finding with data for some other developing countries, which this paper attempts to do in respect of one large developing country (using a somewhat different methodology).

The rest of the paper is organized as follows. The next section discusses the data sources for the study. Section 3 outlines the models used for the econometric analysis. Section 4 presents the basic empirical results. It begins with a preliminary analysis of the data, bringing out the differences between ISO 14001 certified companies and other companies in the sample, and then presents the results of econometric analysis. Section 5 sums up the main findings of the study and concludes.

2. DATA SOURCES

The basic data source for this study is *Capitaline* (www.capitaline.com), which provides data for over 10,000 Indian companies. Data for the year 2004-05, or 2003-04 if data for 2004-05 are not available, are used for this study. Where data for a company were not available even for 2003-04, data for 2002-03 or 2001-02 have been used. Companies for which data were not available for any of the four years have been excluded from the analysis.

Data have been taken on a number of variables including sales, profits before and after tax, fixed assets, inventories, equity, debt, market capitalization, exports, imports of materials, capital goods and technology, advertisement expenditure and R&D expenditure. Certain ratios on which data have been taken from *Capitaline* include share of foreign equity in total equity. These variables are used to assess the stock market performance and profitability performance of companies and analyze the determinants of performance.

As mentioned above, the main aim of the study is to assess the impact of adoption of ISO 14001 standards. For this purpose, one needs to know which companies in the sample have acquired ISO 14001 certification. A list of companies/plants of companies that had acquired ISO 14001 certification till June 2004 was obtained from the Confederation of Indian Industries (CII). The list had about 1000 entries. But, in a large number of cases, different plants of the same company were listed. Also, the list included non-manufacturing companies. Since the focus of the study is on manufacturing companies, those cases were not considered. There were also problems in matching the names of companies in the list procured from the CII and the list of companies in *Capitaline*. Thus, altogether, 209 companies could be identified for which business related data could be obtained from the Captialine and which were present in the CII provided list of ISO 14001 certified companies. The number of companies for which business related data could be obtained from Capitaline but which were not in the list of ISO 14001 certified companies is about 4800. Clearly, the companies that do not have ISO 14001 certification are disproportionately large compared to the companies that have ISO 14001 certification. This may create a problem in making comparison between the two groups. The latter group has many companies that are relatively small in size. Hence, the analysis was confined to the companies that had net sales of over Rs. 500 million. Further, some companies had to be left out as data on all the variables used in the analysis were not available. The total sample size thus reduced to 1624 of which 190 companies had acquired ISO 14001 certification by June 2004.

3. MODEL SPECIFICATION

The models used for regression analysis may be written as:

$$Q_i = \alpha + \beta\, ISO\_D_i + \gamma X_i + \varepsilon_i \qquad ...(1)$$

$$ROA_i = \phi + \mu\, ISO\_D_i + \varphi X_i + \nu_i \qquad ...(2)$$

Q denotes Tobin's q, ROA denotes the rate of return on assets, and ISO_D is a dummy variable taking value one for the companies that had acquired ISO 14001 certification by June 2004, and zero for other companies. X is the vector of other variables included in the regression; these represent various firm characteristics. The subscript *i* denotes company. In these equations, α, β, γ, ϕ, μ and φ are parameters to be estimated and ε and ν are error terms.

The definition of the variables, including the explanatory variables, is as follows:

Q = Tobin's q. This is computed as the market value of assets divided by the book value of assets. The market value of assets is defined as the sum of the book value of assets and the market value of common stock outstanding minus the sum of book value of common stock and balance sheet deferred taxes (following the definition used by Guenster *et al.*, 2005).

ROA = Rate of return on assets. This is obtained as the ratio of profit before tax to assets (net fixed assets and inventories).

Size: Firm size is measured by logarithm of net sales.

Export intensity: Ratio of exports to sales.

Import intensity: Ratio of imports of materials and spares to sales.

Capital goods import intensity: Imports of capital goods as a ratio to sales.

R&D intensity: R&D expenditure divided by sales.

Technology import intensity: Royalty and technical fees paid in foreign exchange as a ratio to sales.

Advertisement intensity: Advertisement expenditure divided by sales.

Foreign equity proportion: Foreign equity as a ratio to total equity.

Debt-asset ratio: Ratio of debt to assets.

Turning to the equations again, the coefficient of ISO_D is expected to be positive, given that a large number of studies have found a positive effect of environmental performance on profitability and market value. It may useful to mention here the reasons that have been given for expecting a positive relationship. First, pollution and waste are reduced by a conscious effort to increase resource efficiency. Many state-of-the-art technologies have high resource efficiency. Such "eco-efficiency" can lower operating costs rather than raise them (*Porter and van der Linde*, 1995; *Hart and Ahuja*, 1996). Secondly, by adhering to high environmental standards, it may be possible to heighten employees' morale and thus productivity. It may also be possible to attract better employees to the firm. Thirdly, the environmental standards in the developing countries would be going up over time, in not-too-distant future. Thus, there is going to be future benefit in adopting a high environmental standard now. To what extent these arguments apply to industrial firms in India, is difficult to say. The econometric analysis presented in the next section is intended to ascertain whether these factors have a significant effect in India.

One estimation issue that needs to be raised here is that the decision of firms to go for ISO 14001 certification cannot be treated as exogenous. The theoretical considerations underlying the models given in equations (1) and (2) above are akin to those involved in the analysis of the impact of EPA's voluntary 33/50 program undertaken by Khanna and Damon (1999). They emphasize the voluntary nature of the 33/50 program, and argue that the decision of a firm to self-select into the program[3] is likely to influenced by the same set of observable and unobservable factors that determines the impact of the program on firm's performance. Thus, an estimation bias arises due to self-selection. To get over this problem, they follow a two-stage least squares technique adopted earlier by Hartman (1988) to analyse the impact of voluntary programs on energy conservation. First, the participation decision of the firm is modelled. A Probit model is used for that purpose. For each firm, the probability of its participation in the program is estimated. Then, the estimated probability is used as an explanatory variable in the equation explaining the impact of the program instead of using a dummy variable to reflect participation of firms in the program.

The estimation issue raised above applies also to the models given in equations (1) and (2) above. Thus, following Hartman (1988) and Khanna and Damon (1999), a set of estimates have been made in which the dummy variable, ISO_D, is replaced by the estimated probability of the firm acquiring ISO 14001 certification, derived from an estimated Probit model.

4. EMPIRICAL RESULTS

4.1 Preliminary Analysis of the Data

Table 1 presents a comparison between ISO 14001 certified companies and other companies in the sample in respect of a number of variables. As mentioned earlier, there are 190 companies in the sample with ISO 14001 certification and 1434 without.

The comparison presented in Table 1 shows that in terms of size, the ISO 14001 certified companies are bigger. Import intensity, advertisement intensity, technology import intensity and the share of foreign equity are relatively higher in such firms. The debt-asset ratio is relatively lower in such firms. Tobin's q and the rate of return on assets are relatively higher in ISO 14001 certified companies than non-certified companies. In respect of other variables, there are no significant differences.

TABLE 1

Comparison of ISO 14001 Certified Companies with other Companies

Indicators	*Average value of indicators*	
	ISO 14001 certified companies	*Other companies in the sample*
Sales (Rs. million)	26703*	3597
Export intensity (%)	12.1	15.4
Import intensity (%)	12.8*	9.6
Capital goods import intensity (%)	1.0	1.1
R&D intensity (%)	0.07	0.08
Technology import intensity (%)	0.4*	0.1
Advertisement intensity (%)	1.1*	0.5
Foreign equity share (%)	5.2*	2.7
Debt-asset ratio (%)	34*	44
Tobin's q (ratio)	2.2*	1.5
Rate of return on assets (%)	13.7*	6.1

* The difference between the means of two groups of firms is statistically significant at 5% level or higher.

4.2 Firms' Decision to Acquire ISO 14001 Certification

A Probit Model has been estimated to explain the decision of firms to acquire ISO 14001 certification. The following explanatory variables have been used: firm size, advertisement intensity, technology orientation (based on R&D expenditure plus payment of royalty and technical fees for imported technology as a ratio to sales), age of the firm, and the ratio of labour cost to sales. To represent the age of the firm, a proxy measures is used, formed by the ratio of net fixed assets to gross fixed assets (varies inversely with the age). The ratio of labour cost to sales (LC) is found to bear a non-linear relationship with the dependent variable. Therefore, the variable and its squared term (LC^2) have been included in the equation.

In addition to the variables listed above, industry dummies have been included in the estimated model to capture inter-industry differences. The sample firms have been divided into 17 groups, and 16 dummy variables have been included in the estimated model. The groups are: (1) Basic chemicals, (2) Petrochemicals, (3) Oil refineries, (4) Distilleries, (5) Pharmaceuticals, (6) Dyes and intermediates, (7) Fertilizers, (8) Pesticides, (9) Iron and Steel basic metal, (10) Aluminium, (11) Copper, (12) Zinc, (13) Cement, (14) Paper, (15) Leather and Products, (16) Sugar, and (17) Other industries.

The estimated Probit model is shown in Table 2 below. The results indicate that large firm size and technology orientation are positively related with the firms' decision to acquire ISO 14001 certification. Interestingly, after controlling other factors, foreign ownership is not found to be positively related with the firms' decision to acquire ISO 14001 certification. Rather, the results suggest that other things remaining the same, a local firm is more likely to go for ISO 14001 certification than a foreign firm.

TABLE 2

Factors Determining Firms' Adoption of ISO 14001 Standards; Results of Probit Model

Explanatory variables	*Regression 1*
Size	0.424(9.51)***
Export intensity	-0.282 (-1.27)
Technology orientation	9.808 (2.28)**
Foreign equity share	-1.091(-1.76)*
Advertisement intensity	0.586(0.42)
Age (Net fixed assets/Gross block)	-0.683(-2.30)**
Ratio of labour cost to sales (LC)	11.391(3.33)***
LC^2	-45.846(-2.51)**
Constant	-3.565(-10.25)****
Industry dummies	Yes
Pseudo R-squared	0.200

t-ratios in parentheses (based on heteroscedasticity corrected standard errors); n=1618

*** Statistically significant at one percent level, ** 5 percent level, * ten percent level.

Note: Some observations are dropped, as one or more explanatory variables take very high values in those observations.

The probability of a firm acquiring ISI 14001 certification is found to bear an inverted-U relationship with labour intensity. It seem that beyond a stage, increases in labour intensity tend to lower the probability of acquiring ISO 14001 certification. The observed negative coefficient of the variable formed by taking the ratio of net fixed assets to gross block may be interpreted as signifying that among the newly established firms the proportion of certified firms is relatively lower than that among the older firms.

4.3 Impact of ISO Certification—Regression Results

The regression results are presented in Tables 3 and 4. The t-ratios of the coefficients are shown in parentheses. The standard errors have been corrected for heteroscedasticity.

TABLE 3

Impact of ISO 14001 Certification on Firm Value, Regression Results

Explanatory variables	*Regression 1*	*Regression 2*	*Regression 3*
ISO 14001 Dummy	0.273(2.60)***	0.272 (2.59)***	
Predicted probability of the firm acquiring ISO 14001 certification			1.255(3.04)***
Size	0.191 (5.77)***	0.194(6.00)***	0.099 (2.25)**
Export intensity	0.072 (0.70)		
Import intensity	0.136(0.66)		
Capital goods import intensity	1.012(0.99)	1.035(1.00)	0.876 (0.78)
Foreign equity share	3.899(6.11)***	3.923 (6.10)***	4.079 (6.36)***
Advertisement intensity	5.884 (2.49)**	5.751 (2.47)**	5.606(2.40)**
R&D intensity	11.734(2.38)**	11.955(2.43)**	9.827(1.91)*
Technology import intensity	10.787(1.37)	11.056(1.42)	8.214(1.05)
Constant	0.296(1.87)*	0.306(1.94)*	0.687 (3.49)***
R-squared (F value)	0.203(18.88)	0.203(23.71)	0.205(22.30)

t-ratios in parentheses (based on heteroscedasticity corrected standard errors); n=1607

*** Statistically significant at one percent level, ** 5 percent level, * ten percent level.

Note: Some observations are dropped, as one or more explanatory variables take very high values in those observations.

TABLE 4

Impact of ISO 14001 Certification on Profitability, Regression Results

Explanatory variables	*Regression 1*	*Regression 2*	*Regression 3*
ISO 14001 Dummy	0.044(3.19)***	0.044(3.22)***	
Predicted probability of the firm acquiring ISO 14001 certification			0.093(1.87)*
Size	0.011(2.49)**	0.011(2.52)**	0.006(1.00)
Export intensity	0.035(1.62)	0.038(1.88)*	0.041 (1.99)**
Import intensity	0.021 (0.61)		
Capital goods import intensity	0.116(1.46)	0.116(1.45)	0.091 (1.03)
Foreign equity share	0.114(2.19)**	0.108(2.15)**	0.111(2.21)**
Advertisement intensity	-0.122(-0.63)		
R&D intensity	-0.338(4.06)		
Technology import intensity	0.963(1.06)	1.005(1.14)	1.074(1.19)
Debt asset ratio	-0.143(-2.96)***	-0.143(-2.96)***	-0.143 (-2.94)***
Constant	0.060(1.76)*	0.059(1.74)*	0.078(2.14)**
R-squared (F-value)	0.251(7.09)	0.251(9.75)	0.248 (9.82)

t-ratios in parentheses (based on heteroscedasticity corrected standard errors); n=1616

*** Statistically significant at one percent level, ** 5 percent level, * ten percent level.

Note: Some observations are dropped, as one or more explanatory variables take very high values in those observations.

It is seen from Tables 3 and 4 that most of the coefficients have expected sign and are statistically significant. In particular, it may be noted that the coefficients of the dummy variable for ISO 14001 certification are positive and statistically significant. This is in conformity with the results of such studies undertaken for developed countries. This result is consistent also with the findings of Dasgupta *et al.* (2001) and Gupta and Goldar (2005). It may therefore be inferred that the adoption of environmental management practices in industrial firms in India has a positive impact on firm profitability and value. This could also be taken to mean that better environmental performance of corporate sector industrial firms in India was associated with higher profitability and enhanced market value.[4]

Replacing the ISO dummy variable by the estimated probability of the firm acquiring ISO 14001 certification (derived from an estimated Probit model, results reported above) does not cause any qualitative change in the results. The coefficient of the ISO 14001 variable expressed in terms of the probability of acquiring it (hereafter, ISO_prob) is found to be positive and statistically significant. It should noted, however, that the coefficient of ISO_prob is statistically significant at one percent level in the equation for market value, but statistically significant only at ten percent level in the equation for profitability. This perhaps indicates that the market anticipates long-term benefits from the environment management system well beyond the short-run impact it may have.

Turning to other variables, firm size is found to be an important determinant of both profitability and market value; bigger size is associated with higher profitability and market value. The results show that foreign equity, advertisement, R&D efforts, and technology imports result in higher market value. Foreign equity, imports of capital goods and exports are found to have a favourable effect on profitability. A significant negative relationship is found between debt-asset ratio and profitability.

5. CONCLUSION

A large number of studies undertaken for developed countries have shown that environmental performance of firms has a favourable effect on profitability and market value. The econometric results presented in this paper indicate that such a relationship probably holds true also for Indian industrial firms. In particular, the results show that financial costs associated with a good environmental management system in a corporate sector industrial firms are more than compensated by the financial gains that the system provides. In a sense, therefore, the market rewards good environmental performance.

The possible loss of competitiveness due to stricter imposition of environmental regulation is sometimes raised as a concern in the context of developing countries, as they are getting increasingly exposed to international competition in the process of globalization. The empirical evidence presented for India in this paper could be interpreted to mean that high environmental standards need not cause a serious loss of competitiveness of Indian industrial firms; rather they may gain in terms of competitiveness from better environmental performance.

NOTES AND REFERENCES

1. At the same time, it should be noted that there are studies that did not find a favourable effect of corporate environmental performance on their financial performance. See, for example, Takeda and Tomozawa (2006) and Zhang and Stern (2007).
2. There is an implicit assumption here that the adoption of ISO 14001 standards by a firm leads to improved environmental performance. This does not seem an unreasonable assumption to make. Some studies on this specific issue do find a positive association between the two. See, for example, Arimura *et al.* (2008). See also the study by Anton, *et al.* (2004), who find that a comprehensive environmental management system leads to lower toxic emission per unit of output. Such analysis is not available for Indian Industrial firms. However, a comparison of 'green rating' of ISO 14001 certified paper firms and other paper firms without such certification points to a positive correlation between ISO 14001 certification and environmental performance. Using the scores for environmental performance given to Indian paper mills by the Center for Science and Environment in their 2004 study, the average score is found to be 33 (out of 100) for ISO 14001 mills and 25 for non-certified mills. While the evidence presented is inadequate to establish conclusively the existence of a positive correlation between ISO 14001 certification and environmental performance among Indian industrial firms in general, it provides some support the assumption that such correlation probably exits.
3. What induces firms to adopt good environmental management systems, has been a subject of research in several studies. See, for example, Anton *et al.* (2004); Khanna and Speir (2007); and Nakamura *et al.* (2001).
4. It would be noticed from Table 1 that Tobin's q for ISO 14001 certified companies is 2.2 on average while that for other companies in the sample is 1.5 on average. The difference is 0.7. Of this, about 0.44 is explained by ISO certification *per se* (i.e. adoption of ISO 14001 standards) as indicated by the estimated regression coefficients; the rest is explained by differences in other variables, say size or foreign ownership, between the two groups of companies. A similar pattern is observed in respect of the rate of return on assets.

REFERENCES

Anton, W.R.Q., Deltas, G., and Khanna, M., 2004. Incentives for Environmental Self-Regulation and Implications for Environmental

Performance. *Journal of Environmental Economics and Management*, 48: 632-54.

Arimura, T.H., Hibiki, A., and Katayama, H., 2008. Is a Voluntary Approach an Effective Environmental Policy Instrument? A Case for Environmental Management Systems. *Journal of Environmental Economics and Management*, 55(32): 281-95.

Cohen, M.A., Finn, S.A., and Naimon, J.S., 1995. Environmental and Financial Performance: Are They Related, Washington DC: Investor Responsibility Research Center.

Cormier, D., Magnan, M., and Morard, B., 1993. The impact of corporate pollution on market valuation: Some empirical evidence. *Ecological Economics*, 8: 133-55.

Dasgupta, S., Laplante, B., and Mamingi, N., 2001. Pollution and Capital Markets in Developing Countries. *Journal of Environmental Economics and Management*, 42: 310-35.

Dowell, G.A., Hart, S., and Yeung, B., 2000. Do Corporate Global Environmental Standards Create or Destroy Market Value? *Management Science*, 46(8): 1059-74.

Feldman, S., Soyka, P., and Ameer, P., 1996. Does Improving a Firm's Environmental Management System and Environmental Performance Result in a Higher Stock Price? Washington: ICF Kaiser.

Grand, M.C., and D'Elia, V.V., 2005. Environmental News and Stock Markets Performance: Further Evidence for Argentina. CEMA working paper no. 300, University del CEMA.

Guenster, N., Derwall, J., Bauer, R., and Koedijk, K., 2005. The Economic Value of Corporate Eco-Efficiency. Academy of Management Conference Paper, 2005.

Gupta, S., and Goldar, B., 2005. Do Stock Markets Penalize Environment-Unfriendly Behaviour? Evidence from India. *Ecological Economics*, 52: 81-95.

Hamilton, J., 1995. Pollution as news: Media and Stock Market Reactions to the Toxics Release Inventory Data. *Journal of Environmental Economics and Management*, 28: 98-113.

Hart, S. and Ahuja, G., 1996. Does it pay to be green? An empirical Examination of the Relationship between Emission Reduction and Firm Performance. *Business Strategy and the Environment*. 5: 30-37.

Hartman, R.S., 1988. Self-selection Bias in the Evaluation of Voluntary Energy Conservation Programs. *Review Economics and Statistics*, 70: 448-58.

Khanna, M., and Damon, L.A., 1999. EPA's Voluntary 33/50 Program: Impact on Toxic Releases and Economic Performance of Firms. *Journal of Environmental Economics and Management*, 37: 1-25.

Khanna, M., Quimio, W.R.H., and Bojilova, D., 1998. Toxics Release Information: A Policy Tool for Environmental Protection. *Journal of Environmental Economics and Management*, 36: 243-66.

Khanna, M., and Speir, C., 2007. Motivations for Proactive Environmental

Management and Innovative Pollution Control. Paper presented at the American Agricultural Economics Association Annual Meeting, Portland, OR, July 29-August 1, 2007.

Klassen, R., and McLaughlin, C., 1996. The Impact of Environmental Management on Firm Performance. *Management Science*, 42: 1199-1214.

Konar, S., and Cohen, M.A., 2001. Does the Market Value Environmental Performance? *Review of Economics and Statistics*, 83(2): 281-89.

Mahoney, L., and Roberts, R., 2002. Corporate Social and Environmental Performance and Their Relation to Financial Performance and Institutional Ownership: Empirical Evidence on Canadian Firms. AAA Seventh Symposium on Ethics Research in Accounting, San Antonio, Texas.

Nakamura, M., Takahashi, T., and Vertinski, I., 2001. Why Japanese Firms Choose to Certify: A Study of Managerial Responses to Environmental Issues. *Journal of Environmental Economics and Management*, 42: 23-52.

Porter, M.E., and van der Linde, C., 1995. Green and Competitive. Ending the Stalemate. *Harvard Business Review*, September-October, 120-35.

Russo, M., and Fouts, P., 1997. A Resource-based Perspective on Corporate Environmental Performance and Profitability. *Academy of Management Journal*, 40: 534-59.

Takeda, F., and Tomozawa, T., 2006. An Empirical Study on Stock Price Responses to the Release of the Environmental Management Ranking in Japan. *Economics Bulletin*, 13(5): 1-4.

White, M., 1995. Does it pay to be green? Corporate Environmental Responsibility and Shareholder Value. Working paper, University of Virginia, Charlottesville, VA.

Zhang, R., and Stern, D., 2007. Firms' Environmental and Financial Performance: An Empirical Study. CSR paper no. 19, 2007, Fondazione Eni Enrico Mattei, Milano.

Corporate Social Responsibility and Sustainable Business

SHRAWAN KUMAR SINGH

The fact of corporate power is clear. Business has become, in the last half century, the most powerful institution on the planet. The dominant institution in any society needs to take responsibility for the whole. Every decision that is made, every action that is taken, must be viewed in light of that kind of responsibility. In the absence of a universally accepted definition for Corporate Social Responsibility (CSR), there are some myths which surround the concept. For the sake of analysis, the paper has been organized into following sections. *Section I* provides nature, concept and dimension of CSR; *Section II* is devoted to the need for CSR; factors contributing towards CSR are presented in *Section III; Section IV* discusses objections to CSR; *Section V* analyses CSR and India; and finally, *Section VI* concludes with a view that business of the 21st century will have no choice but to implement CSR.

I. THE CONCEPT OF CSR

No universally acceptable definition of CSR exists. Some suggest that CSR is about what business puts back—and can show it puts back—in return for the benefits it receives from society. This implies that the rights society bestows on business organizations come as an inclusive package that contains certain obligations to behave in a way society finds acceptable. A similar but more general definition says CSR is about the interaction of the corporation with the legal and social obligations of the societies in which it operates, and how it accounts for those obligations. This *implies an objective concern for the community that restrains corporates from taking on destructive and harmful activities, however, profitable they may be, and leads to positive contributions to human betterment.* This underlines the fact that corporate business activities damage the environment and contribute to health hazards because of the nature of the products and the work conditions in factories. Corporate social responsibility suggests a synthesis of not just enterprise blended with a spirit of philanthropy, but a much broader concept of social empowerment as a philosophy of life. *Gone are the days when profits and ethics were accepted as an un-mixable like oil and water. Today, business is expected to make not only a profit but also a difference—in the workplace, market, and the community. Social responsibility of business is less programmatic than philosophic. CSR according to the Conference Board of Canada, is the overall relationship of the corporation with all of its stakeholders. Elements of social responsibility include investment in community outreach, employee relations, creation and maintenance of employment, environmental responsibility, human rights and financial performance.* Fortunately, companies seem to have realized their folly in hankering after short-term financial gains and have recognized how strategically important it is to be socially responsible.

The concept of CSR is based on the idea that corporations can no longer act as isolated economic entities detached from broader society. If the business enterprise is viewed an institution of society, then the central theme of corporate citizenship would be based on a positive correlation of business with other stakeholders, sustaining the environment, and addressing the issues of poverty, illiteracy and ill-health, at large. This is based on the simple *mantra* that a corporate pays attention to its shareholders, consumers, labour, government and community and adheres to sound business and industrial practices and is environment friendly. A more formal definition emerged from an international meeting the WBCSD organized with 60 opinion formers from within and outside business. *'Corporate social responsibility is the continuing commitment by business to behave ethically and contribute to economic development while improving the quality of life of the workforce and their families as well as of the local community and society at large'*. However, the lack of an all-embracing definition should not deter business from grappling with the issue. A formal definition of the concept may well eventually emerge, with or without the cooperation of business.

II. WHY TO GO FOR CSR

The primary goal of any enterprise is profit-maximisation, necessary to fulfil the aspirations of the several constituents. According to *Paul Samuelson, 'pollution preventive' measures were less costly than 'pollution cure' measures, post-damage. Corporates, he said, have a special obligation to the public, which they cannot disregard. Whatever the economic system the corporates operate in, they cause in the process of production serious damage to society, in varying degrees, depending on the nature of the enterprise.* The pollution effects of corporate activities have come to the fore only in the 1980s. It must be made clear that *social responsibility does not preclude profitability, much less regard it as 'dirty'*. Being profitable compels efficiency in operations and profits create and widen a company's base for future growth and enhance its capacity for being more and more socially responsible. Thus, *profit is itself an aspect of social responsibility. What is unacceptable is converting social irresponsibility into profits. Peter F. Drucker* considers profitability the first and the basic social responsibility of business as no other responsibility, social or otherwise, can be fulfilled by any losing business. A company has a responsibility to instil a sense of interdependence among its stakeholders, and to communicate with all of them more often, more openly and more compassionately. *"The aim of business"*, said *Peter Drucker, "is the exploitation of socially desirable opportunities profitably"*. The American Management Association went even further and defined management itself as *"the efficient achievement of desirable ends through acceptable means"*. And that, ultimately, is what social responsibility is all about. In the modern context, it connotes the business-society interface.

The very fact of the intense interest generated in CSR proves that corporates all over the world are convinced that *it not only makes sound business sense, but helps in building and buttressing their brand equity.* India's business and industry too have not been slow to catch on to the beneficial effects of CSR. There has been no dearth of seminars and the National Summit on CSR. Whether they are sensitive or not, corporations interact with civil society in five domains *(Arun Maira,* 2007):

1. *Accountability to investors and lenders*—the financial domain, the domain of corporate accounting, auditing, corporate law, and stock market regulators, and the principal focus of 'corporate governance'.
2. *Accountability to the direct participants in the corporate 'value creation' process*—customers, employees, vendors, the domain of consumer protection, labour laws, and commercial contracts. Along with the first, this is the principal focus of corporate management.
3. *Accountability for the effect of their operations on the physical environment*—the domain of *environmental regulations.*
4. *Accountability for the 'human condition' around their operations*—health, education, employment, and cultural needs in the community; wherein corporate responsibility is not much regulated and which is the focus of most *corporate philanthropy.*
5. *Accountability for the political health of the societies in which they operate*—human rights, fair democratic practices, etc. This gets to the question of corporations' *responsibility as political citizens in their societies.* Are they merely takers of permissions from society or also creators of fair conditions?

These five domains are like steps of a ladder of corporate social responsibility. Many corporations are still on the first two rungs. To be seen as responsible citizens commensurate with the powers granted to them, they must move up the ladder to the fifth level. Today there is increasingly a realization among many that CSR is good for business. Further, there is growing evidence that the *larger the firm the greater its social responsibility.* Any failure to measure up to the requirements, expectations and desire of the stakeholders, including the wider society, will have implications for the firm's reputation even when such failure does not result in any shortcomings or limitation concerning product or service quality.

III. FACTORS CONTRIBUTING TOWARDS AWARENESS OF CSR

Social responsibility needs a much more holistic perspective, a vision that values positive interaction with all the members of society and not just with consumers and shareholders. The rules of the game have changed and new factors have emerged:

(i) *Markets became global; competition intensified as multi-nationals swept across borders. Companies restructured, re-engineered and slashed jobs. Redundant employees charged re-engineered firms with betrayal and loss of trust, while the existing ones worked under a cloud of uncertainty.*

(ii) Images of *gas-poisoned victims* and oil-soaked birds in the aftermath of the *Bhopal gas disaster* and the *Exxon Vaidez* spill made the world sit up and take notice of the impacts that business could have on the external world. *Environment and human rights pressure groups* campaigned extensively against major oil companies operating in the developing countries.

(iii) *'Consumer statisfaction', 'consumer delight' and 'consumer service' are some of the freely bandied about terms, not without reason.* While *stakeholders of business* demand increased transparency and openness from them, their requests are consistent: *reveal more, deliver more, and do it more quickly and responsibly.*

(iv) *Media publicity of good and bad corporate performance has placed companies in the public glare, at times embarrassing and disconcerting. It is in this background that the social responsibility of business in the prevailing context has to be understood.*

(v) *A new equation is emerging between the government and business. In the prevailing liberalized and globalised climate, the government is readying to shed and vacate the dominant space it occupied in the economy in favour of the business sector.* This comes out of the conviction that the market system is a better allocator of resources and the government's role should be that of a facilitator and umpire. In this new dispensation corporates have tremendous opportunities to pursue their profit-objective, qualified by their commitment and obligations to society. And their *activities are carried out not only for the benefit of shareholders, employees, suppliers, customers and the government but for society at large. It is in this sense that corporates have to be viewed—not as legal entities, but as corporate citizens.*

(vi) A decade ago when the concept of *"eco-efficiency"* was invented—producing more with less; less resources, less waste and less pollution—it excited business and caught their fancy. This was due to two reasons: the term contained the word *'efficiency'*, and the suffix *'eco'* recalls both *economics and ecology*. The concept became popular. The most radical transformation of the simple concept of eco-efficiency can be envisaged in the evolution—from meaning *'producing more with less' in the 1990s to 'making more money by selling less stuff today'. This is the shift form products to services.* Likewise, a chemicals company may not sell paint to a car company, but offer instead the service of painting cars. A classic example here is of *Dupont Canada* striking a deal with their customer Ford to get paid for the number of automobiles painted, rather than the liters of pairit. Consequently, costs of Ford have been reduced and waste volumes cut. *Ford* realized cost savings of 35-40 per cent while emission of volatile organic compounds were reduced by 50 per cent. For Dupont Canada, meanwhile, the lower volume of paint supplied was offset by improved efficiencies. *Clearly, companies are no longer perceived to be environmentally responsible if they continue to be socially irresponsible.*

(vii) Reducing poverty and improving equity was one of the six core themes debated at the *World Economic Forum* in New York in January 2002. Philanthropy aside, the private sector has a role in helping to create sustainable livelihoods for the poor. In "the words *of Marcel Engel,* leader of the Sustainable Livelihood project of the World Business Council for Sustainable Development (WBCSD), *"There are three possible motivations for a company to invest in sustainable livelihood for the world's poor: to manage the company's risk and reputation; to generate bottom-line benefits; and to achieve strategic change by developing new business approaches to meet the needs of the poor".*

(viii) After the announcement of the *Principles of Responsible Investment (PRI)* on April 27, 2006 by the then Secretary General of the UN, *Kofi Annan,* international funds worth $4 trillion have now endorsed the same. The backing of such a large fund to the PRI confirms that the integration of environmental, social and corporate governance considerations is now becoming an essential part of global investment business. *Responsible investing, socially responsible investing, socially aware investing, ethical investing, values-based investing, mission-based investing...all describe the same concept.* These terms tend to be used interchangeably within the investment industry to describe an approach to investing which combines the intentions to maximize both financial return and social good. In general, *Socially Responsible Investing (SRI) favours corporate practices which are environmentally responsible, community friendly, support workplace diversity and increase product safety and quality.*

The globalization of the marketplace, rapid advancement in technology, the changing role of government, changing societal expectations of business, and the rise of civil society and its relationship with business have all made *corporate activity an increasingly challenging, complex and possibly even risky undertaking.* At the same time, it made corporate responsibility an increasingly *challenging, complex and critical aspect of good business practices,* with no place to hide from perceived irresponsible behaviour.

IV. OBJECTIONS TO CSR

The fundamental objection against CSR is that to apply the shareholders' funds in any way other than for the advancement of the company's business is contrary to the fiduciary duty of a company's directors and thus diminishes rather than enhances any claim they may have to be acting in an ethical manner. *Milton Friedman* argues that *'there is one and only one social responsibility of business—to use (its) resources and engage in activities designed to increase its profits so long as it stays with in the rules of the game, which is to say, engages in open and free competition without 'deception or fraud'*. He suggests that where directors, whose responsibility is to manage the business for the benefit of the shareholders, spend money for a *'general social interest'* they are usurping the functions of government in taxing and spending, but without any democratic mandate and without any particular expertise in the areas concerned. He does, however, make the point that if there is a genuine business case for CSR expenditure it is legitimate for the directors to incur it, in the same way as any other business expenditure. In practice, despite the conceptual differences, it seems that such an approach may not always produce significant variation in behaviour between its advocates and those who see directors as having a wider responsibility to a variety of stakeholders.

Other commentators object to the CSR concept on the economic ground that it interferes with efficient resource allocation, and that it is precisely by its profitable commercial activity that a company contributes to the welfare of society. This in turn may reflect a particular stance on the respective roles of the state and of private enterprise, and lead on to a debate, on taxation. Once companies take on *'state'* responsibilities such as education and vocational training they may see this as being to some extent in tension with the continued obligation to contribute to the state through taxation.

The fact of corporate power is clear. However, calls for corporate executives to use that power with responsibility all too often side step a number of important questions (*David C. Korten, 1996)*; (i) Do the managers of public corporations have the option of managing them in the public interest? (ii) Should we assume that a person who happens to head a powerful corporation has the wisdom and the motivation to make decisions for the whole? (iii) Do global corporations, their chief executives, or their owners have a natural right to hold such power over the rest of society? (iv) Is rule by corporations desirable? Is it inevitable?

In the absence of government oversight, corporations are formally accountable only to their owners, which in our present day means global financial markets. Here we confront the implications of how the *world's financial system* has transformed itself. The social and environmental consequences of their actions never register on their computer screens. Theirs is purely a world of money. This is the system to which contemporary corporate managers are accountable: They in turn are under enormous pressure to produce instant financial results. Is corporate rule inevitable? Only if the laws we chose to put into place allow it. Citizens have the right to change those law's whenever they chose to do so. *The matter of business responsibility requires some basic rethinking. Political reform* to get corporations out of politics would be an important first step. Citizens, acting through their governments, must reassert their right to set the rules for those who do business within their political jurisdiction. If we are serious about business responsibility, then we must create a system of business that rewards those firms that are responsible in the eyes of the broader community and eliminates the irresponsible—a system almost the mirror opposite of what we now have (*David C. Korten, 1996*). Corporate responsibility in recent years has been driven by *globalization*. If markets stay open, it will continue to spread. But openness should not be taken for granted: "The day markets close, CSR is over" (*The Economist,* January 19, 2008).

In the absence of a well-defined and authentic statement of standards, there is no framework by which a company can be held accountable for its failure in meeting its social responsibilities. Whose interest, or which interest, should the corporate support? Social responsibilities are ambiguous. They are composed of an amalgam of moral ideals and legal strictures formulated by different action groups to meet their individual goals and objectives. But the real rub is in evolving a matrix to make a comparative evaluation of the efforts made by the corporates. *Argentina, Australia, Britain and Canada* are examples of countries which, in conjunction with business enterprises, have gone in for measurement of CSR based on agreed parameters, such as, *corporate vision and mission, labour conditions, accountability and transparency, quality of stakeholder relations, accuracy, relevance and reliability of information, concern for environmental protection, product safety, redress of complaints and grievances, and funding of projects of vital social importance relating, for instance to, education, health, sanitation, disease prevention, basic amenities and so on.*

V. CSR AND INDIA

CSR is not a concept Indian corporates are unfamiliar with, though their activities may not always have borne the CSR tag. The reforms wave that swept across the country has changed the industry and trade environment. Indian corporates can take legitimate pride in taking CSR along directions which are germane to the needs of society. It was heartening to know of examples of corporates working for farmers development, raising livelihood standards of rural communities, harnessing micro-enterprises to increase the penetration of consumer products in rural markets and coming out with software as aids to teachers and pupils to improve educational standards and promote adult literacy.

A latest survey by the Tata Energy Research Institute (TERI) called *'Altered Images: the 2001 State of Corporate Responsibility in India Pall'* traces back *'The History of CSR in India'* and suggests that there *are four models* of CSR[2]: (i) *Ethical model;* (ii) *Statist Model;* (iii) *Liberal Model;* and (iv) *Stakeholder Model.* The former President of India Dr. *A.P.J. Abdul Kalam*[3] has suggested the corporate India to consider participating in the eight identified missions of the world knowledge platform as a *business opportunity and simultaneously fulfil their corporate social responsibility.* Corporate houses can make an important contribution by adopting the schools particularly in rural areas in their region providing infrastructure for the schools in the form of clean drinking water, toilet facilities, transportation facilities for children coming from far away distances, equipping the sport complexes and providing computing facilities for technology assisted learning. The industrial houses can take up urgent action for conservation of energy, promoting use of renewable energy to the maximum extent in their plants and facilities. They can also work in the development of solar energy systems and wind energy systems either on stand alone mode or in partnership with multinationals for providing cost effective energy sources to the community.

The CSR should not be merely a statement of intent. It should be made compulsory for the corporate operating in India. This will definitely help in upholding human rights. In India, most of the corporates do not have a clear policy on social responsibility. While developed countries like *England have separate ministries to look after the issue of corporate social responsibility,* in India, the government does not have a clear policy on the issue. Out of very few companies who contribute to the social development, the basic intention was not to ensure the good of the nation, rather a business policy to *stay away from the tax net*. The concept of corporate social responsibility (CSR) has so far failed to take deep root in India because the nomenclature is not properly defined. The CSR is in a nascent stage.

'The *why, what and how—an Indian perspective*'[4] of the journey has begun. But the real challenges are to apply fundamental business principles to make CSR sharper and focused. The five-point strategy suggested includes focusing on *priorities, allocating finance for treating CSR as an investment from which returns are expected, optimizing available resources by ensuring that efforts are not duplicated and existing services are strengthened and supplemented; monitoring activities and liaising closely with implementation partners such as NGOs to ensure that initiatives really deliver outputs and reporting performance in an open and transparent way so that all can celebrate progress and identify for further action.*

An index was launched to track stocks of 50 Indian companies that score high on issues such as corporate governance and business ethics as well as responsibility towards employees, environment and community.[5] The index was constituted on a three-stage screening of 500 liquid stocks. The quantitative and qualitative results were then compiled to get a final *'The Environment, Social Governance Index* (ESG)' score. However, companies in India were still not *'very willing'* to disclose all the information that does not pertain to shareholder interest today. According to *Subir Gokarn*, (Chief Economist, S&P), in India companies are evolving from a stage where corporate social responsibility was a mere public relations exercise and are now *"trying to align profit motives with public interest*[1]*"*. Measuring is not a simple task, but once a company has a proper baseline it can see what can be changed. Commitment from the top is crucial. The companies that feature in the index have performed largely in line with the National Stock Exchange's 50-share index, the S&P CNX Nifty. Crisil officials believe that any investor who feels the need to invest in a company that gives prime importance to social and governance issues will not be rewarded any lesser in terms of stock market performance (*Mint, January 1, 2008*).

The Prime Minister's Ten Point Commandments at the recent

CII annual conference (24th May, 2007) created quite a stir. The debate was, however, hijacked on the limited issue of resisting excessive pay. However, one believes that the prime minister intended to re-engage on broader issues of *Corporate Social Responsibility*. Trade and industry should produce a blueprint on what the government and the private sector can do in partnership to strengthen the culture of philanthropy and Corporate Social Responsibility. It is time to articulate a programme on Corporate Social Responsibility which reflects both contemporary needs and capacity of the private sector *(N.K. Singh*, 2007). The foremost change is in attitude towards social responsibility among the companies has taken place.

VI. CONCLUSION

The reasons for companies becoming interested in social responsibility remain diverse. According to Stephen MacGregor, 'Risk protection, market positioning, recruitment, political-social relationship—each displaying an inverse relationship between immediate economic impact and degree of commitment remain crucial'. Management expert *Michael Porter* observed recently: "The fact is, the prevailing approaches to CSR are so fragmented and so disconnected from business and strategy as to obscure many of the greatest opportunities for companies to benefit society. If, instead, corporates were to analyse their prospects for social responsibility using the same frameworks that guide their core business choices, they would discover that *CSR can be much more than a cost, a constraint, or a charitable deed—it can be a source of opportunity, innovation, and competitive advantage*". In the same article, he also says that the proponents of CSR typically, "... focus on the tension between business and society rather on their interdependence". Globally there are many companies that have woken up to this potential and have married their social and business goals with amazing efficiency.

CSR is firmly on the global public policy agenda and is climbing ever higher. The momentum of the debate has often been driven by those outside the business community. Such pressures—driven largely by the perception that business is indifferent to and out of touch with the values of society—reflect a shift in what society expects of both business and government. Clearly, *the forces of globalization, rapid improvements in technology and dramatic changes in world order have caused considerable confusion over exactly what is—and is not—expected of business. Where do the boundaries of responsibility lie, particularly in relation to government? There are no clear answers—much depends on the political, cultural and historical context of the questions.*

Skepticism of corporate social responsibility and sustainable development claims is sometimes reinforced by corporate executives themselves. The McKinsey Company's 2006 *"Global Survey of Business Executives"* based on responses from 4,238 corporate CEOs and CFOs in 116 countries found strong evidence of a continuing gap between the recognition of corporate responsibility principles and business practices. "Business executives across the world overwhelmingly (84 per cent) believe that corporations should balance their obligations to shareholders with explicit contributions to the broader public good". However, most of the executives saw corporate social activities *"as a risk, not an opportunity, and frankly admit that they are ineffective at managing this wider social and political issue"*.

Shri R.C. Bhargava believe that the CSR of a company should be undertaking all actions as would maximize the probability of its long-term survival and sustained growth. Making profits on a sustained basis is a necessary condition for any company to survive for long. In today's globalised and increasingly competitive world, sustained profitability is not possible unless all direct stakeholders recognize the changes taking place and work towards ensuring sustained profitability. They have also to create a positive brand image which attracts customers to the products and services offered by the company. Following all laws and caring for the environment makes good business sense, and helps in image building. These matters have to be the core of the CSR of a company.

The truly responsible business never loses sight of the commercial imperative. It is, after all, by staying in business and providing products and services people want that firms do most good. *If ignoring CSR is risky, ignoring what makes business sense is a certain route to failure.* The business of the 21st century will have no choice but to implement CSR. The real question about corporate responsibility today is *"not whether but how". Doing well by doing good* has become *a fashionable mantra.* Business have eagerly adopted the jargon of *embedding* CSR in the core of their operations, making it *part of the corporate DNA* so that it influences decisions across the company (*The Economist*, January 19, 2008). *Being socially responsible is not just good business practice but also makes good business sense.* CSR has positive effects on the economics of the company, its public relations, customers, employees and shareholders. 'CSR is a cost effective, and a potent business tool'.

Notes and References

1. "I pretty much got thrown out of the room by the promoter of a mining company because we asked for environment audits" said Ms. Naina Lal Kidwai, Group General Manager and Country Head, India of the HSBC Bank. She mentioned this anecdote while addressing a seminar on climate change and environmental risks organized by the Madras Chamber of Commerce and Industry (MCCI) at Chennai on August 20, 2008. Three months after this episode, the promoter agreed for the audits. And two years later, he was actually thanking HSBC for insisting on the audits and raising his awareness because it helped the smooth passage of his equity issue. Reason for this change of heart on the part of this promoter, (when he could have gone to other banks), the promoter needed their services because he was looking at global opportunities and hoping to buy mines elsewhere. Often promoters didn't know better because of the general levels of ignorance about best practices in energy efficiency, environment protection and conservation. "There is often no need to cajole. We just need to raise their awareness. Clean business is good business for them and by extension, for us too". If HSBC would consider providing incentives in the form of lower interest rates for companies that adopt energy conservation and environment-friendly practices, such practices may form one ingredient in the parameters that rating agencies would consider while determining the sustainability of business models and, therefore, prove beneficial (*The Hindu Business Line*, August 21, 2008).
2. A survey was conducted by ORG-MARG for TERI-Europe in several cities of India in 2001. The basic purpose of the survey was to capture perceptions and expectations (related to corporate responsibility) of the following three sets of stakeholders such as general public, workers (skilled, semiskilled and unskilled) and corporate executives (head of corporate relation, labour relations, welfare department and manufacturing department in MNCs, large and medium sized Indian companies). The poll gathered that people believe that companies should be actively engaged in social matters.
3. While inaugurating the First International Summit jointly organized by the Corporate Affairs Ministry and ASSOCHAM in Delhi on January 30, 2008.

4. A study jointly brought out by The Associated Chambers of Commerce and Industry of India (ASSOCHAM) and KPMG on 'Corporate Social Responsibility': The Why, What and How.
5. A subsidiary of credit rating firm Standard and Poor's (S&P), Crisil Ltd. launched the Environment, Social Governance (ESG) Index, in association with environmental research firm, KLD Research and Analytics, is a pilot project initiated and sponsored by the International Finance Corp., the finance arm of the World Bank that encourages sustainable economic growth in developing countries. The top 10 companies by weight in the index are Infosys Technology Ltd., ITC Ltd., Aditya Birla Nuvo Ltd., Dr. Reddy's Laboratories Ltd., Wipro Ltd., Jubilant Organosys Ltd., Axis Bank, GTL Ltd., Reliance Industries Ltd., and Hindustan Unilever Ltd. A company such as ITC finds a high weightage on the index despite being the largest tobacco maker in the country because it scores high on several parameters such as governance issues and employee initiatives, even though it has a negative scoring on its product. Qualitative aspects such as employee unrest or loss of key staff, health and safety violations, regulatory penalties, loss of brand value and loss of reputation were key issues that were taken into consideration while computing scores (*Mint*, January, 2008).

REFERENCES

Atkins, Besty (2006): Is Corporate Social Responsibility Responsible? *Journal of Corporate Citizenship*, November.

Bhargava, R.C. (2008): The Real Meaning of CSR, *The Economic Times*, June 16.

Daily, Herman E. (1966): 'Sustainable Growth? No thank you' in *The Case of the Global Economy* (Eds.) Jerry Mander, Edward Goldsmith, Sierra Book Club, 1996.

David Logan, Delwin and Laurie Regelbrugge (1997): *Global Corporate Citizenship—Rationale and Strategies*, Washington, D.C., The Hitachi Foundation.

The Economist (2008): A Report on Corporate Social Responsibility, January 19.

Fisherman-Hillard/National Consumers League Study (2006): *Rethinking Corporate Social Responsibility*, Fisherman-Hillard.

Friedman, Milton (1970): 'The Social Responsibility of Business is to Increase its Profits', *The New York Times Magazine*, September 13.

Hediger, Werner (2007): Framing Corporate Social Responsibility and Contribution to Sustainable Development, *Center for Corporate Responsibility and Sustainability at the University of Zurich, Zurich, Switzerland*, March.

Holme Richard & Phil Watts (2002): Corporate Social Responsibility: Making Good Business Sense, *World Business Council for Sustainable Development*.

Korten, David C. (1996): Limits to the Social Responsibility of Business; PCD Forum Article, No. 19, June 1.

Maira, Arun (2007): Moving up the CSR ladder, *The Economic Times*, February 8.

Nadkarni, Anant G. (2006): From Social Responsibility to Development-driven Business: The Ongoing Experience of the Tata Group in Reed, Darryl and Sanjoy Mukherjee (eds.), *Corporate Governance, Economic in Reforms and Development: The Indian Experience*, Oxford University Press, New Delhi.

Nelson, J. (1996): *Business as Partners in Development*, Prince of Wale's Business Leaders' Forum, London.

Porter, Michael E. and Mark R. Kramer (2002): The Competitive Advantage of Corporate Philanthropy; *Harvard Business Review*, December.

Roddick, Anita (1999): The Quakers 'ran successful businesses, made money because they offered honest products and treated their people honestly, gave honest value for money, put back more than they took and told no lies', *KLM Herald Magazine*, August.

Rosabeth Moss Kanter notes in *'From Spare Change to Real Change:* The Social Sector as a Beta Site for Business Innovation', *Harvard Business Review.*

Ruggie, John Gerard (2004): 'The Theory and Practice of Learning Networks: Corporate Social Responsibility and the Global Compact', *Journal of Corporate Citizenship.*

Shireman, W.K. (2000): Keynote Address at the *Asian Productivity Organisation's Conference* in Tokyo, April.

Singh, N.K. (2007): Just what the Doctor Ordered, *The Indian Express*, June 4.

Srivastava, Harish and Shankar Venkateswaran (2000): *The Business of Social Responsibility*, Books for Change, Bangalore.

UNCTAD (1999): *The Social Responsibility of Transnational Corporations*, New York and Geneva, United Nations.

Venkateswaran, Shankar (2006): 'Role of Business in Society Business—NGOs Partnership for Development' in Reed, Darryl and Sanjoy Mukherjee (eds.), *Corporate Governance, Economic in Reforms, and Development: The Indian Experience*, Oxford University Press, New Delhi.

www.globalcompact.org

Index